# Automating UNIX and Linux Administration

KIRK BAUER

Apress™

Automating UNIX and Linux Administration
Copyright ©2003 by Kirk Bauer

ISBN (pbk): 1-59059-212-3

Printed and bound in the United States of America 9876543

Technical Reviewers: Nate Campi, Erik Melander, Alf Wachsmann

Editorial Board: Dan Appleman, Craig Berry, Gary Cornell, Tony Davis, Steven Rycroft, Julian Skinner, Martin Streicher, Jim Sumser, Karen Watterson, Gavin Wray, John Zukowski

Assistant Publisher: Grace Wong

Copy Editor: Rebecca Rider

Production Manager: Kari Brooks

Proofreader: Laura Cheu

Compositor: Susan Glinert Stevens

Indexer: Kevin Broccoli

Cover Designer: Kurt Krames

Manufacturing Manager: Tom Debolski

Distributed to the book trade in the United States by Springer-Verlag New York, Inc., 175 Fifth Avenue, New York, NY, 10010 and outside the United States by Springer-Verlag GmbH & Co. KG, Tiergartenstr. 17, 69112 Heidelberg, Germany.

In the United States: phone 1-800-SPRINGER, email orders@springer-ny.com, or visit http://www.springer-ny.com. Outside the United States: fax +49 6221 345229, email orders@springer.de, or visit http://www.springer.de.

For information on translations, please contact Apress directly at 2560 Ninth Street, Suite 219, Berkeley, CA 94710. Phone 510-549-5930, fax 510-549-5939, email info@apress.com, or visit http://www.apress.com.

The source code for this book is available to readers at http://www.apress.com in the Downloads section.

*To my parents, especially my father, who started and supported my interest in computers, and my loving wife Amber, who has supported me throughout this process.*

# Contents at a Glance

# Contents

# About the Author

**Kirk Bauer** has been using computers and programming since 1985. He has been using and administering UNIX systems since 1994. Although his personal favorite UNIX variant is Linux, he has administered everything from FreeBSD to Solaris, AIX, and IRIX.

Kirk has been involved with software development and system/network administration since his first year at Georgia Tech. He has done work for the Georgia Tech Residential Network, the Georgia Tech Research Institute, and the Fermi National Accelerator Laboratory. Kirk was one of the founders and the CTO of TogetherWeb in 2000, which was purchased in 2003 by Proficient Systems. Kirk is currently a software architect with Proficient Systems and continues to support and develop the collaborative browsing software and Linux-based network appliance created by TogetherWeb.

Kirk's latest development is a fully automated installation, configuration, management, and monitoring system that is used to deploy Proficient's software on RLX ServerBlades. Saving time through automation has always been his passion, as evidenced by his collection of open-source software—the most popular being AutoRPM and Logwatch.

Shortly after graduating from Georgia Tech in 2002 with a bachelor's of science in Computer Engineering, Kirk married Amber, the love of his life. They currently live in Peoria, AZ with their two dogs and four cats. When not using a computer, Kirk can be found involved in one of his many hobbies. Kirk enjoys reading, playing strategy games, taking pictures, and watching movies. He likes to snow ski, water ski, and scuba dive when he gets the opportunity. Skydiving is his favorite sport—Kirk has made over 1,400 jumps to date.

# About the Technical Reviewers

**Nate Campi** is a UNIX and network administrator in Silicon Valley. He is currently employed at a (Linux-based) network appliance vendor, running all aspects of their internal IT, helping guide development of products, and designing DNS architectures for customers.

Past jobs include postmaster, hostmaster, and webmaster duties at Terra Lycos, UNIX and network administrator at several Silicon Valley web hosting companies, and a tour as a hospital corpsman in the US Navy. While in the Navy, Nate developed a love of teaching as a instructor for basic and advanced life support, and also pediatric advanced life support for the American Heart Association.

He is married, has a son and a daughter, lives in the San Francisco East Bay, and dreams of one day owning a home in the area.

**Erik Melander**, Managing Architect of Central Systems at Wyndham International, has a decade of experience with UNIX systems, including time working with the University of Minnesota and IBM Global Services. Currently, he is evolving Wyndham's IT infrastructure to realize a shared vision of autonomic computing.

**Alf Wachsmann** holds a doctorate of natural science in Computer Science from the University of Paderborn in Germany. He wrote his thesis about parallel and distributed computing.

He then worked at DESY, Germany's national high-energy physics lab, where he learned system software programming and system administration in a very heterogeneous UNIX environment. His specialty became automation.

Wachsmann then moved from Germany to the San Francisco Bay area, where he now works at the Stanford Linear Accelerator Center, a site with fewer UNIX versions but with a lot more computers. His main focus is again automating system administration and system infrastructure tasks.

Other professional interests include the OpenAFS filesystem and Kerberos 5 authentication.

# Acknowledgments

I HAVE USED COMPUTERS since I was very young and have always loved them, thanks in large part to the support of my parents throughout my childhood. They have always helped me learn and have supported me in whatever I wanted to do. I have to particularly thank my father who, much to my Mom's chagrin, came home one day with my very first computer—a Commodore Vic 20. My life was never the same after that.

I also thank my lovely wife, Amber, who has shared me with this book for many, many months. She has been supportive and understanding, even though I started writing the book just after our honeymoon was over.

In addition, my friend and colleague Moshe Jacobson has been very helpful in this process. He quickly answered my many questions and even did some of the technical review. He helped make writing this book the learning experience that it was.

Finally, I must thank everybody at Apress for helping me through my first book—especially my editor, Jim Sumser, who has stuck by me through this long and arduous process.

# Preface

ADMIT IT. YOU ARE READING this book because you are lazy. Lazy system administrators are wonderful people—who else is willing to spend so much time now in order to do nothing later? We all dream of waking up in the morning, grabbing the laptop from the bedside table, checking our email, and then heading off to the lake for the day.

Using the techniques in this book, you can get closer to the ideal world of fully automated system administration. Although unexpected things always go wrong, we can at least delegate all of the mundane and repetitive tasks to the computer (whose purpose, of course, was to make our lives easier). I will leave it up to you to convince your boss that you only need to come in to work one day per week.

## Benefits of Automation

In most cases, the motivation behind automation is saving time. We are busy people and our time is valuable. We would rather write a script to add a user than add one manually a few times a day. We can then take that time we save and spend it doing things that aren't as easy to automate (or things that are much more entertaining). There are other benefits of automation, however, that are not quite as apparent.

In many cases, automation allows others to do things that they don't have enough direct knowledge to do themselves. These other people range from inexperienced system administrators working under you to support staff manning the corporate help desk. Your automation makes everybody's lives much easier. They don't have to bother you so much, and you don't have to answer the same questions every day.

Equally important is the unintentional documentation that can result from automation. For example, to add a new account, you have to add it to the passwd, shadow, and group files, as well as create a home directory on the file server and set up the automount tables. Although you normally thoroughly document and follow step-by-step procedures for most of your administration tasks, you somehow manage to neglect this particular task.

This is where automation is very helpful. If you write a script to do all of the tasks required to create a user, you have effectively written a step-by-step guide explaining how to create a new account. If you put some good comments in the script, you have documented the process as well. The script comes in handy when you haven't added a new account for three months. Even if the script is dated and fails to operate correctly, you still know what was supposed to happen and that it was supposed to work. Instead of having to re-create the process from scratch, you can just tweak the script so that it will work this time and the next.

## Uses for Automation Techniques

Automation can be beneficial even when it is limited to one system. Regardless of how simple the system is or how little it does, menial tasks still need to be done, logs need to be monitored, and so on. Of course, the benefits of automation really start to outweigh the costs when it is deployed across several systems.

Managing hundreds or even thousands of machines can be fun. It can also be a nightmare if things are not done right. To avoid this and reduce your future workload, make sure to do things correctly from the start. However, there are also many things you can do to make life easier when you are managing existing sets of machines. So even if you can't start from scratch, you may still find this book very helpful. For example, as we will discuss later, you can use methods to automatically standardize machines in your existing network.

If you are managing more than one machine, you probably think that it would be nice if all of the machines had the same hardware, operating system, and software. Sometimes this is possible (if you are using Beowulf clusters, for instance); usually it is not (especially in a software engineering company with 1,000 programmers). This book deals with both uniform and mixed UNIX environments. Although the examples I use only directly apply to Linux and UNIX environments, you can apply these ideas to any situation.

## Who Will Benefit?

I have written this book for the experienced system administrator. This doesn't mean that you have to be an expert, it just means that you need to have a little experience before you will find this book valuable. For instance, if you can't remember how to mount a filesystem without looking it up in a reference manual, then this book may be too advanced for you.

In addition to assuming that you can perform basic system administration tasks, I assume that you are familiar with both Perl and/or bash scripting. In addition, I expect you to understand basic regular expression syntax.

If you are a student and are running a Linux server, then this book could be for you. If you have a few UNIX boxes at work, then you will probably find this book useful. If you administer a few UNIX workstations, a set of UNIX servers, a web farm, or a Beowulf cluster, then this book could be a lifesaver.

# Techniques Covered

You can take one of three approaches when you go to solve the automation problems I present in this book:

> **Open-source software:** Open-source solutions exist for many of the problems I present in this book, but I do not attempt to cover every open source solution to every problem. Instead, I cover the most popular and mature software in each category. Some programs I cover include GNU cfengine, Logwatch, Swatch, AutoRPM, and NetSaint (which is currently being developed as Nagios). This book is not a complete instruction manual for any of this software, but it does provide enough information for you to consider and begin to use these programs.

> **Custom scripts and software:** Another focus of this book involves custom solutions. Why am I advocating custom solutions when open-source solutions already exist? I'm not. I definitely recommend that you use existing solutions when possible. However, there are many cases in which existing solutions are too complicated, are not powerful enough, or are too restrictive for your particular needs. In addition, there are also plenty of areas within automation where existing solutions are hard to come by. This is usually because the situation is significantly different in each case or the solution is too simple to release as a product.

> **Commercial software:** I do not cover commercial software in this book— not because there is anything wrong with the software, it is just too costly for many situations (especially when you consider the consulting costs typically associated with this type of software). In addition, not enough information is available on the commercial solutions for me to fully discuss them within this book. However, for some situations commercial software may be the best solution and I suggest that you consider it if it fits your needs.

# Chapter Summary

The book begins with introductory chapters that you should be very familiar with before you move on to the meat of the text. It then proceeds with one chapter on each core area of automation. Each chapter fully discusses the area in question, describes both existing and custom solutions to each problem, and provides numerous examples.

> **Chapter 1: Introducing the Basics of Automation** covers the methodology behind system administration. automation.

**Chapter 2: Using SSH to Securely Automate System Administration** covers the basics of using Secure Shell (SSH), discusses SSH security concerns, describes how to set up passwordless SSH, and delves into various other related topics.

**Chapter 3: Creating Login Scripts and Shell Scripts** discusses some more advanced features of bash and how you can use them to customize your prompt, create command aliases, enhance tab completion, and otherwise enhance your shell experience. This chapter also provides scripts that allow commands to run across multiple systems.

**Chapter 4: Pre-Installation: Network Preparation and Management** discusses the tasks you need to complete to add a new system to your network and provides a custom, modular shell script you can use to automate these tasks.

**Chapter 5: Automating and Customizing Installation** discusses the options available to you when you want to automatically perform operating system installations. This chapter also discusses your options for customizing your operating systems and provides scripts that allow a new system (even without a custom operating system) to quickly and easily join your automation system.

**Chapter 6: Automatic System Configuration** covers the automatic configuration all of the systems on your network, regardless of the operating systems they run or the tasks they perform. This chapter provides both a custom solution and a comprehensive discussion of GNU cfengine.

**Chapter 7: Sharing Data Between Systems** discusses many methods you can use to share data among your various systems and talks about network filesystems such as the Network File System (NFS), Network Information Services (NIS/NIS+), GNU cfengine, rsync, Concurrent Versioning System (CVS), and the Hypertext Transfer Protocol (HTTP) and the File Transfer Protocol (FTP) protocols.

**Chapter 8: Packages and Patches** discusses the issues involved in updating many systems. This chapter also talks about both Solaris and custom patches, the Red Hat Package Manager (RPM) and Debian package formats, and a custom package solution. In addition, it covers automatic package installation with AutoRPM and introduces the OpenPKG system, which provides packages that can be installed on many different operating systems.

**Chapter 9: System Maintenance and Changes** covers the various maintenance tasks inherent in most modern operating systems. This includes time synchronization, account management, log file rotation, and general system cleanup.

**Chapter 10: System Monitoring** introduces techniques for monitoring your systems. This chapter presents Logwatch and swatch for log monitoring and NetSaint for network monitoring.

**Chapter 11: Improving System Security** discusses tools that can enhance your system's security with minimal maintenance on your part. This chapter also shows you how to use and configure Tripwire, how to create automatic firewall configurations, and how to use GNU cfengine to increase your system and network security.

**Chapter 12: Backing Up and Restoring Data** presents simple and inexpensive solutions for automatically backing up your systems' data.

**Chapter 13: User Interfaces** shows you how to create both console- and web-based user interfaces for your automation system using bash, Perl, and Mason.

**Appendix A: Introduction to Basic Tools** provides a basic introduction to the tools used throughout the book and provides a good starting point for understanding and utilizing the examples presented in this text. This appendix covers the following tools: bash, Perl, grep, sed, and awk.

**Appendix B: Customizing and Automating Red Hat Linux Installation** shows you how to automate the installation of Red Hat Linux. Also this appendix shows you how to create your own custom Linux distribution derived from Red Hat Linux.

**Appendix C: Building Red Hat Package Manager (RPM) Packages** houses comprehensive instructions on how to build your own RPMs.

## Additional Resources

The process of automating system administration covers a wide range of topics. Throughout the book, I will suggest additional reading material. Also, there are several additional books that you will most likely find helpful and I would like to mention them here:

- *UNIX System Administration Handbook (3rd Edition),* by Evi Nemeth, Garth Snyder, Scott Seebass, Trent R. Hein (Prentice Hall, 2000). This book covers almost anything you ever wanted to know about UNIX system administration.

- *Principles of Network and System Administration,* by Mark Burgess (John Wiley & Sons, 2000). This book discusses the theory and principles behind *good* network and system administration.

- *Unix Storage Management,* by Ray A. Kampa and Lydia V. Bell (Apress, 2002). This book covers everything you ever wanted to know about storing data on UNIX systems.

- *Learning the bash Shell,* by Cameron Newham and Bill Rosenblatt (O'Reilly and Associates, 1998). This book covers the bash command shell as well as bash shell scripting.

- *Learning Perl,* by Randal L. Schwartz and Tom Phoenix (O'Reilly and Associates, 2001). This is the first place to start if you want to learn Perl, a very powerful scripting language that is used extensively throughout this book.

- *Programming Perl,* by Larry Wall et al. (O'Reilly and Associates, 2000). This more advanced guide to Perl provides extensive reference material.

- *Perl for System Administration,* by David N. Blank-Edelman (O'Reilly and Associates, 2000). You already know we use Perl extensively in this book. By looking at the title, you also probably know that this book is about automating system administration. Any questions?

- *Practical UNIX & Internet Security,* by Simson Garfinkel, Alan Schwartz, and Gene Spafford (O'Reilly and Associates, 2003). This book discusses security, which should always be on your mind, especially when you automating system administration.

## Conventions Used in This Book

I have used several special font and formatting conventions in this book. This section reviews these conventions and how they are applied.

Here are some of the most common formatting conventions you will come across:

**NOTE**   Notes call attention to important issues or interesting facts about the given subject.

**TIP**   Tips provide additional information about the subject that you may find useful.

 **CAUTION**   Cautions serve to alert you about potentially dangerous side effects your actions or the presented scripts may cause.

 **WARNING**   Warnings provide important information that you must be aware of before proceeding, such as potentially serious side effects.

### Sidebars

Sidebars are used to provide larger amounts of related information that you may or may not be interested in reading.

This book contains a large number of program listings. Sometimes they are shown as a block of code:

```
#!/bin/bash
echo "hello, how are you?"
```

Other times they may be broken into sections. I may first define a function:

```
say_hello() {
   echo "Hello, how are you?"
}
```

and then provide the code that calls the function:

```
case $0 in
   hello)
      say_hello
      ;;
esac
```

To try these examples, you can download the code samples from the Downloads section of the Apress web site (http://www.apress.com). Alternatively, you can create your own script file by combining the separate parts of the script into one file, with the proper interpreter declaration at the top (such as #!/bin/bash).

Finally, some code listings will have their lines numbered and some of the numbered lines will be bold. These lines will be discussed in more detail after the code. Here is an example:

```
1   #!/bin/bash
2
3   echo "Hello, how are you?"
```

**Line 1:** Run this using bash as the interpreter.

**Line 3:** Output the string to stdout using the echo command.

Throughout the book, you will often see examples of commands being run as follows:

```
% ./hello
echo "Hello, how are you?"
```

Note that a constant-width font is used, just like on a terminal. Anything that you should type is **presented in bold**.

Here are some of the most common font conventions you will come across:

Monospaced: Monospaced font is used for a variety of purposes in this book. I use it to identify literal strings, such as Hello, how are you?. I also use it for URLs (such as http://www.apress.com), commands (like grep), filenames (/etc/passwd), and within program listings.

**Bold:** Bold is used to indicate something the reader or user should type, usually at a command prompt.

*Italics*: Italics is used to emphasis something or to indicate that a term is being defined.

## We'd Like to Hear from You

We have gone through several stages of proofreading and error checking during the production of this book in an effort to reduce the number of errors. We have also tried to make the examples and the explanations as clear as possible.

There may, however, still be errors and unclear areas in this book. If you have questions or find any of these errors, please feel free to contact me at kirk.bauer@apress.com. You can also visit the Apress web site at http://www.apress.com to download code from the book and see any available errata.

# CHAPTER 1

# Introducing the Basics
# of Automation

WHEN I WAS IN HIGH SCHOOL, I got my first part-time job keeping some of the
school's computers running. It was great. I did everything by hand. And since there
were only two or three computers, doing everything by hand wasn't a big issue. But
even then, as the number of systems grew to five, six, and finally more than ten,
I realized just how much time you can spend doing the same things over and over
again. This is how my love of automation was born.

In this chapter you will learn the basics of automating system administration
so that you can begin to make your life easier—as well as the lives of everybody
who uses or depends on your systems. The topics covered in this book are applicable to a wide variety of situations. Whether you have thousands of isolated
systems (sold to your customers, for example), a large number of diverse machines
(a large company or university campus), or just a few servers in your home or
small business, most, if not all, of the techniques covered will save you time and
make you a better administrator.

Throughout this book, I have assumed that the reader has a basic set of UNIX
skills and some prior experience as a systems administrator. I used numerous
tools throughout the book to provide example automation solutions. These tools
include the following:

- The bash shell

- Perl

- Regular expressions

- The grep command

- The sed Stream Editor

- awk

If you are not very familiar with one or more of these tools, I urge you to read
their introductions in Appendix A before you proceed.

## 1.1 Do I Need Automation?

If you have one Linux system sitting on your desk at home, you don't *need* automation. You can take care of everything manually—and many people do. But, you may *want* automation anyway because tasks like performing backups, applying security updates, and a variety of other routine activities are a pain to do and are easy to forget.

Likewise, you don't need automation if you only have one server in your company. However, you may want it because backups and timely security updates are easy tasks for a busy system administrator to neglect, even in this most basic setup. In addition, if your company's server is a file or mail server, its drives will tend to fill up and cause problems. In fact, any security or stability problem with this type of computer will likely result in expenses for the company and any loss of data could be disastrous. An automation system can also help out your replacement one day, or the person covering for you while you are on vacation.

So, back to the question—do you *need* automation? A variety of situations are described here in which automation is almost always required and will therefore be discussed throughout the book.

### 1.1.1 Large Companies with Many Diverse Systems

The most traditional situation involves a large company or organization with hundreds or even thousands of systems. These systems range from web servers to file servers to desktop workstations. In such a situation, you tend to have numerous administrators and thousands of users.

You may treat the systems as several groups of specialized servers (i.e., all workstations in one group, all web servers in another) or you may administer all of them together. Either way, with a large number of different systems, automation is the only option. GNU cfengine is especially suited to this type of environment. It uses a very high-level configuration file and allows each system to pull its configuration from the configuration server. cfengine is discussed thoroughly in section 6.4 and following chapters.

### 1.1.2 Medium-Sized Companies Planning for Growth

Any medium or small company is in just about the same situation as the large companies. Even though you may only have 50 servers now and some basic solutions may work for you, you probably hope to expand. If this is the case, you should always keep an eye on scalability and maintainability as you implement your automation system. Again, cfengine is usually your best friend in this situation.

### 1.1.3  Internet Service Provider

You may work at an Internet Service Provider (ISP). If this is the case, you probably have more computers than employees. You also (hopefully) have a large number of customers who pay you money for the service you provide. Your systems may run a wide variety of services and keeping them all running is very important. At other types of companies, although there are some critical servers, most systems are individual workstations, testing systems, and so on, that are not extremely critical for the company's success. At an ISP, almost all of your systems are critical, so you really need to create an automation system that promotes system stability and availability. There are a variety of solutions for you presented in this book; which one you should choose depends on how many systems you currently have and how many you plan to have later.

### 1.1.4  Application Service Provider

You may be an application service provider (ASP). You may have hundreds of systems that all work together, or you may have numerous groups of independent systems. Your system administration tasks probably include deploying and config-uring complex, custom software. Such changes need to be synchronized among the various systems and happen only on demand. Stability is very important, and by minimizing changes you can minimize downtime. You may have a central administration system or a separate administration for each group of systems (or both). When you create your automation system, be sure to keep an eye on scalability—how many systems do you have now, and how many will you have in the future?

### 1.1.5  Web Server Farms

Automation within web clusters is common today. If you have only a couple of load balancers and a farm of web servers behind them, all of your systems will be virtually identical. This makes things easier because you can focus your efforts on scalability and reliability without needing to support differing types of systems. In a more advanced situation, you also have database systems, back-end servers, and other additional systems. In this case, you need a more flexible automation system, such as cfengine. Regardless of the underlying infrastructure, the web servers themselves will be plentiful. You need a quick and efficient way to install and con-figure new systems (for expansion and recovery from failures).

### 1.1.6  Beowulf Clusters

Beowulf clusters are large groups of Linux systems that can perform certain tasks on par with a traditional supercomputer. People also make computational clusters with other types of systems. Regardless, each cluster usually has one control system and hundreds of computational units. To be able to set up and maintain the cluster efficiently, you need to be able to install new systems with little or no interaction. You have a set of identical systems, which makes configuration easy. You also usually have maintenance periods in which you can do what you want on the systems, which is always nice. But when the systems are in use, making any changes to them might be disastrous. For this reason, you will usually want to control the times when any modifications are made to the systems.

### 1.1.7  Network Appliances

Finally, many companies out there produce what I call network appliances. These are systems that run some UNIX variant (often Linux or FreeBSD) and are sold to customers as a "drop-in" solution. Some current examples of these products include load balancers and search engines. The end user administers the systems but may know very little about UNIX. They also usually do not have root access to the system. For this reason, the system must be able to take care of itself, performing maintenance and fixing problems automatically. It will also need to have a good user interface (usually web-based) that allows the customer to configure its behavior.

## 1.2 What Will I Gain?

Since this book applies to such a wide range of people and situations, not all of the material will be of interest to all readers. If you haven't yet created an automation system, then many of the examples will provide you with a good starting point. You will also learn the principles that should guide you in your quest for automation. As your skills and experience grow, you will become more interested in some of the more advanced topics the book discusses and find that it points you in the right direction on others.

If you already have an automation system of some sort, this book will provide you with ideas on how to expand it. There are so many ways to perform any given task that you are sure to encounter new possibilities. In many cases, your current system will be advanced enough to leave as is. In other cases, though, you will find new ways to automate old tasks and you'll find new tasks that you may have never considered automating.

When it comes to computer systems, every environment is different—each has different requirements and many unique situations. Instead of attempting to provide the unattainable "one solution fits all," this book shows you your options. You will learn the pros and cons of each option and see how to use them; there is really no single "right" answer for all situations. After you have learned these options, you will be able to make an informed choice about what should be automated in your environment and how it should be automated.

Many of the scripts in this book will not work right "out of the box" on your systems. For each example, a certain scenario will be used. Your setup will probably not match the scenario exactly, but you should find plenty of similarities. With the example as a starting point, you can make any necessary changes so that the script works in your environment.

An example may connect using several hosts via Secure Shell (SSH) and perform certain configuration tasks. You may need to add a few tasks for your environment, and remove a few others. You may be setting up an isolated system that manages itself, in which case you could remove the remote access component.

Or, your situation may require several thousand systems to be configured all at once. If the example pushes the configuration (see section 1.5.2) to the various systems in series, you may need to configure systems in parallel. Alternatively, you may want to modify the script to pull from a master configuration server instead of pushing to individual systems. Better yet, you may want to consider one of the other options presented (maybe GNU cfengine) that might fit your needs better.

## 1.3 What Do Sysadmins Do?

Life as a system administrator can usually be broken down into three categories:

- Tedious, repetitive tasks (a.k.a. boring tasks)

- New, innovative tasks (a.k.a. why you love the job)

- Answering users' questions (a.k.a. pulling your hair out)

The goal of this book is to help you create new and innovative solutions to eliminate those tedious and repetitive tasks. As far as answering users' questions go, if you find a way of automating that task, please let me know! But even if you can't, you can at least create a system that detects and even fixes many problems before the users even notice. Also, any task that you have automated is a possible task that the users can perform on their own.

The tedious tasks can be broken down into the following categories:

**Pre-Installation:** Assigning IP address, configuring existing servers and network services, and so on.

**Installation:** Installing a new operating system and preparing it for automation.

**Configuration:** Performing initial configuration and reconfiguration tasks.

**Managing Data:** Duplicating or sharing data (user's home directories, common scripts, web content, etc.), backups, and restores.

**Maintenance and Changes:** Rotating logs, adding accounts, and so on.

**Installing/Upgrading Software:** Using package management and/or custom distribution methods.

**System Monitoring and Security:** Performing log analysis and security scans, monitoring system load, disk space, drive failures, and so on.

## 1.4 Providing a User Interface

All of the automation techniques in this book, by their very nature, make system administration easier. This means that you simply need to place a user interface in front of these techniques to allow even novice users to perform these tasks.

Once you have a task automated, making a user interface for that task is a great idea. Even if the automation documents the task pretty well, if nobody can find or use that automation, your efforts are almost pointless. Automation can also allow others to do your work for you, and most people will not miss waiting on a system administrator to get simple things done.

These techniques are also very useful for embedded systems or network appliances. Network appliances almost always have a web interface that can be used by less technical people. Network appliances are also expected to monitor and possibly even repair themselves with little or no user intervention.

How you provide the user interface depends on your situation. Personally, I am a big fan of web-based interfaces. They are easy to create, easy to use, and they can be accessed from all operating systems. Even better, you can create a system that provides both a web-based and a command-line interface (a technique I try to use when possible), without duplicating too much work.

User interfaces will be covered in the last chapter because they are most useful after you have created some tasks (as described in the rest of this book) for which to provide interfaces.

# 1.5 Methodology: Get It Right from the Start!

Automating tasks is much more useful when you apply a consistent methodology. Not only will you have less direct work (by having code that is easier to maintain and reuse), but you will save yourself (and others) time in the future. Whenever possible, I have chosen and developed techniques in this book that allow these basic methodologies to be followed:

- Activities you have performed must be reproducible.

- Any system's state must be verifiable.

- Problems should be detected as they occur.

- Problems should be repaired automatically, if possible.

- The automation methods must be secure.

- The system should be documented and easy to understand.

- Changes should be testable in a safe environment.

- Every system change should be examined for side effects that also must be handled automatically.

Perhaps the most important aspect of any automated system is reproducibility. If you have two machines configured just the way you like them, you should be able to add a third machine, identically configured, to the group with minimal effort. If somebody makes an incorrect change or a file is lost, restoring the system to full functionality should be relatively easy. These nice capabilities all require that you can quickly and perfectly reproduce what you have done in the past or to other systems.

You also need to be able to verify a system's status. Does it have the latest security updates? Is it configured correctly? Are the drives being monitored? Is it using your newest automation scripts or old ones? These are all important questions and the answers should be easy to determine if your automation system is implemented properly.

In many cases, detecting problems is a great step forward in your automation process. But how about automatically fixing problems? This too can be a very powerful technique. If systems fix their own problems, you will get more full nights of sleep. But, if your auto-repair methods are overzealous, you might end up causing more problems than you solve. We will definitely explore self-repair whenever appropriate.

An administrator always has to consider security. With every solution you implement, you must be certain you are not introducing any new security issues. Ideally, you want to create solutions that minimize or even eliminate existing security concerns. For example, although you might find it very convenient to set up SSH so that it uses private keys without any passphrase, this usually opens up serious security holes.

There will always be people who follow in your footsteps. If you ask them, the most important component of your work is good documentation. I already mentioned that automation techniques, in many cases, provide automatic documentation. It is important to take full advantage of this easy documentation whenever possible. Consider, as an example, a web server under your control. You can either manually configure the web server and hopefully document the process for yourself and others in the future, or you can write a script to configure the web server for you. With a script, nothing can be neglected—if you forgot to do something, the web server does not run properly.

As obvious as it may sound, it is important to test out your automation before you deploy it on production servers. One or more staging machines are a must. I will discuss techniques for propagating code across machines and explain how these techniques can also be used for pushing code to your staging server(s).

Whenever you automate a task, it is important to consider dependencies. If you automated the installation of software updates and Apache is automatically upgraded on your systems, that is great. But, if the configuration files are replaced in the process, will they be regenerated automatically? This is just one example of the type of questions you need to ask yourself when you automate a task.

What do you do about these dependencies? They should be your next project. If you can automatically upgrade but can't automatically configure Apache, you may want to take on that task next. Even if you have already automated this task, you need to make sure the automation event is triggered after the software is updated. You may also need to update a binary checksum database or services on your systems. Whether or not these tasks are automated, you need to be sure they will not be forgotten.

## 1.5.1 Homogenizing Your Systems

Most people reading this book will have a variety of UNIX systems within their network. If you are lucky, they will all run the exact same operating system. In most cases, though, you will have different systems because there are a wide variety of commercial UNIX systems as well as FreeBSD and Linux. Even with one type of UNIX, there may be different varieties (called distributions in Linux). Even if all of your systems run the same UNIX system, some may run older versions than others.

When it comes to automation, the more similar your systems, the better. Sure, you can have a shell script that behaves differently on each type of system. You can also use classes in cfengine to perform different actions on different systems (as discussed in section 6.4). These approaches will be necessary to some degree, but your first and best option is to minimize these differences between your systems.

Your first step should be to provide a certain base set of commands that operate the same on all systems. The GNU project (http://www.gnu.org) will be very helpful because the GNU developers have created open-source versions of most standard UNIX commands. These can be compiled to run on any system, but most of them are binary programs, so you will pretty much need to compile each program for each platform. You can then distribute these programs using the methods discussed in Chapter 7. Once they are present on all of your systems, and in a standard location (like /usr/local/), you should use them in all of your scripts.

Some operating systems will provide other helpful commands that you may want to have on all of your systems. If you are lucky, these commands will be shell or Perl scripts that can be modified to operate on other systems. Even if they are binary commands, they may be open source and can be used on commercial UNIX systems.

In addition to consistent commands, a consistent filesystem layout can be helpful. As I already mentioned, placing custom commands in the same location on all systems is a must. But what else is different? Do some of your systems place logs in /var/adm/ and others in /var/log/? If so, this is easy to fix with symbolic links.

What I recommend is that you consider each difference separately. If it is easy to modify your systems to make them similar, then do so. Otherwise, you may be able to work around the differences, which is what you should do. Finally, if it isn't too difficult to add a specific set of consistent commands to all of your systems, try that approach. In most cases, you will have to use some combination of all three of these approaches in your environment.

## 1.5.2  Push vs. Pull

When configuring, maintaining, and modifying systems, there are two main approaches you can take. The first is to have one central system contact other systems and perform the necessary tasks. This is considered the "push" method. The alternative "pull" method is implemented by having the systems contact the central server on a regular basis and configure themselves.

Both methods have their advantages and disadvantages. As usual, the one you should choose depends on your situation. If you want precise control over when a system is modified in any way, you may prefer the push method. This allows you to automatically configure, update, or modify your systems, but only when you (or some other trigger) cause it to happen.

The push method sounds great, right? Well, not exactly—there are plenty of drawbacks. For instance, what if you have over a thousand systems? How long would it take to contact every system when a change needs to be made? What happens if some systems are currently unavailable? Are they just forgotten?

This is where the pull method really shines. If you make a change on a configuration server, all of your systems will pick up those changes whenever they can. If a system is a laptop at somebody's home, it might not get the changes until the next day. If a system has hardware problems, it might not get the changes until next week. But all of your systems will eventually have the changes applied—and most almost immediately.

So, does your environment consist of several systems that are intricately related? Do these systems need to be updated and modified together at all times? Does the update process unavoidably cause some amount of service outage? If so, you probably want to push any changes to these systems. If these aren't issues for you, and especially if you have a large number of systems, then the pull method is generally preferable.

Regardless of the method you choose, you still must be aware of the loads that will be placed on your systems, your network, and especially your servers. If you push in series (one system at a time), you are probably okay. If you push in parallel (all systems at once), though, the server might suffer. If your clients pull from a server, be sure they don't all pull at the same time. Consider adding a random delay before the task begins. GNU cfengine, which uses the pull method, provides the `SplayTime` option that does just this.

## 1.6 Dealing with Users and Administrators

Every person that uses your systems is either a user or an administrator (where an administrator is usually a user as well). At an ISP, most employees are administrators but the customers are actually the users. At a traditional company, a small number of people are administrators and all other employees are users.

Your more technical users may also be administrators of their own desktop systems. Since these systems can still be security risks, they should be included in your automation system. You have to be aware of conflicts that may arise between your automation system and the user's own actions. The user might destroy something that was done by your system; in this case, it should automatically be done again. Similarly, your automation might destroy changes the user wanted to make on their system—you would have to work with the user to find a different way make the change.

What you have to worry about the most are any interactions that may cause problems with the system. If, for example, your automation system assumes that a certain account is present on the system, it may not operate without it. This isn't a problem—unless, of course, somebody manually deletes that user.

Ideally, you would have a list of every assumption your automation system makes about every system. You would then enhance your automation system to check all of these assumptions and repair any problems. Realistically, you would have a hard time reaching this ideal, but the more hands you have in the pot (i.e., the more administrators), the harder you should try.

Another concern, if you have more than one or two administrators for a system, is an audit trail. Who has been accessing each system and what have they been doing? Most systems provide process accounting—a log of every process that is executed, what user executed it, and how long it was running. You usually have to enable this logging because it can consume quite a bit of drive space.

The problem is that when you see that root executed the command rm -rf /home/*, how do you know *who* did it? You know that it was run by the root user, but who was logged in as root at that time? Did you make an unfortunate typo, or did the pissed off employee who quit yesterday do it on purpose?

The easiest solution when you have multiple administrators is to give the root password to everybody, but this provides no audit trail at all. A better option is to specify which SSH keys should provide access to the root account. Each user has their own private SSH key and, assuming the logging is turned up slightly, the SSH server records the key used for each login. This allows you to determine who was logged in as root at any given time. Information on this approach can be found in section 2.6.

There is still a chance that multiple people will be logged in as root when a problem has occurred. The only way to know exactly who ran which commands is to use Sudo.

## 1.6.1 Sudo to the Rescue

Sudo is a program that allows specified users to execute specified commands as root (or any user, really). Using it is easy:

```
kirk % sudo /etc/init.d/httpd start
Password:
Starting httpd:                                    [ OK ]
```

Note that Sudo prompted me for a password. It wants me to enter the password for my user account, not the root account. This request helps verify that the person using the kirk account is still me (Kirk). The authentication will last for some period of time (usually five minutes) or until the command sudo -k is executed.

Executing that command as kirk resulted in the following log entry (sent through syslog, which ends up in /var/log/secure on my system):

```
kirk : TTY=pts/13 ; PWD=/tmp ; USER=root ; COMMAND=/etc/init.d/httpd start.
```

---

 **NOTE**   You can find the code samples for this chapter in the Downloads section of the Apress web site (http://www.apress.com).

---

None of this will work, however, without the proper permissions in the Sudo configuration file: /etc/sudoers. This file can be edited manually, but if more than one person may edit the file at the same time, you should use the visudo command. This command also checks the file for valid syntax on exit.

Here is the entry that allowed kirk to start the web server:

```
kirk ALL = /etc/init.d/httpd
start
```

This line says that the user kirk is allowed, on any host (ALL), to run the command /etc/init.d/httpd start. I could also allow the web server to be stopped and restarted by allowing any parameter to be specified to this script:

```
kirk ALL = /etc/init.d/httpd
```

I can also limit this command so that it can only be executed on the web server:

```
kirk www = /etc/init.d/httpd
```

This would allow the same /etc/sudoers file to be used on all of my systems (if this is the way I wanted it). I can even allow certain users to execute commands as other specific users:

```
kirk www = (nobody) ls
```

This allows kirk to list directories as the user nobody. I find this useful for verifying permissions within web content. If I can list directories with this command, the web server can also get into the directory. I could also apply this rule to all users in a specific group:

```
%users www = (nobody) ls
```

This command allows anybody in the group users to execute the command ls (with any arguments) as the user nobody on the host www. I could even remove the password prompt as well:

```
%users www = (nobody) NOPASSWD: ls
```

Now the users won't have to enter their password at all when they run this command. Since this command is not really that dangerous in most cases, it is nice for the users to not have to enter their password.

With Sudo, you can run certain commands without a password to allow scripts that are running as a user other than root to execute system commands. This is the most beneficial way to use Sudo when it comes to automation.

---

 **WARNING**  It may be tempting to just provide unlimited *root* access to certain users through Sudo. Although this will allow the users to execute commands as root with full logging enabled, it is not usually the most secure thing to do. Since each user can run commands as root with their *user* password, you effectively have several root passwords for the system.

---

There are many more options available to you within the /etc/sudoers file. I'm not going to attempt to cover them here, but you can view the sudo and sudoers man pages as well as the web site: http://www.courtesan.com/sudo/ for more information.

# CHAPTER 2

# Using SSH to Securely Automate System Administration

THE SECURE SHELL (SSH) protocol has revolutionized system administration ever since it became popular in the late 1990s. It facilitates secure, encrypted communication between untrusted hosts over an insecure network. This entire chapter is devoted to SSH because it plays such an important part in *securely* automating system administration.

Since this book is not about installing programs, I assume that you already have SSH installed and operating properly. I have based the examples in this book on OpenSSH 3.1 using version 2 of the SSH protocol. If you are using another version of SSH, the principles are the same, but the implementation details might be different.

For a more thorough and complete discussion of SSH, I highly recommend *SSH, The Secure Shell: The Definitive Guide* by Daniel J. Barrett and Richard Silverman (O'Reilly and Associates, 2001).

## 2.1 The Basics of Using SSH

If you are already familiar with the basic use of SSH, you might want to just skim this section. If, on the other hand, you are an SSH novice, you are in for quite a surprise. SSH is very easy and efficient to use and can help with a wide variety of tasks.

The commands in this section work fine without any setup (assuming you have the SSH daemon running on the remote host). If nothing has been configured, all of these commands use password authentication just like Telnet; except with SSH, the password (and all traffic) is sent over an encrypted connection.

To initiate a connection to any machine as any user and to start an interactive shell, use this command:

```
% ssh user@host
```

In addition to connecting to remote hosts, I often use SSH to log in as `root` on my local machine because it is quicker then using `ssh-agent`, as discussed later in this chapter.

You can also execute any command in lieu of starting an interactive shell. This displays memory usage information on the remote host:

```
% ssh user@host free
                total        used        free      shared     buffers       cached
Mem:           126644      122480        4164        1164       29904        36300
-/+ buffers/cache:          56276       70368
Swap:          514072       10556      503516
```

Finally, there is the `scp` command that allows you to copy files between hosts using the SSH protocol. The syntax is very similar to the standard `cp` command, but if a filename contains a colon, it is a remote file instead of a local file. Like the standard `ssh` command, if no username is specified on the command line, your current username is used. If no path is specified after the colon, the user's home directory is used as the source or destination directory. Here are a few examples:

```
% scp local_file user@host:/tmp/remote_file
% scp user@host:/tmp/remote_file local_file
% scp user1@host1:file user2@host2:
```

The last example copies the file named `file` from user1's home directory on host1 *directly* into user2's home directory on host2. Since no filename is given in the second argument, the original filename is used (`file`, in this case).

## 2.2 Enhancing Security with SSH

Before SSH, `telnet` was widely used for interactive logins. Telnet works fine, except that the password (well, everything actually) is sent in plain-text over the network. This isn't a problem within a secure network, but you rarely encounter secure networks in the real world. On an insecure network, other machines on the network can capture account passwords by monitoring Telnet traffic.

## Is Your Network Secure?

Some people define an insecure network as the Internet and a secure network as anything else. Others think that as long as there is a firewall between a private network and the Internet that the private network is secure. The truly paranoid (such as myself) just assume that all networks are insecure. It really depends on how much security you need. Are you a likely target for crackers? Do you store important, private information? Since nothing is ever 100 percent secure, I find it easier just to assume networks are not secure and skip the rest of the questions.

If you do think you have a secure network, be sure you consider all of the possible security vulnerabilities. Remember, employees within a company are often not as trustworthy or security-conscious as you would like. Somebody might have plugged in a wireless access point, for example. A person with more malicious intentions might intentionally tap into your private network, or exploit a misconfigured router or firewall. Even a fully switched network with strict routing can be vulnerable. I always try to be on the paranoid side because I'd rather be safe than sorry.

When it comes to automating system administration tasks across multiple systems, passwords are a real pain. If you want to delete a file on ten different machines, logging into each machine with a password and then deleting the file is not very efficient. In the past, many system administrators turned to rsh for a solution. Using a .rhosts file, rsh would allow a certain user (i.e., root) on a specific machine to log in as a particular user (again, often root) on another machine. Unfortunately, the entire authorization scheme relies on the IP address of the source machine, which can be spoofed, particularly on an insecure network.

The most secure way to use SSH is to use password-protected public/private Rivest, Shamir, and Adelman (RSA) or Digital Signature Algorithm (DSA) key pairs. Access to any given account is granted only to users that not only possess the private key file, but also know the passphrase used to decrypt that file.

Another component of SSH is a program called ssh-agent, which allows you to log in and enter your passphrase. This passphrase is used to decrypt your private key, which is stored in memory for the duration of your session. This eliminates the need to enter the passphrase every time you need to use your private key.

## 2.3 Using RSA Authentication

Many people are more than happy to use SSH with its default password authentication. In this case, SSH is simply used as a more secure version of Telnet. The problem is that you need to manually enter a password for every operation. This can become quite tedious, or even impossible, when you are automating system administration tasks. For most of the activities throughout this book, you must use RSA (or DSA) authentication.

Even if you use RSA authentication, you still have a passphrase that is used to encrypt the private key. You can avoid entering the passphrase every time you use SSH in one of two ways. You can use an empty passphrase or you can use the ssh-agent command as discussed in the next section. One major disadvantage of empty passphrases is that they are very easy to guess, even by people with very little skill.

---

### Should I Use an Empty Passphrase?

Some people think that using an empty passphrase is one of the seven deadly sins of system administration. I think that it can be appropriate within a very isolated environment, especially when the security implications are minimal. For example, a Beowulf cluster generally has an internal private network containing only one machine with an external network connection. For instance, if the cluster is being used by a university for research, then it might not be a very high target for intrusion. In this case, having an unencrypted private key on one of the cluster machines might not be too much of a concern.

However, if the same cluster were being used by a company that is doing important and confidential research, then, at the very least, the key should not be on the one machine with an external connection. Of course, it would be even better to use an encrypted key along with ssh-agent. This key could be placed on a machine completely separate from the cluster, yet it could be used to access both the gateway and the individual nodes. This would also remove the need to have the private key file on the cluster at all, whether encrypted or not.

The most important thing to consider is what access the key provides. If the key provides root access to every system in your entire network, then the risks of leaving the key unencrypted (i.e., with no passphrase) are pretty great. But if the key only allows the Dynamic Host Configuration Protocol (DHCP) server to be restarted on one host, then what will an attacker do with it? Perpetually restart your DHCP server? Maybe—but that is not the end of the world, and it is easy to fix (change keys).

---

Version 2 of the SSH protocol supports two types of public key encryption: RSA and DSA. The two encryption schemes are similar and are generally considered to provide equivalent security. For no particular reason (apart from the fact that I am most familiar with it), I will use RSA for the examples within this book.

## 2.3.1 Generating the Key Pair

The first step in the key generation process is to create your public and private key pair. OpenSSH provides a command just for this purpose. The following command creates a 2,048-bit RSA key pair. The default output files are ~/.ssh/id_rsa and ~/.ssh/id_rsa.pub for the private and public keys, respectively. The command prompts you for a passphrase (which can be left blank if you so desire).

```
% ssh-keygen -t rsa -b 2048
Generating public/private rsa key pair.
Enter passphrase (empty for no passphrase):
Enter same passphrase again:
Your identification has been saved in ~/.ssh/id_rsa.
Your public key has been saved in ~/.ssh/id_rsa.pub.
The key fingerprint is:
3a:85:c7:e4:23:36:5c:09:64:08:78:b3:72:e0:dc:0d kirk@kaybee.org
```

### What Size Key Should I Use?

The bigger the key is, the harder it is to crack, but the slower it is to use. Most people say a 1,024-bit RSA key is good enough and almost impossible to crack. If a 1,024-bit key is almost impossible to crack, then a 2,048-bit key is even more difficult to crack, but I use the bigger key just in case.

When choosing a key size, you must consider the value of the information or capabilities that the key protects. As long as your key would take more effort to crack than the data (or power) is worth, you are okay. An excessively large key places an unnecessarily large load on your systems.

If you are protecting data, you should also consider how long that data will be valuable. If the data will be worthless in one month and the key would take three months to crack, then the key is big enough. But be sure to consider that the attacker may have specialized hardware or advanced algorithms that can crack your key faster than you may expect.

The size of the key makes the biggest speed difference during the actual key generation process. Large keys are also more work (and therefore slower) when the computer encrypts and decrypts data. Since SSH only uses RSA/DSA when it is initiating a new connection, the RSA key size does not affect the performance of a session once it is established, just the initial session negotiations.

Throughout this book, I will generally show you examples that use the SSH key to access your systems. The actual data being sent is usually not important; it will typically contain commands to be executed and other control data. If somebody later decrypts this traffic, it will probably be of little value.

But in some cases, the data being transferred *is* sensitive. In these instances, the RSA (or DSA) key is only one thing to consider since these protocols are only used to exchange keys for the algorithm used to encrypt the actual data. If they have logged the SSH session, attackers can either crack the public key (by determining its associated private key) and determine the encryption key, or they can crack the actual encrypted data directly.

You can use the -c switch to ssh to control which cipher is used for encrypting your session. Your options are des, 3des, and blowfish. You should avoid des unless you need to use version 1 of the SSH protocol. The default is 3des, which is believed to be secure, while blowfish is faster and is also believed to be secure.

## 2.3.2 Specifying Authorized Keys

Now that you have a public key file, you can simply place that key in any account on any machine running the SSH server (sshd). Once the account is properly set up, your private key will allow easy access to that account. Since it is virtually impossible to determine the private key from a public key, only a person that possesses the private key can access the account.

To allow access to an account, simply create ~/.ssh/authorized_keys. The file contains one key per line (although the lines are very long—the 2,048-bit RSA key created in the previous example is almost 400 characters long in its ASCII representation). If the file does not currently exist, you can simply make a copy of your public key file.

You should also be careful with your permissions because sshd is usually very picky. In general, your home directory and the ~/.ssh directory must be only writable by the user (and not their group, even if they have their own group). The directory must be owned by the user as well—this can be an issue if root's home directory is / and it is not owned by root. If your RSA key is not accepted, look in the logs on the system you are connecting to; it will usually tell you why.

Here is an example that assumes that you have already copied your public key file into your home directory in another account.

```
% mkdir -p ~/.ssh
% chmod 0700 ~/.ssh
% cp ~/id_rsa.pub ~/.ssh/authorized_keys
% chmod 0600 ~/.ssh/authorized_keys
```

To add a second key, simply append it to the file. Once you have the file in place, your private key alone allows you to access the account. Of course, by default, the account password also allows access to the account. You can disable this feature in the OpenSSH sshd by modifying /etc/ssh/sshd_config (or the equivalent on your system) and adding this line:

```
PasswordAuthentication no
```

Alternatively, you could completely disable the account password (usually stored in /etc/shadow and allow only RSA-authenticated logins. However, this isn't a good idea if the user needs that password for other services such as POP3 mail access, FTP file transfers, and so on.

## 2.4 Using the ssh-agent

If you can use ssh-agent to allow passwordless operation instead of leaving your private key unencrypted, then you will greatly add to the security of your systems. The ssh-agent allows you to enter your passphrase only one time per "session" and your private key remains in memory, allowing passwordless connections for the rest of the session.

### 2.4.1 Basic ssh-agent Use

Using ssh-agent is simple. You actually start your command shell or your X session using the agent. Once logged in, you can run

```
ssh-agent bash
```

and you will have a new shell running through the agent. Or, if you use the wonderful screen program (included with most Linux installations and available from http://www.gnu.org/directory/screen.html, you can use

```
ssh-agent screen
```

to begin your screen session. I use the following script as my ~/.Xclients (or ~/.xinitrc) to allow easy use of ssh-agent within X:

```
#!/bin/bash

cd ~
exec ssh-agent bin/startx-continue
```

As you can see, `ssh-agent` runs my `startx-continue` script. That script runs `ssh-add </dev/null` to add the key and prompt for a passphrase (the `/dev/null` causes the program to use an X window for the passphrase entry). The `startx-continue` script also performs other startup tasks and finally starts the window manager.

Once you are running the agent, you can add your private key(s) with `ssh-add`:

```
% ssh-add
Enter passphrase for /home/kirk/.ssh/id_rsa:
Identity added: /home/kirk/.ssh/id_rsa (/home/kirk/.ssh/id_rsa)
```

You can also use the `ssh-add` utility to list the fingerprints of the keys currently stored in the agent by running `ssh-add -l`.

When you use `ssh-agent` to run another command, that `ssh-agent` session exists for as long as that command runs (such as your X session). Once that command terminates, any stored keys are lost. This is fine when you can start your entire X session as we just saw, but what if you can't? You can use the command shown in the next section to start a new `ssh-agent` for each login. This works well, unless you have a good number of simultaneous logins, in which case you will have to add your SSH keys for each session. If you are in this situation, consider using a tool called keychain that allows all of your logins on the same system to share the same `ssh-agent` easily. You can find information about this tool at `http://www-106.ibm.com/developerworks/library/l-keyc2/`.

## 2.4.2 *Advanced ssh-agent Usage*

You can also use `ssh-agent` without starting a new process. In the bash shell (or any POSIX-compliant shell) you can, for example, start `ssh-agent` like this:

```
% eval `ssh-agent`
```

Note that those are backticks around `ssh-agent`; they cause the output of this command to be passed to the `eval` command that will execute the code. In fact, all `ssh-agent` really does is start itself and print out some environment variables to be set by the shell. When you use `ssh-agent` to start a new process (as shown in the last section), it just sets these variables and then creates a new process with the variables already set. It is easy to see what is set by running `ssh-agent` by itself:

```
% ssh-agent
SSH_AUTH_SOCK=/tmp/ssh-XXoND8EO/agent.26962; export SSH_AUTH_SOCK;
SSH_AGENT_PID=26963; export SSH_AGENT_PID;
echo Agent pid 26963;
```

The SSH_AUTH_SOCK environment variable contains the path to the named socket created by ssh-agent to allow communication between the SSH program and the agent. The SSH_AGENT_PID variable contains the process ID of the agent so that it can be killed at some point in the future.

The main disadvantage of running ssh-agent this way is that you must kill the agent through some external method if you want it to stop running once you have logged out. The more basic usage causes the agent to die once the process it executed completes.

As an example, let's say that you have a script that executes numerous SSH operations and you only want to enter the passphrase once. You could create the following script:

---

 **NOTE** You can find the code samples for this chapter in the Downloads section of the Apress web site (http://www.apress.com).

---

```bash
#!/bin/bash

# Start the agent (don't display PID)
eval `ssh-agent` >/dev/null
# Now, ask for the key once
ssh-add

# Now, perform a bunch of SSH operations
ssh host1 'command1'
ssh host1 'command2'
ssh host2 'command3'

# Finally, kill the agent and exit
kill $SSH_AGENT_PID
exit 0
```

You could then run this script and it would prompt you for the passphrase only once, store the private key in the agent, perform several operations, and then kill the agent when it was finished.

## 2.4.3  Key Forwarding

You can configure your SSH client to *forward* your ssh-agent as well. If you enable this option, you can connect from machine to machine while your private key is only in memory on the original machine (the start of the chain). The key itself is never transmitted over the network. The agent is very useful when connecting to machines on private networks. You can connect to the gateway machine and then connect to internal machines that you cannot access directly from your workstation. For example, you can connect to one machine as root, and then run a script that connects to other machines using your private key, yet your key does not actually exist on that machine.

---

### Be Careful with ssh-agent Forwarding!

You should never forward your ssh-agent connection to untrusted hosts (hosts where untrusted users have root access). The root user on other systems can not obtain your actual private key, but they *can* use your forwarded ssh-agent connection to access other machines using *your* private key. OpenSSH lets you specify different options for different hosts (in ssh_config) so that you can forward your ssh-agent to only trusted hosts.

In addition, once you connect to another host and then use the ssh command on that host to connect to a third host, you are using the SSH client configuration of the second host, not the first host. That host may have been configured to forward ssh-agent connections anywhere—including untrusted hosts.

So, a prudent user only forwards their agent to specific hosts. These selected machines only allow trusted users access to the root account, and they also limit to which hosts they will forward the ssh-agent session. You can also do this on the command line instead of modifying the actual ssh_config file; just specify the option -o "ForwardAgent no|yes" to the ssh command.

Also note that, in the authorized_keys file, you can restrict which remote hosts are allowed to connect with the specified key with the from directive (discussed next in the "Restricting RSA Authentication" section). If you only forward your key to certain systems, you can only allow login from those systems. If you accidentally forward your key to some other host, it won't work from that system anyway.

---

Some people also use ssh-agent in a noninteractive environment. For example, you might have a system monitoring script that needs to connect to other machines continuously. You could manually start the script through ssh-agent, and then the script could run indefinitely using the passphrase that you entered at startup. You could even place something like this in your system's startup scripts:

```
# start the ssh agent
/usr/bin/ssh-agent | /usr/bin/head -2 > ~/.ssh/agent-info

# alert oncall person to the system reboot
echo "$(hostname) rebooted, need to ssh-add the ssh keys into the ssh-agent" \
  | /bin/mail -s "$(hostname) rebooted" oncall@page.example.com
```

Any scripts that need access to this SSH agent can source `~/.ssh/agent-info`.

## 2.5 Restricting RSA Authentication

The `authorized_keys` file can contain some very powerful options that can limit the amount of access to the account the private key is granted. You can also use these options to prevent your agent from being forwarded to an untrusted host. To do so, place these options in the `authorized_keys` file at the beginning of the line, and follow it with a space character. No spaces are allowed within the option string unless they are contained within double quotes. If you specify multiple options, you must separate them with commas. The following is a list of the options and a brief description of each. The man page for sshd contains more detailed information.

> `from="pattern-list"`: Can specify a list of hosts from which the connection must be made. This way, even if the key (and the passphrase) is stolen, the connection still must be made from the appropriate host(s). The pattern could be `*.myoffice.com` to allow only hosts from the office to connect using that key.

> `command="command"`: If specified, the given command always runs, regardless of what the SSH client attempts to run.

> `environment="NAME=value"`: Environment variables can be modified or set with this command (which can be listed multiple times).

> `no-port-forwarding`: SSH allows ports on the server (or any machine accessible by the server) to be forwarded to the remote client. So, if a user can SSH into a gateway machine, they can forward ports from your private network to their remote machine, possibly bypassing some or all security. This prevents a specific key from forwarding any ports over its connection.

> `no-X11-forwarding`: SSH can also forward X11 connections over the encrypted connection. This allows you (and also the `root` user if they so desire) to run X11 applications that display on the computer initiating the SSH connection. This command disables this feature for this particular key.

> `no-agent-forwarding`: This prevents an `ssh-agent` connection from being forwarded to the host when a user connects to it with the specified key.

`no-pty:` Prevents the allocation of a tty (so that an interactive login is not possible).

`permitopen="host:port":` Allows only a given host and port to be forwarded to the remote client.

These options can be used for a lot of interesting tasks, as the following sections illustrate.

### 2.5.1  Dealing with Untrusted Hosts

When adding your public key to the `authorized_keys` file on an untrusted host, you could add some of the options just discussed to prevent agent and X11 forwarding. This is a good idea, but it should not be relied upon— if an untrusted `root` user on the machine can hijack your forwarded X11 or agent session, they can probably also modify your `authorized_keys` file. That being said, you can prevent the forwarding on both ends (client and server) to be extra safe. To do so, put the following in your `authorized_keys` file on the remote host (the key has been trimmed down for easier reading):

```
no-X11-forwarding,no-agent-forwarding,from="*.kaybee.org" ssh-rsa AB...YZ
```

This example also limits connections to this account. Only if the canonical hostname is `something.kaybee.org` will the key be granted access.

### 2.5.2  Allowing Limited Command Execution

Let's say that you have a script that monitors a set of servers. Root access is not necessary for monitoring the systems. The script does, however, need to reboot the machines in some cases, which does require root access. The following configuration, when placed in `~root/authorized_keys`, only allows this specific key to reboot the system and nothing more.

```
no-port-forwarding,command="/sbin/reboot",no-pty ssh-rsa AB...YZ
```

Whoever possesses the specified private key cannot open an interactive shell or forward ports. They can only do one thing: run the `/sbin/reboot` command. In this specific example, you must be careful because if you connect to the account with the specified key, the system will reboot (regardless of what command the remote client attempts to run). You must also make sure you use an absolute path for the command. If you do not, a malicious user might be able to place a command with the same name earlier in the search path.

## 2.5.3  Port Forwarding

There are plenty of situations in which forwarding a port between two machines is very useful. If the port is not encrypted, for example, you can use SSH to forward it over an encrypted channel. If the machine is behind a firewall, that machine can connect to an outside machine and forward ports to enable outside access.

### Accessing a Server Behind NAT

Let's say that you want to view a web page on a machine that is on a private network but can initiate outgoing connections (i.e., is using Network Address Translation [NAT]). You can connect from that web server to your local machine using SSH as follows:

```
% ssh -R 8080:localhost:80 user@your-desktop-system
```

The command says to connect from the web server (which is behind the NAT router) to the client (your desktop) and connect port 80 on the server to port 8080 on the client. Once this command has been executed, a user of the desktop system can point a browser to port 8080 and view the content on port 80 of the web server.

The hostname localhost could be replaced with any other hostname that the initiating host (the web server in this example) can access. This can be used to provide connectivity between two systems that could not normally communicate with each other. Let's say, for example, that there was a router in that same private network as the web server that allows Telnet access via port 23. The web server could map port 23 on that router to port 2323 on some other system:

```
% ssh -R 2323:my-router:23 user@some-host
```

Once you run this command, you will actually have an interactive login session on the destination system. As long as that session is open, the port forwarding is active.

### Encrypting Mail Traffic

To forward unencrypted port 25 (mail) traffic from your client to a server over an encrypted channel, you could run this command as root on your local machine:

```
% ssh -L 25:localhost:25 user@mailserver
```

This does not work if a mail server is already running on the local machine because it is already using port 25. When the command is executing, you could send mail to port 25 of your local machine and that traffic would really go to the mail server over the encrypted connection.

### Configuring authorized_keys

If you wanted to create a special account on the mail server that allows users to forward traffic to port 25 and nothing else, you could configure the authorized_keys file to restrict access to the account as follows:

```
command="while true; do sleep 1000; done",no-pty,
 permitopen="localhost:25" ssh-rsa AB...YZ
```

Please note that the preceding code would be only one line in the actual authorized_keys file, with no space after the no-pty,. This configuration allows you to make a connection that only runs an infinite loop and only forwards port 25. When connecting with this specific key, you can not do anything else with this account.

## 2.6 Using SSH for Common Accounts

One interesting way to use SSH involves allowing several users to access one or more common accounts. This is perhaps the most useful for the root account (when there are multiple administrators), but you could use it for other accounts (such as a special account to do software builds, etc.). The advantage of this approach is that each user does not have to know the account password to access the account. In addition, the logs can tell you who is actually logging into the account.

Another, and perhaps better, solution is to have each user login with their user account. They can then use Sudo to execute certain commands as root (Sudo was introduced in section 1.6.1). But, there are times when Sudo is not an option—particularly if you don't want to create a user account on the system for each user who needs to run commands as root.

### 2.6.1 Preparing for Common Accounts

The setup is actually very simple. You generate a key pair for each user and then list the appropriate public keys in the account's authorized_keys file. However, it can be frustrating to manually maintain this system when you have a large number of accounts and/or users. It is much easier to create a configuration file as follows:

```
# The account name is given first, followed by a colon,
# with each user who should be able to access that account
# listed afterward, and separated by commas.
root:amber,bob,frank,jill
build:amber,bob,susan
```

Then create a script that can process the configuration file and generate all of the authorized_keys files. This particular script assumes that each person's public key is in their home directory and they are using RSA:

```perl
#!/usr/bin/perl -w
use strict;

# Set the location of the configuration file here
my $config = "/usr/local/etc/ssh/accounts";

# Where the key fingerprints will be stored
# (for purposes of log analysis)
my $prints = "/usr/local/etc/ssh/prints";

# Set the path to a user's public key relative to
# their home directory
my $public_key = ".ssh/id_rsa.pub";

# This function takes one scalar parameter (hence the $
# within the parenthesis). The parameter is stored in
# the local variable $username. The home directory
# is returned, or undef is returned if the user does
# not exist.
sub GetHomeDir ($) {
    my ($username) = @_;
    my $homedir = (getpwnam($username))[7];
    unless ($homedir) {
        print STDERR "Account $username doesn't exist!\n";
    }
    return $homedir;
}

# This function takes in an account and the home directory and logs
# the key fingerprint (by running ssh-keygen -l), which has output:
# 2048 85:2c:6e:cb:f6:e1:39:66:99:15:b1:20:9e:4a:00:bc ...
```

```perl
sub StorePrint ($$) {
    my ($account, $homedir) = @_;
    my $print = `ssh-keygen -l -f $homedir/$public_key`;
    # Remove the carriage return
    chomp($print);
    # Keep the fingerprint only
    $print =~ s/^\d+ ([0-9a-f:]+) .*$/$1/;
    print PRINTS "$account $print\n";
}


# This function takes one line from the config file and
# sets up that specific account.
sub ProcessLine ($) {
    my ($line) = @_;
    # A colon separates the account name and the users with access
    my ($account, $users) = split (/:/, $line);
    my $homedir = GetHomeDir($account);
    return unless ($homedir);

    print "Account $account: ";

    # First, make sure the directory exists, is owned
    # by root, and is only accessible by root
    my $group = 0;
    if (-d "$homedir/.ssh") {
        $group = (stat("$homedir/.ssh"))[5];
        system("chown root:root $homedir/.ssh");
        system("chmod 0700 $homedir/.ssh");
    } else {
        mkdir("$homedir/.ssh", 0700);
    }

    # Remove the existing file
    unlink ("$homedir/.ssh/authorized_keys");

    # Create the new file by appending other users' public keys
    my ($user, $homedir2);
    foreach $user (split /,/, $users) {
        # Get this other user's home directory too
        $homedir2 = GetHomeDir($user);
        next unless ($homedir2);
```

```perl
        if ((not -f "$homedir2/$public_key") or
            (   -l "$homedir2/$public_key") ) {
            print "\nUser $user public key not found or not a file!\n";
            next;
        }

        print "$user ";
        my $outfile = "$homedir/.ssh/authorized_keys";
        system("cat $homedir2/$public_key >> $outfile");
        StorePrint($user, $homedir2);
    }
    print "\n";

    # Now, fix the permissions to their proper values
    system("chmod 0600 $homedir/.ssh/authorized_keys");
    system("chown $account $homedir/.ssh/authorized_keys");
    system("chown $account $homedir/.ssh");
    if ($group) {
        # We saved its previous group ownership... restore it.
        system("chgrp $group $homedir/.ssh");
    }
}


# Open the fingerprint file
open (PRINTS, ">$prints") or die "Can't create $prints: $!\n";

# Open the config file and process each non-empty line
open (CONF, "$config") or die "Can't open $config: $!\n";
my $line;
# The angle operators (<>) read one line at a time
while ($line = <CONF>) {
    chomp($line);
    # Remove any comments
    $line =~ s/\#.*$//;
    # Remove leading and trailing whitespace
    $line =~ s/^\s+//;
    $line =~ s/\s+$//;
    # Process the line (if anything is left)
    $line and ProcessLine($line);
}
close (CONF);
close (PRINTS);
exit 0;
```

## Always Watch for Race Conditions!

You might find it odd that the authorized_key file generation script changes ownership of the .ssh directory to user root and group root and then changes it back to the proper user later in the script. The script makes these ownership changes to prevent any race condition exploits by the user of that account. Even if you trust all of your users now, you might not trust them all in the future, and it is much easier if you worry about the problems when you are writing the original script.

The script first makes sure the directory is owned by root and writable by nobody else. Then it removes the current authorized_keys file. If this is not done, the current authorized_keys file could be a symbolic link to a system file that is overwritten when you create the file.

The script also checks the user's public key file to make sure it is a regular file (the -f operator) and not a symbolic link (the -l operator). If the user's public key file was a symbolic link, the user of the account could point that link to any system file they could not normally read (such as the shadow password file). Then, when the script was run, it would copy the contents of that file into an authorized_keys file.

Note that you must remove the current authorized_keys file and check the public key file after the ownership and permissions of the .ssh directory have been changed. If you do not, the user could theoretically change the files after you have checked them but before you access them, effectively bypassing all of the security in the script.

As you can see, the script assumes all of the home directories are on this particular machine. There are various methods you can use to synchronize home directories among multiple machines as discussed in Chapter 7. Alternatively, you could easily modify this script to manage accounts on other machines using scp to transfer the actual authorized_keys files. Here is the output from this script when it is run with the sample configuration file:

```
% ./account-ssh-setup.pl
Account root: amber bob frank jill
Account build: amber bob susan
```

The script also creates a file that lists all of the key fingerprints and their associated account names. Later, you can use this file to aid in the analysis of the sshd log entries. The file, as you will notice, may contain duplicate entries, but that won't affect how it is later used.

## 2.6.2 Monitoring the Common Accounts

If you want to monitor which users are logging into which accounts, you must first keep a log of which key logs into which account. Unfortunately, OpenSSH does not do this by default. You need to turn up the logging level of sshd by adding this line to /etc/ssh/sshd_config (or wherever it is on your system):

```
LogLevel VERBOSE
```

Once you have added this configuration line and restarted sshd, you will see these logs (in /var/log/secure or wherever you have your other sshd logs). The headers have been removed for easier reading:

```
Found matching RSA key: cc:53:13:85:e5:a0:96:c9:24:f5:de:e0:e3:9e:9b:b6
Accepted publickey for test1 from 10.1.1.1 port 55764 ssh2
```

Unfortunately, the information we need for each login spans two lines in the log file, which makes analysis slightly more complicated. Here is an example script that can analyze a log file and summarize user logins. As with every example in this book, this script is only an example; you should modify it as necessary for your specific needs.

```perl
#!/usr/bin/perl -w
use strict;

# The logfile to analyze
my $log = "/var/log/secure";

# Where the key fingerprints are stored
my $prints = "/usr/local/etc/ssh/prints";

# First, read and store the fingerprints in a hash table
# Duplicate lines will not hurt anything
open (PRINTS, "$prints") or die "Can't open $prints: $!\n";
my (%Prints, $line);
while ($line = <PRINTS) {
   chomp($line);
   my ($account, $print) = split / /, $line;
   $Prints{$print} = $account;
}
close (PRINTS);
```

```perl
# Open the logfile and process each line
# Store results in a two-tier hash table
open (LOG, "$log") or die "Can't open $log: $!\n";
my (%Results, $user);
while ($line = <LOG>) {
    chomp ($line);
    if ($line =~ /Found matching \S+ key: ([0-9a-f:]+)/) {
        # Determine user from print-lookup hash (if possible)
        if ($Prints{$1}) {
            $user = $Prints{$1};
        } else {
            $user = 'Unknown';
        }
    } elsif ($line =~ /Accepted publickey for (\S+)/) {
        $Results{$1}{$user}++;
    }
}
close (LOG);

# Display the results
my $account;
foreach $account (keys %Results) {
    print "$account:\n";
    foreach $user (keys %{$Results{$account}}) {
        print "   $user: $Results{$account}{$user} connection(s)\n";
    }
}
exit 0;
```

The script is fairly simple, but you could expand it to support date ranges or to report the dates of the various logins. But, here is an example of the script, as shown, being executed:

```
% ./sshreport.pl
root:
    amber: 2 connection(s)
    bob: 1 connection(s)
build:
    susan: 4 connection(s)
```

# CHAPTER 3

# Creating Login Scripts and Shell Scripts

**IN A PERFECT WORLD,** you could spend a few weeks creating a system and the result would be a system that never required manual maintenance or modifications. Whether this ideal will ever be achieved is debatable, but it definitely won't happen in the near future. In the meantime, we still have to do things manually, even if only once in a while.

When I must do things manually, I'm not usually happy about it. In fact, it usually means that there has been an emergency, so other people aren't happy about it either. In times like this, it is nice to have a consistent and efficient user interface on every machine.

The information and examples presented in this chapter assume that you are using the bash shell. However, you can modify all of the scripts so that they work in other shells. In some cases, they might even work unmodified (like in the standard Bourne Shell [sh]). Other shells will also work, but they might have different methods for changing the prompt and creating command aliases. The principles in this chapter should be relatively easy to adapt to the shell of your choice.

What I want you to learn from this chapter, even if you don't use bash, is that many shells are very powerful and most of us use very little of that power to our advantage. It is worthwhile to spend some time becoming familiar with your shell and learning some of its advanced features—those that can help make your life more efficient.

## 3.1 Tailoring the Command Prompt

Some people have no desire to modify their command prompt. They may consider such a change as only aesthetic or a waste of time. It is true that the appearance of the command prompt is purely entertainment for some, but for me, it is crucial that it be informative and clear.

If you, like most administrators, run the X Window System with 10 or more terminals open, or you run screen and have so many windows that you lose some here and there, then you will also appreciate a detailed prompt. If you have accounts on 100 machines, for example, it is nice to know what machine you are running commands on at all times. If you have both root and regular user accounts, it is nice to know when you have superpowers. It is also very important to know exactly what directory you are in when you run commands such as `rm -rf *`.

## 3.1.1 *Making Your Prompt More Informative*

The default prompt on many systems is a single character. I can find no good reason to use such a prompt any longer than necessary. Prompts should be informative so that they help you work more efficiently and make fewer mistakes.

You are probably thinking I am being a hypocrite right about now because every single prompt I have used in every example thus far has been a single character. It may go without saying, but the examples in this book do not usually require context (i.e., user, host, or directory) and a more descriptive prompt would only add unnecessary clutter to the examples.

Any good prompt should include the following information:

- Current directory

- Username

- Hostname

- Return code (of the last command)

Many prompts do not include the return code of the last command. Although such information is not completely necessary, it might help you see whether a previous command succeeded or failed. So, a simple, informative prompt that is easy to read can be set as follows (in the bash shell):

```
export PS1="-\$?-(\u@\h) \w > "
```

If you have never set a custom prompt before, this might be just about the most cryptic thing you have ever seen. Here are the important parts:

\$?: The environment variable $? always expands to the return code of the last command. The backslash (/) preceding the $ character prevents the shell from expanding it when you set the prompt; instead the shell expands the $? variable each time the prompt displays. Without the backslash, you would always have the same return code in your prompt (whatever it happened to be when you set the prompt).

\u: This expands to your current username.

**\h:** This expands to your current hostname. In some cases, this can be too long or too short (and therefore, not descriptive enough). If that is the case, you should, in your login script, come up with a better value (using the hostname command), store it in an environment variable (such as $host), and use that in your prompt instead.

**\w:** This special sequence expands to your full current working directory.

This prompt will make much more sense when you see what it looks like in action. You'll notice that many of the special characters are simply literal parts of the prompt. Here is what the prompt looks like (or you could just run the command and see for yourself):

```
-O-(kirk@kaybee) /tmp >
```

Some people have their prompt display only the last portion of the current directory (accessed in bash with the \W sequence). I find this almost useless because I prefer to see the entire pathname (\w in bash). The full pathname, however, can sometimes be quite long. So long, sometimes, that no room is left to actually type commands. For this reason, I personally use a two-line prompt. This may seem ridiculous to some, but I can put all of the variable-length data on the first line and reserve almost the entire second line for my actual commands. Here is an example of a two-line prompt:

```
export PS1="[\u@\h]: \w\n\$?> "
```

The only new thing in this prompt is the carriage return (\n), which starts the second line. As you can see, the full current directory can be pretty long, yet the prompt is still very usable:

```
[kirk@kaybee]: /usr/local/m68k-palmos/include/sys
O>
```

Some people hate two-line prompts, but I think using them is better than cutting off most of the current directory.


## 3.1.2  Using Colored Prompts

The use of colored prompts is another area of great disagreement among UNIX users. Some think they are distracting and a waste of time. I think they significantly add to the readability of the prompt (well, assuming an appropriate color scheme is chosen). I like to put important information in bright colors and background text in dull colors.

One problem with colored prompts is that a certain color scheme will look great on a black background, but it will be virtually unreadable on a white background. Since I always use a black background for my terminals, I use colors that look good on a black background. I force the background under the prompt to be black (using the code 40) just in case I use the prompt on a terminal with a white background. So, on a white terminal, you would have a white background everywhere except for the characters under your prompt, which would have black backgrounds and colored text.

### 3.1.2.1 *Using ANSI Color Codes*

ANSI escape sequences look quite ugly at first glance, but they are not actually too difficult to use. An actual ANSI sequence can be as simple as \033[37m ("white" text) or as complicated as \033[4;37;40m (underlined, "white" text on a black background). The \033 is actually the octal value for the escape character. Then comes an open bracket, followed by one or more numbers (separated by semicolons), and then terminated with the m character.

I use the term "white" in quotes because it is usually displayed as gray, and bright white is usually what you would consider to be white. Likewise, "yellow" is typically orange and bright yellow can usually be considered yellow. The actual color displayed is dependent on the terminal itself. So, just because the colors aren't quite what you expected does not mean you made a mistake in your escape sequence.

Table 3-1 is a list of all the common ANSI color codes. Some of them may not work on all terminals. Remember, you can include several codes, separated by semicolons.

*Table 3-1. ANSI Color Codes*

| Code | Effect |
| --- | --- |
| 0 | All attributes off |
| 1 | Bold (or Bright) |
| 2 | Light (default) |
| 4 | Underline |
| 5 | Blink |
| 7 | Invert |
| 30 | Black text |
| 31 | Red text |

*Table 3-1. ANSI Color Codes (Continued)*

| Code | Effect |
|------|--------|
| 32 | Green text |
| 33 | Yellow text |
| 34 | Blue text |
| 35 | Purple text |
| 36 | Cyan text |
| 37 | White text |
| 40 | Black background |
| 41 | Red background |
| 42 | Green background |
| 43 | Yellow background |
| 44 | Blue background |
| 45 | Purple background |
| 46 | Cyan background |
| 47 | White background |

When placing nonprintable characters (such as ANSI color codes) within your bash prompt, remember to enclose them with \[ and \] sequences. If you forget, the characters will be counted as printable characters and the prompt will be corrupted during command editing.

### 3.1.2.2 Defining a Colored Prompt

You will see that I like to define the actual colors in separate environment variables to make the prompt definition easier to read. The colors are provided using American National Standards Institute (ANSI) escape sequences and may not work on all terminals.

**NOTE**  You can find the code samples for this chapter in the Downloads section of the Apress web site (http://www.apress.com).

```
#!/bin/bash
# This should go in your ~/.bashrc file

# Define ANSI color sequences
NORMAL="\[\033[0m\]"
WHITE="\[\033[0;37;40m\]"
MAGENTA="\[\033[0;35;40m\]"
BRIGHTBLUE="\[\033[1;34;40m\]"
BRIGHTWHITE="\[\033[1;37;40m\]"
BRIGHTMAGENTA="\[\033[1;35;40m\]"

# Find out if we are root
if [ $UID -eq 0 ] ; then
    # The # character serves as an extra reminder that I am root
    SYM='#'
else
    SYM='-'
fi

# Define the actual prompt
# This is split up for easier reading within this book
P1="$MAGENTA$SYM$BRIGHTMAGENTA-$BRIGHTBLUE($WHITE\u$MAGENTA@$WHITE"
P2="\h$BRIGHTBLUE)$BRIGHTMAGENTA-$BRIGHTBLUE($BRIGHTWHITE\w$BRIGHTBLUE"
P3=")$BRIGHTMAGENTA-$MAGENTA$SYM$NORMAL\n$MAGENTA$SYM$BRIGHTMAGENTA-"
P4="$BRIGHTBLUE($BRIGHTWHITE\$?$BRIGHTBLUE)$MAGENTA>$NORMAL "
PS1="$P1$P2$P3$P4"
```

There is a little utility written by Moshe Jacobson called, aptly enough, color. This is a C program that you can call from within your shell scripts to make using color easier, and the resulting scripts easier to read. Here is the previous example using the color program. It is more verbose, but easier to read.

```
#!/bin/bash
# This should go in your ~/.bashrc file

# Find out if we are root
if [ $UID -eq 0 ] ; then
    # The # character serves as an extra reminder that I am root
    SYM='#'
else
    SYM='-'
fi
```

```
# Define the actual prompt
# This is split up for easier reading within this book
P1="$(color magenta)$SYM$(color ltmagenta)-$(color ltblue)"
P2="($(color white)\u$(color magenta)@$(color white)"
P3="\h$(color ltblue))$(color ltmagenta)-$(color ltblue)"
P4="($(color ltwhite)\w$(color ltblue))$(color ltmagenta)-"
P5="$(color magenta)$SYM$(color off)\n$(color magenta)$SYM"
P6="$(color ltmagenta)-$(color ltblue)($(color ltwhite)\$?"
P7="$(color ltblue))$(color magenta)>$(color off) "
PS1="$P1$P2$P3$P4$P5$P6$P7"
```

Unfortunately, colored prompts will not look particularly exciting when they are printed in a black and white book, so you will have to try these out for yourself to see the results. Here is what the colored prompt looks like without color:

```
--(kirk@kaybee)-(/home/kirk)--
--(0)>
```

I also like to make root's prompt stand out just a little bit more, so I have the script check to see if I'm root and change the prompt accordingly:

```
#-(root@kaybee)-(/home/kirk)-#
#-(0)>
```

As you can see, the possibilities for colored prompts are endless. There is no point in giving other examples because the actual formatting and color choices are personal preferences. However, I do think that it is worthwhile to spend an hour modifying your prompt because it will serve you well for many years to come.


## 3.2 Using Tab Completion

Most shells have some form of completion, typically initiated by the TAB key. Shells will typically complete things such as command names, filenames, users, and environment variables. If you do not use tab completion very often, you are missing out on a real time saver. How much should you use tab completion? A good sign that you are using it enough is when you catch yourself trying to tab-complete the directory in the mkdir command or the target for the make command.

## 3.2.1  Configuring Tab Completion

Once again, the following information is specific to the bash shell. Other shells (most notably zsh) are similar. Tab completion has become so important to me that I rarely use the ls command any more, because I can use tab completion instead to list the contents of a directory.

The bash shell uses the GNU readline library for its command-line interface. A variety of other programs also use the readline library. In all cases, the library reads its configuration from the .inputrc in your home directory. At the very least, I recommend that you try these options in your .inputrc. Some people like them, but others don't (maybe that's the reason they are not enabled by default). Give them a shot and see what you think:

```
set show-all-if-ambiguous on
set visible-stats on
```

The first option immediately shows possible matches the first time you hit the TAB key (normally you have to hit it twice to see the list). The second option appends characters to filenames in completion lists, just like ls -F does (* on the end of executables, / on the end of directories, etc.).

## 3.2.2  Programmable Tab Completion

Some shells, such as bash and zsh, have fully programmable completion systems. Although nobody has come up with a function that guesses your new directory names for you quite yet, you *can* have your shell complete make targets or CVS modules. In fact, the number of specialized completion functions people have written is mind-boggling.

In most cases, it is probably not worth the effort to write custom completion commands for every program you use. It might take you hours to get it right and you usually don't run any given command enough for it to be worth it. Other people have, however, written quite a number of these custom completion functions, and using their hard work to your advantage may very well be worth the effort.

Ian Macdonald maintains a package that includes many custom completion functions that add special support for commands such as cvs, rpm, make, mount, man, kill, and almost every other command in existence. I definitely recommend trying out his package, which can be found at http://www.caliban.org/bash/.

### 3.2.3  Using Custom Completion Functions

Although you can probably find custom completion functions for most commands, you may have a command that you wrote yourself or you may run across one that most people just do not use very often. In this case, it might be worthwhile to write your own custom completion function.

The first thing you need to do is check out several existing functions to get ideas about what functionality you want to provide. In most cases, you could also copy code from existing functions to make your new one. To add the functionality, you have to enable custom completion in your bash shell and associate your custom function with the appropriate command.

The following example (taken from Ian Macdonald's bash-completion package mentioned in the previous section) adds special functionality for the umount command. Once you type the command, you can hit the TAB key and a complete list of currently mounted partitions will be displayed. This is much more pertinent for the umount command than the standard filename completion.

```
1   # Turn on programmable completion
2   shopt -s progcomp
3
4   # umount(8) completion. This relies on the mount point being
5   # the third space-delimited field in the output of mount(8)
6   _umount()
7   {
8       local cur
9
10      COMPREPLY=()
11      cur=${COMP_WORDS[COMP_CWORD]}
12
13      COMPREPLY=($(compgen -W '$( mount | cut -d" " -f 3 )' -- $cur))
14
15      return 0
16  }
17  complete -F _umount -o dirnames umount
```

**Line 2:** This shell setting enables programmable completion functionality.

**Line 10:** This initializes $COMPREPLY as an empty array. bash expects to see a list of completion options in this array when the function returns.

**Line 11:** $COMP_CWORD is the index of the word on which the cursor is currently located. This line takes that word out of the $COMP_WORDS array and stores it in the local variable cur.

**Line 13:** The compgen command is used to populate the $COMPREPLY array with the completion list. The cut command is used to isolate the third column in the output of the mount command.

**Line 17:** This tells the bash shell to call the _umount when attempting to complete the command umount. The dirnames option tells the complete function to attempt to match directory names if the completion function does not return any matches.

You should place your custom completion code in your ~/.bashrc (or in a separate file executed by your login script). Once activated, you can type umount , followed by a space, and hit the TAB key, which will result in a list of all currently mounted filesystems being immediately displayed.

This is a relatively simple example and many other commands can be more complicated. The nice thing is, like many things in life, the more complicated your completion function is, the more useful it will be. So, pick a command and look around for an existing completion function. If you don't find one, try writing one and see how well it works out.

## 3.3 Creating Command Aliases

Most, if not all, shells provide *command aliases*, which are basically virtual commands that you can run as if they are real commands. When you execute an alias, it runs one or more real commands (or other aliases) usually with prespecified arguments. You could accomplish the same thing with shell scripts, but command aliases are more efficient and can be placed within your login scripts (such as ~/.bashrc) instead of requiring you to create one file per command.

### 3.3.1  Increasing Efficiency with Aliases

Most people use command aliases to shorten or simplify often-used commands. This is a terrific way to make your life more efficient. For example, if you use Network Information Services (NIS) to manage accounts on your network, and you want to check the entry for a specific account, you would run the following:

```
% ypcat passwd | grep -i username
username:XXXXXXXXXXX:500:500:Some User:/home/username:/bin/bash2
```

It is much more convenient to define a command alias to make this kind of operation less cumbersome, like this:

```
alias gypp='ypcat passwd | grep -i'
```

Once defined, you can run the same query with much less typing:

```
% gypp username
username:XXXXXXXXXX:500:500:Some User:/home/username:/bin/bash2
```

The actual string gypp is expanded, by the shell, to ypcat passwd | grep -i. Therefore, every parameter to the gypp command is actually passed along to the grep command.

## 3.3.2  Improving Consistency with Aliases

When you frequently use machines running different variants of UNIX (i.e., System V, BSD, Linux), you will find having a consistent command-line interface very helpful. Regular users, in addition to administrators, can benefit from such consistency. As you may have experienced, it is frustrating when you have to try two or three times before you get a complete process listing because of differing syntax for the ps command across different platforms. In addition, inconsistency can be downright dangerous—think what would happen if you ran the killall on Solaris (which, not surprisingly, kills every process on the system as the command's name implies) when you meant to just kill only programs with a specific name (as is the behavior on Linux systems). You can use command aliases to eliminate or at least help reconcile these differences.

### 3.3.2.1  Detecting the System

The first step is to determine the class of system you are currently using. In most cases, differentiating between the three major variants is enough. This is very easy to do with the following segment of bash commands which, once again, can be placed in your ~/.bashrc file.

```
case $(uname -s) in
    Linux) os=linux ;;
    *[bB][Ss][Dd]) os=bsd ;;
    *) os=unix ;;
esac
```

Once these commands have been executed, the $os environment variable contains the string linux, bsd, or unix. You can then use this information at a later time (such as when you are defining command aliases) to alter your behavior based on operating system type. In many cases, you must also modify the shell environment based upon the actual hostname. For example, you might want to have different settings for the $CVSROOT environment because each machine might have different locations for the CVS repository.

```
1   HOSTNAME=$(hostname -f 2>/dev/null || hostname)
2   case $HOSTNAME in
3     *kaybee*)
4         CVSROOT="/var/cvs"
5         HOST="kaybee"
6         ;;
7     *work*)
8         CVSROOT="/data/cvs"
9         ;;
10  esac
11  export HOST=${HOST:-${HOSTNAME%%.*}}
```

**Line 1:** Since the -f (fully qualified domain name) option to the hostname command is only valid on some systems, it is attempted, but if it fails, the hostname command is run again without any arguments.

**Line 3:** For any host with the string kaybee contained in its full hostname, the $CVSROOT will be set to /var/cvs. The $HOST environment variable will also be set to the string kaybee.

**Line 7:** For any host with the string work within its full hostname (normally this would be the domain of your work computers), CVSROOT will be set to /data/cvs/.

**Line 11:** This cryptic line will set $HOST to the current value of $HOST if it is non-empty (i.e., if it was set in the case statement). If it is empty, it will set $HOST to the value of HOSTNAME with everything after the first dot removed.

The $HOST environment variable can be used within your prompt instead of the standard \h sequence. This allows you to customize what hostname appears within your prompt, since some hostnames are not clear or are just too long.

### 3.3.2.2   The ls Command

On many systems, the ls command does not display colors by default (or it may not even be capable of displaying colors). Most implementations of the ls command can also be configured to "classify" the files displayed (such as adding a * on the end of executables and a / on the end of directories). When you add the following code to your login scripts it will cause ls to use color and/or classify the files on many different systems. This script assumes the $os environment variable is configured as was shown in the previous section.

```
# Find out if we are root
unset ALL
if [ $UID -eq 0 ] ; then
    ALL='-a'
fi


if [ "$os" = "linux" ] ; then
    alias ls='/bin/ls $ALL --color=auto --classify'
elif [ -x /usr/local/bin/ls ] ; then
    alias ls='/usr/local/bin/ls $ALL --color=auto --classify'
else
    alias ls='/bin/ls $ALL -F'
fi
```

The first thing this script does is set $ALL to -a if you are logged in as root. This causes all file listings as root to show hidden files. Then, if the system is Linux, the script assumes /bin/ls is GNU ls, which supports the options --color=auto and --classify. If the system is not Linux, the script checks for /usr/local/bin/ls instead, and, if it finds it, it assumes *this* is GNU ls (on many non-Linux systems, GNU utilities are installed in /usr/local/bin). If all else fails, the script settles on a non-GNU /bin/ls and only uses the -F flag (same as --classify).

Once this initial alias is configured, many people like to have a few other aliases as follows:

```
alias ll='ls -l'
alias lla='ls -al'
alias la='ls -a'
```

The ls command specified within these aliases will actually be the previously defined ls alias, not the system command, so the appropriate flags will already have been defined.

### 3.3.2.3 The ps Command

The ps command is probably the best example of a command that is used significantly differently among various systems. The following aliases (again, assuming you have the $os variable properly configured) provide consistent ps output (of all processes) on a variety of systems.

```
case $os in
 linux)
  alias psa='ps axo "user,pid,ppid,%cpu,%mem,tty,stime,state,command"'
  ;;
 bsd)
  alias psa='ps axo "user,pid,ppid,%cpu,%mem,tty,start,state,command"'
  ;;
 unix)
  alias psa='ps -A -o "user,pid,ppid,tty,stime,s,comm"'
  ;;
esac
```

A complete process listing is rarely what I want to see. Usually, I want to filter the list based on one thing or another. So I use the following function when I am looking for a certain process (or everything a certain user is running):

```
function is () {
   case $os in
       linux|bsd)
          psa ww | grep "$@" | grep -v "grep"
          ;;
      *)
          psa | grep "$@" | grep -v "grep"
          ;;
   esac
}
```

This is a function and not an alias. The reason for the added complexity is that I need to insert the arguments passed to the is command within a command sequence. By using a function, I can reference the arguments anywhere I want to with the $@ variable, which preserves the exact tokenization of the original arguments. With command aliases, the arguments to the actual aliased command are always placed on the end of the substituted command, which would not work in this case.

On systems where it will work properly, this function adds ww to the ps command to provide very wide output for better filtering. Then, the search pattern (the argument to the actual is command) is applied against the ps output. Finally, any matches of the actual grep command are removed (of course, any line with the string grep in it is removed, which could inadvertently remove a valid result).

## 3.4 Creating Commands That Affect Multiple Systems

The first step in automating the administration of multiple machines is to implement a set of basic commands that operate on multiple machines. The most important of these commands are the ssh and scp commands, which are extended to operate on multiple remote hosts instead of just one.

### 3.4.1 Simple Multi-SSH

Simple multi-SSH is a simple shell script that executes the specified command on every machine listed in a configuration file. The configuration file contains exactly one hostname per line.

```
#!/bin/bash

# This file should have one host per line
host_list='/usr/local/etc/all_hosts'

# Check for required argument
[ $# -gt 0 ] || {
    echo "usage: $0 command ..." >&2
    exit 1
}

# Execute the command(s) on each host
for host in `cat "$host_list"` ; do
    echo " ** $host **"
    ssh "$host" "$@" || {
        echo "ERROR: Could not execute $* on $host!" >&2
    }
done
```

The arguments to this command can be one or more shell commands, separated by semicolons, but enclosed within quotes (if any spaces or semicolons are used). The command(s) are run on every host, and the output is displayed locally with a line separating each host.

### 3.4.2 Group-Based Multi-SSH

In many cases, you may want to run a command on a certain subset of machines instead of being forced to run it on every machine in every circumstance. The following scripts execute an arbitrary command on (or copy files to) one or more groups of hosts.

### 3.4.2.1  The Host Files

A directory (such as /usr/local/etc/hosts/) should contain one file per group of hosts. Each file should contain one host per line. The same host can be present in any number of files because the commands will eliminate duplicates. An example grouping of hosts is shown in Table 3-2. As you can see, some machines are in multiple groups because, in the real world, machines usually have several roles.

*Table 3-2. Example Host Groups*

| Group | Hosts | Description |
| --- | --- | --- |
| desktops | amber, bill, moshe, jill | Users' desktop machines |
| web | bill, wsw1, wsw2 | Machines that run web servers |
| external | amber, wsw1, www2 | Machines that are externally accessible |

### 3.4.2.2  Executing Commands

The following script runs any command (or multiple commands) on the machines in each specified group. The first argument must be the command, so it must be enclosed in quotes if it contains spaces (i.e., if you want to run a command with arguments). Multiple commands may be separated by semicolons, but they must all be within the quotes. As you can tell, it is a good idea to always enclose the command(s) in quotes to avoid any confusion. Following the command(s) to be executed are one or more group names. These must be the names of files within the configured host group directory.

```
#!/bin/bash

# Directory containing host file(s)
host_dir='/usr/local/etc/hosts/'

# Check for required arguments
[ $# -gt 1 ] || {
    echo "usage: $0 \"command(s)\" hostgroup ..." >&2
    exit 1
}
```

```
# Take the command(s) off of the parameter stack
cmd="$1"
shift


# Place full paths to each hostfile in $hostfiles
# This will loop once for every (remaining) argument
for hostfile ; do
    if [ -r "$host_dir/$hostfile" ] ; then
        hostfiles="$hostfiles $host_dir/$hostfile"
    else
        echo "INVALID GROUP: $hostfile" >&2
    fi
done


# Make sure we actually have hosts to operate on

[ -n "$hostfiles" ] || exit 1

# Execute the command(s) on each host
for host in `sort $hostfiles | uniq` ; do
    echo "  ** $host **"
    ssh "$host" "$cmd" || {
        echo "ERROR: Could not execute $cmd on $host!" >&2
    }
done
```

This shell script is actually too simple, considering how useful it is. All it does is build a list of files containing hosts based on its parameters and then stores this list in the $files variable. It then sends these files through the sort and uniq programs (uniq eliminates duplicate lines, but it requires them to be sorted first). The result is a complete list of unique hosts, based on the groups specified on the command line). The script then executes the requested command on each of those hosts and the resulting output is displayed to the screen.

### 3.4.2.3 Copying Files

The following shell script copies one or more local files, recursively, to a given directory on multiple machines. The first argument in this script must be the local file, or a list of local files contained within quotes. The second argument must be a destination directory. Following the file(s) and destination directory is one or more group names. These must be the names of files within the configured host group directory.

```bash
#!/bin/bash

# Directory containing host file(s)
host_dir='/usr/local/etc/hosts/'

# Check for required arguments
[ $# -gt 2 ] || {
    echo "usage: $0 \"local file(s)\" remote_dir hostgroup ..." >&2
    exit 1
}

# Take the local and remote files off the parameter list
lfile="$1"
shift
rdir="$1"
shift

# Place full paths to each hostfile in $hostfiles
# This loop will loop once for each (remaining) parameter
for hostfile ; do
    if [ -r "$host_dir/$hostfile" ] ; then
        hostfiles="$hostfiles $host_dir/$hostfile"
    else
        echo "INVALID GROUP: $hostfile" >&2
    fi
done

# Make sure we actually have hosts to operate on
[ -n "$hostfiles" ] || exit 1

# Execute the command(s) on each host
for host in `sort $hostfiles | uniq` ; do
    echo "  ** $host **"
    scp -r "$lfile" "$host:$rdir" || {
        echo "ERROR: Could not copy $lfile to $host:$rdir!" >&2
    }
done
```

This script is very similar to the script we discussed in the previous section, so please refer to that script for an explanation of how the scripts actually work. Make sure you note, however, that this script is slightly different because here a recursive copy will be performed if the local file is a directory.

## 3.5 Distributing Your Login Scripts

One of the most difficult things you could do is maintain independent login scripts for each of your accounts. Depending on how you configure your systems, you may have a unique home directory on each. This is almost always true with the root account—and the root account may be used the most frequently and is the most critical account for an administrator.

If you write a new function for one account and want that feature on every account, you have to manually merge the files to make this happen. This might be manageable if you only have a few accounts and simple login scripts, but when your login scripts grow to over 500 lines and are deployed in 30 accounts, it will be an absolute nightmare.

You must establish a master copy of your login scripts, and only make changes to these scripts in that location. If you need to make changes that are specific to only a subset of machines, you should use detection code, which I explain in section 3.3.2.1.

If a change is only specific to a single machine, you could have code in your login script that tries to source a particular file. If the file doesn't exist, the login script should not complain. If the file does exist, it should contain commands specific to a single host. This sourced file can be different on each host, but your main login script will still be the same everywhere.

### 3.5.1  Tracking Different Versions

As your login scripts become more complicated, you need to use versioning of one type or another. This could be as simple as adding a version and a date at the top of each file (in the comments). Alternatively, you could get the script to display its version when you log in (only when the shell is interactive), which is the method I like to use. I use the following code:

```
VERSION="6.2.1"
VDATE="06/16/2002"
case $- in
   *i*)
      echo "Kirk's Login Scripts -- Version $VERSION ($VDATE)"
      ;;
esac
```

In the bash shell, the $- environment variable contains the letter i when the shell is running interactively. So, if the shell is interactive, the version of the login scripts is displayed on every login. If you use Revision Control System (RCS) or Concurrent Versioning System (CVS) to manage your login scripts, you could use the $Id substitution string to have the version automatically updated.

## 3.5.2 Distributing Login Scripts

A script that distributes your login scripts (and other related files) to any or all of your accounts helps you maintain a single version. When you make significant changes, you can distribute those changes to every account with one command. Likewise, when you make a host-specific change in your master copy, you can distribute that change to its needed location.

### 3.5.2.1 Creating a Central Configuration File

A configuration file that is easy to create, read, and maintain is crucial to any script that is supposed to make your life easier. In this case, the configuration file uses one line per account. Each line contains one entry in the following format: user@host. Here is an example configuration file:

```
kirk@kaybee.org
root@kaybee.org
kirk@desktop.work.com
root@desktop.work.com
root@www1.work.com
root@www2.work.com
amber@sca.org
```

As you can see, on many machines, you might have a normal user account as well as access to the root account. Both accounts are listed as separate entities within this configuration file. If other people use the root account as well, they also have to be happy with your login scripts.

---

### Sharing the root Account

If the root account is shared among several users, you can have your login scripts execute when you log in to the root account. This removes the need to modify root's home directory at all. For example, on some systems, you can use the following alias for the su command:

```
alias su="su -c 'bash -rcfile ~$USER/.bashrc'"
```

When connecting via SSH, you can also execute bash and specify a specific rcfile instead of the one in the account's home directory.

A word of caution--be sure that your personal .bashrc does not do anything strange that might create a bad environment for your root login (such as placing the current directory in your path). Also, be sure any scripts you run depend as little as possible on root's environment because it will not always be the same if several different users use this approach.

---

### 3.5.2.2  Creating the Distribution Script

The following script assumes the model of one or two highly protected private keys that allow access into many accounts. In such a case, you want the same authorized_keys file on each host.

The first thing the script does is set up the SSH authorized_keys file in the remote account. This lets the remaining file transfers occur without you entering a password (assuming your ssh-agent is running). The umask statement is important because most SSH servers ignore the authorized_keys if the permissions are too open. Note that the file's contents are transferred using the same session, so you only have to enter the password once.

Once passwordless access is enabled, scp is used to transfer any remaining files. Here is the script:

```
#!/bin/bash

# This file should have one account per line
acct_list="$HOME/etc/accounts"

# Files to copy
copy_files='.vimrc .inputrc .bashrc .bash_profile .emacs'

# Go to our home directory
cd ~

do_account() {
    # $1 contains string "user@host"
    echo "  ** $1 **"

    # Create ~/.ssh (if necessary), copy authorized_keys file
    ssh -T "$1" \
        'umask 077; mkdir -p $HOME/.ssh; dd of=$HOME/.ssh/authorized_keys' \
        < $HOME/.ssh/authorized_keys 2>/dev/null || {
        echo "Failed to create directory on $1!" >&2
        return 1
    }
```

```
    # Now, copy other files over
    scp $copy_files "$1:~/" || {
        echo "Failed to copy files to $1!" >&2
        return 1
    }
}


for account in `cat "$acct_list"` ; do
    if [ -z "$*" ] ; then
        # No arguments specified, so do every host
        do_account $account
    else
        for arg ; do
            if [ "$arg" = "${account#*@}" ] ; then
                # Host was specified on command line
                do_account $account
            fi
        done
    fi
done
```

If no arguments are given, the script updates every host in the configuration file. If arguments are given, the script assumes they are hostnames, and only those hosts are updated. The sequence `${account#*@}` in the script is expanded to the $account variable with the username (and @sign) removed from the beginning.

Note that this script works with an account it has never been run on before, but it can also run repeatedly against any single account without causing harm (unless, that is, you have made a local change in that account, in which case that change will be lost).

# Pre-Installation: Network Preparation and Management

BEFORE YOU CAN add a new system to a network, you must do many things and you can automate most, if not all, of them. The most common of these include:

- Classifying the new computer

- Allocating an IP address

- Adding the new host to system lists

- Configuring the Dynamic Host Configuration Protocol (DHCP) server

- Configuring the Domain Name System (DNS)

- Updating the /etc/hosts file

As with most other automation tasks, different sites will want to automate different tasks. Some sites will not use all of the features I discuss in this chapter. Other sites will want to automate additional tasks. As a result, the scripts described here will be modular so that they can be trimmed down or expanded as necessary.

In this chapter, you will learn how to create a modular network preparation script. You will also see how to develop a set of modules that perform common tasks, and you will learn how to add your own functionality. Conversely, I will also present a modular script for removing systems from your network at the end of this chapter.

## 4.1 Deciding Between Static and Dynamic IPs

Most networks contain a mix of servers with static IP addresses and workstations with dynamic IP addresses. The servers provide a variety of services, such as web, mail, DNS, and so on, and generally they require static IP addresses to be operated properly.

The workstations include personal desktop machines, laptops, lab, and testing machines. Typically they don't need static IP addresses, so assigning them dynamic IPs using DHCP is a good option.

From an administrative perspective, you would prefer that any machine that is part of your automation system have a static IP address. Although you could also manage hosts with dynamic IPs, doing so is more difficult, so try to provide static IPs for all of your systems. If necessary, you can modify the examples in this book to work with dynamic hosts by pulling IP addresses from your DHCP server's log files.

So, for each system that doesn't inherently require a static IP address, you have to make a choice. If its operating system is compatible with your automation system, then usually using a static IP address is the best choice. For all other systems, dynamic IPs may be your easiest option, or you can just stick with one approach and assign static IPs to all your systems. DHCP can configure clients with either static or dynamic IPs, so the use of static IPs does not prevent your users from enjoying its convenience.

Keep in mind that dynamic IP addresses have one big drawback. If a system on your network has been hacked or is causing a problem of some sort, how do you find the system that has been compromised? If it has been assigned a dynamic IP, all you know is its Media Access Control (MAC) address. If you only have 30 systems in your company, it might only take you an hour to locate the problem. But if you have 1,000 employees in 2 buildings and almost 2,000 systems, finding the troubled system would pretty much be impossible (unless your network hardware can help you narrow it down, which is a possibility).

My favorite solution is to use DHCP for all hosts, but assign static IPs to as many systems as possible. This way, you can still allow dynamic addresses to be assigned if you want visitors to be able to use your network. Just be careful—with dynamic IPs available, most users do not really need to request a static IP for their systems. As a result, your network can quickly degrade into a set of unknown systems with dynamic IP addresses.

## 4.2 Creating and Using Modular Shell Scripts

It should already be clear that, when handling system pre-installation tasks, one solution will not fit all. This is a perfect situation for a modular shell script. My favorite way to create modular scripts is to create a special directory that contains several separate shell scripts. I then define an interface (by setting certain environment variables, for example) and write a central script to execute each of the component scripts. Each shell script performs a certain task or logical group of tasks.

If you need the script to perform a new task, you do not need to modify the main script. Instead, you can place a new script within the component script directory. If you need to have a certain activity removed, you can remove the script from the directory (or, even better, you can make it nonexecutable by running chmod a-x on the file). Another big advantage of a modular shell script is that you can write each component script in whatever language is appropriate for its specific task.

The main script, which the user runs directly, is responsible for initializing tasks and executing each module. It usually sets (and exports) certain environment variables and passes certain parameters to the modules. If modules should be run in a certain order, numbers can be prepended to their filenames (such as 01allocate_ip, 05dns, etc).

One problem with executing separate shell scripts as components of a program is that they are unable to set environment variables that can be accessed by other components or the main script. We will resolve this problem by having the components output their desired variables on stdout; then the main script will eval any output generated, causing the variables to be set in the scope of the main script. The main script (and other components, assuming the variable was exported) can then access these environment variables. If this is a bit confusing to you, don't worry, some of the examples later in this chapter should clear this up.

In general, I like using separate scripts to provide more flexibility than a monolithic shell script. It allows different people to separately maintain the different scripts. You can also add new functionality without modifying any of the current, well-tested scripts; just add a new script to the set and leave the rest alone. In addition, if you use packages to install software, each package can add scripts to the directory if necessary, regardless of which other packages are installed and which other scripts are present.

You can also create modular systems by creating separate functions within one main script. Although you lose some of the benefits of separate scripts if you do this, you gain the advantage of having a single file to manage and distribute. If this appeals to you, then you should know that there is nothing inherently wrong with creating one big script with multiple functions.

## 4.3 Using Locking to Prevent Conflicts

One important thing that is often overlooked when you are writing a script of this nature is locking. Locking can be used to prevent more than one person (or process) from doing the same thing at once. If you are the only administrator, then it is not critical to have a lockfile. Even so, such a file could prevent you from having two sessions of the program running at the same time (i.e., one session is still waiting for user input, yet you have started a second session). With multiple administrators, eventually two of you will try to add a new system at the same time. This may or may not cause problems, but it is better to be safe than sorry.

You could get into advanced locking where each individual operation is locked as it occurs. For a system that will be run often by many users, this is important. But, in this specific system preconfiguration script, we know that only a limited number of people will be adding systems at any given time. In addition, in most situations, this script will not be run more than a few times per day (and usually much less).

So, here is a simple locking system that can be added to the top of this script (or to any other script) to prevent it from being run multiple times simultaneously on the same system. For this reason, you should make sure this script only exists on one system.

 **NOTE** You can find the code samples for this chapter in the Downloads section of the Apress web site (http://www.apress.com).

```
lockfile="/var/lock/myprogram"
[ -f "$lockfile" ] && {
    pid="$(cat "$lockfile")"
    if ps $pid >/dev/null ; then
        # Still running
        echo "ABORTING: Another instance is running ($pid)" >&2
        exit 1
    else
        # No longer running, remove stale lockfile
        rm -f "$lockfile"
    fi

}
# We can proceed... write our PID into the lockfile
echo "$$" > "$lockfile"
```

Likewise, you could make sure the script is being run by root just to be safe:

```
[ "$UID" -eq 0 ] || {
    echo "Must be run as root!" >&2
    exit 1
}
```

## 4.4 Base Pre-Installation Script

The following script asks for the hostname that has been assigned to the new machine. It then performs the necessary configuration and setup tasks (through the component scripts). In many cases, this can be done before the operating system is even installed, but it could also be done after the machine is up and running.

The script's operation is fairly straightforward:

1. Request, validate, and format a new hostname.

2. Check for a duplicate hostname.

3. Add the hostname to the list of hosts.

4. Execute all scripts in the module directory.

The main script should be similar to the following:

```
1  #!/bin/bash
2
3  set -u
4  component_dir="/usr/local/lib/prepare_system/"
5  export data_dir="/usr/local/var/prepare_system/"
6
7  echo
8  echo "New System Preparation"
9  echo
10
11  echo -n "Enter the system's hostname: "
12  read -e new_hostname
13
14  # First, convert all letters to lowercase in $new_hostname
15  # Be sure to export the variable for use by component scripts
16  export new_hostname="$(echo $new_hostname | tr 'A-Z' 'a-z')"
17
18  # Make sure the hostname contains only valid characters
19  if ! echo "$new_hostname" | egrep -q '^[0-9a-z_-]+$' ; then
20      echo "Invalid hostname: $new_hostname" >&2
21      exit 1
22  fi
23
```

```
24  # Make sure the hostname is not already in use
25  if grep -q "^$new_hostname$" "$data_dir/hosts" 2>/dev/null ; then
26    echo "Hostname already exists: $new_hostname" >&2
27      exit 1
28  fi
29
30  # Record the new hostname
31  echo "$new_hostname" >> "$data_dir/hosts"
32
33  # Now, execute all component scripts
34  for script in $component_dir/* ; do
35      # Go to next file if this is a directory
36      [ -d $script ] && continue
37      # Go to next file if this is not executable
38      [ -x $script ] || continue
39      # Execute this script, execute its output, abort on failure
40      eval `$script` || {
41          echo "$script returned error" >&2
42          exit 1
43      }
44  done
45
46  echo
47  echo "System preparation complete for $new_hostname"
48  echo
49
50  exit 0
```

**Line 3:** This causes any undefined variables to be treated as errors, which is a nice way to identify problems in the scripts.

**Line 4:** This is the directory that contains all of the subcomponents that should be executed by this script.

**Line 5:** This is the directory that contains all of the data files used by the script. Note that this variable is exported so subcomponents can have access to the value.

**Line 12:** Reads input from the user (the -e switch tells the read to use readline for user input, if possible).

**Line 16:** The tr (translate) command is used to convert all letters to lowercase. The $new_hostname variable is set to the output of the commands within the $(...) sequence. Within that sequence, the current value of the variable is sent through the tr command, which does the actual conversion.

**Line 19:** Checks the hostname for validity. The egrep command is used to make sure the hostname consists entirely of one or more of the following characters: a-z, 0-9_, and -. The q switch causes the egrep command to produce no output.

**Line 34:** This loops through every file or directory within the directory stored within the $component_dir environment variable. The $script variable is set to a different file or directory name on each loop.

**Line 36:** The -d operator returns true if the file specified is a directory. If true is returned, the continue command is executed to skip to the next directory entry (because we want to ignore any directories).

**Line 38:** Similar to the -d operator, the -x operator returns true if the file is executable. Since directories have already been eliminated, if the file is executable, we can assume it is a script we want to run. Users can turn off the execute bit on a particular script to prevent its execution without having to delete the entire script.

**Line 40:** The component script is executed by the backticks. The standard error output (stderr) of the command is then executed by the eval command to set environment variables as discussed earlier in this chapter.

This base program, along with the component scripts described in the next section, will complete a variety of setup tasks for a new machine. Here is a sample run of the program:

```
# add_system

New System Preparation

Enter the system's hostname: some-new-hostname
Enter the system's MAC address (no colons!): abcdef012345
IP Address Allocated: 192.168.1.14

Select one or more groups for this host (Q to quit):
 1) web
 2) desktop
 3) linux
#? 1
```

```
Current List: web

 1) web
 2) desktop
 3) linux
#? 2

Current List: desktop web

 1) web
 2) desktop
 3) linux
#? q

Enter the system's contact: Kirk Bauer

Host some-new-hostname added to group(s): desktop web
Added some-new-hostname to hosts file
some-new-hostname added to dhcpd.conf
DNS entries created for some-new-hostname (192.168.1.14)

System preparation complete for some-new-hostname
```

## 4.5 The Pre-Installation Component Scripts

The script in the previous section would be pretty useless without some component scripts in the specified directory. The base script does not store or generate any data (except for the master host list), nor does it make any direct changes. This section contains several component scripts that can and should be used to perform the real setup tasks, as required by your specific situation. They should also make great examples that can be modified for your own purposes.

Each script can expect two environment variables to be set by the base script: $data_dir and $new_hostname. Each script can interact with the user, but each must limit its output on stdout to commands that should be executed by the base script (such as export new_variable=value; to set a new variable). Each script should output either the string true; or the string false; on stdout as its last command to indicate its return status. Obviously any output on stdout needs to be limited to valid commands that can be executed by the shell.

These scripts have been written with the assumption that all operations should be performed on the machine on which the specific service is running. For example, the DHCP and DNS changes are made locally. In the real world, these changes would usually need to be made on other machines. In that case, the script can simply be split into two parts, and one part of it can be placed on another system. The local script can then execute the remote script via Secure Shell (SSH) to perform any operations that must be performed remotely.

Another option is to create the files in a directory that is shared among your systems. Any system running a service, such as a DNS or DHCP server, can periodically check to see if the configuration file has changed. If it has, the service can be restarted or reloaded as appropriate.

In some cases, an infrastructure may already exist for making remote changes. With DNS, for example, you can use the nsupdate utility to make changes to zones on a remote DNS server running the Berkeley Internet Name Daemon (BIND). The command set for this utility is pretty flexible and you can easily use it from an automation script.

Several of the changes (again, such as the DHCP and DNS configuration changes) will need you to restart the server using those configuration files. This has been left out of these system pre-installation scripts because it is very system dependent. Each component script could restart its associated daemon process, or it could be restarted periodically by an outside process.

Finally, changes such as those made to the hosts file, will almost certainly need to be distributed to other machines. I will discuss a variety of ways to do this in Chapter 6 and Chapter 7.

## 4.5.1 Requesting the MAC Address

This component requests the MAC address from the user and performs the following tasks:

1. Requests the MAC address

2. Formats the MAC address

3. Checks for a duplicate MAC address

4. Logs the new MAC address

5. Exports the MAC for use by other components

It needs to run first and should be named 00getmac.sh (or another name that comes alphabetically first) so that this script is run before all of the other component scripts. Many computer manufacturers provide a sticker with the MAC address for the system. If you do not have one, you will need to use the ifconfig command on the system to determine its MAC address. Be sure to add any zeros necessary to bring the address to 12 digits, and remove the semicolons.

```bash
1  #!/bin/bash
2
3  echo -n "Enter the system's MAC address (no colons!): " >&2
4  read mac_address
5
6  # First, convert all letters to lowercase in $mac_address
7  mac_address="$(echo $mac_address | tr 'A-Z' 'a-z')"
8
9  # Next, make sure it contains exactly 12 valid characters
10 if ! echo "$mac_address" | egrep -q '[0-9a-f]{12}' ; then
11     echo "Invalid MAC address: $mac_address!" >&2
12     echo "false;"
13     exit 1
14 fi
15
16 # Finally, insert colons within the MAC address
17 mac_address="$(echo $mac_address | sed \
18     's/\(..\)\(..\)\(..\)\(..\)\(..\)\(..\)/\1:\2:\3:\4:\5:\6/')"
19
20 # Make sure the MAC address has not already been specified
21 if grep -q "^$mac_address " "$data_dir/macs" ; then
22     echo "MAC address already exists: $mac_address" >&2
23     echo "false;"
24     exit 1
25 fi
26
27 # Record new hostname
28 echo "$mac_address $new_hostname" >> "$data_dir/macs"
29
30 echo "export mac_address=$mac_address;"
31 echo "true;"
32 exit 0
```

**Line 4:** Note that, in this read command, the -e switch is not used because it does not work well with all the redirects done in the main script.

**Line 10:** Here, `egrep` is used to make sure the MAC address contains only numbers and the letters a through f and that it contains exactly 12 characters.

**Line 17:** The `sed` command is used here to replace the 12 characters with 6 groups of those same characters, separated by colons.

**Line 21:** The `macs` file, which contains a list of already used MAC addresses, is scanned by `grep` and looks for the provided MAC address already in the file, at the beginning of a line, and followed by a space. The `-q` switch causes `grep` to not actually produce any output, but it will still return `true` (exit code 0) if a match is found.

**Line 30:** As is required by all of the components, an exit result of `true` is returned. In addition, the `$mac_address` is also returned so that it will be exported for use by other component scripts.

After this script has executed, a fully formatted MAC address will be stored in the `$mac_address` environment variable and exported for use by other component scripts. In addition, the MAC address (and the provided hostname) are logged in the `macs` file in the data directory (as specified in the main script by the `$data_dir` environment variable).

## 4.5.2 Allocating an IP

The script in this section allocates an IP address for the new machine. Once the address has been allocated, it is removed from the list of available IPs. The `available` file (in the data directory) contains one available IP address per line. You could generate this file by running the following on the command line:

```
data_dir="/usr/local/var/prepare_system/"
for i in `seq 10 250` ; do
    echo "192.168.1.$i"
done > $data_dir/available
```

After this is run, the `available` file contains all the IPs from `192.168.1.10` to `192.168.1.250`. Obviously your environment may warrant more entries in your file.

```
1  #!/bin/bash
2
3  available_list="$data_dir/available"
4  allocated_list="$data_dir/allocated"
5
```

```
6   [ -s $available_list ] || {
7   # File is empty or nonexistent, return false
8       echo "No IP Addresses Available ($available_list is empty!)" >&2
9       echo "false;"
10      exit 1
11  }
12
13  # Pick the first IP address from the available list
14  ip_address="$(head -n1 $available_list)"
15
16  # In addition, write the new available list
17  tail +2 "$available_list" > "$available_list.new" && \
18      mv "$available_list.new" "$available_list"
19
20  # Now, log the new allocation
21  echo "$ip_address $new_hostname" >> "$allocated_list"
22
23  # Display the IP address to the user
24  echo "IP Address Allocated: $ip_address" >&2
25
26  # Finally, return the IP, and return true
27  echo "export ip_address=$ip_address;"
28  echo "true;"
```

**Line 14:** Here, the head command is used to return the first line of the file (using the -n1 argument). This line is the new IP address and is stored in the $ip_address variable.

**Line 17:** The new available file is written using every line from the original file, apart from the line that contains the IP address we just allocated to the new host (which was the first line). The tail command is useful because it can provide us with every line in the file starting at line two.

After this script runs, a newly allocated IP address will be stored in the $ip_address environment variable so that it can be used by other components. In addition, the IP address (and the provided hostname) are logged in the allocated file in the data directory (as specified in the main script by the $data_dir environment variable).

## 4.5.3 Classifying the System

The classify component script (which can be named anything and can execute in any order, but which I call 10classify.sh) lets the user place the new host in one or more groups. Each group should contain systems with something in common. For example, you could have one group for each operating system and another group that contains all systems that are running a web server, regardless of operating system. You can use these lists of hosts in each group to perform commands on groups of machines as shown in Chapter 2.

This script displays a list of possible groups (as read from /usr/local/etc/group_list) and the user can pick one of the groups. The list is displayed again and the process continues until no more groups are selected by the administrator.

```bash
#!/bin/bash

host_dir='/usr/local/etc/hosts/'
group_list='/usr/local/etc/group_list'
host_list='/usr/local/etc/all_hosts'
groups=''

echo >&2
echo "Select one or more groups for this host (Q to quit):" >&2
select group in `cat $group_list` ; do
    if [ -n "$group" ] ; then
        groups="$group $groups"
        echo >&2
        echo "Current List: $groups" >&2
        echo >&2
    else
        break
    fi
done


# Add to group files
for group in $groups ; do
    # Make sure the host is not already in the group
    grep -q "^$new_hostname$" "$host_dir/$group" || {
        echo "$new_hostname" >> "$host_dir/$group"
    }
done


# Always add to "all_hosts" file
echo "$new_hostname" >> "$host_list"

echo >&2
echo "Host $new_hostname added to group(s): $groups" >&2
```

```
# Generate output data on STDOUT
echo "export groups='$groups';"
echo "true;"
exit 0
```

The `select` command is a bash built-in. Each of the options specified on the command line is presented and the user can choose any of them. If the user does not choose an option, or if they make an invalid choice, the variable ($group in this case) will be empty. On the other hand, if the user makes a valid choice, the actual value displayed in the option list will be stored in the environment variable. Either way, the commands within the "do done" loop execute. The list then displays again, unless the `break` was executed.

This script ultimately places the new hostname in the file associated with each selected group (each group has one file that contains a list of hosts within that group). The environment variable $groups is also exported by this component script. It isn't actually used by any of the example scripts provided, but it is available if you were to find it useful.

## 4.5.4  Gathering Contact Information

You should always know who is using or is responsible for a system. Maintaining a simple list of machines and their contacts can go a long way. The script I describe here asks you to enter the contact for a new system and stores it in a file. You could enter a name, an email address, and/or a phone number.

```
#!/bin/bash

echo -n "Enter the system's contact: " >&2
read contact

# Record the contact
echo "$new_hostname $mac_address $contact" >> "$data_dir/contacts"
echo

echo "export contact=$contact;"
echo "true;"
exit 0
```

## 4.5.5  Adding to the /etc/hosts File

This is about as simple as a component script could be. The provided hostname and allocated IP address are simply added to the end of the /etc/hosts file. This script must run after the IP address has been allocated, so it should be named something like 20hosts_file.sh.

Adding entries to the hosts may or may not be appropriate in your environment, but the following script is presented as a simple example and will be useful in some environments. You will want to either use this method or the DNS method, but usually not both.

```
#!/bin/bash

hosts_file="/etc/hosts"

echo "$ip_address $new_hostname" >> "$hosts_file"

echo "Added $new_hostname to hosts file" >&2

# Indicate success on stdout
echo "true;"
exit 0
```

## 4.5.6  Configuring a DHCP Server

Adding an entry to the standard UNIX DHCP server configuration file is not as easy as adding a line to the end of the file. In this section, I need to add several lines in the middle of the file, which is a bit more difficult.

Although you could use either awk or even sed to perform this task, the implementation would have been fairly complicated and cryptic. Also, by writing this module in Perl, I can illustrate the benefits of having separate modules that can be written in different languages.

Here is a sample configuration file for the DHCP server from the Internet Software Consortium (usually located in /etc/dhcpd.conf). This example configuration file enables dynamic IPs on the specified subnet. In addition, one static host is already defined in this file:

```
subnet 10.1.0.0 netmask 255.255.0.0 {
    option routers          10.1.1.1;
    option subnet-mask      255.255.0.0;
    option domain-name      "sample.com";
    option domain-name-servers 10.1.1.1;
    option time-offset      -5;

    range dynamic-bootp 10.1.2.1 10.1.2.254;
    default-lease-time 21600;
    max-lease-time 43200;

    host example {
        hardware ethernet a0:a0:c0:c9:46:9b;
        fixed-address 10.1.1.10;
    }
}
# The } above must remain in column 1!
```

Some configuration files might have more than one subnet declaration, but the following script only adds the static hosts to the first subnet. Obviously you can modify the script to alter a subnet declaration other than the first one, or you can enhance it to parse the actual subnet declaration so that it can look for a specific network address and not depend on the order of the file.

The following Perl script should be placed into the same component directory and named 30dhcp_config.pl because it will need to run after the IP allocation and MAC request scripts. Here is the script:

```
#!/usr/bin/perl -w
use strict;
my $dhcpd_conf='/usr/local/etc/dhcpd.conf';

# Open up the input and output files
open(IN, "$dhcpd_conf") or die "Could not open $dhcpd_conf: $!\n";
open(OUT, ">$dhcpd_conf.new") or
    die "Could not open $dhcpd_conf.new: $!\n";

# Now, go through the file, looking for } at beginning of line
my $line;
my $done = 0;
while ($line = <IN>) {
    if ((not $done) and ($line =~ /^\}/)) {
        # Found closing brace at beginning of line
```

```
        print OUT " host $ENV{'new_hostname'} {\n";
        print OUT " hardware ethernet $ENV{'mac_address'};\n";
        print OUT " fixed-address $ENV{'ip_address'};\n";
        print OUT " }\n\n";
        $done = 1;
    }
    # Always print the line out
    print OUT $line;
}
close(IN);
close(OUT);

# Copy the new file over
unless (rename("$dhcpd_conf.new", $dhcpd_conf)) {
    die "Could not replace $dhcpd_conf: $!\n";
}

print STDERR "$ENV{'new_hostname'} added to dhcpd.conf\n";

# Indicate success on STDOUT
print "true;\n";
exit 0
```

Note that this particular script is not very robust because it requires the closing brace for the subnet declaration to be at the very beginning of the line. No other closing braces must be at the beginning of the line. If another closing brace was found at the beginning of the line, it would assume that was the end of the subnet declaration and probably corrupt the file.

As long as you are careful when you manually edit the file, this restriction shouldn't be too much of a concern. Of course, placing a comment in the file, as I showed you in the example configuration file, is also a good idea. In addition, the Perl script could use some more powerful parsing to reduce the need for such strict formatting restrictions (it could actually parse the syntax of the file, noticing the beginning of the block and finding the matching closing brace).

## 4.5.7 Updating your DNS Configuration

For most hosts, you want both a forward and reverse lookup entry in DNS. Assuming you have control of both zones and are running BIND, you would have two zone files, such as the following:

```
$TTL 86400
; Forward-lookup zone for sample.com
sample.com. 1D IN SOA @ root (
                    ; WARNING: do not change formatting of next line
                    1 ;serial
                    3H 15M 1W 1D )
            IN NS @
somehost.sample.com. IN A 192.168.1.1

$TTL 86400
; Reverse-lookup zone for 192.168.X.X
168.192.in-addr.arpa. 1D IN SOA @ root (
                    ; WARNING: do not change formatting of next line
                    1 ;serial
                    3H 15M 1W 1D )
            IN NS @
1.1.168.192.in-addr.arpa. IN PTR somehost.sample.com.
```

Fortunately, we can just add new entries to the bottom of these files. Unfortunately, we also have to increment the serial number after every change. To help in this effort, the serial number in these files has been placed on a line by itself, and the comment ;serial was added after the serial number (separated by whitespace).

The following component script updates the serial numbers in these zone files and adds the appropriate entry to the end of each file. It should be named 40dns_config.sh so that it runs after the IP address has already been allocated:

```
1   #!/bin/bash
2
3   domain="sample.com"
4   forward_zone="/usr/local/var/named/sample.com"
5   rev_zone="/usr/local/var/named/hosts.rev"
6
7   # This function requires that the serial number be on
8   # a line by itself and be followed by " ;serial"
9   increment_serial() {
10      [ -w "$1" ] || {
11          echo "File $1 doesn't exist or is not writable!" >&2
12          return
13      }
14      awk '/;serial/ {print "                    " $1+1 " ;serial"} \
15          !/;serial/ {print $0}' "$1" > "$1.tmp" && \
16              mv "$1.tmp" "$1"
17  }
18
```

```
19  # First, increment the serial numbers
20  increment_serial "$forward_zone"
21  increment_serial "$rev_zone"
22
23  # Determine reversed-ip
24  rev_ip=`echo "$ip_address" | sed \
25     's/^\(.*\)\.\(.*\)\.\(.*\)\.\(.*\)$/\4.\3.\2.\1.in-addr.arpa./'`
26
27  # Now, add new entries
28  echo "$new_hostname.$domain.   IN A $ip_address" >> "$forward_zone"
29  echo "$rev_ip   IN PTR $new_hostname.$domain." >> "$rev_zone"
30
31  echo "DNS entries created for $new_hostname ($ip_address)" >&2
32
33  # Indicate success on STDOUT
34  echo "true;"
35  exit 0
```

**Line 9:** Since the serial number has to be incremented in two separate files, a function is defined so that it can be called twice.

**Line 15:** This awk command looks for two different patterns. One matches lines containing the string ;serial; the other pattern matches lines not containing that string. If the string is found within a line, some whitespace is printed, followed by the first field of the line (the serial number) incremented by one, followed by the string ;serial. If that string is not found within the line, the line is printed to the output stream unmodified.

**Line 24:** This sed command takes the four numbers within the IP (which are separated by periods) and reverses their order in the output stream (and adds the necessary .in-addr.arpa. suffix). This is the format you must use within the reverse-lookup zone file.

If you wanted to, you could use the named-checkzone command (included with modern versions of BIND) to verify the new zone file. You could then force a reload of the zone file on your name server.

## 4.6 What About Errors?

One disadvantage of the modular approach is that it has a reduced capability to cleanly handle errors. If a particular component fails, it can (and does) cause the entire process to fail. Unfortunately, other components might have already made changes and, when the script exits, the new system may have only been partially added.

There are a few solutions to this problem. The best method involves separating each components into two parts. The first part prepares for an action (asking for a MAC address, for example) and performs any error checking that can be done before things are modified. Once every component is properly prepared, the second part of each component is called to actually make the changes. This two-step process provides each component with an opportunity to abort the process before any changes actually take place. The two parts of the scripts may be placed in different directories or prefixed with strings such as `prepare_` and `perform_`.

You have a second option—you can allow the setup script to fail at anytime. One side effect is that such a failure could result in incomplete changes. Each component of the *remove* script, however, can be written to handle these incomplete changes. If the remove scripts work correctly whether an action is necessary or not, you can run them to remove any changes that have been made, even if some changes were never completed. If adding a new system fails and results in incomplete changes, the same system can simply be removed, which eliminates any changes that may have been made. Basically, the point is that if you are in doubt, you can just remove the system and then add it again.

Since adding new systems is not typically done very frequently and is not usually time critical, the simpler (second) option is used within this chapter. This allows our scripts to be shorter and easier to understand while being just as effective for this situation.

## 4.7 Removing Machines

Since we want to be able to remove a system even if it has not been added completely (if there was an error in the preparation process, for example), we only perform minimal error checking in the removal process. If the removal attempt fails, we can just ignore the error and assume that the change we are removing was never properly completed. The following system removal script is very similar to the base script you used to add a new system, so you should refer to the discussion in section 4.4 to understand the basic operation of this script.

```
#!/bin/bash

component_dir="/usr/local/lib/remove_system/"
export data_dir="/usr/local/var/prepare_system/"

echo
echo "Remove System"
echo
```

```
echo -n "Enter the system's hostname: "
read -e old_hostname

# Convert all letters to lowercase in $old_hostname
# Be sure to export the variable for use by component scripts
export old_hostname="$(echo $old_hostname | tr 'A-Z' 'a-z')"

# Make sure the hostname *is* already listed
if ! grep -q "^$old_hostname$" "$data_dir/hosts" 2>/dev/null ; then
 echo "Hostname does not exist: $old_hostname" >&2
 exit 1
fi

# Now, execute all component scripts
for script in $component_dir/* ; do
   # Go to next file if this is a directory
   [ -d $script ] && continue
   # Go to next file if this is not executable
   [ -x $script ] || continue
   # Execute this script, execute its output, abort on failure
   eval `$script` || {
      echo "$script returned error" >&2
      exit 1
   }
done

# Remove the hostname from the host list
grep -v "^$old_hostname$" "$data_dir/hosts" > "$data_dir/hosts.new" \
   && mv "$data_dir/hosts.new" "$data_dir/hosts"

echo
echo "System removal complete for $old_hostname"
echo

exit 0
```

**NOTE**  Note that this removal script does perform a quick check to make sure the host exists before it attempts to remove it. It does not, however, remove the host from that list until the removal component scripts have successfully completed. If it did, and one of the scripts failed, the system could no longer be removed, even though its existence might not have been completely eliminated.

Like the system preparation script, this script also would be fairly useless without component scripts to do the various specific removal tasks. The following component scripts need to go in the component directory specified in the remove system base script.

## 4.7.1  Removing MAC Addresses

This component script for the removal process should be named 00rmmac.sh so that it will execute first. This script can look up the hostname and set the $mac_address environment variable that can be used by other removal component scripts. Once it finds the MAC address for the specified hostname, it removes that line from the file.

```
#!/bin/bash

# We must find the MAC address for other removal components
mac_address=`cat "$data_dir/macs" | sed -n \
    "s/^\([0-9a-f:]\+\) $old_hostname$/\1/p"`

# Now, remove this host from the MAC listing
egrep -v "^[0-9a-f:]+ $old_hostname$" \
    "$data_dir/macs" > "$data_dir/macs.new" && \
        mv "$data_dir/macs.new" "$data_dir/macs"

# Return the MAC address in case other components need it
echo "export mac_address=$mac_address;"
echo "true;"
exit 0
```

The sed command used in this script does not print lines by default (because of the -n option). However, the p flag specified after the substitute pattern causes any *matched* lines to be printed. So, unless there are duplicate hostnames in the file, only one line will be printed.

The sed command also isolates the MAC address by marking it with \ ( and \) delimiters and by referencing it with the \1 in the substitution string (this is known as backreferencing). This allows the script to isolate the desired line *and* format that line using only one sed command.

## 4.7.2 Reclaiming IP

This script is almost identical to the previous script that removes the MAC address record. This script should be named 05take_ip.sh. It finds the IP assigned to the hostname, removes the record, and returns the IP address for future use. It also adds the IP back to the end of the available IP list so that it will be reused.

```bash
#!/bin/bash

available_list="$data_dir/available"
allocated_list="$data_dir/allocated"

# We must find the IP address for other removal components
[ -w "$allocated_list" ] && {
  ip_address=`cat "$allocated_list" | sed -n \
    "s/^\([0-9][0-9.]*\) $old_hostname$/\1/p"`

  # Now, remove this IP from the allocated list
  egrep -v "^[0-9.]+ $old_hostname$" \
    "$allocated_list" > "$allocated_list.new" && \
      mv "$allocated_list.new" "$allocated_list"
}

# And add the IP back to the available list
echo "$ip_address" >> "$available_list"

# Finally, return the IP, and return true
echo "export ip_address=$ip_address;"
echo "true;"
```

## 4.7.3 Declassifying a System

This is almost the simplest script of the bunch. It should be named 10declassify.sh. It doesn't return any data. All this script does is look through all of the host group files and remove the specified hostname from each file.

```
#!/bin/bash

host_dir='/usr/local/etc/hosts/'
host_list='/usr/local/etc/all_hosts'

# Remove this host from any groups it might be in
cd $host_dir
for file in * $host_list ; do
    if [ -f $file ] ; then
        grep -v "^$old_hostname$" $file > $file.new && \
            mv $file.new $file
    fi
done

# Indicate success on STDOUT
echo "true;"
exit 0
```

## 4.7.4  Removing Contact Entry

Here we just remove the contact entry that was recorded for this system.

```
#!/bin/bash

# Now, remove the contact entry for this host
egrep -v "^$old_hostname $mac_address" \
    "$data_dir/contacts" > "$data_dir/contacts.new" && \
        mv "$data_dir/contacts.new" "$data_dir/contacts"

echo "true;"
exit 0
```

## 4.7.5  Modifying Hosts File

For the second time in this chapter, modifying the /etc/hosts has won the award for the easiest task to automate. In an all-UNIX environment, the simplicity of the automatically maintained hosts might be a good excuse to avoid DNS completely!

This simple script, which I would name 20hosts_file.sh, doesn't return anything and simply removes the host from the hosts file.

```
#!/bin/bash

hosts_file="/etc/hosts"

[ -w "$hosts_file" ] && {
    # First, create the new file with the same permissions
    cp -p "$hosts_file" "$hosts_file.new"
    grep -v "^$ip_address *$old_hostname$" \
        "$hosts_file" > "$hosts_file.new" && \
            mv "$hosts_file.new" "$hosts_file"
}

# Indicate success on STDOUT
echo "true;"
exit 0
```

**NOTE** Note that the permissions on the /etc/hosts file are preserved because the new file is copied over the old version. If any disk errors occur during the process, the entire process aborts.

## 4.7.6  Configuring DHCP

Good things usually come in pairs; this holds true for Perl scripts that modify DHCP configuration files. Since we used a Perl script to add entries to the DHCP file, we can save ourselves some effort by using much of the same code to remove entries from DHCP. Again, I recommend naming this file 30dhcp_config.pl:

```
#!/usr/bin/perl -w
use strict;
my $dhcpd_conf = '/usr/local/etc/dhcpd.conf';
my $host = "$ENV{'old_hostname'}";

# Open up the input and output files
open(IN, "$dhcpd_conf") or die "Could not open $dhcpd_conf: $!\n";
open(OUT, ">$dhcpd_conf.new") or
    die "Could not open $dhcpd_conf.new: $!\n";
```

```
# Now, go through the file, looking for deleted host
my $line;
LOOP: while ($line = <IN>) {
    if ($line =~ /host\s+$host\s+{/) {
        # Found the host we are removing
        while ($line = <IN>) {
            # Loop through file until closing brace found
            # near beginning of line
            next LOOP if ($line =~ /^\s+}/);
        }
    }
    # Print other lines out
    print OUT $line;
}
close(IN);
close(OUT);

# Copy the new file over the original
unless (rename("$dhcpd_conf.new", $dhcpd_conf)) {
    die "Could not replace $dhcpd_conf: $!\n";
}

# Indicate success on STDOUT
print "true;\n";
exit 0
```

The only new thing in this component is the logic within the main loop. Once the script finds the line that begins the block for the specified host, it starts a second loop. That loop continues until it finds a } immediately after any whitespace at the beginning of a line (that would be the closing brace for the block). The script then skips to the next iteration of the outside loop, which continues to output the rest of the file.

The string LOOP: might not be familiar to all readers. It is a label that allows program execution to jump back to that particular line in the program. This allows the inside loop to skip to the next iteration of the outside loop (thus avoiding an unwanted printing of the } line). Some programmers think labels are evil incarnate, but I think they are appropriate (at least in Perl) when dealing with nested loops.

## 4.7.7  *Updating your DNS Configuration*

This script, which could be named `40dns_config.sh`, contains much of the same code as the script that adds the DNS entries. In fact, in a real environment, I would recommend putting the common code in an include file that each script could include (by using the `source` command at the top of each script).

```bash
#!/bin/bash

domain="sample.com"
forward_zone="/usr/local/var/named/sample.com"
rev_zone="/usr/local/var/named/hosts.rev"

# This function requires that the serial number be on
# a line by itself and followed by " ;serial"
increment_serial() {
    [ -w "$1" ] || {
        echo "File $1 doesn't exist or is not writable" >&2
        return
    }
    awk '/;serial/ {print " " $1+1 " ;serial"} \
        !/;serial/ {print $0}' "$1" > "$1.tmp" && \
            mv "$1.tmp" "$1"
}


# First, increment the serial numbers
increment_serial "$forward_zone"
increment_serial "$rev_zone"

# Determine reversed-ip
rev_ip=`echo "$ip_address" | sed \
    's/^\(.*\)\.\(.*\)\.\(.*\)\.\(.*\)$/\4.\3.\2.\1.in-addr.arpa./'`

# Now, remove entries
[ -w "$forward_zone" ] && {
    # First, copy original file, to preserve permissions
    cp -p "$forward_zone" "$forward_zone.new"
    egrep -v "^$old_hostname\.$domain\. +IN A $ip_address" \
        "$forward_zone" > "$forward_zone.new" && \
            mv "$forward_zone.new" "$forward_zone"
}
```

```
[ -w "$rev_zone" ] && {
   cp -p "$rev_zone" "$rev_zone.new"
   egrep -v "^$rev_ip +IN PTR $old_hostname\.$domain\." \
      "$rev_zone" > "$rev_zone.new" && \
         mv "$rev_zone.new" "$rev_zone"
}


# Indicate success on STDOUT
echo "true;"
exit 0
```

As you can see, most of the removal scripts are very similar. They just remove known lines from their respective files.

# 4.8 Generating Reports

Placing new hosts into groups during their installation process is very useful when administering the machines in the future. These groups can be used to perform a wide variety of tasks on these hosts based on which groups they belong to. Another big benefit you gain from all this pre-installation configuration effort is the ability to generate useful reports. How many machines are there? How many IPs are available? What MAC addresses should you be seeing on your network?

If you have been following the examples in this section, you already know that you can quickly get the answers to these questions from the data files stored in /usr/local/var/prepare_system (or wherever you decided to place them). Because these are text files, processing them is easy.

I will provide a few examples of reports that you can generated using this information. If you are experienced with this type of activity, it may not even be worth creating scripts for these reports because the commands are simple enough to manually enter whenever you need them. Either way, useful data can be quickly retrieved from your text-based data files.

## 4.8.1 How Many Machines Are There?

Since there is one line in the allocated file for each host, you can determine how many hosts there are by running this command:

```
% cd /usr/local/var/prepare_system

% wc -l allocated
    14 allocated

% wc -l allocated | awk '{print $1}'
14
```

The first command shows you how many hosts there are by counting the number of lines in the allocated file (using wc -l). The second command pipes that output through the awk program to display only the actual count and hide the unneeded filename.

## 4.8.2  How Many IPs Are Available?

Determining how many IPs are available is as simple as counting the number of lines in the available file, as we did in the last example.

```
% cd /usr/local/var/prepare_system

% wc -l available
    239 available

% wc -l available | awk '{print $1}'
239
```

## 4.8.3  What MAC Addresses Should Be in Use?

Ask many people what MAC addresses they expect to see on their network and they would have no clue. Yet, as I write this example, I feel that it is really too simple to even bother writing about. This really helps illustrate how simple tasks become once you have a good infrastructure in place. But, to be complete, let me just explain that you can answer this question by simply listing the first column of the macs file:

```
% cd /usr/local/var/prepare_system
% cut -f1 -d' ' macs
aa:bb:cc:dd:ee:ff
ab:bc:cd:de:ef:fa
ff:ee:dd:cc:bb:aa
aa:aa:aa:aa:aa:aa
bb:bb:bb:bb:bb:bb
ba:ba:ba:ba:ba:ba
```

Although I could have used the awk command, the cut command is fine in this case. The awk command is great when the whitespace between elements on a line is variable in size and in type (i.e., tabs and spaces, possibly mixed). The cut command, however, works best when there is only one specific delimiter between items on a line. In this case, we tell cut to use the space character as the delimiter (the -d option) and to take the first field (the -f option).

# Automating and Customizing Installation

ONCE YOU HAVE PREPARED your network infrastructure for a new system, you must still install the actual operating system. Automating the installation can be as simple as coming up with a printed set of instructions that you or somebody else can follow. For a larger number of installations, your operating system may allow you to make some or all of the decisions in advance, which allows you to partially or completely automate your installations.

If you are lucky, you are in a position in which you can choose an operating system that can be customized. If you are really lucky, you might even be able to customize the operating system you are already using. Either way, adding custom software to the operating system can be very useful and can save you time and effort in the future.

Regardless of how the operating system is installed or how much it has been customized, the system needs to be configured so that it fully cooperates with your automation system. In most cases, this can be done completely automatically (with a fully customized operating system or a post-install script). In other cases, at least a little manual intervention will be required (enough to allow a remote system to connect and finish the system preparation).

The system configuration discussed in this chapter is just enough to get your new system up and running so that your regular automation system can take over. You should try to minimize the things you configure at this stage—do as much as you can do with your main automatic configuration tools, as discussed in Chapter 6.

## 5.1 Automating Installations

A broad range of decisions traditionally require user input during the installation of an operating system; yet, in many situations, you can make these decisions in advance. For example, you can pick your network settings or decide the software you want to include once, and then automatically apply these choices to future installs. If you are fortunate and have very similar or identical systems, the entire installation process can require little or no user intervention.

There are two reasons why you might want to automate the installation process: to reduce necessary user input on similar systems, or to eliminate user input on identical systems. You may install a large number of systems with a number of settings (such as network settings) that are constant. In this case, you could predefine these settings and as a result, reduce the number of questions that must be answered during the installation process. This is also nice if less technical people are performing the installs because they might not readily know the answers to these questions.

The more common reason for automating installations is to reduce or eliminate user input requirements when you are installing numerous identical (or nearly identical) systems. You might be setting up a 1,000-node Beowulf cluster or preparing network appliances that will be sold to customers, or you might have numerous testing machines that need to be reinstalled daily. In all of these cases, automating the installation process saves a lot of time.

Many operating systems natively support automated installations in one form or another. Red Hat Linux and Sun Solaris are two examples. I discuss how to automate a Red Hat Linux installation using its Kickstart mechanism in Appendix A. You can find information on Solaris's JumpStart facility in *JumpStart Technology: Effective Use in the Solaris Operating Environment* by John S. Howard and Alex Noordergraaf (Prentice Hall, 2001).

In other cases, third party software may facilitate such automation. One example of this is the Fully Automatic Installation (FAI) software that you can use to automate Debian GNU/Linux installations (information can be found at `http://sourceforge.net/projects/fai/`).

## 5.2 Customizing Your Operating System

When I talk about customizing an operating system installation, I am referring to your ability to add, remove, or modify the software included with that operating system. For example, you may want to add custom software, especially software that aids in your automation tasks. You may also want to upgrade certain included software to newer versions or remove unneeded software to reduce clutter, security risks, or disk usage.

Before spending too much time thinking about customization, there are two questions you should ask yourself:

- Is it worth your effort to customize your operating system?

- Is this something you can do with the operating system of your choice?

If Linux is your operating system of choice, customization and automation abilities will be almost guaranteed, due to Linux's open-source nature. The only question to answer is how difficult customization will be. Other UNIX variants may or may not be customizable and answering that question will require some research on your part.

Remember that, even if your operating system can't be customized in the traditional sense, you can probably make changes in a post-install script. You can also make these changes using your regular automation tool (such as GNU cfengine), which could be executed from a post-install script.

So, if you want the newest version of the bash shell on your systems, you can possibly modify your operating system to include it upon installation. If not, you can copy it from an NFS or FTP server in the post-install script. Better yet, you can have your configuration system install the program when it performs its other configuration tasks on the system.

If you are using Red Hat Linux or are interested in creating your own custom Linux distribution, Red Hat has made it fairly easy to customize its Linux distribution, so if you are interested, check out Appendix B.

## 5.2.1  Should I Customize?

Whether or not you should customize your operating system is a much more difficult question. Several factors should be included in your decision-making process:

- How many machines will use the customized operating system?

- How much work is the customization?

- What amount of customization would you be performing?

- How do you solve the problems now?

Most of these questions should be easy to answer if you have an existing set of systems. If you are planning for a new environment (such as a new cluster of systems), on the other hand, these answers might require more thought.

Obviously your decision requires you to weigh the rewards against the effort required. If you only have 2 computers, the rewards will be too small. If you have 1,000 computers (all running the same operating system), and the customization process is not too difficult, then it will probably be worth the effort.

Let's say, for example, that you just want to add a few new packages to Red Hat Linux, and they can already be found in Red Hat Package Manager (RPM) format.

If this is the case, you can accomplish this task with minimal effort. If you want to include a custom kernel, you have to modify and rebuild the kernel RPM and *then* substitute that custom kernel in the distribution, which requires a bit more effort. And if you have to modify the source for the actual installation program, then things might become even more difficult.

There are many benefits to a custom distribution. For instance, you can include exactly what software you want (including custom software) so that it does not have to be installed after the installation. If many people are responsible for system installs (or if installs are performed in different geographical regions), a custom installation makes the systems more consistent since everybody will be following the same procedure. It is also easier to standardize your environment on a single operating system when you can customize that operating system to fit your environment exactly.

Keep in mind that companies (like Red Hat) spend a tremendous amount of time making sure the packages work together properly. Every time you change, add, or upgrade a particular package, you need to repeat this effort. You definitely want to keep as much of the Quality Assurance (QA) burden as possible on the operating system vendor, not on you. In addition, if your changes are significant and nonstandard, new administrators will have a higher learning curve.

Unfortunately, whether or not you customize your operating system is a question that I can't answer for you, nor can I give you a formula you can use to calculate that answer. I can, however, give you some generalizations. For example, a large company or university often finds a custom distribution invaluable because they have a large number of systems. Even though each system may perform different tasks, a single customized operating system can often be used to fill a wide variety of roles. If you are running a Beowulf cluster full of identical systems, a custom distribution is still worth the effort, but, if you only have 30 employees in your company and everybody uses a different operating system, it probably isn't (unless you could convince everybody to switch to your new operating system).

## 5.2.2  Maintaining a Custom Distribution

You also have to consider how you plan to maintain your custom distribution. Many people overlook this important and (possibly) time-consuming task when they decide to produce a custom operating system distribution. If security or bug fixes are released for programs you have added to a distribution, you have to update those components. If the operating system vendor releases a security patch, you should be able to apply it to your distribution easily (assuming you watch for them, or are notified by the vendor). But, if a security patch is released for a component that you have modified, you might have to merge that patch into your modified distribution, which could take much more effort.

Even more work may be necessary when a new version of your original operating system is released. Although your custom distribution might be able to lag behind the most current distribution available, you eventually need to upgrade your distribution to take advantage of new features in that base operating system. When you upgrade to the newer base operating system, you may find that some of your added software is not fully compatible with the newer operating system. If you modified some of the original software, you might need to make those same changes to the newer versions of that software.

For many people, custom operating system distributions are still worth the effort, but maintenance requirements should definitely be considered in your decision-making process.

## 5.3 Preparing for Automated Administration

Once you have it installed, you will want to make sure the new system works with your automation system. You first need to decide between using a "push" or "pull" method to accomplish this task. You don't have to use the same method for all of your tasks, but how you will automatically configure your systems later affects the method you should use to prepare new systems for that automation. Both the push and pull method will be discussed extensively in Chapter 6.

If your automation system generally works by connecting to each system and performing any necessary tasks, then you are using the push method of system automation. This method works fine when the number of systems is small, or when there are many independent groups of systems that are each configured independently.

If you use the push method of system configuration, then you need to enable remote access to the system and run a script on your configuration server that pushes data to the new system. Once remote access has been established, your configuration server can perform whatever tasks it needs. This is also a good solution if you don't have control over the actual software installation process—that is, you have to configure the system after somebody else installed it.

If your automation system uses the pull method, each system is responsible for configuring itself using data from a configuration server. (This is how the popular cfengine program works; it is particularly useful in large-scale environments.) In this case, you should let the system configure itself immediately after installation (either by adding your configuration system to the operating system or by installing it using the post-install script).

## 5.3.1  Remotely Configuring a New System

If your automation system works by pushing configuration to other systems, it won't work unless the remote systems allow access from the configuration server. To get things going, you must first manually allow access into the new system, and then your configuration server can connect and perform any one-time modifications that it needs to make to the system.

Immediate remote access is also useful if you don't personally install the operating system on the machine. You may receive a new workstation with an operating system pre-installed, for example. In a large company, you may wipe it out and reinstall it, but in smaller companies, this might be too much trouble. If the rest of your system configuration relies on the pull method, however, you should also consider using a manual post-install script as discussed later in the "Manual Post-Install" section.

You also may have employees that install their own operating systems. If you have a customized operating system (that includes custom software) or a post-install script, this method becomes easier—but probably not as easy as using the pull method, as I discuss later.

Configuring a new system from afar consists of three distinct steps:

1. Enable remote access to the system.

2. Transfer data to the system.

3. Configure the system for automated configuration.

### 5.3.1.1  Enabling Remote Access

When enabling remote access, the goal is to enable remote access to the system so that all future tasks that need to be performed on the system can be executed remotely. In some cases, this might be something that you can do during the automated system installation process. If not, you will have to enable remote access manually after the installation is complete.

I would recommend using whatever software is included with the operating system for this initial configuration task. This reduces the amount of manual work that needs to be done and reduces the chances for mistakes. Once remote access is enabled, you can install better software if necessary. For example, if your system comes with Remote Shell (RSH), you can use that to provide initial access to the system (which will allow you to install and configure Secure Shell [SSH] later).

**NOTE**   If you have decided to use initial remote access to perform initial system setup tasks and you have the ability to execute a post-install script when the system is installed, you can enable remote access in that process automatically. (I discuss transferring data and programs to a system from a post-install script in "Manual Post-Install".) If you can't add a post-install script, you will have to manually enable remote access this first time.

### 5.3.1.1.1  *Using SSH*

If the operating system you installed comes with SSH (or if you have a custom operating system to which SSH could be added), I recommend using SSH for all of your remote access needs. It provides more than enough functionality for initial system configuration and will probably be a crucial part of continuing system maintenance in the future.

You have a few choices when you configure the SSH daemon to allow remote access. You can either place an appropriate public key in the `~/.ssh/authorized_keys` file, use (temporarily) the `~/.shosts` file, or just use password authentication for the root account over SSH. You also, of course, have to make sure the SSH daemon is running.

#### 5.3.1.1.1.1  *Using the* authorized_keys *Approach*

This approach is the safest, especially if the system might be left in an incomplete state for a significant period of time. If you use only one public/private key pair in your setup, then this initial configuration step might be all of the SSH configuration you ever need to perform.

The disadvantage of this approach is that you need to find a way to get the public key onto the new machine. Since the ASCII representation of the key usually exceeds 200 bytes, it is not something you want to type in manually. If you are able to customize your operating system or its installation, you may be able to include the public key in the distribution, or transfer it from a remote server during the installation process.

If you cannot customize the operating system to include the public key, I recommend placing it on an FTP, HTTP, or NFS server and transferring it to the `~/.ssh/authorized_keys` file. If your operating system is running Linux, it is very likely that it includes wget, ncftpget, or lftpget, allowing you to use the FTP or HTTP protocols. You could also transfer the file to the new server using SSH or RSH.

Once the proper public key is in place (and the SSH server is running and properly configured), you can continue the system's initial setup from a remote system.

### 5.3.1.1.1.2 *Using the* `.shosts` *Approach*

The SSH protocol allows `.rhosts` authentication that works almost the same as the RSH version. The `.rhosts` file, however, is called `.shosts` and is placed in the user's home directory (root in our case). The only advantage over RSH is that the connection is encrypted.

Unfortunately (well, it is good for security, but not good for us), most SSH servers disable this form of authentication by default. So, you may have to change the server's configuration file to be able to use it. With OpenSSH, you should add the following lines to the configuration file (such as `/etc/ssh/sshd_config`):

```
RhostsAuthentication yes
IgnoreRhosts no
```

After (re)starting the SSH server, the following `.shosts` file can be created in root's home directory:

```
server.mydomain.com root
```

This allows the `root` user on `server.mydomain.com` to connect, without a password, to the root account on this new system. The connecting machine, however, must use protocol version 1 and connect from a privileged port. Here is how the connecting machine would do this (again, with the OpenSSH client):

```
% ssh -1 -o 'UsePrivilegedPort yes' newsystem.mydomain.com
```

I strongly recommend removing the `.shosts` file and disabling the `.rhosts` authentication once your normal authentication mechanism is in place. This authentication method was fine for initial system setup, but it is not something you want to leave in place because it is not secure. This is the perfect first task for your initial setup script as discussed later in this chapter.

### 5.3.1.1.1.3 *Using Password Authentication*

Using password authentication over SSH when you are connecting to the new system is the easiest approach and is probably a better choice than using the `.shosts` approach. You just have to set the `root` password on the remote machine and make sure the SSH daemon (sshd) is running. You also need to make sure root logins via password authentication are allowed by default with the your operating system of choice. With OpenSSH, you should have the following settings in your `/etc/ssh/sshd_config`, or equivalent. Note that they may be the default settings, and if they are, they do not actually need to be contained within the file:

```
PermitRootLogin yes
PasswordAuthentication yes
```

The only particular disadvantage of using password authentication is that you must enter the password several times when you transfer files to and execute scripts on the new machine (at least until a passwordless connection method is configured).

### 5.3.1.1.2 Using RSH

All UNIX variants that I am aware of come with the Remote Shell (RSH) and Remote Copy (RCP) utilities, which are the predecessors to Secure Shell (SSH) and Secure Copy (SCP). Assuming the RSH server is active (usually launched on demand by inetd), you only have to create the `.rhosts` in root's home directory. It should contain the following line:

```
server.mydomain.com root
```

You can then connect to the new system remotely without a password. In this case, I would recommend that the initial setup script (as described later in this chapter) install and configure SSH for remote access and then disable the RSH protocol completely (unless it is needed for other purposes).

### 5.3.1.2 Transferring Data

Once your server has SSH or RSH access to the new system, you can use SCP or RCP to transfer files to that system. If you have a completely customized installation process, this step may not be necessary. In other cases, you will need to, at the least, transfer an initial setup script to the new machine that can be executed on that system.

You may also need to transfer other files to the system. I recommend transferring only what is necessary to allow the system to operate with your regular automation system. Once this is possible, the regular system configuration mechanisms can complete the remaining configuration tasks.

As an example, we will consider a set of Linux systems that use the RPM package format for their software. For one reason or another, they use a standard Linux distribution, so no custom software is installed initially. For our example, our systems use AutoRPM to install RPMs on each system from a central server.

This takes care of any custom software because it is already packaged into RPMs. Each system is also expected to have a sysadmin account that has a certain cron entry. We also assume that the public key has not been transferred to the new system and needs to be transferred as well (SSH is, however, already installed and running).

The following files need to be transferred to each new system:

initial_setup.sh: This script performs the initial setup of the new system. The contents of this script are discussed in the next section.

ssh_public_key: This is the public key that needs to be placed in ~root/.ssh/authorized_keys to allow future system administration access.

autorpm-2.9-1.noarch.rpm: This is the AutoRPM program, packaged in the RPM package format.

sysadmin_crontab: This is a crontab file that needs to become the sysadmin user's crontab.

The following prepare_system.sh script copies the files to the new system. It also copies every RPM in /usr/local/lib/sys_prep_files/. The packages are also installed on the remote system. We install only a minimal number of packages at this point. Once the automatic installation program is installed (AutoRPM, in our case), that program can install any additional custom RPMs.

---

 **NOTE** You can find the code samples for this chapter in the Downloads section of the Apress web site (http://www.apress.com).

---

```
1   #!/bin/bash
2
3   # Local directory containing files to be transferred
4   file_dir='/usr/local/lib/sys_prep_files'
5
6   # Assumes .shosts is configured on new system
7   alias rsh="/usr/bin/ssh -1 -o 'UsePrivilegedPort yes'"
8   alias rcp="/usr/bin/scp -1 -o 'UsePrivilegedPort yes'"
9
10  die() {
11      echo >&2
12      for i in "$@" ; do
13          echo "$i" >&2
14      done
15      echo >&2
```

```
16    exit 99
17 }
18
19 echo ' ** New System Preparation ** '
20 echo
21 echo -n "Enter new system's hostname: "
22 read -e HOST
23
24 echo "Checking hostname: $HOST"
25 RESULT=`ping -w2 $HOST 2>&1`
26 if [ $? -ne 0 ] ; then
27    if echo $RESULT | grep -q 'unknown host' ; then
28       die 'Host does not exist (no DNS entry)'
29    fi
30    IPADDR=`host "$HOST" | sed 's/^.* \([0-9.]*\)$/\1/'`
31    die 'Host not responding... is the correct IP configured?' \
32       "The registered IP address for $HOST is $IPADDR"
33 fi
34
35 # Create new directories (if necessary)
36 rsh -l root $HOST 'mkdir -p ~/.ssh ~/setup' || \
37    die 'Could not create ~/.ssh and ~/setup dirs'
38
39 # Copy files
40 cd $file_dir 2>/dev/null || die "Directory $file_dir 41  not found!"
42 rcp ssh_public_key root@$HOST:~/.ssh/authorized_keys || \
43    die 'Could not create authorized keys file'
44 rcp *.rpm sysadmin_crontab initial_setup.sh \
45    root@$HOST:~/setup || die 'Could not transfer files'
46
47 # Make sure permissions on .ssh and contents are correct
48 rsh -l root $HOST 'chmod og-rwx ~ ~/.ssh ~/.ssh/*' || \
49    die 'Could not set permissions on .ssh directory'
50
51 # Install any RPMs that were copied over
52 rsh -l root $HOST 'rpm -Uvh ~/setup/*.rpm' || \
53    die 'Failed to install RPMs'
54
55 # Now, run initial setup script
56 rsh -l root $HOST 'bash ~/setup/initial_setup.sh' ||
57    die 'Execution of initial_setup script failed!'
58
59 echo "Host $HOST Configuration Complete"
60 exit 0
```

**Line 7:** These aliases can be changed depending on how you configure the temporary access to your new systems.

**Line 10:** This function displays each argument on a separate line and exits the program with a non-zero exit code to indicate an error.

**Line 25:** This `ping` command allows two seconds for a response (using the `-w2` option). If no packets are returned, the program exits with a failure. You might have to modify this command to work properly on your variant of UNIX.

**Line 30:** We look up the IP address here out of convenience. If the machine is not responding, the person running the script should be able to quickly verify the hostname/IP mapping.

This example assumes you created a `~root/.shosts` file on the new system. If this isn't the case, you could change the two alias lines in the script to support other types of authentication. If you have already created `~root/.ssh/authorized_keys` on the new system, for example, you can replace those lines with the following:

```
alias rsh='ssh'
alias rcp='scp'
```

Or, if you created `~root/.rhosts` on the new system, you would change the lines to:

```
alias rsh='rsh'
alias rcp='rcp'
```

### 5.3.1.3 Configuring the System

The specific contents of the `initial_setup.sh` script are different for every system. You can obviously do anything you want on the new system from within the script in this section. I recommend, however, sticking to tasks that your normal automation script does not perform.

You should also avoid making any changes that are dynamic (such as creating normal user accounts). If the data changes frequently, you need to update that data in the future when you are not initializing a new system. For this type of data, you should write a script that runs on your server and adds and modifies any such data. This script could even be called from the `prepare_system.sh` script discussed in the previous section, and be called in the future when the data needs to be updated.

Finally, I recommend that you make the script fault-tolerant so that you can run it on any given system any number of times. This way, if the script fails (very likely during the development process), you can simply fix it and run it again. More importantly, if the script is changed (i.e., new tasks are added or existing ones are done differently), you can run the new script on any existing systems to bring them up-to-date.

```
1    #!/bin/bash
2
3    # First, run 'autorpm' to install additional new software
4    autorpm auto
5
6    # Add 'sysadmin' account if it doesn't exist
7    grep -q '^sysadmin:' /etc/passwd || {
8        useradd sysadmin
9    }
10
11   # Update the sysadmin user's crontab
12   crontab -u sysadmin ~/setup/sysadmin_crontab
13
14   # Disable .rhosts/.shosts authentication on this host
15   rm -f ~/.rhosts
16   rm -f ~/.shosts
17   cp -p /etc/ssh/sshd_config /etc/ssh/sshd_config.new
18   sed -e 's/RhostsAuthentication.*/RhostsAuthentication no/' \
19       -e 's/IgnoreRhosts.*/IgnoreRhosts yes/' \
20       /etc/ssh/sshd_config > /etc/ssh/sshd_config.new && \
21         mv /etc/ssh/sshd_config.new /etc/ssh/sshd_config
22
23   /etc/init.d/sshd restart
```

**Line 4:** In this example, AutoRPM is being called to install new software on the system automatically. We are assuming it is already configured properly. AutoRPM is explained in detail in section 8.6.

**Line 7:** If a sysadmin's account does not yet exist, it is created. As with almost everything in this example, this command does not work on all systems, but you should have some equivalent command on your system.

**Line 12:** We are replacing any existing crontab with our new one, so this command can be run repeatedly.

**Line 18:** This multistage command removes both the .rhosts and .shosts files from root's home directory (if they exist), then it disables .shosts authentication (whether it was enabled or not). The SSH daemon is then restarted.

## 5.3.2  New Systems That Configure Themselves

This section will be of interest to you if the following statements are true (or if they could be true if you so desired):

- You use cfengine for your system configuration (as discussed in section 6.4), or a similar method that allows each system to configure itself while pulling information from a configuration server.

- You use a customized operating system or a post-install script that allows software to be added to the system at installation time.

If you use cfengine but have no control over the installation process (or the software that is installed), you may have to manually initiate the first system configuration as discussed in the upcoming "Manual Post-Install" section. But, you should also consider the simple, yet effective, manual post-install code provided in the next section.

If you push configuration changes to systems, yet you have your own custom operating system or post-install script, you should still follow the tasks in "Manual Post-Install". The only difference is that you can perform almost all of those tasks in the post-install script instead of doing anything manually.

---

 **NOTE**  Most of the examples in this section were inspired by code from Alf Wachsmann.

---

### 5.3.2.1  Manual Post-Install

If you are used to having your systems configure themselves, you may find it very frustrating to get the process going the first time manually. The best thing to do is have your operating system installation program do this for you in its post-install routine. But, if the operating system is already installed, you have missed out on this opportunity. This is especially true if you are introducing automation to an already existing set of systems—how do you quickly integrate your current machines into your automation system?

One great option is to write a post-install script (or use your existing post-install script) and place it on an internal web server. You can then log in to a new system as root and run the following command:

```
# lynx -dump http://internal-www/linux/prepare.sh | sh
```

This retrieves the specified URL (the file /linux/prepare.sh from the web server internal-www) and executes it with the sh shell. The contents of this script would be virtually the same as the script discussed in the next section.

This example assumes you have the text-based web browsing program Lynx on your system. If it is a Linux or FreeBSD system, you probably have this program. If you don't have it, see if you have wget, which can do the same thing for you. If all of this fails, you might need to use another method to access the file (such as NFS, FTP, SSH, etc.). You can find information about all of these options in Chapter 7.

### 5.3.2.2 Creating the Automatic Preparation Script

You need to create a script that allows a new system to configure itself for the first time. It probably needs to perform some initial setup tasks so that your automation program will be able to execute (which may include transferring data), and then it should trigger the automatic configuration.

This script could be transferred to the system and executed manually (as discussed in the previous section). If you have a customized operating system, you can install this script along with every other file on the system. It can even be embedded in a post-install script, as follows:

```
/bin/cat >/etc/rc.d/init.d/prepare_system << __EOF__
# You can place any sh commands here...
__EOF__
# now make it executable...
/bin/chmod +x /etc/rc.d/init.d/prepare_system
# ...and let it be executed as the last rc script in the very first
# reboot after the install
/bin/ln -s /etc/rc.d/init.d/prepare_system /etc/rc.d/rc3.d/S99prepare_system
```

The comment "You can place any sh commands here" would be replaced with the actual contents of your system preparation script. You should have this script perform whatever tasks are necessary to start your regular automation system. The contents of this script are completely dependent on your specific situation, but I can provide a simple example for Linux systems:

```
1   #!/bin/sh
2
3   # Mount Linux data and binaries via NFS
4   mount nfsserver:/linux/usr/local /usr/local
5
6   # Configure SSH access
7   mkdir -p ~/.ssh ~/setup
8   cp /usr/local/etc/global_auth_keys ~/.ssh/authorized_keys
9   chmod og-rwx ~ ~/.ssh ~/.ssh/*
10
11  # Install any RPMs that need to be added
12  rpm -i /usr/local/src/RPMS/to_install/*.rpm
13
14  # Now, run 'autorpm' to install system updates
15  /usr/local/sbin/autorpm auto
16
17  # Generate cfengine key for this client (and copy to server)
18  mkdir -p /var/cfengine/ppkeys
19  /usr/local/sbin/cfkey
20  MY_IP=`ifconfig eth0 | sed -n 's/.*inet addr:\([^ ]*\).*/\1/p'`
21  cp /var/cfengine/ppkeys/localhost.pub \
22      /usr/local/var/cfengine/ppkeys/root-$MY_IP.pub
23
24  # Finally, run cfengine to perform all other configuration tasks
25  /usr/local/sbin/cfagent
26
27  # All done (prevent this script from running again)
28  rm -f /etc/rc.d/rc3.d/S99prepare_system
```

**Line 4:** First, we mount a common /usr/local for Linux systems.

**Line 7:** Now we copy an authorized key list from /usr/local/etc. This file presumably contains whatever keys should be allowed to log in to this system.

**Line 12:** Presumably some RPMs in this directory need to be installed on all new systems. This *could* include packages for both AutoRPM and cfengine, but in this example, we execute these programs from the NFS mounted directory.

**Line 15:** We are executing this to apply system updates. It could also have installed new packages in lieu of the previous command.

**Line 18:** A new public/private key pair is generated for this client to use with cfengine. The key is then copied to the NFS server and given a name based on this system's IP address (as described in section 6.4.2.5.1. This is a bit contrived; you would usually mount /usr/local as read-only. Your master cfengine server(s) would also have to consolidate these keys (because other types of systems wouldn't be mounting this Linux-specific NFS directory, so they couldn't copy their keys there). You could use a variety of other methods to copy the public key instead.

**Line 25:** We finally run the cfagent command to let cfengine finish the system's configuration. Much of this example script could be done from within cfengine if you so desired (such as the SSH setup and the RPM installations).

**Line 28:** The SysV-style link to this init script is removed so that it is not run again.

Keep in mind that there is a risk here—if the configuration server or NFS servers are down, the script will fail. This might leave your new system in a unusable state or, even worse, in an insecure state. I recommend verifying that each new system has been properly configured when using this method.

# CHAPTER 6

# Automatic System Configuration

YOU HAVE JUST INSTALLED and configured a fresh copy of an operating system on a new system and you are now ready to automate its configuration. A UNIX system's configuration is usually contained in hundreds, if not thousands, of individual files. Many of these files contain system-level configurations such as network settings, device information, drive mappings, and so on. The rest of the configuration belongs to various applications you have installed on the system, such as web servers and user applications.

A thousand configuration files might seem a bit overwhelming at first. Luckily, most of these files will never need to be modified because the defaults are suitable for most situations. One significant advantage to automating the administration of UNIX systems is that most of the configuration files are text and not binary. In some cases, it doesn't matter because you will use a utility program to create the file for you. In other cases, however, you will have to directly modify the file, and then you will be glad when the file is plain text.

This chapter first explores a custom solution that can be adapted exactly to your needs. The custom solution may be perfect for small groups of systems, stand-alone "network appliances," and situations with very specific or unique requirements. I expand on the concept of system grouping throughout the custom solution examples. Also, I supply many examples of files that should be configured on most systems. For these reasons, even readers who have decided to use cfengine may want to skim through this chapter's custom examples.

The latter half of this chapter provides a comprehensive introduction to the GNU cfengine. This system automation/configuration application is very powerful, flexible, and useful—particularly for larger networks of differing systems. cfengine uses the pull method that allows each system to configure itself independently of other systems. This is more reliable and scalable in most situations than the push method used in the custom example. Regardless of your thoughts on cfengine right now, you should read through the introduction starting in section 6.4, "Configuring Systems with GNU cfengine," which fully describes all of the benefits it can provide.

## 6.1 What Do I Configure?

The configuration on a system can be divided into several categories:

**Customized files:** Files whose contents differ from system to system.

**Dynamic files:** Files that are not the system default and may change several times over the life of a system.

**Default files:** Files whose default contents are adequate for your purposes.

**Static files:** Files that need to be customized only once.

**Filesystem components:** Symbolic links, directories, device files, file permissions, and so on (filesystem components).

### 6.1.1 Customized Files

There are certain files that are going to be different on each machine. The most obvious are the network settings, particularly the system's IP address. Other settings that might be different include the firewall configuration, the services that should be run at startup, and so on.

These files are the most important part of the configuration automation system. Even on a relatively small number of systems, any files that are different from system to system can be major sources of difficulties. Attempting to manually create those files is bound to result in errors. If you want to make a change to such a file, you have to make the change on each system manually. Or, in some cases, you may copy the new file onto each system and make the customizations manually on each machine.

Since the file on each system is, by definition, different, it is nearly impossible to verify that any given file is correct, apart from painstakingly examining each file manually. For these reasons, customized files are the focus of this chapter.

### 6.1.2 Dynamic Files

These files are the same on each machine, yet they are modified from time to time. For these files, you could simply maintain a master system and then copy any new versions of the file(s) out to the other systems using a program such as Secure Copy (SCP). It is, however, easy to forget to perform the copy, or neglect a particular system in the copy process. It is also easy to make changes to one of the systems and forget to make those changes to the master system.

You can usually distribute these dynamic files using the methods within this chapter. Alternatively, the methods for data synchronization discussed in Chapter 7 can be used for this type of file. The size and number of files determine which approach is best in your situation. The methods in this chapter are, in general, suited for smaller numbers of smaller files *or* files that don't change too often. You should usually accomplish sharing or distributing applications and their data with the tools in Chapter 7.

## 6.1.3  Default Files

In an ideal world, our automation system would handle every file on any system. We would be able to verify that any given file is, indeed, correct. If, in the future, we decided to modify a new file, it would already be part of the automation system and could just be modified on the configuration server.

In the real world, however, it is not usually worth your effort to worry about files you don't expect to change. If you change your mind in the future, you can always expand your automation system. If you still want to verify that the other files have not been changed from their original values, you can use the tools discussed in Chapter 11.

## 6.1.4  Static Files

You need to modify some files' content from their default, but after you do, this content will remain static from that point forward. You can handle these files in a variety of ways:

- You can configured the file during the system's initial setup as discussed in Chapter 5. root's static `~/.ssh/authorized_keys` file is a good candidate for this method.

- You can handle the file the same as other data as discussed in Chapter 7.

- You can distribute the file using the techniques discussed in this chapter.

You may want to consider using the most appropriate of these methods for each individual file. Alternatively, you can choose one method for all files for simplicity and consistency.

## 6.1.5  Filesystem Components

Although most system configuration takes the form of configuration files, the actual filesystem itself can also be important. The `~/.ssh/authorized_keys` file is a configuration file, for example, but before it can be created, the `~/.ssh` directory must already exist. In addition, the permissions on the directory and the file must be correct, otherwise the SSH daemon ignores the file.

Another example of making configuration changes directly on the file system involves operating systems using System V init scripts. System V init scripts use symbolic links to determine which services start at bootup. These symbolic links are also part of the system's configuration, but they don't really make up a configuration file.

I also discuss the creation, management, and verification of these filesystem-level configuration items in this chapter.

## 6.2 Configuration Principles to Follow

The principles you will follow when you build your configuration automation system are the same as those you will continue to see throughout this book:

- The system should operate on as many different operating systems as necessary.

- The system should enable you to place systems into one or more classes and treat each class differently.

- The system should allow you to update the configuration on each system whenever and as often as you like. If nothing needs to be done, nothing should be changed.

- The system should be able to automatically update the various machines and/or update machines on demand, and possibly even update individual machines on demand.

- The system needs to be self-documenting. At the very least, you should be able to see what you changed two years ago. Hopefully, you will also know why.

- The system should be self-repairing. If a file on a system is deleted or the permissions are changed, the system should repair that problem.

- If you are automating a site that has many system administrators or has a high turnover rate, then having a single tool for almost everything is very important.

Normally, I would include a verification requirement in that list. For example, it would be nice to have a command that could verify that every system is properly configured. In this case, however, we have specified that the system should be able to be run on demand and not cause any harm. So, in lieu of verifying the system's configuration, you could just activate it and, after it runs, you will know everything is configured just as it should be.

In some situations, however, you still may want to have real verify abilities. You might want to see if something has changed, possibly back up that change, and then update the configuration. If this is required, you could always back up the original version of every configuration file before you update it. You could then use the diff command (or equivalent) to determine if the files differ (and to get the actual differences). This facility could be added to the methods described in this chapter with a little additional effort.

## 6.3 Creating a Custom Configuration Approach

In this section, we develop a system that configures a variety of machines based on a master set of configuration files and scripts. This configuration information, along with the files, scripts, and templates that compose the system, resides on a master server. This server is assumed to have passwordless Secure Shell (SSH) access to each system it needs to configure.

I am a big fan of directory structures. By using a complex directory structure, I actually make the contents of each file much simpler. The script that must process the data also tends to be simpler. It also makes the whole system more modular and easier to manage with source-control systems like CVS.

On the negative side, directory structures can be intimidating at first. Instead of one configuration file, you have to look through various directories, which is particularly difficult if you don't have a guide to get you started. It also can be a pain when you have to modify several different files to make a small change (which sometimes does happen).

All in all, I feel that directory structures are worth it. I like the structure and order. I like having simple text files that can be edited and managed by shell scripts. Also, I often find that I only edit a small subset of files subset of files—most files are generally left alone.

For these reasons, the custom approach in this chapter uses a directory structure. As with any program, there are many ways this structure could be written, each with its own advantages and disadvantages. The following example should provide you with a good starting point and/or good ideas for a script of your own.

## 6.3.1 Defining the Files and Directory Structure

For this example, all files will be under the /usr/local/etc/ directory. The following directory layout will be used for this example and its associated scripts:

```
/usr/local/etc/
|-- all_hosts
|-- group_list
|-- hosts/
|   |-- desktop
|   |-- linux
|   `-- web
`-- sysconfig/
    |-- conf/
    |   |-- all
    |   |-- groups/
    |   |   |-- desktop
    |   |   |-- linux
    |   |   `-- web
    |   `-- systems/
    |       |-- host1
    |       |-- host2
    |       `-- host3
    |-- files/
    |   |-- all/
    |   |-- desktop/
    |   |-- linux/
    |   `-- web/
    |-- scripts/
    |   |-- all/
    |   |-- desktop/
    |   |-- linux/
    |   `-- web/
    `-- templates/
        |-- all/
        |-- desktop/
        |-- linux/
        `-- web/
```

The all_hosts file contains a list of all hosts (by name) in your network. The group_list file contains a list of all possible groups (each system can be a member of one or more of these groups—i.e., one system might run Linux, be used as a desktop, and run a web server, so it would be a member of all three example groups).

The hosts/ directory contains one file per group that contains the list of hostnames of the systems in each group. All of these files were created and some were used in previous chapters.

The sample groups used for this example are desktop, linux, and web. These example groups were also discussed and used in Chapter 4.

Everything under the sysconfig/ directory is new for this chapter. I recommend using CVS to manage this directory. If you make a bad modification and corrupt a template, you can always use CVS to see what you changed and/or revert back to the working template. CVS will be introduced in section 7.9.

### 6.3.1.1  The conf/ Directory

Each file within this directory and its subdirectories contains any number of configuration settings. Each file is in a format that can be sourced directly by bash scripts. It can also be easily parsed by any other language. Here is a sample system-specific file:

```
IP_ADDRESS=192.168.10.11
NETMASK="255.255.0.0"
HOSTNAME='host1'
```

As you can see, quotes can be omitted if there are no spaces or special characters (such as ;, !, &, and others). Double quotes escape these characters but still allow for variable expansion. Single quotes disable any processing of the argument completely.

The conf/all file contains settings that are common for all hosts. Like any setting, they may be static or they may change from time to time.

The conf/groups/ directory contains settings specific to a given group. Any settings in that file override any settings in the all file for hosts in that group. In most cases, this directory also contains settings that are not found in the all file because they do not apply to all hosts. Each group does not need a file, so groups that do not have any special settings need not be represented here.

If settings within different group files conflict, the situation is a bit more tricky. Obviously there is only a problem if a system is in two groups that have different values for a specific setting. It is best if this doesn't happen. If it does, the groups are processed alphabetically so that the setting in the last alphabetical group is used.

The conf/systems/ directory contains one file per host. The filename needs to be the system's hostname. Not all systems need to be present—only the systems with specific settings. Any values in a system-specific file override any values in any other file (the global or group-specific files).

### 6.3.1.2 The files/ Directory

The files/ directory contains several subdirectories. One of them contains files that belong on all hosts (the all/ directory). Also one directory per group contains files that belong on hosts within that group.

Each file should be the exact file you want on the proper hosts. The file is placed on each host unmodified except for certain metadata that is removed from the file. This metadata specifies the destination location and permissions for the file. It needs to be in a format that is not likely to be found in any normal file. In this case, I use the sequence __:VAR=VALUE that must appear first in a line. Here is an example /etc/resolv.conf file:

```
__:LOCATION=/etc/resolv.conf
__:PERMS=0755
__:USERGROUP=root.root
search mydomain.com
nameserver 192.168.1.2
```

This example file should be named resolv.conf and be placed in the sysconfig/all/ directory. This causes this file to be placed on every host as /etc/resolv.conf and its permissions to be set to 0755. The first three lines are not present in the destination file (nor are any lines of this format) because this metadata does not belong in the final configuration files.

### 6.3.1.3 The scripts/ Directory

Just like the files/ directory, this directory has an all/ directory and one directory for each group. Each directory can have any number of scripts (or any executable program) that are executed on the appropriate systems based on their group membership. Both the groups and each set of scripts in each group are processed alphabetically.

### 6.3.1.4 The templates/ Directory

The templates/ directory structure is identical to the files/ directory. The only functional difference is that each file in the templates/ directory is processed for possible substitution of the various settings from the configuration files. That is what separates templates from regular files—templates can contain any number of tokens that are replaced with real values during the configuration process.

The substitutions are actually made by processing the file using the bash shell. This allows us to have a wide variety of powerful substitution operators (everything that the bash shell supports). Here is an example template:

```
IP_ADDRESS="${IP_ADDRESS}"
SUBNET="${SUBNET}"
```

This template is very simple and contains just some host-specific network configuration parameters. The values for these particular settings would be in a host-specific file in conf/systems/. Here is an example line in a template file that uses one of the more powerful substitutions the bash shell supports:

```
SUBNET="${SUBNET:-255.255.0.0}"
```

The ${var:-default} substitution string uses the value in the SUBNET configuration item. If that value is not set, 255.255.0.0 is used as the default value. With this method, only a system with a unique netmask has its netmask set in its system-specific configuration file. Any other systems have the default value substituted in place of this substitution string.

Of course, you can also put a default value in the conf/all file, which operates in the same way. You have the option of using whichever method you think is the best for values such as this that are usually the same across multiple systems but can be different in some cases.

Here is another possible line from a template:

```
IP_ADDRESS="$(sed -n 's/ $HOST$//p' /usr/local/var/prepare_system/allocated)"
```

This line uses the $(cmd) substitution string, which causes the specified command to be executed and the output to be substituted in its place. In this example, the template assumes the HOST variable is set to the system's hostname (and it will be set by the main script that will be processing the template). The file containing the list of IP addresses and the host to which they are assigned (created by our scripts in Chapter 4) are processed and the host's IP address is isolated using the sed command. Remember that in this custom configuration system, the template is processed on the central configuration server, not on the destination system.

One disadvantage of this particular template system is that certain reserved environment variables cannot be used to store settings. You should not, for example, have a variable named PATH or IFS. The bash man page has a complete listing of the special environment variables used by the shell. As long as you avoid using these as variable names, you will not have any problems.

The greatest disadvantage of this type of template system is that you cannot usually push any shell scripts out using this system. A shell script is likely to have substitutions that will be processed when the template is parsed, and as a result, the script will be corrupted. This limitation can be overcome by pushing the shell script out as a file (and not as a template). The script could then read any configuration from a separate configuration file. This is, arguably, a better way to do it anyway.

You could also use a completely different method for the template files. I often use a Perl script to process templates and use something like __VARIABLE__ for substitution values. Note that this method requires more coding and does not allow nested substitutions (although it could if I chose unique opening and closing delimiters such as __{VARIABLE}__).

## 6.3.2  Defining the Configuration Logic

We will have one configuration script (config_all_systems) that runs on a central server and performs various actions on the remote systems based on the information in the directory structure discussed in the previous section.

The logic for this script is lengthy but straightforward. The list of hosts will be read from /usr/local/etc/all_hosts and the following actions will need to be performed for each host:

1. Determine which groups the host belongs to by processing the files in the hosts/ directory.

2. Load the configuration from the conf/all file.

3. Load the configuration from each necessary group file in the conf/groups/ directory.

4. If it exists, load the system-specific configuration from the appropriate file in the conf/systems/ directory.

5. Transfer any files in the files/all/ directory to the remote system and into the location specified in each file.

6. For each group the system belongs to, transfer any files in the files/groupname/ directory to the remote system and into the location specified in each file.

7. Process any templates in the templates/all/ directory locally and then transfer them to the remote system and into the location specified in each file.

8. For each group the system belongs to, process any templates in the `templates/groupname/` directory locally and then transfer them to the remote system and into the location specified in each file.

9. Transfer any scripts in the `scripts/all/` directory to the remote system and then execute them on the remote system.

10. For each group the system belongs to, transfer any scripts in the `scripts/groupname/` directory to the remote system and then execute them on the remote system.

## 6.3.3  Presenting the Configuration Script

This system is divided into two scripts: one script, called `config_all_systems`, executes the `configure_system` script for each system and summarizes the results. The `configure_system` script, does the actual configuration on any one system.

One good reason for this separation is simplicity (each smaller script is simpler than one big script would be). A better reason for separate scripts is that they isolate environment variables. Each host needs to start with a clean slate for its variables. One host might, for example, have a special SUBNET value, while the next host wants that variable unset so that the default variable will be used (when using the `${var:-default}` substitution string). By executing each host in a separate shell, you will not have any problems with the settings for one host being left over when you configure other hosts.

I present the `config_all_systems` script first because it is fairly simple. Next in this section I cover the `configure_system` script and explain all of the components within that complicated script.

### 6.3.3.1  The config_all_systems Script

The `config_all_systems` script presented in this section simply executes the second script for each host. It finishes by summarizing the results, displaying any failed hosts by name, and exiting with 0 only if all hosts were successful.

```
#!/bin/bash

# This file should have one host per line
host_list="/usr/local/etc/all_hosts"
```

```
# This is the script that configures each host
configure_system="/usr/local/sbin/configure_system.sh"

# Process each host
success_count=0
failure_count=0
failure_list=''
for host in `cat $host_list` ; do
    echo
    if $configure_system "$host" ; then
        echo " Host $host Configuration Successful!"
        success_count="$[$success_count+1]"
    else
        echo " Host $host Configuration FAILED!"
        failure_count="$[$failure_count+1]"
        failure_list="$failure_list $host"
    fi
done

# Display summary
echo
echo "Total of $[$success_count+$failure_count] systems processed:"
echo " $success_count Success(es)"
echo " $failure_count Failure(s)"
echo
[ -n "$failure_list" ] && {
    echo "$failure_count host(s) failed:"
    for host in $failure_list ; do
        echo " $host"
    done
    exit 1
}
exit 0
```

**NOTE**  You can find the code samples for this chapter In the Downloads section of the Apress web site (http://www.apress.com).

There shouldn't be much in this script that you have not seen before. One exception might be the use of bash's mathematical capability. The $[expr] expression evaluates expr as a mathematical equation. The results are substituted in its place. This is used to count the successes and failures to be reported at the end of the script.

## 6.3.3.2 The configure_system Functions

Although there are many distinct steps for each host, many of them are related and can be implemented using functions to reduce the amount of code in the script. As any developer knows, functions are a very good thing. Using them means that you have less code to write, debug, and maintain.

The following functions should be placed into a file that can be included (sourced) by the configure_system:

```
# Abort the program, displaying an error
die() {
    echo " ERROR: $*" >&2
    exit 1
}


# arg1: full path of configuration file to read
read_conf() {
    if [ -f "$1" ] ; then
        source "$1" || die "Could not source $1"
        echo " Processed Config: $1"
    fi
    return 0
}
```

These functions are very simple but perform useful functions and help clean up the main code. The die function displays a properly formatted error message and exits the script (with an unsuccessful return code). The read_conf function checks for a configuration file, sources the file (if found), and aborts if it finds the file but cannot read it.

### 6.3.3.2.1 The do_template Function

The following do_template function also needs to be placed in the function file that is sourced by the configure_system script:

```
# arg1: full path of local source file
# arg2: full path of local destination file
do_template() {
    local src="$1"
    local dest="$2"
    [ -z "$src" -o -z "$dest" ] &&
        die "do_template called with empty parameter(s) ($*)"
```

```
# Process the template
sed 's/\\/\\\\\\\\/g; s/"/\\\\"/g;' "$src" | while read line; do
    eval echo "\"$line\"";
done > "$dest" || die "Could not process template $src"
echo " Processed Template: $(basename "$src")"
}
```

One part of this function definitely requires an explanation. You saw that I had to use the sed command to escape backslashes and double quotes. Using this is necessary if I want to preserve these characters throughout the echo command, followed by the eval command. Additionally, since the sed command also requires backslashes to be escaped, the actual sed substitution pattern contains eight backslashes. This is the first part of the sed expression (s/\\/\\\\\\\\/g). Here is what happens at the various stages:

Original      \
After sed     \\\\
After echo    \\
After eval    \

The translation of the double quotes should also seem very similar. This is the second half of the two-part sed command (s/"/\\\\"/g). The journey of the double quote character through all of these steps is as follows:

Original      "
After sed     \\"
After echo    \"
After eval    "

### 6.3.3.2.2 The push_file Function

The push_file function is provided in this section. It also needs to be placed in the function file that is sourced by the configure_system script that I will provide you with later in this chapter.

The push_file function is the most complex of the helper functions. It has to parse information out of the source file, remove that metadata, transfer the file, and possibly set ownership and permissions.

As mentioned earlier in this chapter, any file that is being pushed to the remote system may have any number of the following lines containing metadata to be used by the script:

```
__:LOCATION=/etc/resolv.conf
__:PERMS=0755
__:USERGROUP=root.root
```

In fact, the script is written so that any line starting with __: will be evaluated (to set these variables) and removed from the pushed file. If, for some reason, one of your files is supposed to have a line that begins with that sequence, you will need to modify the script to use a different sequence than the one used in the example.

---

**NOTE** The line numbers in this code and other code sections in this chapter are for display purposes only and are not part of the actual program code.

---

```
1   # arg1: full path of local source file
2   # arg2: hostname of remote system
3   # arg3: [optional] destination file on remote system
4   push_file() {
5       local src="$1"
6       local host="$2"
7       local dest="$3"
8       [ -z "$src" -o -z "$host" ] &&
9           die "push_file called with missing parameter(s) ($*)"
10
11      # Read configuration items from file
12      eval `sed -n 's/^__:://p' "$src"`
13
14      # Override location if necessary
15      [ -n "$dest" ] && LOCATION="$dest"
16
17      # Push the file now
18      grep -v '^__:' "$src" | ssh -T "root@$host" "cat > $LOCATION" ||
19          die "Could not place remote file $LOCATION"
20
21      # Set the permissions, if necessary
22      [ -n "$PERMS" ] && ssh "root@$host" "chmod $PERMS $LOCATION" ||
23          die "Could not set permissions on remote file $LOCATION"
24
25      # Set the ownership, if necessary
26      [ -n "$USERGROUP" ] && ssh "root@$host" \
27          "chown $USERGROUP $LOCATION" ||
28          die "Could not set permissions on remote file $LOCATION"
29
```

```
30    [ -z "$dest" ] && {
31        # Only produce output if third arg was not given
32        # (third arg is given when pushing scripts to execute)
33        echo "   Pushed File: $LOCATION"
34    }
35  }
```

**Line 12:** The sed command is used only to print lines in the file that begin with the special __: sequence. In addition, that sequence is stripped from the beginning of the lines, leaving a series of commands suitable for being evaluated by the shell. This output is then processed by the eval so that the variables are set. So, for example, the line __:PERMS=0755 is converted by sed to PERMS=0755, which is evaluated by the eval command, which causes the PERMS environment variable to be set with the value 0755.

**Line 15:** If a third parameter was provided to the function, the dest variable will not be empty, and the -n test will succeed. The LOCATION variable will be set to that value whether it was specified in the file or not.

**Line 18:** The inverse (-v) grep command is used to remove the metadata lines from the file. The output stream is sent through SSH to the remote system. Although scp could have been used, it would have required another temp file. The ssh command works fine for transferring files (as long as you use the -T switch to disable tty allocation). On the remote side, the cat command takes its stdin and outputs it to stdout, which is redirected to the destination file.

### 6.3.3.3   The configure_system Script

This shell script configures a single remote host. It uses the host directory specified (such as /usr/local/etc/hosts) to determine the system's associated groups. It uses all of the files and directories in the /usr/local/etc/sysconfig directory as described in section 6.3.1. It also requires all of the functions shown in the previous section to be in the specified file (/usr/local/sbin/configure.functions).

```
1  #!/bin/bash
2
3  # The base directory
4  host_dir='/usr/local/etc/hosts'
5  base_dir='/usr/local/etc/sysconfig'
6  source '/usr/local/sbin/configure.functions'
7
```

```
 8  # Specify any necessary options for ssh here
 9  alias ssh="/usr/bin/ssh"
10
11  [ $# -lt 1 ] && die "Usage: $0 host"
12  host="$1"
13  echo "Configuring host $host:"
14
15  # We need a safe local and remote temp file
16  localtemp=`mktemp /tmp/sysconfig-XXXXXX` ||
17      die "Could not create local temp file"
18  remotetemp=`ssh $host 'mktemp /tmp/sysconfig-XXXXXX'` ||
19      die "Could not create remote temp file"
20
21  # First, retrieve group list for the host
22  cd "$host_dir" || die "Host directory $host_dir not found"
23  groups="$(grep -l "^$host$" *)"
24
25  # Read settings for this host
26  read_conf "$base_dir/conf/all"
27  for group in $groups ; do
28      read_conf "$base_dir/conf/groups/$group"
29  done
30  read_conf "$base_dir/conf/systems/$host"
31
32  # Now, push out any necessary files
33  for dir in all $groups ; do
34      for file in "$base_dir/files/$dir/"* ; do
35          if [ -f "$file" ] ; then
36              push_file "$file" "$host"
37          fi
38      done
39  done
40
41  # Next, push out any necessary templates
42  for dir in all $groups ; do
43      for file in "$base_dir/templates/$dir/"* ; do
44          if [ -f "$file" ] ; then
45              do_template "$file" "$localtemp"
46              push_file "$localtemp" "$host"
47          fi
48      done
49  done
50
```

```
51  # Finally, execute any necessary scripts
52  for dir in all $groups ; do
53    for file in "$base_dir/scripts/$dir/"* ; do
54      if [ -f "$file" ] ; then
55        push_file "$file" "$host" "$remotetemp"
56        ssh "root@$host" "chmod u+x $remotetemp ; $remotetemp" ||
57          die "Execution of script $(basename "$file") failed"
58        echo "   Executed Script: $(basename "$file")"
59      fi
60    done
61  done
62
63  # Clean up
64  rm -f "$localtemp"
65  ssh "root@$host" "rm -f $remotetemp"
66
67  exit 0
```

**Line 16:** The mktemp command is used to create both a local and remote temporary file, using /tmp/sysconfig-XXXXXX as its pattern (the X characters are replaced by random characters). The mktemp command returns the name of the actual file created on stdout. It would even be better to put these temporary files in a directory that normal users cannot access.

**Line 23:** The -l switch for the grep command causes a list of filenames with matching lines to be printed. This list is the list of groups associated with the specified host.

**Line 26:** Each necessary configuration file is read, in order, by the read_conf command. If a setting is defined in more than one file, the last value read will be used.

**Line 33:** Each file in the all/ directory, as well as each file in any appropriate group directories, is pushed out to the remote system using the push_file function.

**Line 42:** This loop is just like the files loop, but for templates. Each template is first processed using the do_template function, and then it is pushed to the remote system using the push_file function.

**Line 52:** This loop is the same as the files and templates loop. Each local file is a script or other executable program. The file is pushed out as the remote temporary file, made executable, and then executed.

## 6.3.4  Exploring Example Configuration File Creation

The actual configuration script might be a relatively minor part of your custom configuration system. Depending on how many configuration files you need to push to your various systems, you can end up spending most of your time creating the actual configuration files and templates. Unfortunately, most UNIX variants have their own method for configuring much of the system. Applications, of course, also have widely varied configuration methods, file formats, and so on, so I will not be able to provide a set of templates that will work with your specific set of systems. I will, however, provide a couple simple examples that should help you start creating your own template system.

### 6.3.4.1  The /etc/resolv.conf File

For our first example, we will consider the /etc/resolv.conf file, which is found on just about every UNIX system. A typical system will have the following /etc/resolv.conf file:

```
nameserver 192.168.2.2
nameserver 192.168.2.3
search mydomain.com
```

You would place the following lines in the conf/all file:

```
SEARCH_DOMAIN="mydomain.com"
NAMESERVER1="192.168.2.2"
NAMESERVER2="192.168.2.3"
```

Let's say that all desktop machines should also have dev.mydomain.com in their search domains. You would put this line in conf/groups/desktop:

```
SEARCH_DOMAIN="${SEARCH_DOMAIN} dev.mydomain.com"
```

Finally, you would create the following template in templates/all/resolv.conf:

```
__:LOCATION=/etc/resolv.conf
__:PERMS=0755
__:USERGROUP=root.root
nameserver ${NAMESERVER1}
nameserver ${NAMESERVER2}
search ${SEARCH_DOMAIN}
```

### 6.3.4.2 The /etc/mail/access File

Let's say that you run sendmail on several hosts in your network. Each of those hosts is in the sendmail group. Let's say all of your IP addresses are in the 192.168.0.0/255.255.0.0 subnet (which contains addresses from 192.168.0.0 through 192.168.255.255). You want to place /etc/mail/access on each of these hosts to allow mail to be received from any other host in your network. Since there is no variable information in this particular example, you use a static file. The files/sendmail/access file should be as follows:

```
__:LOCATION=/etc/mail/access
__:PERMS=0755
__:USERGROUP=root.root
localhost.localdomain                      RELAY
localhost                                  RELAY
127.0.0.1                                  RELAY
192.168                                    RELAY
```

In this case, however, the binary /etc/mail/access.db file needs to be rebuilt after the access is updated. So, you need a script to be run on each remote system. This script should be placed in scripts/sendmail/update_db.sh:

```
#!/bin/bash

cd /etc/mail
make >/dev/null 2>&1
exit 0
```

This script will be run on each host in the sendmail group after the /etc/mail/access file is placed on the system. The script shown always exits with a positive return value. You may want to remove the exit command so that the script exits with the return value of the make command. This way, if the make fails, the configuration process terminates, and you can determine what went wrong. Of course, this might not be desirable if you run the configuration script automatically.

## 6.4 Configuring Systems with GNU cfengine

GNU's cfengine satisfies all of the requirements mentioned in this chapter and many more. In addition to system configuration, it can also perform a range of monitoring and maintenance tasks that I will discuss in future chapters.

Although it can be a bit overwhelming at first, installing and configuring cfengine is going to be easier than making your own system in many cases. The larger your network of systems, and the more diverse they are, the greater the advantages of using cfengine. Since many environments tend to grow bigger and faster than you expect, cfengine may be worth the effort in most cases.

That being said, there are still some situations in which you might be better off using a custom approach. A stand-alone network appliance is a good example. Although cfengine could indeed do the job, it might be overkill when you have only one machine. You might only need to do a few things that could be done with custom scripts rather quickly. The important thing is to evaluate your available options and choose the best one for your particular situation.

The single biggest drawback (as well as one of the best features) of cfengine is its complexity. It would probably take an average system administrator a week to get cfengine operating fully on only a few systems. Of course, once you have accomplished that feat, expanding its operations to hundreds of systems is relatively painless.

The most current version of cfengine at the time of this writing was 2.0.4 and it is the version used within this chapter. The 2.*X* series has quite a few changes from the 1.*X* series, so you will see differences between the examples in this book and older versions of cfengine. If you are just getting started, I would recommend that you use a newer version of cfengine.

## 6.4.1 cfengine Overview

In this section, I provide a brief overview of cfengine, its files, its methods, and its most important concepts.

### 6.4.1.1 cfengine Concepts

The GNU cfengine program was designed to save time and reduce headaches in the long run. It may take some time to set up and configure, but you will be happier when everything has been said and done. At least at first, performing new tasks with cfengine will take longer than performing the same task manually. But, when you upgrade the operating system and loose some change, you will be glad you used cfengine because it will simply perform the change again. Or, when you realize a few other systems need the same change, you can use cfengine to make this happen in seconds (by adding the new systems to the appropriate class).

If you made the change manually, on the other hand, it might take some time before you even notice that the change needs to be made again. Once you notice, you'll have to make the change manually all over again—that is, of course, if you remember how you did it the last time. If ten new systems need a specific change, you might spend an hour changing each system yourself, whereas cfengine could have just done it for you.

One major design principle for cfengine was that it should operate using one central set of configuration files. This enables the same set of configuration files to be executed on every host on the network in their original form. Each host also transfers the configuration files from the server (if possible) before each run. As long as you make all the changes in that central set of configuration files, then everything else will happen automatically. You will not have any more manual changes to systems that you may forget about. You will no longer have to use special scripts for special systems and/or scripts that have so many conditionals (based on hostname, operating system, etc.) that they have become unreadable and difficult to maintain. Perhaps most importantly, this central set of configuration files documents every change you have done to every system. If you put a few comments in the files along with the commands, you will not only document what you have done, but also document *why* you did it.

For some tasks, cfengine abstracts the actual desired action from the technical specifics of the underlying operating system. For other tasks (namely editing files), cfengine provides a high-level language that allows you to exactly specify the actual modifications.

For other tasks, cfengine does not provide any native support. It does, however, allow you to execute external scripts based on a system's class membership. When possible, you should use the internal commands provided by cfengine. If you do not, you can use custom shell and Perl scripts, but you should still get cfengine to execute them on your behalf.

Once you decide to use cfengine, it is in your best interest to use it for as many tasks as possible. This usually means that you will need to change your habits because it will always be tempting to just "fix it real quick" instead of going through the proper cfengine process. However, once you switch fully to cfengine, you will enjoy many benefits:

- A standardized, centralized configuration that all hosts on your network can use.

- Systems that can be classified using a variety of methods and classes that can specify certain behavior.

- Changes that when made to systems are recorded and performed again, if necessary.

- Systems that may have intermittent uptime or network connectivity but will eventually make any necessary changes.

### 6.4.1.2 Push vs. Pull

Yet another advantage to using cfengine is that it pulls from a server instead of pushing from the master system. This doesn't make a big difference when you have a local set of servers that are reliable and usually up and running; if, however, your systems are spread out over an unreliable network and/or may not always be running, the pull method is much more reliable.

For example, if some systems can boot to either Linux or Windows, they can pull from the server whenever they are running in Linux. If you used a push technique instead, the system might get neglected if it was running Windows at the time the push was attempted. Here is another example: you might have UNIX running on one or more laptops that are not always connected to the network. A system like this might never be updated using the push method, because it would have to be connected to the network at the exact time a push occurs. With the pull method, the laptop would automatically pull the configuration changes the next time it could contact the configuration server.

There is, of course, no reason why the custom method just discussed couldn't be adapted to use the pull method. If you need to use the pull method, but you don't want to use cfengine for some reason, try using the custom scripts earlier in this chapter—they would be a good place to start. Either way, you will be able to make changes on a server and have each client pull those changes from the server at their next opportunity.

Although cfengine typically pulls from a server and executes every hour, it also supports the ability to force updates to all or any subset of the systems on demand. Obviously, you will find this very useful when you are performing mission-critical bug fixes (e.g., something else you did messed up a system or two and you need to fix them very quickly).

You can also run cfengine directly on each system by logging in and manually running the cfagent command. I think cfengine follows a good theory in system administration automation: the more ways you can initiate changes to a system, the better—as long as they are done in the same way. In other words, cfengine provides several methods for updating each system, but all of them use the same configuration files and operate exactly the same way (once initiated).

### 6.4.1.3 The Components of cfengine

The cfengine suite consists of several compiled programs. I will not list all of these programs here, only the ones that we will discuss in this book. These programs are typically installed in a location that is common to all systems (such as an NFS-mounted /usr/local). Alternatively, they can be directly installed on each system by a package management system. In either case, the important binaries (cfagent, cfexecd, and cfservd, described momentarily) are copied to a local directory such as /var/cfengine/bin/ to make sure that they are always available, even when there may be problems with the network.

> cfagent: The autonomous configuration agent (the heart of the program). This command can be run manually (on demand), by cfexecd on a regular basis, and/or by cfservd by remote command.

> cfservd: The file transfer and remote activation daemon. This must be run on any cfengine file servers and on any system that you would like to be able to execute cfagent remotely.

> cfexecd: The execution and reporting daemon. This is either run as a daemon or run as a regular cron job. In either case, it handles running cfagent and reporting its output.

> cfkey: Generates public/private key pairs and needs to be run only once on every host.

> cfrun: This command needs to be run from a server that will contact the clients (through cfservd) and tell them to execute cfagent.

For any given command, you can see a summary of its options by using the -h command-line option. When running a command, you can always specify the -v switch to see more (or in many cases, any) detail. When debugging a program, you should use the -d2 switch to view debugging information (and, for daemons, the -d2 switch prevents it from detaching from the terminal).

### 6.4.1.4  *cfengine Directory Structure*

The binaries need to be installed in a directory mounted on every host or they need to be installed independently on each host. Everything cfengine uses during its normal operation is located under the /var/cfengine/ directory. Its contents are as follows:

> bin/: Important binaries (cfagent, cfexecd, and cfservd) are copied here to ensure that they are available when needed.

> inputs/: This is the standard location for all of the configuration files cfengine needs. We will be using three files from this directory: cfagent.conf, cfservd.conf, and update.conf.

> outputs/: This is where the output files from each run cfexecd performs are placed.

> ppkeys/: This is where this system's public and private keys, as well as other systems' public keys, are located.

### 6.4.1.5  cfengine Configuration Files

Each system must have a minimal number of configuration files. These are found in the `/var/cfengine/inputs/` directory on each system, but they should be maintained in a central location.

> **update.conf:** This file must be kept simple. It is always parsed and executed by `cfagent` first. Its main job is to copy the set of configuration files from the server. If any of the other configuration files contain an error, this file should still be able to update files so that the next run will be successful. If there is an error in this file, you will have to manually fix any affected systems.
>
> **cfagent.conf:** This file contains the guts of your automation system. It contains all of the actions, group declarations, and so on. Although our examples in this book are simple enough to neatly fit into one file, this file could include any number of separate files to make things simpler (using the `import` section).
>
> **cfservd.conf:** This, as may be obvious, is the configuration file for the `cfservd` daemon. It defines which hosts can remotely execute `cfagent` and which remote hosts can transfer which files.

The master copy of the configuration files should be managed with a source control system like CVS. This way you have a record of any changes made and you have the ability to revert to an older configuration file if you introduce a problem into the system.

### 6.4.1.6  Identifying Systems with Classes

The concept of classes is at the heart of cfengine. Each system belongs to one or more classes. Or, if you think of it another way, many classes are defined each time `cfagent` runs based on a variety of different kinds of information. Each action in the configuration file can be limited to only certain classes. So, any given action could be performed only on one host, or only on hosts that are running a specific operating system, or on every host. cfengine uses both built-in and custom classes, both of which will be discussed within this section.

#### 6.4.1.6.1  Predefined Classes

The host itself determines many of the classes that are defined—its architecture, hostname, IP address(es), and operating system. Several classes are also defined based on the current date and time.

To determine which standard classes are defined on any give system, run this command:

```
# cfagent -p -v | grep Defined
Defined Classes = ( any redhat redhat_7 redhat_7_2 Sunday Hr16 Min58
Min55_00 Q4 Hr16_Q4 Day11 August Yr2002 linux kaybee_org org kaybee
32_bit linux_2_4_9_31smp i686 linux_i686 linux_i686_2_4_9_31smp
compiled_on_linux_gnu ipv4_10 10_1_1_1 10_1_1 ipv4_10_1_1_1
ipv4_10_1_1 ipv4_10_1 )
```

As you can see, there are quite a number of predefined classes for my system. They can be divided into a few categories:

**Operating System:** redhat redhat_7 redhat_7_2

**Kernel:** linux linux_2_4_9_31smp

**Architecture:** i686 linux_i686 linux_i686_2_4_9_31smp

**Hostname:** kaybee_org kaybee org

**IP Address:** 10_1_1 10_1_1_1 ipv4_10 ipv4_10_1 ipv4_10_1_1 ipv4_10_1_1_1

**Date/Time:** Sunday Hr16 Min58 Min55_00 Q4 Hr16_Q4 Day11 August Yr2002

Every system is a member of the any class, for obvious reasons. As you can see, cfengine provides quite good granularity with its default class assignments. I cannot possibly list all the classes that could be assigned to your systems, so you will have to check the list on each of your systems (or, at least, each type of system on your network).

The time-related classes probably require some additional explanation. The Min55_00 class specifies the current five-minute range. The Q4 class is always set in the last quarter of the hour. The Hr16_Q4 class says we are currently in the last quarter of the 16th hour.

### 6.4.1.6.2 Custom Classes

Custom classes are defined in the classes section of the cfagent.conf configuration file. Here is an example:

```
classes:
    # Check to see if X11R6 is installed
    X11R6 = ( '/usr/bin/test -d /usr/X11R6' )

    # Mail servers must be explicitly defined
    mail = ( mail1 mail2 )
```

```
# DNS and web servers are obvious by their configuration files
dns = ( '/usr/bin/test -f /etc/named.conf' )
web = ( '/usr/bin/test -f /etc/httpd/conf/httpd.conf' )

# Any critical servers are a member of this class
critical = ( mail dns web )
```

When a class definition contains a quoted string, that is a command to be executed. If it returns an exit code of 0, then this system will be part of that class.

Class definitions can (and usually do) list other classes. If a system is a member of any of the listed classes, then it is also a member of the new class.

Some cfengine commands can define new classes in certain situations. If, for example, a particular drive is too full, a class can be defined (and a warning can also be printed). Other parts of the configuration file may take further actions if that class is defined. I explore this further later in this chapter.

### 6.4.1.7 More Information About GNU cfengine

GNU cfengine can be downloaded from its web site http://www.cfengine.org/. The web site includes a tutorial, a comprehensive reference manual, mailing lists, and archives.

You should also examine the large number of sample configuration files that are included with the cfengine distribution. These sample files, when combined with the web-based reference manual, should get you going on even the most advanced uses of cfengine.

## 6.4.2 Basic Setup

Within this section, I illustrate and discuss a simple cfengine setup that will provide a good framework for customization and expansion. These simple configuration files will not make many changes to your systems, but they will still show some of the power of cfengine.

This simple setup includes one central server and one other host. With cfengine, all hosts are set up identically (even with only slight differences on the server), so this example could be extended to any number of systems. I would recommend, though, that you start out with just two systems. Once you get cfengine up and running on those systems, it is easy enough to expand the system to other hosts.

### 6.4.2.1 Setting Up the Network

Before starting with cfengine, you should make sure that your network is properly prepared. It is difficult, if not impossible, to use cfengine with dynamic IP addresses. Even if you use the Dynamic Host Configuration Protocol (DHCP) to assign addresses to some or all of your systems, it should always assign the same IP address to systems that will be controlled with cfengine. In other words, it doesn't matter which method you use to assign the IP addresses, as long as each system that is going to be managed has a consistent IP.

The next task is to make sure your Domain Name System (DNS) is properly configured for your hosts. Although you can always work around DNS problems, it is best to have properly configured DNS for your testing hosts. Each host should have a hostname, and a DNS lookup of that hostname should return that host's IP address. In addition, if that IP address is looked up in DNS, the same hostname should be returned.

If this setup is not possible, I recommend that you add every host to the /etc/hosts file on every system. If you are using a multihomed host, you have to pay attention to which IP address will be used when your host is communicating with other cfengine hosts.

### 6.4.2.2 Running Necessary Processes

In the most simplistic setup, you can use cfengine by running cfagent on each system manually. You will, however, benefit more from running one or two daemons on each system.

#### 6.4.2.2.1 The cfexecd Daemon

Although you could, theoretically, only run cfagent on demand, it is better to run it automatically on a regular basis. This is when cfexecd comes in handy; it runs as a daemon and executes cfagent on a regular, predefined, schedule. This schedule can be modified by adding time classes to the schedule setting in the control block in cfagent.conf. The default setting is Min00_05, which means cfagent will run in the first five minutes of every hour. To run twice per hour, for example, you could place the following line in the control section of cfagent.conf:

```
schedule = ( Min00_05 Min30_35 )
```

The cfexecd daemon does not have its own configuration file, but it does use this setting out of cfagent.conf.

You can also run cfexecd on a regular basis using the system's cron daemon. The following entry could be added to the system crontab (usually /etc/crontab) to execute (and report) cfagent every hour:

```
0 * * * * root /usr/local/sbin/cfexecd -F
```

The -F switch tells the cfexecd not to go into daemon mode because it is being run by cron.

For the ultimate in reliability, run cfexecd as a daemon and also run it from cron (maybe once per day). You can then, in cfagent.conf, check for the crontab entry and check to see if the cfexecd daemon is running. The following lines, if placed in cfagent.conf, perform these checks and correct any problems:

```
editfiles:
   { /etc/crontab
     AppendIfNoSuchLine "0 * * * * root /var/cfengine/bin/cfexecd -F"
   }
```

```
processes:
   "cfexecd" restart "/var/cfengine/bin/cfexecd"
```

With this technique, if either of the methods is not working properly, the other method ultimately repairs the problem.

### 6.4.2.2.2 The cfservd Daemon

The cfservd daemon is not required on all systems. It needs to run on any cfengine file servers, which, in our case, is the central configuration server only. It also allows you to remotely execute cfagent from other systems. If you want this functionality, then cfservd needs to be running on every system. In either case, you should always check to make sure it is running with the following command in cfagent.conf:

```
processes:
   "cfservd" restart "/var/cfengine/bin/cfservd"
```

## 6.4.2.3  Creating Basic Configuration Files

These configuration files need to be placed in the master configuration directory on the configuration server (as explained in the next section). They are common files and will be used in their exact original form on every server in your network.

### 6.4.2.3.1 *Example cfservd.conf*

This is the configuration file for the cfservd daemon. It allows clients to transfer the master set of configuration files and also allows cfagent to be remotely executed using cfrun. Obviously only one system needs to allow access to the central configuration files (the server), but having cfservd allow access to those files does not hurt anything on other systems (because they don't have the files there to copy). All systems, however, can benefit from allowing remote cfagent execution, since it allows you to execute cfagent on demand from remote systems.

So, the following cfservd.conf can be used on all systems, which is what we want:

```
control:
    domain = ( mydomain.com )
    AllowUsers = ( root )
    cfrunCommand = ( "/var/cfagent/bin/cfagent" )

admit:
    /usr/local/var/cfengine/inputs *.mydomain.com
    /var/cfagent/bin/cfagent       *.mydomain.com
```

The cfrunCommand setting specifies the location of the cfagent binary to be run when a connection from cfrun is received. The admit section is very important because it specifies which hosts have access to which files. You must grant access to the central configuration directory and the cfagent binary. You also need to grant access to any other files that clients need to transfer from this server.

### 6.4.2.3.2 *Basic update.conf*

The update.conf file must be kept as simple as possible and should rarely, if ever, be changed. This file is parsed and executed by cfagent before cfagent.conf. If you put out a bad cfagent.conf, the next time the clients execute cfagent they get the new version because their update.conf file is still valid. Distributing a bad update.conf would not be a very good idea, so I recommend thoroughly testing any changes before you place the file in the central configuration directory.

Again, this file is run on every host, including the server. The cfagent command is smart enough to copy the files locally (instead of over the network) when running on the configuration server. Several variables are defined in the control section and then used in the copy section. Variable substitution can be accomplished with either the $(var) or ${var} sequences.

```
1  control:
2  actionsequence  = ( copy tidy )
3  domain          = ( mydomain.com )
4  workdir         = ( /var/cfengine )
5  policyhost      = ( server.mydomain.com )
6  master_cfinput  = ( /usr/local/var/cfengine/inputs )
7  cf_install_dir  = ( /usr/local/sbin )
8
9  copy:
10      $(cf_install_dir)/cfagent      dest=$(workdir)/bin/cfagent
11                                     mode=755
12                                     type=checksum
13
14      $(cf_install_dir)/cfservd      dest=$(workdir)/bin/cfservd
15                                     mode=755
16                                     type=checksum
17
18      $(cf_install_dir)/cfexecd      dest=$(workdir)/bin/cfexecd
19                                     mode=755
20                                     type=checksum
21
22      $(master_cfinput)              dest=$(workdir)/inputs
23                                     r=inf
24                                     mode=644
25                                     type=binary
26                                     exclude=*.lst
27                                     exclude=*~
28                                     exclude=#*
29                                     server=$(policyhost)
30  tidy:
31      $(workdir)/outputs pattern=* age=7
```

**Line 5:** The string server.mydomain.com should be replaced with the host-name of your configuration server.

**Line 6:** This is the directory on the master configuration server that contains the master configuration files.

**Line 7:** This is the location, on every server, of the cfengine binaries.

**Line 23:** This specifies that the source directory should be copied recursively to the destination directory with no limit on the recursion depth.

**Line 25:** This option is misleading at first. It specifies that any local file should be compared byte-by-byte with the master copy to determine if an update is required.

**Line 29:** This option causes the files to be retrieved from the specified server.

**Line 31:** This command in the `tidy` section removes any files in the `outputs/` directory that have not been accessed in the last seven days.

The permissions (modes) on each file are checked on each run even if the file already exists.

### 6.4.2.3.3 Framework for cfagent.conf

This is the meat of the cfengine configuration. Hopefully, any change you need to make on any system will be done using this file. The sample `cfagent.conf` given here is very simple for testing purposes, and more advanced `cfagent.conf` uses will be discussed further in section 6.4.4.

If you call any scripts from cfengine and those scripts produce any output, that output will be displayed (when executed interactively) or logged and emailed (when executed from `cfexecd`). Since it is typical to execute `cfagent` every hour, any scripts should only produce output if there is a problem or if something changed and the administrator needs to be notified.

```
1   control:
2       actionsequence  = ( files directories tidy disable processes )
3       domain          = ( mydomain.com )
4       timezone        = ( EDT EST )
5       access          = ( root )
6       # Where cfexecd sends reports
7       smtpserver      = ( mail.mydomain.com )
8       sysadm          = ( root@mydomain.com )
9
10  files:
11      /etc/passwd mode=644 owner=root action=fixall
12      /etc/shadow mode=600 owner=root action=fixall
13      /etc/group  mode=644 owner=root action=fixall
14
15  directories:
16      /tmp mode=1777 owner=root group=root
17
18  tidy:
19      /tmp recurse=inf age=7 rmdirs=sub
20
```

```
21  disable:
22     /root/.rhosts
23     /etc/hosts.equiv
24
25  processes:
26     "cfservd" restart "/var/cfengine/bin/cfservd"
27     "cfexecd" restart "/var/cfengine/bin/cfexecd"
```

**Line 2:** The `actionsequence` command is very important and easy to overlook. You must list each section that you wish to process in this variable. If you add a new section but forget to add it to this list, it will not be executed.

**Line 4:** cfengine will make sure the system is configured with one of the time zones in this list.

**Line 10:** This section checks the ownership and permissions of a few important system files and fixes any problems it finds.

**Line 15:** This section checks the permissions on the /tmp/ directory and fixes them, if necessary. It also creates the directory, if necessary.

**Line 18:** This section removes everything that has not been accessed in the past seven days from the /tmp/ directory. It only removes subdirectories of /tmp/ and not the directory itself.

**Line 21:** These files are disabled for security reasons. They are renamed if they are found. If they are executable, the executable bit is unset.

**Line 25:** This section verifies that the cfservd and cfexecd daemons are running and starts them if they are not.

### 6.4.2.4  Creating the Configuration Server

The configuration server contains the master copy of the cfengine configuration files. It also processes that configuration file on a regular basis just like all of the client systems. The server must run a properly configured cfservd so that the client systems can retrieve the master configuration from the system.

The configuration server needs to have a special place to keep the master cfengine configuration files. In this example, that directory is /usr/local/var/cfengine/inputs/. It could be any directory, but not /var/cfengine/inputs/ because the master host copies the files to that directory when executing, just like every other host.

Like all systems, the server should also run cfexecd either as a daemon or from cron (or, even better, both).

### 6.4.2.4.1  *Generating Server Keys*

You need to run cfkey on the server system to create its public and private key files. These files will be in the /var/cfengine/ppkeys/ directory and will be named localhost.priv and localhost.pub. You then need to copy the localhost.pub to a new file in the same directory. This file should be called root-10.1.1.1.pub, assuming your IP address is 10.1.1.1. This is only necessary to allow the cfrun command to connect to itself, but it is good to do anyway.

The server also needs each client's public key in the appropriate file, based on the client's IP address as described in the next section.

## 6.4.2.5  Preparing the Client Systems

Each client system is relatively simple to configure. Once you install the actual cfengine binaries, you need to generate and copy the appropriate public keys (as discussed in this section). You also need to manually copy the update.conf file from the master server and place it in /var/cfengine/inputs/. Once this file is in place, you should manually run cfagent to download the remaining configuration files and complete system configuration.

Each client should run cfexecd either as a daemon or from cron. You probably want to run cfservd on each client as well to allow remote execution of cfagent using cfrun. Assuming this is already configured in the cfagent.conf file on the server, these daemons will be started after the first manual execution of cfagent.

### 6.4.2.5.1  *Generating Client Keys*

You need to run cfkey on each client system. This creates localhost.priv and localhost.pub in /var/cfengine/ppkeys/. You then need to copy the central server's public key to the client. If the server's IP address is 10.1.1.1, then you should copy its public key to root-10.1.1.1.pub in the /var/cfengine/ppkeys/ directory on the client.

Finally, you need to copy the client's public key (localhost.pub) to the server's /var/cfengine/ppkeys/ directory. Again, this file should be named according to the client's IP address (if its IP address is 10.2.2.2, then the file should be named root-10.2.2.2.pub on the central server. This can be done manually, or it can be done automatically from your initial system configuration script (as discussed in section 5.3).

## 6.4.3 Debugging cfengine

When you are trying to get cfengine up and running, you will probably run into a few problems. Network problems are common. This includes the processes of transferring configuration files from the master server and initiating cfagent execution on remote systems with cfrun.

For any network problems, you should run both the server (cfservd) and the client (cfrun or cfagent) in debugging mode. You can accomplish this by using the -d2 command-line argument. For cfservd, this switch not only provides debugging output, but it also prevents the daemon from detaching from the terminal.

When you are trying new things in your cfagent.conf, you should always try it with the --dry-run switch to see what it would do without making any actual changes. The -v switch is also very useful if you want to see what steps are being taken by cfagent. If it is not doing something you think it should be doing, the verbose output will probably tell you why.

If you are making frequent changes or trying to get a new function to work properly, you probably want to be able to run cfagent repeatedly on demand. By default, cfagent will not do anything more frequently than once per minute. This helps prevent both intentional and accidental denial-of-service attacks on your systems.

You can eliminate this feature for testing purposes by placing this line in the control section of cfagent.conf:

```
IfElapsed = ( 0 )
```

It is also helpful to only run a certain set of actions by using the --just command-line option. For example, to check only on running processes, you can run the command cfagent --just processes.

## 6.4.4 Creating Sections in cfagent.conf

There are, as of cfengine version 2.0.4, 24 possible sections in cfagent.conf. I only cover some of these sections in this chapter. Other sections will be covered later in this book, while some will not be covered at all. In addition, some of the sections can be quite powerful and will not be fully explored in this book. For additional information, refer to the comprehensive reference manual that can be read on the cfengine web site at http://www.cfengine.org/.

Every section can contain one or more class specifications. For example, the files section could be:

```
files:
    /etc/passwd

    any::
        /etc/group
    redhat::
        /etc/redhat-release
    solaris::
        /etc/vfstab
```

Both /etc/passwd and /etc/group will be processed on all hosts (because the default group is any when none is specified). In addition, the /etc/redhat-release file will be checked only on systems running Red Hat Linux, and the /etc/vfstab will be checked only if the operating system is Sun's Solaris.

The period (.) can be used to "and" groups together, whereas the pipe character (|) can be used to "or" groups together. The exclamation character (!) can invert a class and parentheses ((/)) can be used to group classes. Here is a complex example:

```
files:
    (redhat|solaris).!Mon::
        /etc/passwd
```

In this case, the /etc/passwd file will only be checked if the operating system is Red Hat Linux or Sun's Solaris and today is not a Monday.

### 6.4.4.1  Using Classes in cfagent.conf

The classes section can be used to create user-defined classes as described in section 6.4.1.6.2. A system's class membership can be determined by a shell command as follows:

```
classes:
    X11R6 = ( '/usr/bin/test -d /usr/X11R6' )
```

If the command returns true (exit code 0), this machine will be a member of that class (for the current run). Classes can also be defined to contain specific hosts or any hosts that are a member of another existing class, as follows:

```
classes:
    critical = ( host1 host2 web_servers )
```

Here are a few more possibilities that could be placed in the `classes` section:

```
classes:
    notthis = ( !this )
    ip_in_range = ( IPRange(129.0.0.1-15) )
    ip_in_range = ( IPRange(129.0.0.1/24) )
```

### 6.4.4.2  The directories Section

The `directories` section checks for the presence of one or more directories. Here is an example:

```
directories:
    /etc mode=0755 owner=root group=root syslog=true
        inform=true
    /tmp mode=1777 owner=root group=root define=tmp_created
```

If either directory does not exist, it will be created. The permissions and ownership will also be checked and corrected, if necessary. In this example, the administrator will be informed (through mail or the terminal) and a syslog entry will be created if the /etc/ directory does not exist, or if it has incorrect permissions and/or ownership.

For the /tmp/ directory, the class `tmp_created` is defined if the directory was created. You could then use this class in another section of the configuration file to perform certain additional tasks if the directory was created.

### 6.4.4.3  The disable Section

The `disable` section causes cfengine to disable any number of files. This simple section disables two files that you probably would never want around because they are used to allow access to the `root` account via Remote Shell (RSH) using only the source IP address as authentication:

```
disable:
    /root/.rhosts
    /etc/hosts.equiv
```

If either of these files exist, they will be disabled by being renamed with a `.cfdisabled` extension. The permissions will also be changed to `0600`, so this command is also suitable for disabling executables. At one point, for example, there was a local root exploit with the `eject` command on Solaris. Until there was a patch available, you could have disabled that command using the following sequence:

```
disable:
  solaris::
    /usr/bin/eject inform=true syslog=true
```

This would not only disable the command, but it would inform the administrator and make a log entry using syslog.

Let's say that you want to remove /etc/httpd/conf/httpd.conf, if it exists, and create a symbolic link pointing to the master file /usr/local/etc/httpd.conf. The following command sequence can accomplish this task:

```
disable:
  /etc/httpd/conf/httpd.conf type=file define=link_httpd_conf
links:
  link_httpd_conf::
    /etc/httpd/conf/httpd.conf -> /usr/local/etc/httpd.conf
```

The disable section would only remove the file if it is a normal file (and not a link, for example). If the file is disabled, the link_httpd_conf class will be defined. Then, in the links section, a symbolic link will be created in its place.

It is important to remember that cfengine does not execute these sections in any predefined order. The actionsequence setting in the control section controls the order of execution. So, for this example, we need to make sure that the file is disabled before the symbolic link is created:

```
control:
  actionsequence = ( disable links )
```

You can also use the disable section to rotate log files. The following sequence rotates the web server access log if it is larger than five megabytes and keeps up to four files:

```
disable:
  /var/log/httpd/access_log size=>5mbytes rotate=4
```

This, and other method of rotating files, are further discussed in Chapter 9.

## 6.4.4.4  The editfiles Section

The editfiles section can be the most complex section in a configuration file. There are approximately one hundred possible commands that can be used in this section. These commands allow text files (and, in a few cases, binary files) to be checked and modified. Here is an example:

```
editfiles:
   { /etc/crontab
      AppendIfNoSuchLine "0 * * * * root /usr/local/sbin/cfexecd -F"
   }
```

This command adds the specified line of text to /etc/crontab. This makes sure that cron runs cfexecd every hour. You also might want to make sure that other hosts can access and use the printers on your printer servers as follows:

```
editfiles:
   PrintServer::
      { /etc/hosts.lpd
         AppendIfNoSuchLine "host1"
         AppendIfNoSuchLine "host2"
      }
```

In your environment, perhaps a standard port is used for another purpose. For example, you might want to rename port 23 to myservice. To do this, you could change its label in /etc/services on every host:

```
editfiles:
   { /etc/services
      ReplaceAll "^.*23/tcp.*$" With "myservice 23/tcp"
   }
```

If you are using inetd and want to disable the TELNET application, for example, you could comment out those lines in /etc/inetd.conf:

```
editfiles:
   { /etc/inetd.conf
      HashCommentLinesContaining "telnet"
      DefineClasses "modified_inetd_conf"
   }
processes:
   modified_inetd_conf::
      "inetd" signal=hup
```

Any line containing the string telnet will be commented out with the # character (if not already commented). If such a change is made, the inetd process is sent the HUP signal in the processes section.

### 6.4.4.5  The files Section

The files section can process files (and directories) and check for valid ownership and permissions. It can also watch for changing files. Here is a simple example:

```
files:
    /etc/passwd mode=644 owner=root group=root action=fixall checksum=md5
    /etc/shadow mode=600 owner=root group=root action=fixall
    /etc/group mode=644 owner=root group=root action=fixall


web_servers::
      /var/www/html r=inf mode=a+r action=fixall
```

We accomplish several tasks with these entries. On every system, the ownership and permissions are checked (and fixed) on /etc/passwd, /etc/shadow, and /etc/group. The md5 checksum of /etc/passwd is also calculated and recorded.

On any system in the class web_servers, the permissions on /var/www/html/ are checked. The directory is scanned recursively and all files and directories are made publicly readable. The execute bits on directories will also be set according to the read bits; so, since we requested files to be publicly readable, directories will also be publicly executable.

The checksum option requires a little more explanation. Since the file's checksum is stored, if the checksum changes at a later date, the administrator will be warned. In fact, the administrator will be warned every hour unless you configure cfengine to update the checksum database. In that case, the administrator will only be notified once, and then the database will be modified. You can enable this by adding the following command in the control section:

```
control:
    ChecksumUpdates = ( on )
```

Here are some other options you may want to use in this section:

links: Can be set to traverse to follow symbolic links pointing to directories. Alternatively, this can be set to tidy to remove any dead symbolic links (links that do not point to valid files/directories).

**ignore:** The ignore option can be specified multiple times. It requires a regular expression pattern or a simple string. Any file or directory matching this pattern is ignored. For instance, ignore="^\." would ignore all hidden files and directories.

**include:** If any include options are listed, any files must match one of these regular expressions to be processed.

**exclude:** Any file matching any of the exclude regular expressions will not be processed by cfengine.

**define:** If any changes are made to any file, this class will be defined. You can also list several classes, separated by colons.

**elsedefine:** If no changes are made to any files, this class will be defined. You can also list several classes, separated by colons.

**syslog:** When set to on, cfengine will log any changes to the system log.

**inform:** When set to on, cfengine will log any changes to the screen (or sent via email if so configured).

### 6.4.4.6 The links Section

With the links section, cfagent can create symbolic links.

```
links:
    /usr/tmp -> ../var/tmp
    /usr/local/bin +> /usr/local/lib/perl/bin
```

In this example, the first command creates (if it doesn't already exist) a symbolic link from /usr/tmp to ../var/tmp (relative to /usr/tmp).

The second command creates one link in /usr/local/bin/ pointing to each file in /usr/local/lib/perl/bin/. Using this technique, you could install applications in separate directories and create links to those binaries in the /usr/local/bin/ directory.

There are plenty of possible options in the links section but, in practice, they are rarely used, so I will not cover them in this book. See the cfengine reference manual for more information.

### 6.4.4.7 The processes Section

System processes can be monitored and manipulated in the processes section. Here is an example from earlier in this chapter:

```
processes:
    "cfservd" restart "/var/cfengine/bin/cfservd"
    "cfexecd" restart "/var/cfengine/bin/cfexecd"
```

For the `processes` section, cfengine runs the `ps` command with either `-aux` or `-ef` switches (as is appropriate for the specific system). This output is cached and the first part of each command in the `processes` section is interpreted as a regular expression against this output. If there are no matches, the `restart` command is executed.

You can specify the following options when using the `restart` facility: `owner`, `group`, `chroot`, `chdir`, and/or `umask`. These affect the execution environment of the new process as started by the `restart` command.

You can also send a signal to a process:

```
processes:
    "httpd" signal=hup
```

This signal would be sent on every execution to any processes matching the regular expression `httpd`. It is also possible to specify limits on the number of processes that can match the regular expression. Let's say, for example, that you wanted to make sure there were not more than ten `httpd` processes running at any given time:

```
processes:
    "httpd" action=warn matches=<10
```

## 6.4.4.8 The shellcommands Section

For some custom and/or complex operations, you will need to execute one or more external scripts from cfengine. You can accomplish this with the `shellcommands` section. Here is an example:

```
shellcommands:
    all::
        "/usr/bin/rdate -s ntp1" timeout=30
    redhat.Hr02_Q1::
        "/usr/local/sbin/log_packages" background=true
```

On all systems, the `rdate` command is executed to synchronize the system's clock. This command is terminated by cfengine in 30 seconds if it has not completed. On systems running Red Hat Linux, when it is between 2:00AM and 2:15AM, a script runs to log the currently installed packages. This command is placed in the background and cfengine does not wait for it to complete. This allows cfengine to perform other tasks or exit while the command is still running.

You can specify the following options to control the environment in which the command is executed: owner, group, chroot, chdir, and/or umask.

If these scripts want to access the list of currently defined classes, they can look in the CFALLCLASSES environment variable. Each active class will be listed, separated by colons.

Scripts, by default, are ignored when cfengine is performing a dry run (with --dry-run specified). You can override this by specifying preview=true. The script should, however, not make any changes when the class opt_dry_run is defined.

## 6.4.5 Using cfrun

The cfrun command allows you to execute cfagent on any number of systems on the network. It requires a configuration file in the current directory named cfrun.hosts (or a file specified with the -f option). The contents of the file should be as follows:

```
domain=mydomain.com
server.mydomain.com
client1.mydomain.com
client2.mydomain.com
```

Apart from the domain setting, this file is just a list of every host, including the configuration server. You can also have the output logged to a series of files (instead of being displayed to the screen) by adding these options to the top of the file:

```
outputdir=/tmp/cfrun_output
maxchild=10
```

This tells cfrun to fork up to ten processes and place the output for each host in a separate file in the specified directory. You can normally run cfrun without arguments. If you do want to specify arguments, the format is as follows:

```
cfrun CFRUN_OPTIONS HOSTS -- CFAGENT_OPTIONS -- CLASSES
```

CFRUN_OPTIONS is optional and can contain any number of options for the cfrun command. Next, you can specify an optional list of hostnames. If some hostnames are specified, only those hosts will be contacted. If no hosts are specified, every host in the cfrun.hosts file is contacted.

After the first -- are any options that you want to pass to the actual cfagent command run on each remote system. After the second -- is an optional list of classes. If some classes are specified, only hosts that match one of these classes will actually execute cfagent (although each host is contacted because each host has to decide if it matches one of the classes).

# CHAPTER 7

# Sharing Data Between Systems

IF YOU HAVE MORE than one system, there is a good chance you will want to transfer data between them at some point. If you have the systems connected by a network, you will probably want to transfer data over the network on a regular basis.

Automating system administration is a great thing and can save you lots of time. It is not, however, a necessity. It is often something that is done on the side as time permits. For this reason, it is not completely surprising that many of these tasks require software that does not come with most operating systems. In fact, many of these tasks even require custom scripts as shown throughout this book.

Sharing data, on the other hand, has been a central function of computers since the beginning of their existence. All operating systems have native support for synchronizing (or at least sharing) data. Also, other popular programs can be installed on most systems and they will take care of many of your needs "out of the box."

In addition, you can use plenty of standard protocols to share data, such as scp and ftp. By themselves, however, these protocols allow only manual file transfers; they don't really share or synchronize data—they just transfer files.

Despite their simplicity, these tools are used by a larger set of tools that can automatically synchronize data. The most obvious of these tools are network file-systems, such as NFS, that allow the same set of files to be used, simultaneously, on any number of systems. Also, programs like rsync use the ssh protocol to synchronize files between two systems.

This chapter covers many methods you can use to share data between systems. The techniques in this chapter assume at least one of these is true for your environment:

- The clients can mount network filesystems, or can access other network services, directly from the server.

- The server can actively connect to and push data to each client.

- Each client has software that connects to the server and pulls the files to the client.

## 7.1 Types of Data

Shared data usually falls into one of the following categories:

**Shared applications:** Common applications that you can use on several systems. The /usr/local/ or /opt/ directories are often shared between systems and contain additional applications that did not come with the operating system.

**User data:** The users' home directories that contain all of their data and personal files.

**Application data:** In distributed computing environments, application data is often shared between systems. A cluster of web servers, for example, usually needs to share the same content.

**System information:** System information includes network configuration, mail aliases, host listings, and so on.

**Account information:** Account information includes users, groups, and passwords.

I discuss each of these types of data, and options for its distribution, in this section. I discuss each distribution method in detail in the remainder of the chapter.

### 7.1.1  Shared Applications

As may be obvious from their name, shared applications are used on multiple systems. These applications are usually located in one directory, such as /usr/local/ or /opt/. These applications are usually software that does not come with the original operating system and is added based on the specific needs of the local users. Shared applications may also include utilities and customized shell scripts that users and administrators use.

All of these applications are usually placed into one common directory. This directory is either mounted directly on all systems via a network filesystem, or it is stored directly on each system but is regularly synchronized using the methods discussed in this chapter.

In networks with mixed operating systems and processors, a different structure is often used. Programs that are not architecture-dependent, such as shell scripts and Perl programs, are placed in one common location. These scripts are used on all systems in the network. Binary programs that are architecture and operating system dependent, however, are separated into directories based on architecture. Each system uses only the binary programs compatible with its architecture.

When you are deciding how to share these applications, you must consider several things:

- How many systems will be using the applications?

- What is the network bandwidth between the systems?

- How critical are the applications?

- How often are the applications used?

- How reliable is the network?

- How often do the applications change?

- How many files are there and how large are they?

If the network bandwidth is adequate for the number of systems that need the applications and the amount the applications are used, a network filesystem can be used (such as NFS). Of course, with modern filesystem caching, the frequency of application use might not be very important. If there is a large number of files, the applications are large in size, or the files change frequently, network operating systems are often preferable.

Alternatively, if the applications are very important or if the network is not reliable, copying every file to every system is usually the way to go. It helps if the files are relatively static and smaller in size, but these are not strict requirements. For example, in many cases, the synchronization can be done at night so that the amount of data that needs to be transferred is of little significance. You can also use efficient transfer techniques (such as the methods used by rsync) that can significantly reduce the amount of data that gets transferred during the synchronization process. Placing all data on every system can require significant drive space on each machine but, considering the low cost of drive space, the enhanced reliability and performance may be worth the cost.

## 7.1.2 User Data

User data is usually contained within each user's home directory. It is usually very convenient (for your users, at least) if your users can log in to any system and be able to access all of their data. Users also want to be able to modify their data on one system and have that modified data available on all other systems.

Some systems have only a few user accounts. A web server, for example, might only have the root account and a web account. The root account is used to manage the system (as usual). The web account could be used to update the web content. Each of these users would need very little, if any, data in their home directories. The data would also be fairly static. So, for a cluster of web servers, the user data would probably not need to be synchronized in any way. At the most, an automated or semi-automated method could be employed to synchronize the web user's init scripts or any other necessary files.

In an environment where numerous systems are available to many users, each user's home directory usually needs to be directly available on each system. This is typical of many research and engineering environments and an ideal situation for networked filesystems such as NFS.

## 7.1.3  Application Data

Although application data is closely tied to the applications themselves, it usually changes much more frequently. When I told you about frequently changing applications, I recommended that you use a network filesystem, so that would appear to be the proper solution for application data.

Distributed application data, however, is usually distributed purely for performance reasons. For instance, you may have a cluster of web servers and the same content needs to be available to every system. The reason there are many servers is to distribute the system load and/or provide high reliability. A traditional network filesystem would require one file server, which could be a bottleneck and a single point of failure.

You can still use a network filesystem as long as you have a high performance file server that can properly handle the load. These file servers are often highly specialized commercial solutions that can provide high throughput and reliability. This type of advanced setup, although something to consider, is not within the scope of this book, because it will be very specific to your environment.

Distributed web content is almost always modified from one central location and not directly on each server. This means that a system such as rsync could be used to copy the content from the central location and store it directly on each server. You can even use a source control system like CVS to provide a change history for the content (which is always nice to have with frequently changing files) and also do the actual file distribution.

Other applications require distributed data that can be modified directly on any individual system. For smaller amounts of data with relatively few changes, a network filesystem is one good option. If you will not be making conflicting changes to the same files at the same time on different systems, then you could use CVS to synchronize the data.

If you have applications that need to share a large amount of dynamic data that is frequently being changed on multiple systems and a network filesystem is not an option, then you will probably need a fully customized solution. In some cases, the application can be written so that it can exchange data in an efficient manner with other systems in a cluster. Beowulf clusters can also solve this problem by providing shared memory across cluster machines. Due to their highly specialized nature and their potential for complexity, I do not discuss these types of solutions within this book.

## 7.1.4  System Information

System information poses a unique problem for synchronization. You usually can't store this type of information on a network filesystem. The files are generally spread out over various directories on the system, so they can't be consolidated into one directory (or even a few directories) very easily. Even more bothersome is the fact that most of this information is critical for system operation. If the information is not available, the system might not be able to operate properly or even boot.

Most system information can be distributed using the methods discussed in. Some information, however, changes frequently and cannot be expressed easily using templates. These files usually need to be distributed using one of the techniques discussed in this chapter.

Two good options are rsync or cfengine as discussed in section 7.8 and section 7.7, respectively. Alternatively, you could use the NIS or NIS+ systems as discussed in section 7.4.

## 7.1.5  Account Information

Account information presents a special problem—the users' passwords are particularly sensitive pieces of information. For this reason, especially when you have a large network of systems, you should consider using Kerberos as your authentication system. Kerberos is introduced in section 7.6 later in this chapter.

Apart from the passwords, user and group listings are really system information, and as such, they can be distributed just like any other system information (cfengine, rsync, NIS, or NIS+). If you do transfer files that include passwords with these methods, you should be careful. You can use encrypted transfers in cfengine and rsync. I don't recommend storing passwords in an NIS map, but NIS+ has addressed some security issues and is an option.

Another option is the Lightweight Directory Access Protocol (LDAP). You can set up an LDAP server that contains a variety of information about your users including their usernames, full names, phone numbers, office locations, and so on. If it is supported on all of your systems, you can use this LDAP server as your source of user account information. If a system supports Pluggable Authentication Modules (PAM), then LDAP support is likely. LDAP is introduced in section 7.5.

## 7.2 Using Network Filesystems

Network filesystems can be very convenient, but they can also be a major source of headaches. When the server is up and running and the network is operating properly, network filesystems are perfect for most situations. The same applications and data can be accessed from multiple systems. The files can be modified on any system and the changes are instantly available on all other systems.

Problems with network filesystems begin to appear when there are server or network problems. Network filesystems do not operate at 100 percent efficiency when these problem occur. In many cases, the network filesystem may not work at all and could even hang the system.

There are a variety of network filesystems that are available depending on the operating systems you are using on your network. I have attempted to cover all of the major network filesystems in use, but you should explore any additional options you may have with your specific set of operating systems.

This section just provides an overview of each network filesystem and sometimes a few brief examples. The actual implementation details of these filesystems are often system dependent and you should consult the documentation for your specific operating systems.

### 7.2.1 *Sharing Data with NFS*

The Network File System (NFS) is the oldest distributed filesystem still in common use today. Its single greatest advantage is its native support in most, if not all, UNIX variants. It is also generally easier to configure and use than other network filesystems. As with just about any network filesystem, you can make changes on the server or on any client and have them be immediately available on all other systems.

The data on an NFS filesystem is physically located on only one server. Every client mounts the filesystem directly from that server. If a significant number of or highly active clients exist, you may run into performance problems. You will either have to upgrade the server or move a portion of the data into separate NFS filesystems on separate servers to alleviate these problems. All NFS clients have some amount of caching capabilities to help increase performance and reduce the load on the server. Some operating systems, however, will have better caching support than others.

---

 **NOTE**  I only provide a very brief introduction to NFS in this book. For more information, check out *Managing NFS and NIS* by Hal Stern, Mike Eisler, and Ricardo Labiaga (O'Reilly and Associates, 2001).

---

The biggest disadvantage of NFS is that it relies on the network and the single server. Depending on the client's implementation, any network or server downtime can cause the client system to hang, particularly when a process is using the network filesystem. If critical data is shared via NFS, a problem with the server might make all client systems inoperable.

With NFS, it is important that the same users share the same user IDs on each system. All file ownership on an NFS filesystem (well, any filesystem really) is by user and group IDs. If users have different user IDs on each system, then a user will not be able to modify their own files, and possibly will able to modify somebody else's.

Since NFS uses Remote Procedure Calls (RPC), the server and all clients need to run the portmap daemon at all times. The portmap daemon allows RPC connections to be initiated between systems. The use of RPC makes it difficult to use NFS through most firewalls. NFS also uses a variety of helper programs, such as mountd and a locking daemon.

For these reasons, NFS may be difficult to configure and use in your environment. There is an effort underway to create version 4 of NFS, which should address these issues. It uses one well-defined port and does not require so many ancillary programs. Although NFSv4 is not ready for a production environment at this time, it might be by the time you read this, so take a look at http://www.nfsv4.org.

### 7.2.1.1  Configuring the NFS Server

The NFS server usually needs to run one or more daemons. Exactly what daemons need to run depends on the operating system, so you need to consult your operating system's documentation for details.

Any server, however, needs to specify what portion of its local filesystem needs to be shared, or exported, to NFS clients. This is usually accomplished with the /etc/exports file.[1]

Here is a simple example:

```
/export/home @linux(rw,root_squash)
/mnt/cdrom    192.168.0.0/255.255.0.0(ro,no_root_squash)
```

For this example, we are assuming that there are some home directories located under the /export/home/ directory. So, to allow systems to mount users' home directories remotely, the /export/home/ directory (and everything under it) is exported to all systems in the netgroup linux (netgroups are discussed later in section 7.4.3.) The CD-ROM on this system is also exported to all systems with an IP address beginning with 192.168.

---

1.  This file is called /etc/dfs/dfstab on Solaris. It has similar content but a different format. See the dfstab man page for more information.

Each line ends with one or more options in parentheses. The available options are different on every operating system, but there are a few basic ones you can expect to find just about everywhere:

**ro:** Clients can only read from this filesystem, which is the default.

**rw:** Clients can read and write to this filesystem.

**root_squash:** The root user on the client system does not have root privileges on the network filesystem. So, if a file is owned by root, it cannot be deleted by a client. If a file is not publicly readable, it cannot be read by root on the client system. This is the default.

**no_root_squash:** The root users on clients do have special access on the filesystem.

The root_squash option is very important for system security. If a user has root access to a client system, but not the server, he can still bypass system security. A user could simply copy the bash shell, for example, onto the network filesystem and make it setuid root (which means anybody who runs the program runs it as root). The user can do this because the copy is taking place on the client and the user has root access on that system. This user can now log in to the NFS server with a regular user account, execute that bash shell, and gain full root access to the server. So, you should use the root_squash option whenever possible, especially if not-so-trusted users have root access on any systems that are allowed to mount your NFS resources.

### 7.2.1.2 Configuring the NFS Client

Once portmap is running, any client with appropriate permission can mount an NFS partition from a server with the following command:

```
# mount server.mydomain.com:/export/home/kirk /home/kirk
```

On some systems, you may need to specify a -t nfs or -F nfs switch to the mount command. See the mount man page on your system for more details.

A client can also automatically mount NFS filesystems at startup by placing entries in the standard /etc/fstab filesystem table (/etc/vfstab on Solaris or /etc/filesystems on AIX).

## 7.2.2  Using Samba to Share Files

Samba is an open-source implementation of Microsoft's Server Message Block/
Common Internet File System (SMB/CIFS). For most people, the biggest attraction
to Samba is its interoperability with Microsoft's operating systems. The biggest
disadvantage (for UNIX users at least) is the lack of ownership and permissions on
the files shared over SMB. You also can't have symbolic links within these partitions.

The Samba application actually refers to the server software that can run on
most UNIX variants. The Samba server is quite powerful and, consequently, can be
quite complicated. Fortunately, there is a web-based configuration system for
Samba called the Samba Web Administration Tool (SWAT) that can make configuring the server a much easier task. For more information on Samba, you can visit
http://www.samba.org.

In addition to Windows, SMB servers can be accessed from Linux, FreeBSD,
and some other UNIX variants using the smbfs filesystem. Mounting SMB filesystems
on these systems is easy, assuming you have the smbmount command installed
(which comes with Samba):

```
# smbmount //server/share /mnt/tmp -o 'username=kirk,ip=192.168.1.1'
```

This command mounts the SMB share share from the SMB server called
server on the local directory /mnt/tmp/. The username and IP address are also
specified on the command line. The IP address is useful if smbmount has trouble
finding the server. The username is a valid account on the SMB server. You will be
prompted for a password, if one is required.

## 7.2.3  Using the Andrew File System (AFS)

The Andrew File System (AFS) is a distributed filesystem that can be used with most
popular operating systems. Although some operating systems come with AFS as
standard equipment, you will need to install the OpenAFS software on many other
systems. This software can be downloaded from http://www.openafs.org. The web
site also contains comprehensive documentation on the AFS system.

The biggest advantage of AFS is that it supports server replication. Backup file
servers can be configured to keep the filesystem available even when one server is
lost. Servers can also be distributed in different regions around the world so that
clients can communicate with file servers in their local area. Or, in high load situations, multiple local servers can provide the same files, reducing the load on each
server. In addition to server replication, aggressive client-side caching helps increase
filesystem performance and reduce network traffic.

Any group of AFS systems can define a "cell." A cell can be as large or as small as it needs to be for your situation. You can administer each cell separately, but users in one cell can still access data in another cell. AFS also provides transparent access though a uniform namespace. Any given AFS directory always contains the same files, regardless of the system's name or its assigned cell.

Some people consider AFS to be the only alternative to NFS. It is very reliable, stable, and robust. It can handle sharing data on a large scale—that is, tons of data and/or users/clients. AFS is being used in production at some very large sites (Intel, Morgan-Stanley, Carnegie Mellon University, and Stanford University to name a few). In addition to UNIX systems, AFS can be used on some versions of Microsoft Windows and MacOS X. A disconnected mode (where the filesystem can still be used to some degree without access to any servers) is currently being developed.

There is only one book on AFS available, but it happens to be a good one. It is *Managing AFS: The Andrew File System* by Richard Campbell (Pearson Education POD, 1998).

## 7.2.4  Other Networked Filesystem Options

There are two other network filesystems I am including to make sure I completely cover this area: Coda and DFS. Neither of these filesystems is widely used or actively developed, to my knowledge. In most cases, I would stick with NFS, AFS, or Samba.

### 7.2.4.1  Coda

Coda has been in development since 1987 at Carnegie Mellon University. It has many of the features provided by AFS, and it also supports disconnected operation. If a client is disconnected from the network, whether intentionally (laptop) or unintentionally (network failure), it can continue to use the filesystem to some degree. The client can continue to read from the filesystem (at least the portions that have been cached) and can continue to write data at will. When network connectivity is restored, the changes are automatically synchronized with the server. If there are any collisions (the same file was changed by more than one person at the same time) that cannot be resolved automatically, the user is prompted to manually merge the changes.

Although Coda has been around for a while, it is not yet reliable enough for sharing critical data. It also has scalability issues with large filesystems and/or large numbers of clients. Although this situation will probably continue to improve, it is something that you should be aware of when you consider Coda for your systems.

I personally tried installing Coda on my server at home, as well as on my laptop, because I was very interested in the possibilities of disconnected operation. After a couple of days, though, I gave up, not having accomplished much of anything. Whether my experience affects your decision or not is up to you.

Coda is available for Linux, NetBSD, and FreeBSD. It also has limited support for Windows. More information on Coda can be found at http://www.coda.cs.cmu.edu.

### 7.2.4.2 DFS

DFS is a distributed filesystem running on a Distributed Computing Environment (DCE) that yields a single, shared filespace for all authorized users from all possible locations. It is available as part of both Sun Solaris 7 (and higher) and IBM AIX 4.2.1 (and higher). You can also add client (and sometimes server) support for DCE to Microsoft Windows NT/2000, Compaq Tru64, Red Hat Linux, and SGI IRIX.

Like AFS, DFS also supports server replication and provides efficient client-side caching. It also supports a consistent namespace for your systems' files. Refer to the documentation for your specific operating system for more information on DFS or for help installing and configuring DFS in your environment.

As far as I know, DFS is not widely used and does not seem to be going anywhere. I don't see any particular advantages of using DFS over AFS, but your viewpoint may be different than mine.

## 7.3 Automounting Network Filesystems

An automounter is a program that can mount network (and other) filesystems on demand. You can, for example, automatically mount the CD-ROM when somebody tries to access its mount directory. For instance, when a user logs in to a system, their home directory can be mounted automatically from the proper server. Shortly after the user logs out, their directory is automatically unmounted so that unneeded NFS mounts do not build up on the system.

Some automounters do much more than just mount filesystems. In some cases, you can provide more than one server for each filesystem to provide some amount of redundancy. If one of the servers is down, the directory will automatically be mounted from another server. You also might be able to mount entire systems so that you could access any data they might be exporting to your client.

Automounters are particularly useful when you use them to mount user home directories. When you use an automounter, you can make every user's home directory /home/username/ on every system, regardless of the physical location of their data. When you add a new fileserver or a new drive, you can move the user's home directories without affecting its visible location.

Most UNIX variants come with an automounter of one type or another. They all, unfortunately, are somewhat different. In particular, the map files require a different syntax among the various implementations. I cover the basic usage of a few of the most popular automounters in the following pages.

## 7.3.1 Solaris Automounter

The Solaris automounter allows Solaris systems to automatically mount NFS filesystems on demand. You do not have to list the filesystems in /etc/vfstab; you just have to configure and run the automounter.

The Solaris automounter uses /etc/auto_master as its master configuration file.

 **NOTE** You can find the code samples for this chapter in the Downloads section of the Apress web site (http://www.apress.com).

```
# Use this line to include the NIS/NIS+ map for this file
#+auto_master

# /net/${hostname} will automagically contain the host's exported filesystems
/net            -hosts          -nosuid

# Use map file /etc/auto_home to mount home directories under /home
/home           auto_home

# Include a direct-mount file
/-              auto_direct
```

If you use NIS or NIS+, as discussed in section 7.4, you can include the NIS auto_master map in this file using the line +auto_master. The home directories are itemized in the /etc/auto_home file as follows:

```
# Again, you can include the NIS/NIS+ auto_home map
#+auto_home

amber   fileserver.mydomain.com:/export/home/amber
jeff    fileserver.mydomain.com:/export/home/jeff
kirk    kirk.mydomain.com:/export/home/kirk
```

When you are automating home directories with an automounter, the standard method is for each system to have an /export/home/ directory that contains any physical home directories. The entire /export/ directory on each system is usually exported to the other systems on the network (Hence the name, "export"). When a user logs in to a system, their home directory is found in the /etc/auto_home file. If the directory is on the local system, a symbolic link in /home/ is created to the directory; if it is on another system, it is automatically mounted via NFS.

In this example, there are only three users. One user (kirk) has his home directory on his own workstation (kirk.mydomain.com). The other users have their home directories on the file server.

You can also use the automounter to mount any directory via NFS using a direct map file. You can even specify more than one server for each directory. Here is an example /etc/auto_direct:

```
# Mount the mail directory from the mail server
/var/mail        -rw                mail:/var/mail

# Mount /usr/local from one of these servers
/usr/local       -ro,soft           server1,server2:/usr/local
```

Since there is only one mail server, its mail directory is mounted on all systems. For the /usr/local/ directory, however, there are two servers that can be used to mount this filesystem. If the first server is not accessible, the second server is used. The soft option prevents the client from hanging when there is an NFS error.

As you can see, the automounter can be quite useful, especially for home directories and replicated filesystems (that don't change often) like /usr/local/ in this example. When you combine the automounter with NIS or NIS+, you can share the actual map files over NIS and can quickly add new NFS directories that will be mounted on your systems as needed.

## 7.3.2 Linux Automounter (autofs)

The Linux automounter, often called autofs, is very similar to the Solaris version. The Linux automounter uses a special filesystem type that must be supported by the kernel called, strangely enough, autofs. Like the Solaris automounter, autofs needs a master configuration file, but in this case, this file is named /etc/auto.master (instead of /etc/auto_master). Here is an example configuration file:

```
/home /etc/auto.home --timeout=10
/misc /etc/auto.misc --timeout=10
```

You can also use the +map_name expression to include an NIS/NIS+ map in any autofs configuration file. Here is an example /etc/auto.misc file:

```
# Mount the kernel.org FTP site via NFS
# Use soft and intr to avoid hanging on failure
kernel  -ro,soft,intr      ftp.kernel.org:/pub/linux

# Mount the CD-ROM and floppy on demand
cd      -fstype=iso9660,ro,nosuid,nodev  :/dev/cdrom
floppy  -fstype=auto,rw,nosuid,nodev     :/dev/fd0
```

The automounter is very useful for mounting removable media such as floppies and CD-ROMs. You can insert a floppy disk, and then access the /misc/floppy/ directory and it will be mounted. The timeout value in /etc/auto.master (10 seconds in this example) determines how long the filesystem remains mounted once you have left the directory. You want this to be fairly short because you should not (and usually cannot with a CD-ROM) remove the media until it has been unmounted.

When you start the automounter, it starts a separate process for each mount point (the processes are named automount). The mount command (with no arguments) also shows a filesystem of type autofs mounted on each directory. If a filesystem is being used when the autofs is stopped, that filesystem may not be unmounted. You may have to manually unmount the filesystem when it is no longer being used and then restart the automounter (the init script for the automounter is usually /etc/rc.d/init.d/autofs).

## 7.3.3  The am-utils Automounter

According to the am-utils web site (http://www.am-utils.org), am-utils is the next generation of the popular BSD Automounter, Amd. am-utils includes many additional updates, ports, programs, features (such as NFS V.3 support and shared libraries), bug fixes, and more.

am-utils can be used on most UNIX variants because it does not require any kernel support. It can do everything the other automounters can do and more. It can, in fact, do so many things that it is well beyond the scope of this book. The web site does provide a comprehensive manual, however.

The main amd configuration file is /etc/amd.conf. Here is an example:

```
[ global ]
auto_dir    =    /.automount
search_path =    /etc
```

```
[ /net ]
map_name    =    amd.net
map_type    =    file


[ /home ]
map_name    =    amd.home
map_type    =    file
```

The global section contains global settings for all directories. The first configuration item in this section is auto_dir, which is a special directory where amd physically mounts all filesystems. The search_path setting tells amd where to look for its map files. There are many other possible things you may want to set within this section as shown in the man page for amd.conf.

After the global section, there is one section for the /net/ directory and one section for the /home/ directory. The /net/ directory provides a virtual directory hierarchy based on the hosts in your network and the directories that they export. The /home/ directory contains users' home directories that are automatically mounted as each user logs in. Two separate map files exist for the two separate directories and they are explained in the following sections.

### 7.3.3.1  The amd.net File

This map is mounted on the /net/ directory. If you change into the /net/somehost/ directory, the key somehost is applied to the following map file (/etc/amd.net):

```
/defaults opts:=nosuid,nodev
*         rhost:=${key};type:=host;rfs:=/
```

If you use this map, when you change into the /net/somehost/ directory, you can get a directory listing that contains all of the exported filesystems from host somehost.

The first column is the key that should match this entry. In this case, all keys match this single entry (because of the wildcard *). So, for any key, the remote host (rhost) is set to that key. The filesystem type of host tells the automounter to mount all directories that are exported from the host, starting under the directory specified in the rfs option. So, the local directory /net/www.mydomain.com/var/www/html/ is mapped to the /var/www/html/ on the remote host www.mydomain.com.

The /defaults entry specifies options that will be applied to all keys within this map. In this case, device files and setuid files are disabled on all remote hosts (for security purposes).

### 7.3.3.2 The amd.home File

The following map uses the mount type of nfsl for all keys (because it is in the /defaults section). This mount type tells the automounter to create a symbolic link to fs if it is running on the host specified in rhost. If it is not, the directory rfs is mounted from rhost instead.

```
/defaults   type:=nfsl
amber       fs:=/export/home/amber;rhost:=fileserver.mydomain.com;rfs:=${fs}
jeff        fs:=/export/home/jeff;rhost:=fileserver.mydomain.com;rfs:=${fs}
kirk        fs:=/export/home/kirk;rhost:=kirk.mydomain.com;rfs:=${fs}
```

In this code, both the amber and jeff users have their home directories physically located on the server file server.mydomain.com in the /export/home/ directory. The home directory for user kirk is on the workstation kirk.mydomain.com.

If kirk logs into kirk.mydomain.com, the home directory /home/kirk/ will be accessed during the login process. As a result, the automounter will create a symbolic link from /home/kirk/ to /export/home/kirk/. If kirk logs into fileserver.mydomain.com, however, that server will mount /export/home/kirk/ from kirk.mydomain.com on the local directory /home/kirk/.

You can store the home, or any other map, in NIS or NIS+ if you like. You just have to specify the appropriate map type:

```
[ /home ]
map_name    =   amd.home
map_type    =   nis        # or nisplus
```

You then need to create the appropriate map file in NIS or NIS+. The key for the map is the first column (the username in this example). You can find the appropriate code to add to your NIS makefile in the documentation at http://www.am-utils.org.

## 7.4 Sharing System Data with NIS/NIS+

The Network Information Service (NIS) first appeared on SunOS (the predecessor of Solaris) and was called Yellow Pages, or YP. The name was later changed to NIS, but commands such as ypcat cannot hide their heritage.

NIS+ accomplishes many of the same tasks as NIS, but it is much more powerful and secure. It was designed from the ground up to be a major improvement on NIS, particularly from a security standpoint. That said, many people still use the original NIS because of its simplicity and compatibility with a large number of operating systems.

Both of these protocols are designed to share certain system configuration files between hosts on a network. The most common use of NIS is to share account information files such as /etc/passwd and /etc/group. It is also often used to share automounting map files, as discussed in the previous section, as well as many other system files.

 **NOTE**   I only provide a very brief introduction to NIS in this book. For more information, check out *Managing NFS and NIS* by Hal Stern, Mike Eisler, and Ricardo Labiaga (O'Reilly and Associates, 2001).

## 7.4.1  Creating NIS Maps and NIS+ Tables

NIS uses maps, NIS+ uses tables, and both NIS and NIS+ generally have the same map/table names. The name of a map usually resembles the name of a system file the map represents (i.e., the passwd map corresponds to /etc/passwd file). New maps or tables can be added as you need them, but the applications using those files must be NIS-aware.

You could create a new map for the Apache web server, for example, but since the Apache web server is not NIS-aware (well, at least not the last time I checked), the map will not be useful at this time. It would actually be difficult to represent a full Apache configuration in an NIS map. You could, however, include some limited information and use that to fill in certain portions of httpd.conf. The script that starts the web server could use ypcat or niscat to pull the information from the map/table, do the substitutions, and finally start the web server.

Automounter files, such as auto_home and auto_data (which contain mount information for /home/ and /data/, respectively) make up one common type of map that is added to NIS. This is probably because most automounters are NIS-aware. The auto_master file (or, better yet, the auto_master map) obviously needs to be modified to take advantage of these additional maps. More information on automounters can be found in section 7.3 earlier in this chapter.

Here is a list of most of the standard NIS/NIS+ maps that may or may not be used in any specific environment:

**passwd:** Corresponds to /etc/passwd. This is actually an alias for passwd.byname in NIS. There is also a passwd.byuid map where the user ID is the key.

**group:** Corresponds to /etc/group and is an alias for group.byname in NIS. There is also a group.bygid map where the group ID is the key.

**hosts:** Corresponds to /etc/hosts and is an alias for hosts.byname in NIS. There is also a hosts.byaddr map where the IP address is the key.

**ethers:** Corresponds to /etc/ethers and is an alias for ethers.byname in NIS. There is also a ethers.byaddr map where the IP address is the key. The ethers information is used by Reverse Address Request Protocol (RARP).

**networks:** Corresponds to /etc/networks and is an alias for networks.byaddr in NIS. There is also an ethers.byname map where the network name is the key.

**protocols:** Corresponds to /etc/protocols and is an alias for protocols.bynumber in NIS. There is also a protocols.byname map where the protocol name is the key.

**rpc:** Corresponds to /etc/rpc. Actual map names in NIS are rpc.byname and rpc.bynumber.

**services:** Corresponds to /etc/services and is an alias for services.byname in NIS. There is also a services.bynumber map where the protocol name is the key.

**netgroup:** Used to define groups of hosts on the network as shown in section 7.4.3. Actual map names in NIS are netgroup, netgroup.byhost, and netgroup.byuser.

**aliases:** Corresponds to /etc/aliases as used by sendmail and is an alias for mail.aliases in NIS.

As you can see, NIS has two maps covering most files because you can only have one key per map. So, if you need to perform searches on more than one column, which is usually the case, you need two maps. NIS+ does not have this limitation, so it has only one table per logical item.

This list is not a comprehensive guide to the data distributed over NIS and NIS+. One type of information not shown in the list that is sometimes distributed with NIS/NIS+ is printer information, such as /etc/printcap. An NIS-specific map that was not mentioned is the special map ypservers that contains a list of any other YP servers that are part of the network. NIS+ has an important table that I have not mentioned yet called publickey that contains the NIS+ public keys. Each operating system may have additional default maps, such as timezone and locale, for example.

## 7.4.2  The /etc/nsswitch.conf File

Most modern UNIX systems have a Name Service Switch configuration file such as /etc/nsswitch.conf that tells the system where to get certain configuration information. This file is used by library functions such as getpwnam. This file may have a different name and/or different syntax on your system. Here are some typical filenames:

- /etc/nsswitch.conf (Solaris, Linux, HP-UX)

- /etc/netsvc.conf (AIX)

- /etc/host.conf (FreeBSD)

- /etc/svc.conf (Tru64)

Some programs might not be aware of /etc/nsswitch.conf, nor use the getpwnam function (and other similar functions), and they might read the local /etc/passwd file directly. Hopefully none of the system programs would do this, but some third-party applications might do something similar—it is definitely something to watch out for.

The file is fairly self-explanatory, but here is an excerpt from a /etc/nsswitch.conf on a typical Linux system:

```
passwd:     files nisplus nis
shadow:     files nisplus nis
group:      files nisplus nis
```

When a user logs into a system, their entry needs to be read from the passwd file. This is done, in most cases, by your system libraries. First, these libraries look for an entry in the local file. If an entry for the given user is not found there, NIS+ is consulted next. If NIS+ is not available or does not have the appropriate entry, NIS is used. If the entry is not found in any of the locations, the search for the entry fails (i.e., the user is not found).

You can modify the order of the data sources as is suitable for your environment. In most cases, you should never remove the files entry completely; if you do, the system will not have any data if NIS or NIS+ is not operating properly (you should always, for example, have at least the root account in your local /etc/passwd, because it is usually not distributed via NIS/NIS+ anyway). Local files can also allow you to add special entries that are only valid on that one system.

The hosts entry in nsswitch.conf is important because it controls hostname lookups from your clients. Here is a typical entry:

```
hosts:      files nisplus nis dns
```

So, when the system needs to look up a host, the local /etc/hosts file is consulted first. If the host is not found there, NIS+ tables and NIS maps are checked. If neither of those sources can resolve the host, the Domain Name Service (DNS) is used, as controlled by /etc/resolv.conf.

### 7.4.3   The netgroup File

One file commonly shared via NIS/NIS+ is the netgroup file. This file contains groups of systems (and sometimes users) and is commonly used to control which hosts have access to directories exported via NFS. On some systems, the netgroup file can only be used when shared through NIS/NIS+.

Each netgroup contains one or more sets of parentheses. Within each set of parentheses are three values: host, user, and domain. If any field is left blank, it is considered a wildcard (i.e., anything will match). The user field is used for rsh access and is not discussed in this book. The domain field refers to the domain of the *server*. When a host is parsing the netgroup file to determine its appropriate export entries, it ignores an entry if the domain does not match the domain of the server doing the parsing.

In most modern environments, you only use the host field. It simply contains the hostname of a system that is a member of that group. Here is a typical netgroup:

```
linux   (linuxhost1,,) (linuxhost2,,)
solaris (solarishost1,,) (solarishost2,,)
web     (www1,,) (www2,,) (www3,,)
desktop (linuxhost1,,) (solarishost2,,)
```

You can use these groups in /etc/exports to export certain directories only to hosts within the specified netgroup. NFS was discussed earlier in more detail in section 7.2.1.

### 7.4.4   NIS Details

Every NIS server and client needs to be in an NIS domain. This could be the same as your DNS domain, or it could be completely different. It is important, however, that all systems that are sharing data be part of the same domain. This domain is configured in the client (such as /etc/yp.conf) and server (such as /etc/ypserv.conf) configuration files.

The NIS server runs the ypserv process and shares a set of binary maps with other hosts. These maps are generated from plain-text files—usually the appropriate /etc/ files on the server itself. The data files are generated by going to the /var/yp/ directory, modifying Makefile (if necessary), and running make.

Sometimes the makefile is modified by the administrator to use an alternate password file instead of /etc/passwd.

One common situation is to have an NIS server that has accounts that you do not want active on other hosts. Some people solve this by placing all of the source files in a special directory so that the server can't use those files directly and must access the data through NIS (just like the clients). Then any accounts that should only exist on the server are added to the local /etc/passwd file. In fact, you can add local accounts to any system using this method.

Alternatively, most makefiles are configured to ignore accounts with a user ID below a certain threshold when they are creating the database files. Accounts that should only exist on the NIS server and not be included in the map could be assigned user IDs below this threshold. The most important result is that the root account is usually not included in the passwd map.

Once the server is running, you need to start the client (ypbind) on every system (including the server in most cases). Once ypbind is running, you can view an NIS map with the ypcat command:

```
% ypcat -k passwd
test1:x:703:703::/home/test1:/bin/bash
test2:x:704:704::/home/test2:/bin/bash
test3:x:705:705::/home/test3:/bin/bash
```

The -k switch tells ypcat to display the keys as well as the data. In this case, the keys are the usernames. The passwd argument is the name of the map file you want to view.

Once you are using NIS, your users must use the commands yppasswd, ypchfn, and ypchsh to modify their login information. These programs communicate with the yppasswdd process running on the NIS server to make the actual changes. That process changes the text files and rebuilds the data files automatically.

With NIS you can configure multiple servers for one domain. Each client communicates with the first server it can find. One server is the master server and the others are slave servers. Whenever the data files are built on the master server, the Makefile immediately updates the slave servers. They are usually listed in /var/yp/ypservers and are placed into the ypservers NIS map.

## 7.4.5  Security Concerns with NIS

One of the biggest problems with NIS is that each user's encrypted password is available to all users on all systems. Many years ago, a good number UNIX variants switched to a shadow password file (/etc/shadow) that is only readable by root and contains the user passwords. This makes it much more difficult for users to run dictionary attacks against the user passwords because they first have to gain (at least limited) root access to read the shadow file and then crack the encrypted passwords.

Unfortunately, when you use NIS, you lose any benefits the shadow password file provided. You do have some options with NIS, however. For instance, some people use Kerberos for authentication and ignore the password field in the NIS maps. Systems that support PAMs (such as Solaris, Linux, and FreeBSD) make it particularly easy to add custom user authentication techniques. Unfortunately, in a network with a wide variety of operating systems, some of these custom solutions become difficult to implement.

Linux and FreeBSD (and possibly others) have also extended the NIS protocol to provide better security. Linux can, for example, be configured so that requests from unprivileged ports do not show the encrypted passwords. However, this simple security enhancement can be easily circumvented if there are systems on the network where untrusted users have root access. Or, if there are any Windows users on the network, any user can make requests from the Windows systems from a privileged port. As you might guess, these type of solutions do not significantly improve security and can also cause compatibility issues with other operating systems.

## 7.4.6  NIS+ Details

Sun Microsystems created NIS+ as a replacement for NIS, in part to solve the user password problem found in NIS. Several commercial operating systems such as Solaris, AIX, and HP-UX come with full NIS+ client and server software. Other operating systems such as Linux and FreeBSD have decent client support and some server support.

With NIS+, users have to authenticate themselves with the NIS+ server. This is usually done with the user's login password, so you do not need a separate authentication step. Since users are authenticated with the server, you can provide much better control over access to sensitive information. Each NIS+ table can, for example, have different access permissions for each column. So the password column in the passwd table is only visible to the root user. You can use the niscat command on systems running the NIS+ client to examine the NIS tables.

If your network involves a large variety of UNIX variants, NIS+ will be more difficult, if not impossible, to use. Even the semi-secure NIS solutions are also difficult on a mixed network. So, if security is a significant concern on your network and you have a variety of operating systems, it may be that neither NIS nor NIS+ are for you. You could use the techniques discussed in Chapter 6 to distribute this system and account data, or you could even user sync as discussed in section 7.8. You should also consider using NIS to share basic system information, but for secure authentication, use Kerberos (see section 7.6).

# 7.5 Using the Lightweight Directory Access Protocol (LDAP)

The Lightweight Directory Access Protocol (LDAP) allows you to use a central information repository for a variety of system tasks. Although just about any information can be stored in an LDAP server, the most common thing to store is your user listing. For each user, you can specify their account, their full name, their phone number, their office, and any other information you may need.

Any LDAP-aware application can retrieve this data from the LDAP server. The Apache web server, for example, can use this information when it is authenticating users who are visiting a restricted web site. It is even more common to use LDAP to store the actual user accounts for your systems. Your operating system may be able to use a remote LDAP server in addition to the local user list (/etc/passwd). If your system uses PAM, the system itself and many of its utilities may already support LDAP.

If your system does not come with an LDAP server or you need additional LDAP clients, take a look at OpenLDAP (http://www.openldap.org/). It provides an LDAP server as well as client libraries and compiles on a wide variety of systems.

Before you switch to LDAP for your account management, you should make sure it will meet your needs. Does all of your software support LDAP? Most programs use the standard system library calls to access account information. If your system already supports LDAP, then these programs should work fine.

Other programs may require more direct access to this directory information. If they don't directly support LDAP (or indirectly support LDAP by supporting PAM), you may be out of luck. At best, you can create or find an LDAP gateway that allows this program to use LDAP without knowing it. At worst, you can create a script that pulls data out of LDAP on a regular basis and creates a file to be used by the program in question.

I think LDAP is a great system for a medium to large company or other organization. It takes a bit of work to set up, and you have to make sure your systems can take advantage of it, but it is worth it when you have a lot of account information to manage. If you decide to use LDAP, take a look at *DAP System Administration* by Gerald Carter (O'Reilly and Associates, 2003).

# 7.6 Security with Kerberos

Kerberos is an authentication system designed to be used between trusted hosts on an untrusted network. Most commonly, a Kerberos server is used to authenticate remote users without sending their password over the network. Kerberos is a pretty common security system and basic information can be found at http://web.mit.edu/kerberos/www/.

Kerberos is the best option (that I know about) available today for authenticating the same accounts across multiple systems. Unlike many other options, the users' passwords are rarely sent over the network. When they are, they are strongly encrypted.

Using Kerberos for authentication on your systems is not always easy, unfortunately. First of all, you need to set up a Kerberos server, which is beyond the scope of this book. It isn't the hardest thing in the world to do, but it will take you longer than five minutes. Good documentation can be found at MIT's Kerberos site: `http://web.mit.edu/kerberos/www/`.

You will also need to make sure any programs that require user authentication on your systems are able to use Kerberos. Some systems support PAM, which allows you to use Kerberos easily for all system-level authentication. If you do have PAM, it is also likely that most of the applications that came with your systems and require authentication can also use PAM. Other applications, like Apache and Samba may directly support Kerberos as well (with or without PAM).

Another advantage of Kerberos is its ability to use one authentication service from several unique software packages. It is not uncommon for each user to have a separate password for logging into systems over SSH, accessing a restricted web server, and accessing a Samba share. With Kerberos, you can use the same user password for all of these different services and any other services that support Kerberos.

Like LDAP, Kerberos is an excellent choice if you have a large number of user accounts and a decent number of systems. In fact, if you have a large enough number of systems, it can be worth the effort regardless of the number of accounts you use. Considering Kerberos is also the safest way to authenticate users over the network and can be used from such a wide variety of software, it is something you consider using in almost any environment.

## 7.7 Sharing Data with cfengine

GNU cfengine can be helpful in a couple of ways when you are sharing data between systems. First of all, cfengine can manage NFS mounts for you in lieu of an automounter. cfengine can also distribute data to other systems, which means that it can be used instead of NIS/NIS+.

---

 **NOTE**   GNU cfengine was extensively discussed in . If you have not yet read that section and you are interested in fully understanding the examples presented here, I would advise you to go back and learn the basics of cfengine.

---

## 7.7.1 Distributing Files

GNU cfengine can be used to distribute files to systems on your network. One very good use for this facility is to transfer files such as /etc/passwd, /etc/shadow, /etc/group, and other system files from a central server to every other system. The one advantage of this system over NIS/NIS+ is that the network is not used when these files are accessed. With NIS, for example, if the network is down, no users in the passwd map can log in to a system. When the files are copied, however, the local file is always complete (but could be slightly out-of-date).

Here is an example that will cause a client to transfer several system files from a server:

```
control:
    domain        = ( mydomain.com )
    cfserver      = ( cfserver.mydomain.com )

copy:
    !cfserver_mydomain_com::
        /etc/shadow  dest=/etc/shadow
                     mode=600
                     server=${cfserver}
                     encrypt=true
                     verify=true
                     /etc dest=/etc
                     mode=644
                     recurse=1
                     server=${cfserver}
                     verify=true
                     include=passwd
                     include=group
```

This copy section, if placed in cfagent.conf, first transfers the /etc/shadow file on the server to /etc/shadow on each client. This is accomplished by sending the data from the server to the client over an encrypted connection and verified before it is moved to its final location. Next, the passwd and group files are copied from the server, but they are created with more open permissions and are not transferred securely (because this is usually not necessary).

Each file is only transferred if it was changed on the server. cfengine determines this by comparing the timestamps on the files. You can also add the option type=checksum to use a checksum to compare the files. Although this takes longer to process, it is more reliable than using timestamps.

The class declaration line !cfserver_mydomain_com:: makes sure these copies do not occur on the server itself, because if they did, the server would be copying to and from the same file. cfengine does not actually let this happen; instead, it produces an error. The string `cfserver_mydomain_com` is a class that is based on the hostname of the system (dots in the hostname are replaced with underscores when the class definition is created). This class is only defined on the host `cfserver.mydomain.com`, which is the server.

## 7.7.2  Managing NFS Mounts

GNU cfengine has a significant amount of support for controlling and mounting NFS filesystems as is explained in this section. It also requires a very structured setup. If you are already using an automounter, particularly if you are using NIS/NIS+ to synchronize the maps, then it may not be worth your effort to convert to this new type of mounting system. If, on the other hand, you are already using, or are considering using cfengine and do not have any automated mounting on your systems, cfengine provides a good solution.

cfengine understands two types of NFS-mounted directories: home directories and binary directories. Home directories contain user data that can (and usually should) be mounted on every system. Binary directories, on the other hand, should only be mounted on systems of the appropriate architecture.

cfengine will not mount incompatible binary directories on a system (assuming you have it properly configured). This can reduce the number of NFS mounts required on each system by only mounting the necessary directories. Most automounters mount every home directory separately (i.e., `/home/kirk/` and `/home/amber/` are separately mounted filesystems, even if they may be physically located on the same server). cfengine only mounts each directory from each system one time, further reducing the number of NFS mounts. This does mean, however, that the user's home directories cannot be `/home/username`, unless all of your home directories are on one system. Also, unlike an automounter, cfengine makes sure all directories are always mounted (directories will not be unmounted when they are not being used).

The cfengine documentation recommends that you mount every directory in exactly the same place on every system. When you are using cfengine, the usual mounting location for a filesystem is `/site/host/contents/`. For example, let's say your site is named `mysite`, you have a fileserver named `fileserver`, and it exports a directory called `local`. The directory would be physically located in `/mysite/fileserver/local/` on the system `fileserver`. All other systems will mount this directory in exactly the same location via NFS. Each system can then create a symbolic link for `/usr/local/` pointing to this directory, assuming the binaries are compiled for the appropriate architecture/operating system.

I will now present an example `cfagent.conf` that just handles NFS mounting. Obviously this would be merged with (or referenced from within) your existing configuration file. I will present this file in several pieces. Here is the `control` section:

```
control:
   domain     = ( mysite.com )
   sysadm     = ( kirk )
   netmask    = ( 255.255.255.0 )
   actionsequence = (
      mountall
      mountinfo
      addmounts
      mountall
      links
   )
   mountpattern = ( /mysite/$(host) )
   homepattern  = ( u? )
```

The `actionsequence` is obviously a very important part of any `cfagent.conf`. Here is what these actions cause cfagent to do:

> **mountall:** This causes cfengine to look through /etc/fstab (or equivalent) and make sure everything that should be mounted is indeed mounted.
>
> **mountinfo:** This tells cfengine to load information on any actively mounted partitions. This information is required by the `addmounts` action.
>
> **addmounts:** Causes cfengine to add any necessary mount entries to /etc/fstab (or equivalent) and to create any necessary mount points. The actual NFS directories are taken from the `mountables` and `mailserver` sections.
>
> **mountall:** This (again) causes cfengine to look through the possibly modified /etc/fstab (or equivalent) and make sure everything that should be mounted is indeed mounted.
>
> **links:** This section (at least in the context of this chapter) is used to create symbolic links from the mounted partitions to other locations (such as /usr/local/, for example).

The `mountpattern` variable helps cfengine determine which directories are local and which directories are remotely mounted. When combined with the `mountpattern` variable, the `homepattern` variable allows cfengine to determine which directories contain home directories. The `homepattern` variable actually contains a list of patterns, but only one is used in this example.

When `cfagent` runs on the host host1, the directory /mysite/host1/data/ is considered a local directory. The directory /mysite/host2/u1 is considered a remote directory containing users' home directories.

The next section itemizes every server that contains home directories. Any home directories (those matching `homepattern`) on these systems are mounted on all systems.

```
homeservers:
    fileserver1
    fileserver2
```

Two servers export directories containing users' home directories: `fileserver1` and `fileserver2`. In the next section, `binservers` lists the servers that contain binary data (i.e., applications):

```
binservers:
    linux::   linux1
    solaris:: solaris1
    all::     fileserver1
```

So, for this example, all servers will mount all directories on `fileserver1` (they would have already mounted home directories, now they will also mount anything else). This is because `fileserver1` contains scripts that run on all systems.

In addition to `fileserver1` and `fileserver2`, all Linux machines mount all directories (well, all directories listed in the `mountables` section, which will be given momentarily) on the server `linux1`. Likewise, all Solaris systems mount directories off of the server `solaris1`.

The following `mailserver` section lists the location of the mail spool directory that should be mounted on all systems. The path given is the mail directory on the mail server. The directory is actually mounted in the appropriate location on the local machine based on its operating system. On some systems, it is mounted as `/var/mail/`, on other systems it is mounted as `/var/spool/mail/`.

```
mailserver:
    mail:/var/spool/mail
```

The final section directly related to NFS mounts is the `mountables` section that lists all of the exported directories on every server on the network. If a partition is not listed here, it will not be managed by cfengine. Even though all partitions will be listed here, hosts will only mount the appropriate directories based on the `homeservers` and `binservers` sections discussed earlier.

```
mountables:
    fileserver1:/mysite/fileserver1/u1
    fileserver1:/mysite/fileserver1/scripts
    fileserver2:/mysite/fileserver2/u2
    fileserver2:/mysite/fileserver2/u3
    linux1:/mysite/linux1/local
    solaris1:/mysite/solaris1/local
```

As you can see, `fileserver1` contains one directory containing home directories, and one directory containing scripts. The host `fileserver2` contains two separate directories, both containing home directories (presumably on separate physical drives). The host `linux1` contains applications you can use on Linux systems (to be ultimately accessed as `/usr/local/` on each system). Finally, the host `solaris1` contains similar applications for Solaris systems.

The `links` section can be used for many other linking tasks but, in this case, we are just using it to link `/usr/local/` to the binary directory appropriate for this host. The variable `binserver` expands first to the current system's hostname, then to the first applicable server in the `binservers` section, then to the next, and so on. Each expansion of `binserver` is tried, in order, until the specified directory is valid. At that point, the symbolic link is created.

```
links:
    /usr/local -> /mysite/${binserver}/local
```

When `cfagent` runs with this configuration file, it creates all necessary directories, adds any appropriate entries to `/etc/fstab`, and actually mounts the specified filesystems. Here are the directories that will be mounted on all Solaris systems in our example network:

- `mail:/var/spool/mail` is mounted on `/var/mail/`.

- `fileserver1:/mysite/fileserver1/u1` is mounted on `/mysite/fileserver1/u1`.

- `fileserver1:/mysite/fileserver1/scripts` is mounted on `/mysite/fileserver1/scripts`.

- `fileserver2:/mysite/fileserver2/u2` is mounted on `/mysite/fileserver2/u2`.

- `fileserver2:/mysite/fileserver2/u3` is mounted on `/mysite/fileserver2/u3`.

- `*solaris1:/mysite/solaris1/local` is mounted on `/mysite/solaris1/local`, and it is symbolically linked to `/usr/local/`.

A Linux system would have almost exactly the same mounted filesystems. The only difference is that, instead of mounting from the host `solaris1`, `linux1:/mysite/linux1/local` would be mounted on `/mysite/linux1/local`, and symbolically linked to `/usr/local/`. Let's say that `fileserver1` runs Linux. Here is what network filesystems would be mounted on that system:

- `mail:/var/spool/mail` is mounted on `/var/mail/`.

- `/mysite/fileserver1/u1` does not need to be mounted (it is local).

- `/mysite/fileserver1/scripts` does not need to be mounted (it is local).

- `fileserver2:/mysite/fileserver2/u2` is mounted on `/mysite/fileserver2/u2`.

- `fileserver2:/mysite/fileserver2/u3` is mounted on `/mysite/fileserver2/u3`.

- `linux1:/mysite/linux1/local` is mounted on `/mysite/linux1/local`, and symbolically linked to `/usr/local/`.

There is definitely one advantage to using cfengine to manage your home directory mounts. Assuming all of your directories containing home directories match the `mountpattern` and `homepattern` settings in the `control` section, you can use the special pattern `home` in several sections in `cfagent.conf`. Here is an example from the `tidy` section:

```
tidy:
    home                    pattern=core  recurse=inf age=0
    home                    pattern=*~    recurse=inf age=7
    home/.netscape/cache  pattern=*     recurse=inf age=3 type=atime
```

The special path `home` matches all users' home directories. These are all the directories under the home directory partitions, such as `/mysite/fileserver2/u3/`. By default, `cfagent` only operates on home directories that are local to the current system, because I assume that `cfagent` is being regularly run on all systems.

---

## Using the home Pattern Without NFS Mounting

If you do not use cfengine to manage your NFS mounts (i.e., you use an automounter instead), or even if you don't use NFS mounts at all, you still may be able to use the `home` pattern in `cfagent.conf`. If, for example, all of your users' home directories are under `/home/`, you could use these settings in your `control` section:

```
control:
    mountpattern = ( / )
    homepattern = ( home )
```

---

This `tidy` section erases any `core` files found in any users' home directories. Next, it erases any filenames ending in a tilde, which are usually Emacs backup files that are more than seven days old. Finally it deletes Netscape cache files that have not been accessed in the past three days. You can also use the `cfagent` to enhance the security of user's home directories and files:

```
files:
    home            mode=751                 action=fixall
    home            mode=o-w recurse=inf action=fixall
    home/.ssh       mode=600 recurse=inf action=fixall
```

This makes sure that each user's home directory has modes 751. It also makes sure that no publicly writable files are anywhere in the user's home directory (whether this is something you actually want to change is up to you). Finally, the permissions on the `.ssh/` directory are set such that neither the directory, nor any files in it, can be modified or accessed by anybody else.

One final thing that might help out some users is this command:

```
files:
    home/public_html mode=644 recurse=inf action=fixall
```

This makes sure that all files under each user's `public_html/` directory are publicly readable. Directories are also made publicly executable. Some users might intentionally make parts of this directory *not* publicly readable to hide part of their web content. So, depending on your users and your environment, you may not want to use these types of commands that broadly affect the user's home directories.

## 7.8 Synchronizing Data with `rsync`

rsync is a wonderful program that allows files and directories to be transferred from one host to another. I know it doesn't sound very impressive; you are probably thinking you can do all of this yourself with `scp`. You could (rsync, in fact, can use the SSH protocol to do its work), but it would be difficult to do it as well as rsync does.

What rsync adds to the mix is the ability to efficiently mirror files between two hosts. The files are compared using their timestamps or checksums and only the necessary files are transferred. In fact, when files do change, only the portions that have changed are sent over the network. This makes rsync very efficient. I regularly use rsync to synchronize about 1GB of data; it only takes a couple of seconds when there are no (or few) changes.

You can also use rsync to delete files and modify permissions to achieve an exact copy. It can copy device files, create symbolic links, preserve ownership, and synchronize timestamps. rsync also supports both include and exclude patterns that allow you to specify exactly which files you want synchronized.

---

 **TIP**   It is important to remember that the rsync program must be installed on both the remote and local systems to synchronize data between those systems.

---

## 7.8.1 Possible Uses of rsync

rsync is very useful for synchronizing applications and their data. You could, for example, use rsync to synchronize /usr/local/ across several systems. In most environments, /usr/local/ doesn't change very often, so using rsync once per day can be significantly more efficient than using network filesystems. In addition, using rsync reduces network use and improves application access time. However, not surprisingly, it uses much more disk space because each system has its own complete copy of the application directory.

Clusters of web servers have become commonplace in the modern web-enabled world. You may have anywhere from 2 to 50 web servers behind a set of load balancers. A large amount of web content may need to be accessed by each of these web servers. Creating an efficient and reliable network filesystem to store the web server software and content can be very expensive, but because hard drives are so inexpensive these days, each system can simply store all of its content on its local drive and update it daily with rsync. For quicker updates, you can even combine a pull and push method—the servers can check daily for changes (the pull portion), and you could also push new content on demand to update the servers quickly.

Conveniently, you can also use rsync to transfer account data (such as /etc/passwd, /etc/shadow, and /etc/group) among your systems. For this limited number of small files, rsync could be run hourly (or even more often than that) with little performance degradation.

One potential drawback to using rsync is that it has real trouble showing any respect for changes made on the system being updated. This means that any files that were locally modified will be replaced with the copy on the server, and any deleted files will be added again. Also, if you use the --delete switch, any new files will be erased. This means that you must make *all* changes on the master server and never make any of them on the client systems. Anybody who needs to make changes should be trained appropriately or they will have to learn the lesson the hard way.

Some would consider this potential drawback a benefit—when you have ten copies of supposedly identical data, the last thing you want is people making changes in only one place and forgetting to propagate that change to other systems. Another benefit is that you can add debugging or try something on a system and then erase all of those temporary changes by resyncing the data.

You can also tell rsync to dereference symbolic links when copying (the -L switch). If you do, rsync creates a copy of any symbolic link in the source directory as a regular file (or directory) in the destination directory. The destination tree will take up more space as a result, but the elimination of symbolic links can be very useful in some situations. If, for example, you need to regularly replicate data, but the application that uses that data does not work with symbolic links, you can use rsync to solve your problems. You can also use symbolic links to make the management of the original copy easier and then use rsync to make a useable copy (you can even make the copy from and to the same system).

Some examples where the dereferencing of symbolic links might be useful are chroot environments, anonymous FTP sites, and directories that are exported via NFS. Although symbolic links work fine within the anonymous FTP directory, for example, they cannot reference files below the root of the anonymous directory. If you used rsync to transfer some or all of your FTP content into your anonymous FTP directory, however, any symbolic links would be dereferenced during that process (if the -L switch is used).

## 7.8.2 Deciding Which rsync Transport Protocol to Use

By default, rsync uses the RSH protocol to communicate with the remote system. It can, fortunately, be configured to use SSH instead, allowing it to use all of the standard SSH authentication methods and utilize encrypted file transfers. I recommend using SSH if at all possible. You can tell rsync to use SSH by setting the RSYNC_RSH environment variable to the location of your ssh binary (such as /usr/bin/ssh).

If you want to include extra options for the SSH program, you need to create a shell script, such as /usr/local/bin/rsync_ssh, as follows:

```
#!/bin/bash

exec ssh -2 -i /etc/keys/some_rsa_key -o 'CheckHostIP no' \
    -o 'ForwardX11 no' -o 'ForwardAgent no' \
    -o 'StrictHostKeyChecking no' ${1+"$@"}
```

The -2 option specifies that protocol version 2 should be used for this encrypted connection. The -i option is used in this example to provide a special location for your private key file. Since neither X11 nor Agent forwarding are necessary for file transfers, you should turn off the `ForwardX11` and `ForwardAgent` options.

With the options `CheckHostIP` and `StrictHostKeyChecking` disabled, `ssh` never prompts you about a host's public key. This is fine in some cases. For instance, if the information you are pushing is not sensitive, then it doesn't really matter if you push it to an attacker's system. If you are pulling from a server, however, you might not want these options because somebody could spoof your server and push out their own data to your systems.

Don't forget to make this script executable. You can then set `RSYNC_RSH` to point to this shell script, and rsync will now use SSH with your options to perform the file transfers.

## 7.8.3 Basic Use of rsync

By my estimate, there are around fifty command-line options for rsync. I do not attempt to cover each option, but I try to show you some useful examples. When trying these commands out, you may find it very useful to use the verbose switch (-v) and/or the dry-run switch (-n). You should also be careful when trying out rsync because you could accidentally copy large amounts of data to places it does not need to be. The dry-run switch can help with the debugging process because it will cause rsync to not actually transfer any files. This lets you see what would have happened without actually making any modifications to the files.

Here is a simple example that copies `/usr/local/` (recursively, in archive mode, using the -a switch) to a remote system:

```
% rsync -a /usr/local root@remote_host:/usr/local/
```

If you actually ran this command, you would see that it doesn't quite work as expected. The `/usr/local/bin/` directory on the local system is pushed as `/usr/local/local/bin/` on the remote system. The reason this happens is that I forgot the slash on the end of the source directory. I asked rsync to copy the file (or directory) `/usr/local` into the remote directory `/usr/local/`.

Any of the following commands will work the way you might have expected the previous command to operate. Personally, I prefer to use the first one listed here because I think it is the most readable. I would not recommend running any of these other commands unless you really want to copy all of `/usr/local/` to another system (just in case you didn't learn your lesson when you tried the last example).

```
% rsync -a /usr/local/ root@remote_host:/usr/local/
% rsync -a /usr/local/ root@remote_host:/usr/local
% rsync -a /usr/local root@remote_host:/usr/
% rsync -a /usr/local root@remote_host:/usr
```

The -a switch tells rsync to operate in archive mode. This causes it to operate recursively and preserve permissions, ownership, symbolic links, device files, access times, and so on. In fact, using the -a switch works the same as using the options -rlptgoD.

By default, rsync leaves a file alone if it has exactly the same timestamp and size as the source file. You must specify the -a switch or the -t switch to preserve file timestamps. If you do not use either of these options, every file will be transmitted every time you execute rsync. This is fine if you are using rsync for a one-time transfer, but it is not very efficient when you run rsync multiple times.

If you previously used a different method to transfer files and you are not sure the timestamps are correct, but you know that most of the files are already identical, you can use the --size-only option, along with the -a switch, for the first transfer. This option causes rsync to ignore the timestamps and only use the size of the files to find differences. It then sets all timestamps properly (because of the -a switch) so that future runs on the same file do not need the --size-only switch. For a small amount of files this doesn't matter, but if you are transferring lots of data or using a slow connection, this can make the first synchronization less painful.

The only problem with this example is that it does not delete any files on the remote system. Let's say that you used to have /usr/local/program-2.0/, but now you have /usr/local/program-3.0/. You might have deleted /usr/local/program-2.0/ on the server, but it has not been deleted on the other systems.

This is where the --delete switch becomes useful. This switch tells rsync to delete any files in the destination directory that are not in the source directory. You must be very careful with the --delete switch because it has the potential to do major damage. You could, for example, accidentally run this command:

```
% rsync -a --delete /tmp/ root@remote_host:/
```

This command would wipe out everything on the entire remote host and replace it with the contents of the local /tmp/ directory. I have a feeling this is not something you would like to do for fun. However, as long as you are careful when you use this option, you will find that it can be very useful. As a minimal safeguard, rsync will never delete files if any errors occur during the synchronization process.

Our above example could be expanded to remove files that shouldn't be on the destination system. This allows an exact copy of the source files to be created on the destination system. The command you would run follows:

```
% rsync -a --delete /usr/local/ root@remote_host:/usr/local/
```

After running this command, the remote system will have exactly the same files in its /usr/local/ directory as the local system—no less, and no more.

## 7.8.4 Example rsync Usage

Here are a few examples that illustrate how rsync can help with some common problems.

### 7.8.4.1 Pushing /usr/local/

In the last section, you saw how /usr/local/ can be pushed out to another system. This practice could easily be extended to push to all systems on demand. Here is such a script that assumes that all systems are running the same (or compatible) operating system:

```
#!/bin/bash

for host in `cat /usr/local/etc/all_hosts` ; do
    rsync -a --delete /usr/local/ root@$host:/usr/local/
done
```

You would run this script whenever you made a change to the files in /usr/local/. It is also a good idea to automatically run it at least once per week (usually once per day unless the system/network load is a real issue) just in case you forget to manually synchronize data after a change.

### 7.8.4.2 Pulling /usr/local/

You can also have your systems pull /usr/local/ from a server on a regular basis. You could have cron run this script every hour, for example. In this example, I assume that there are several types of operating systems on the network. I use the uname command to determine the type of the local system. Here are some example outputs from the uname command on a few different operating systems:

```
linux% uname
Linux
solaris% uname
SunOS
aix% uname
AIX
```

Now I need to create a configuration file called /usr/local/etc/fileservers. It will contain one entry per operating system, specifying the location of binaries for that system. Here is an example:

```
# WARNING: A mistake in this file could cause all systems to have their
# /usr/local directory wiped out completely or be replaced with bad files
Linux master_linux_system:/usr/local
SunOS master_solaris_system:/usr/local
AIX master_aix_system:/usr/local
```

As you can see, I started the file with the warning as a comment. If somebody edits this file, and then a system updates itself using the file, any mistakes could cause serious problems. The script that should be run regularly (usually daily) on each system is as follows:

```
#!/bin/bash

# First, determine our system type
host_type=`uname`

# Now, isolate our fileserver with sed and remove the beginning of the line
source=`sed -n "s/^$host_type //p" /usr/local/etc/fileservers`

# Make sure a valid remote filesystem was found (would contain a colon)
echo "$source" | grep -q ':' && {
    # Finally, transfer the files
    rsync -a --delete $source/ /usr/local/
}
```

You may note that comments aren't really supported in the configuration file. I'm just assuming that no systems have uname output that begins with a #. This is a pretty decent assumption since typical output from this command is Linux or SunOS. Since this output doesn't begin with #, a line beginning with # could never match.

After seeing the actual rsync command in the script, you can see how destructive a mistake can be. If, for example, the source was an empty directory, the entire /usr/local/ would be wiped out. For this reason, you should test this script thoroughly and be very careful when you make changes.

### 7.8.4.3  Synchronizing Account Information

Here is a command that you can run on every host on your network on a regular basis (hourly, for example) to update its account data files (/etc/passwd, /etc/shadow, and /etc/group) from a master server.

```
rsync -ac --include=/passwd \        # include some files
          --include=/shadow     \
          --include=/group      \
          --exclude='*'         \ # exclude all other files
          root@fileserver:/etc/ \ # source
          /etc/                   # destination
```

You may specify any number of include and exclude options, but be aware that their order is important. Their argument is a pattern that is applied against each file. Every file is compared against the first pattern (/passwd) and, if it matches, it is automatically accepted. If a file passes through all of the include patterns without being matched, it will ultimately be matched by the exclude pattern of *. This entry matches and excludes every other file in the /etc/ directory. This is necessary because any file not matched by an exclude statement is, by default, included in the copy process.

The patterns are relative to the base directory of the transfer. For instance, the pattern /passwd matches the file /etc/passwd because the directory /etc/ is the base directory for the transfer. In addition to literal file or directory names, the patterns may include the * character to match zero or more of any character. The ? character will match any one character. The [] characters can be used to specify a list of characters, any one of which is acceptable.

Remember—unless you are using SSH as the transport layer, you are sending sensitive information (including passwords in this example) in clear-text over the network. For this reason, I recommend that you use SSH as your transport layer as I discussed in section 7.8.2.

## 7.9 Managing and Distributing Data with CVS

According to the Concurrent Versions System (CVS) man page, "CVS is a version control system, which allows you to keep old versions of files (usually source code), keep a log of who, when, and why changes occurred, etc." You may be asking, "What does version control of source code have to do with system administration?" Well, in addition to the obvious uses of keeping track of the changes you make to your system administration tools and related files, you can actually use CVS to distribute files to your systems.

Although you can store binary files with CVS, it is not designed for this and I would not recommend doing this on a large scale. I would not, for example, use CVS to store and distribute your /usr/local/ directory. I would, however, recommend that you use CVS to distribute textual data such as your system administration scripts and web content.

When using CVS, you should never make changes directly on the "client" systems. Unlike rsync, if you make changes on a "client" system, those changes might persist for some period of time. If you add a new file, for example, it remains in place even if it doesn't exist in the repository. Deleted files will be re-added, but modified files can really cause problems. If you are really lucky, CVS will be able to merge the local changes with the changes in the repository (which may or may not be a good thing). If you are not so lucky, CVS will create a file that needs to be manually merged. This file will probably not work at all until the manual merge finishes. Manual merges are something to avoid in an automated distribution system.

## 7.9.1 CVS Basics

If you are not familiar with using CVS, this section gets you started. I do not, however, attempt to provide a comprehensive introduction or reference to CVS. For further information, visit http://www.cvshome.org.

One thing I should mention about CVS and its use for system administration tasks is that it does not allow you to commit files as root. The only way to modify this behavior is to recompile the program with this restriction disabled. The only exception to this rule is when you are using CVS with a remote repository (either a pserver or via RSH/SSH). In this case, you can be root on the local system, as long as you are not connecting as root to the server.

### 7.9.1.1 Creating and Using a CVS Repository

Before you can use CVS, you need to set up your $CVSROOT root environment variable to point to your desired CVS repository. This repository can be a local directory (such as /var/cvsroot), a remote server accessed over SSH (kirk@cvsserver.mydomain.com:/var/cvsroot), or a system running a CVS "pserver" (:pserver:cvsserver.mydomain.com:/var/cvsroot).

The last example (the CVS "pserver") refers to a repository on a host running CVS in a special daemon mode. This type of CVS server requires the most complicated setup and is the least secure, so I will let you explore this option on your own if you feel it is necessary.

A local CVS repository is also not very useful for automating system administration because you usually have more than one machine that needs to access the repository. For this reason, the examples in this chapter will access a remote CVS repository using the SSH protocol.

To access a repository, it is easiest to set your $CVSROOT environment variable to the proper CVS repository. You also need to set CVS_RSH to ssh to tell CVS to use SSH to communicate with the CVS server (as opposed to the traditional RSH, which

I don't recommend using). These environment variables should be set in root's
.bash_profile (or equivalent) on each system, as follows:

```
export CVSROOT='kirk@cvsserver.mydomain.com:/var/cvsroot'
export CVS_RSH='ssh'
```

Once these environment variables have been set, you need to make sure the
directory (such as /var/cvsroot/) actually exists on the specified server. Assuming
it does, you can create a new repository by running cvs init.

Like any other command that uses SSH as its network communications protocol, you may be prompted for a password or passphrase each time you access
the remote repository. You can avoid this by setting up passwordless SSH access as
discussed in the section called "Using the ssh-agent" in Chapter 2.

It is easy to add modules to a CVS repository. First, create a temporary directory
somewhere on your system, then place any number of files and directories inside,
or just leave it empty. You can then change into that directory and import its contents
as a new module:

```
% cd /tmp/newmodule
% cvs import -m 'initial import' newmodule v1 r1
```

The strings v1 and r1 are the vendor and release tags, respectively. The initial
versions of the files will be marked with these tags. Both tags must be specified and
must be different, but any valid tag labels will do. I typically use the actual values v1
and r1.

### 7.9.1.2 Using a CVS Module

Once you have created your CVS repository and one or more modules are present,
you can see how CVS works from the end user's perspective. Again, you must first
make sure your $CVSROOT and $CVS_RSH variables are set properly. You can then check
out a module from the repository as follows:

```
% cvs checkout sample
cvs checkout: Updating sample
U sample/file1
U sample/file2
```

CVS just created a new directory called sample/, which contains all of the files
that are part of the sample module. This directory is your local working directory.
Any changes you make in this directory do not affect the repository until you commit

them. Likewise, any changes made to the repository (such as changes made by other users) do not affect your local working directory unless you perform an update.

Once you have this working directory, you can enter it to view and modify files as necessary. For illustration purposes, let's say that you made a change to file2. If you want to find out what changes you made (maybe you made many changes or made them long ago), you can use the cvs status command:

```
% cvs status
cvs status: Examining .
======================================================================
File: file1              Status: Up-to-date

   Working revision: 1.1    Sat Jan  4 19:22:08 2003
   Repository revision: 1.1    /tmp/blah/sample/file1,v
   Sticky Tag:     (none)
   Sticky Date:       (none)
   Sticky Options:    (none)
======================================================================
File: file2              Status: Locally Modified

   Working revision: 1.2    Sat Jan  4 19:24:11 2003
   Repository revision: 1.2    /tmp/blah/sample/file2,v
   Sticky Tag:     (none)
   Sticky Date:       (none)
   Sticky Options:    (none)
```

You can then see what you changed in a specific file:

```
% cvs diff -u file2
Index: file2
======================================================================
RCS file: /tmp/blah/sample/file2,v
retrieving revision 1.2
diff -u -r1.2 file2
--- file2    3 Jan 2003 19:24:13 -0000    1.2
+++ file2    3 Jan 2003 19:24:17 -0000
@@ -1 +1 @@
-original file2
+new file2
```

So, you can see that you removed the line original file2 and changed it to new file2. You can then commit this change (and any others):

```
% cvs commit -m 'just a test'
cvs commit: Examining .
Checking in file2;
/tmp/blah/sample/file2,v  <--  file2
new revision: 1.3; previous revision: 1.2
done
```

If you don't specify the -m switch, CVS loads a text editor and allow you to enter a message describing the changes you made to the file(s). You can also add files to your CVS repository (you must first create the files in your working directory, of course):

```
% cvs add newfile
cvs add: scheduling file `newfile' for addition
cvs add: use 'cvs commit' to add this file permanently
```

It is important to tell CVS when you are adding a binary file. You can do this by including the -kb switch to the cvs add command:

```
% cvs add -kb c.png
cvs add: scheduling file `c.png' for addition
cvs add: use 'cvs commit' to add this file permanently
```

You can also configure the repository itself to automatically recognize certain file extensions as binary files, but I do not discuss this in this book because I consider it advanced CVS administration. Regardless of the type of files you add, you need to commit them to the repository, as CVS has been so kind to remind us:

```
% cvs commit
cvs commit: Examining .
RCS file: /tmp/blah/sample/c.png,v
done
Checking in c.png;
/tmp/blah/sample/c.png,v  <--  c.png
initial revision: 1.1
done
RCS file: /tmp/blah/sample/newfile,v
done
Checking in newfile;
/tmp/blah/sample/newfile,v  <--  newfile
initial revision: 1.1
done
```

You can also remove files from CVS. When files are removed, they are actually just moved to an Attic directory within the repository. This means that you can still check out any old revisions of the file if necessary. Removing a file is simple:

```
% rm c.png
% cvs remove c.png
cvs remove: scheduling `c.png' for removal
cvs remove: use 'cvs commit' to remove this file permanently
% cvs commit -m 'removed c.png'
cvs commit: Examining .
Removing c.png;
/tmp/blah/sample/c.png,v  <--  c.png
new revision: delete; previous revision: 1.1
done
```

If more than one user is making changes to a module and/or you have more than one active working directory, you need to update each working directory from time to time. I usually update my working directory just before I start making changes to make sure I have the latest version of the files. You can perform a full update by running the following command in the base directory of your working directory:

```
% cvs update -dP
cvs update: Updating .
U file2
U newfile
```

The -dP switches tell CVS to create any new directories and remove any empty directories, as necessary. In this case, file2 had been updated and newfile had been added.

### 7.9.1.3 Understanding File Revisions

Every time you commit a change in CVS, the modified files are assigned a new revision. This revision can later be used to check out any version of any file. If, for example, you commit a file as revision 1.3 with the following command:

```
% cvs commit -m 'just a test' file2
cvs commit: Examining .
Checking in file2;
/tmp/blah/sample/file2,v  <--  file2
new revision: 1.3; previous revision: 1.2
done
```

you can then access the previous version at any time as follows:

```
% cvs update -r 1.2 file2
U file2
% cvs status file2
===================================================================
File: file2              Status: Up-to-date
   Working revision: 1.2   Sat Jan  4 19:47:59 2003
   Repository revision: 1.2    /tmp/blah/sample/file2,v
   Sticky Tag:      1.2
   Sticky Date:       (none)
   Sticky Options:    (none)
```

Note that the file now has a "sticky tag" of 1.2. This means that I can't change the local file and commit it because it is not the newest version. You can remove these sticky tags (and also update the files to the newest version) by running the cvs update -A command.

### 7.9.1.4 Creating and Using Tags

You can also assign an arbitrary tag to one or more files:

```
% cvs tag mytag
T file1
T file2
T newfile
```

Since I didn't specify any specific files, all files in my working directory were tagged. Note that if any local files have been modified, they must be committed before being tagged if you want to tag those modified versions. You can then check out the repository using the tag by running the cvs checkout -r mytag command. You can also update an existing working directory by running cvs update -r mytag. Just like when you check out a specific revision of a file, checking out a specific tag sets the local sticky tag. This prevents you from committing the affected files until the sticky tag has been removed.

Tags are useful for marking specific versions of files that are known to work or have some other special meaning. If I place some code on a production server, I might tag that code so that I can later determine exactly what code was deployed.

### 7.9.1.5  Creating and Using Branches

Branches are a special type of tag that allows tagged files to be modified. If you have a stable set of scripts, for example, you can create a branch at that point. Minor bug fixes can be done on the stable branch while new development can continue on the main trunk. Branches can get very complicated, so I only provide a basic introduction here. See http://www.cvshome.org for all of the gory details about branches and many other CVS topics.

You can create a branch the same way you create a tag, by adding the -b option:

```
% cvs tag -b mybranch
cvs tag: Tagging .
T file1
T file2
T newfile
```

You can then checkout the branched version of the code:

```
% cvs checkout -r mybranch -d mybranch sample
cvs checkout: Updating mybranch
U mybranch/file1
U mybranch/file2
U mybranch/newfile
```

I used the -r option to request the branch mybranch. I also used the -d option to check out the files into the directory mybranch/ instead of the default sample/ directory. I like to use unique directory names when working on a branch so that I don't forget that I'm modifying a branch and not the main code (the "trunk"). You can use the cvs status command to see that you have branched files:

```
% cd mybranch/
% cvs status
cvs status: Examining .
===================================================================
File: file1              Status: Up-to-date
   Working revision: 1.1   Sat Jan  4 19:22:08 2003
   Repository revision: 1.1   /tmp/blah/sample/file1,v
   Sticky Tag:    mybranch (branch: 1.1.2)
   Sticky Date:      (none)
   Sticky Options:   (none)
```

```
===================================================================
File: file2              Status: Up-to-date
   Working revision: 1.4    Sat Jan  4 19:29:15 2003
   Repository revision: 1.4    /tmp/blah/sample/file2,v
   Sticky Tag:     mybranch (branch: 1.4.2)
   Sticky Date:       (none)
   Sticky Options:    (none)


===================================================================
File: newfile            Status: Up-to-date
   Working revision: 1.1    Sat Jan  4 19:38:56 2003
   Repository revision: 1.1    /tmp/blah/sample/newfile,v
   Sticky Tag:     mybranch (branch: 1.1.2)
   Sticky Date:       (none)
   Sticky Options:    (none)
```

You can then make any changes you want in this branched working directory. Everything you do only affects the branch and not the main trunk. You can even add and remove files in the branch without affecting the main trunk. This is the reason you use a branch, of course, but it is both a blessing and a curse.

If you fix a bug in the branch, for example, you usually need to fix the same bug in the trunk. If you add a new file in the branch, you may need to add that same file into the trunk. Managing these differences can be challenging, but a good amount of web-based documentation exists on the subject. For these reasons, I don't use branches unless I need to. Even then, I wait as long as possible before branching, or I even branch only the specific files that I have to (and tag the rest with the same name).

## 7.9.2 *Distributing System Administration Scripts*

Since you will probably collect many configuration files and build many automation scripts in your quest for automation, CVS is something to seriously consider. You get instant revision control and change history for your scripts, as well as a way to distribute them. You can also stage the release of the scripts (i.e., development, testing, and production), which is more difficult to do with some of the other solutions presented in this chapter.

For the example in this section, we assume that you keep your scripts in /usr/local/sbin/ and their configuration files in /usr/local/etc/. Let's assume that your CVS server is a remote system that you access through SSH using the account kirk. In this case, you need to set the following environment variables:

```
export CVSROOT='kirk@cvsserver.mydomain.com:/var/cvsroot'
export CVS_RSH='ssh'
```

You will be using two CVS modules: sbin and etc. You should have a system, maybe even your desktop machine, that you can use to develop and test your scripts. Here is what you would do to get started. I have assumed that you already have your current scripts and configuration files on this system, but you have not yet initialized the CVS root. If you have, just skip the cvs init command. If you have any binary files in these directories, you need to read the information in "Using a CVS Module" before you proceed.

```
% cvs init
% cd /usr/local/sbin
% cvs import -m '' sbin v1 r1

No conflicts created by this import

% cd /usr/local/etc
% cvs import -m '' etc v1 r1

No conflicts created by this import

% cd /usr/local
% mkdir backup
% mv etc sbin backup/
% cvs checkout etc sbin
cvs checkout: Updating etc
cvs checkout: Updating sbin
```

You have now created the new modules in your CVS repository. You have also checked them out to your local system, after moving the existing files to a backup directory. Theoretically, when the process is done, you have exactly the same files that you started with, but it is always a good idea to have a backup until you are sure everything went according to plan.

At this point, you can modify, add, and remove files from these directories. Remember to commit your changes frequently with the cvs commit command. Once you are sure that the directories on your development machine are OK and you want exactly those directories on every other system, you should tag the files with the tag production:

```
% cd /usr/local
% cvs tag -c 'production' etc sbin
cvs tag: Tagging etc
cvs tag: Tagging sbin
```

You have now marked these files with the tag production. The -c switch says to check for uncommitted files while tagging and to abort if any are found. At all times, the revision of any file with this tag should be OK to deploy to other systems. When you are ready to deploy these scripts, log in to every other system and perform these commands:

```
% cd /usr/local
% rm -rf etc sbin
% cvs checkout -r 'production' etc sbin
cvs checkout: Updating etc
cvs checkout: Updating sbin
```

## File Permissions with CVS

When you add a new file to CVS (with the import or add commands), the file in the repository gets the execute permissions of the original file. So, if the file was marked executable, it will be that way in the repository. When the file is checked out of CVS, it will still be executable. Other permissions on the file are generally lost because it is usually created with the write permissions based on your umask, but publicly readable. For this reason, the script that updates your CVS-controlled directories may need to fix the permissions of some or all of the files after they are updated.

You can now modify and test these files on your local system. You should commit changes as often as possible, but you should only tag the files production once you are sure they are safe to deploy to other systems. When you have made changes to some files and you want to retag all of the files, you need to move the tag. You can do this with the -F flag:

```
% cd /usr/local
% cvs tag -Fc 'production' etc sbin
cvs tag: Tagging etc
cvs tag: Tagging sbin
```

You should have a script that runs frequently (every day or so) on every other system that updates these files. This script could be as follows:

```
#!/bin/bash

cd /usr/local
cvs update -dRP -r 'production' etc sbin
```

CVS updates any files that have newer versions, adds any new files or directories (the -d switch) that have been tagged production, and deletes any unneeded files or directories (the -P switch). There is only one thing you really have to watch out for—you must always delete the production tag before you delete a file from the repository. Here is an example of deleting a script from the sbin/ directory:

```
% cd /usr/local/sbin
% cvs tag -d 'production' script.sh
D script.sh
% cvs remove -f script.sh
cvs remove: scheduling `script.sh' for removal
cvs remove: use 'cvs commit' to remove this file permanently
% cvs commit -m 'reason' script.sh
Removing script.sh;
/var/cvs/t/script.sh,v  <--  script.sh
new revision: delete; previous revision: 1.1
done
```

Although CVS might seem like a lot of work for these types of tasks, it may be beneficial in the long run. You are forced to do a two-stage process to deploy new scripts (you make the change and then tag the change when it is ready), which makes it harder to distribute bad changes. If, on the other hand, you make a bad change on an NFS-mounted filesystem, all systems are instantly be affected. You also get automatic version control and change history (whether you like it or not). This can save you one day when you lose a script or make a mistake and need to revert to an older version of that file. Change history and revision tracking are also nice when there are several administrators.

Each administrator can work on the scripts on their own workstation and CVS will help resolve any conflicts. Each administrator just needs to remember to update their own system regularly (run **cvs update** with no tag specified). With multiple administrators checking out untagged scripts, you do need to be a bit more careful about what you commit into CVS. If you commit a nonworking script, the other administrators might get that file and it may cause problems (but your production systems will not be affected).

### 7.9.3  Distributing Web Content

CVS can be quite useful for distributing web content. Most web content usually consists of text files, which are often modified by multiple people at the same time. This content is often deployed first onto a testing server and then onto one or more production servers. CVS can support all of this and also provide full change history and recovery capabilities.

First let's initialize the CVS repository (if necessary):

```
% export CVSROOT='kirk@cvsserver.mydomain.com:/var/cvsroot'
% export CVS_RSH='ssh'
% cvs init
```

Now, let's assume you have a copy of your web content in ~/web. You need to import this data into a new module web and then re-create this directory by checking it out from CVS:

```
% cd ~/web
% cvs import -m '' web v1 r1
% cd ..
% mv web web_bak
% cvs checkout web
cvs checkout: Updating web
```

All web developers should check out the content into their own directory where it can be modified as needed. If the content depends on a complex server configuration, you could set up a development server and check out one copy of the content on that server. A staging server like this, even though not always necessary, is always a good idea. It can be configured almost exactly like the production servers and it can either be the place where development is done or it can be a final testing point before the code is released into the real world.

Once you have content that is ready to be distributed, you need to tag the files so that they will be deployed to the production servers. You can tag the files in this way:

```
% cd ~/web
% cvs tag -c 'production'
cvs tag: Tagging .
```

Let's say that you need to deploy the files to /var/www/html/ on each web server. You need to log in on each system and run these commands (once per system) to perform the initial CVS checkout:

```
% export CVSROOT='kirk@cvsserver.mydomain.com:/var/cvsroot'
% export CVS_RSH='ssh'
% cd /var/www
% mv html html_bak
% cvs checkout -r 'production' -d html web
cvs checkout: Updating html
```

In this case, we are checking out the module web into the directory html. The -d switch specifies an alternate checkout directory (usually the directory name is the same as the module name). At this point, you can make changes in your development directory, commit the files to the repository, and tag those changes when they are ready to be deployed. If you have the staging server as previously discussed, you could also use the tag stage that could be used to mark files as being ready for deployment on the staging server.

The production server (and the staging server) need to update themselves regularly so that they incorporate changes. Information on retagging files, updating servers, and removing files can be found in the previous section.

## 7.10 Transferring Data with HTTP/FTP

Most of the other options discussed in this chapter have problems when going through most firewalls. This is not an issue, in most cases, because the systems are usually all behind the same firewall or you can modify the firewall configuration as necessary. Many of the network filesystems require communication over several ports and possibly even connections each way (i.e., client connects to the server and the server connects back to the client).

Using rsync and scp are good options because they only use port 22 (SSH protocol) and only need one-way connections (i.e., the clients always connects to the server). In some environments, unfortunately, even this might not be possible. This is a case when you have to turn to the File Transfer Protocol (FTP) or the Hypertext Transfer Protocol (HTTP). FTP, in passive mode, only connects to the server on ports 20 and 21, and is more likely than SSH to be allowed through firewalls. HTTP connects to the server over port 80 and is very likely to be allowed through a firewall. It might be redirected through a transparent proxy, but even then, it should still work fine.

Neither FTP nor HTTP are good protocols for transmitting private data that requires authentication unless you have strict control of the initiating system. The reason is that the password needs to be stored on the initiating system in plaintext in order to access the files. Another concern is that the password is sent in plaintext over the network during the HTTP authentication process.

With that being said, there are times when HTTP or FTP are your best options for transferring files. There are three programs that you might find useful, and they may already be installed on your system. They can be added to just about any UNIX system if necessary.

wget: Command-line, noninteractive HTTP transfer and mirroring program. This is handy because it can recursively retrieve files and perform exact mirrors. It can also transfer files via FTP.

lftpget: The lftpget command is part of the lftp FTP client and can transfer single files over FTP and even HTTP.

ncftpget: The ncftpget command is part of the ncftp FTP client and can transfer single files over FTP.

## 7.10.1  Example: Synchronizing Web Content

You may be able to use wget to actually copy your web site from a master server to additional servers. This is really only feasible if you have a simple web site with no authentication and no dynamic content. This type of site is not very common today, so in most cases, you have to use the other methods described in this chapter. But, if your situation permits the use of wget, here is how you would use it (assuming your web content is located in /var/www/html/):

```
% cd /var/www/html
% wget -q --recursive --no-host-directories http://www.mysite.com/
```

The wget command produces quite a bit of output. It was suppressed in the example by using the -q switch.

This command would not delete any old local files. You would have to wipe out the local directory first, which obviously would require retransmitting all files and would cause the web server to have invalid content for a period of time. This is why I urge you to use rsync if at all possible for this type of data transfer.

## 7.10.2  Simple Example: Transferring System Configuration

Let's say, for example, that for some reason you wanted to synchronize some of your system's configuration files over HTTP. You could pull these files to the client with this script:

```
#!/bin/bash

mkdir -p /etc/new_files
cd /etc/new_files

for file in hosts resolv.conf nsswitch.conf ; do
   if lftpget "http://server.mydomain.com/$file" ; then
      if [ -s "$file" ] ; then
         cat "$file" > "/etc/$file"
      fi
   fi
done

rm -rf /etc/new_files
```

First it should be noted that all files are transferred into a safe temporary directory (under /etc/) that cannot be accessed (read: exploited) by ordinary users. This temporary directory is used because you usually do not want to transfer directly on top of the destination file—the file could be wiped out and not replaced if there is a transfer error.

This script does double error checking to help avoid replacing your system configuration files with invalid copies. If the lftpget command fails, the file is not copied into its final location. Even if the lftpget command is successful, the file is only copied if it is greater than zero bytes in size. This is just an additional sanity check to make sure that a file was actually copied, and may not be necessary.

The cat command is used to write the contents of the new file over the contents of the old file. This allows the old file to retain its original permissions and ownership.

The web server would have to have these configuration files in its root web directory, which means that they would need to be regularly copied there from their actual location.

## 7.10.3 Advanced Example: Transferring System Configuration

The simple example in the last section could be extended to transfer all kinds of files. You could even use the recursive feature of wget to transfer several files at once and then move them to their final destination.

This section shows an example of a more robust system configuration method that will work well over HTTP. Before considering this method in your environment, you should read about the security implications in section 7.10.3.3 later in this chapter.

This system can transfer any arbitrary file on the server to any location on each client. You can specify the proper permissions and ownership for each file. It is fairly efficient and would work through just about any firewall or transparent proxy server. It could also be expanded to support symbolic links, device files, and other special files.

One other hidden advantage is that you can tell people that you have created an "automated system administration system that uses XML over HTTP to automatically configure client systems anywhere in the world." It will sound really impressive to management and other nontechnical types.

You actually could use real XML for this entire system if you so desired. Perl has the Net:HTTP and Net:HTTPS modules that you could use to manually perform the HTTP requests. Perl also has a large number of XML parsers that you could use to pull information from the manifest file to decide which files to transfer from the server.

### 7.10.3.1  Setting Up the Server

This is a Perl program that can be run regularly on your server to generate the manifest file for the clients to access when they are ready. It places the manifest file (manifest.html) and all other referenced files into the directory specified in $WebRoot. Your clients need to be able to access this directory through your web server.

This script is written to use the md5sum command to compute checksums. If all of your systems do not have that command, you could use the sum command with little modification to the scripts. Be aware that the sum command does not work the same on all UNIX variants, which is why I prefer to use md5sum whenever possible (the md5 algorithm is standardized).

Here is the Perl program. You should only need to change the $WebRoot and @Files variables. The permissions and ownership are taken from the actual source files. The files will be placed into the same location on the client systems as their original location on the server system.

```perl
#!/usr/bin/perl -w
use strict;
use File::Copy;

my $WebRoot = "/var/www/html/sysconfig";
my @Files = (
    "/etc/hosts",
    "/etc/ssh/sshd_config",
    "/etc/resolv.conf"
    );
```

```perl
# First, erase the manifest file
# (so clients cannot update during this build process)
unlink "$WebRoot/manifest.html";

# Create new manifest file (with temporary name)
open (MANIFEST, ">$WebRoot/manifest.new.html") or
    die "Could not create $WebRoot/manifest.new.html: $!\n";

my $ret = 0;
foreach my $file (@Files) {
    # Get information on the file
    my ($mode, $uid, $gid, $size, $checksum);
    unless (
        (undef, undef, $mode, undef, $uid, $gid, undef, $size) =
        stat $file) {
        # There was an error, skip this file
        print STDERR "WARNING: Could not stat $file: $!\n";
        $ret++;
        next;
    }

    # Isolate permissions from mode and convert to octal string
    $mode = sprintf "%04o", $mode & 07777;

    # Turn UID and GID into user/group names
    $uid = getpwuid($uid);
    $gid = getgrgid($gid);

    # Get a checksum for the file
    $checksum = `md5sum "$file"`;
    chomp($checksum);
    # Strip off everything after the first whitespace
    $checksum =~ s/\s+.*$//;

    # Now, copy the file
    unless (copy "$file", "$WebRoot") {
        print STDERR "Could not copy $file to $WebRoot: $!\n";
        $ret++;
        next;
    }

    # Remove the path from the file
    my $basename = $file;
    $basename =~ s/^.*\///;
```

```
    # Make sure it is publicly readable
    chmod 0644, "$WebRoot/$basename";

    # Okay, create the manifest entry
    print MANIFEST "<A href=\"$basename\" dest=\"$file\"\n",
        "perms=\"$mode\" user=\"$uid\" group=\"$gid\"\n",
        "size=\"$size\" md5sum=\"$checksum\"></A>\n\n";

    print "Packaged $file\n";
}

close (MANIFEST);

# Now rename the file so clients can update themselves again
move "$WebRoot/manifest.new.html", "$WebRoot/manifest.html" or
    die "Could not create $WebRoot/manifest.html: $!\n";

# Make sure it is publicly readable
chmod 0644, "$WebRoot/manifest.html";

print "Packaging Complete!\n";
exit $ret;
```

After this program is run, you should see the following files in the directory specified in $WebRoot:

- manifest.html

- hosts

- sshd_config

- resolv.conf

If you take a look at manifest.html you would see something similar to this file:

```
<A href="hosts" dest="/etc/hosts"
perms="0644" user="root" group="root"
size="154" md5sum="8ea395cc514a22f926d590e32e46c6c0"></A>

<A href="sshd_config" dest="/etc/ssh/sshd_config"
perms="0600" user="root" group="root"
size="2528" md5sum="967cbfaa9f4f48056d4ab94d476bf291"></A>
```

```
<A href="resolv.conf" dest="/etc/resolv.conf"
perms="0644" user="root" group="root"
size="83" md5sum="d7883795c4b1915e2403951ac8b7b18d"></A>
```

What we have here is a pseudo-HTML file that would not look too good in a regular browser. It does, however, link to all required files, as well as provide extra information (such as permissions and checksums) needed by our client script. We can then use wget on the client to retrieve the manifest file and all referenced files automatically.

### 7.10.3.2  The Client Retrieval Script

Each client system would need to run a script on whatever schedule you decide is appropriate. It might be hourly, daily, weekly, or on-demand only. This script retrieves manifest.html from the server and acts according to the data in that file.

There are plenty of modules for Perl that can parse HTML. In our case, since our other script makes the manifest file with a very specific format, we can just parse it manually with minimal effort. We will look for any strings of the format name="value" and store those for the current entry. When we see the string </A>, we will finish the current entry.

```perl
#!/usr/bin/perl -w
use strict;
use File::Copy;

my $URL = "http://configserver.mydomain.com/sysconfig/manifest.html";
my $TempDir = "/usr/local/var/http_update";
my $wget = 'wget -q --recursive --no-host-directories';

unless (-d $TempDir) {
    mkdir $TempDir, 0700 or die
        "Could not create temporary directory $TempDir: $!\n";
}

# Go into our temporary directory
chdir $TempDir or die
    "Could not enter temporary directory $TempDir: $!\n";

# Retrieve the manifest (and other files)
unless (system ("$wget '$URL'") == 0) {
    die "wget could not retrieve $URL\n";
}
```

```
chdir "sysconfig" or die
    "Could not enter sysconfig directory: $!\n";

# Load data from manifest file
my ($line, $entryhash, @Entries, $name, $value);
open (MANIFEST, 'manifest.html');
while ($line = <MANIFEST>) {
    chomp($line);
    # First, look for name/value pairs on this line
    while ($line =~ s/^.*?([^\s=]+)="([^"]+)"//) {
        # Found a name/value pair
        $name = $1;
        $value = $2;
        # Add to hash table
        $entryhash->{$name} = $value;
    }
    if ($line =~ /<\/A>/) {
        # Ending an entry, add what we have to the list
        push @Entries, $entryhash;
        $entryhash = undef;
    }
}
close (MANIFEST);

# Delete manifest file
unlink 'manifest.html';

# Okay, now we have all the information we need in @Entries
# We have one entry per file, and each entry is a hash reference
my $ret = 0;
foreach my $entry (@Entries) {
    my ($uid, $gid, $perms, $checksum);
    my $file = $entry->{'href'};
    print "$file: ";

    # First, make sure the file we received is valid
    unless ((-s $file) == $entry->{'size'}) {
        print "FAILED!\n";
        print STDERR "Size of $file not correct... Skipping.\n";
        $ret++;
        next;
    }
    print "[Size OK] ";
```

```perl
# Check the md5sum
$checksum = `md5sum "$file"`;
chomp($checksum);
# Strip off everything after the first whitespace
$checksum =~ s/\s+.*$//;
unless ($checksum eq $entry->{'md5sum'}) {
    print "FAILED!\n";
    print STDERR "MD5 checksum of $file failed... Skipping.\n";
    $ret++;
    next;
}
print "[MD5 OK] ";

# Next, set the permissions/ownership on the new file
unless (defined($uid = getpwnam $entry->{'user'})) {
    print "FAILED!\n";
    print STDERR "Could not lookup user $entry->{'user'}\n";
    $ret++;
    next;
}

unless (defined($gid = getgrnam $entry->{'group'})) {
    print "FAILED!\n";
    print STDERR "Could not lookup group $entry->{'group'}\n";
    $ret++;
    next;
}

unless (chown $uid, $gid, $file) {
    print "FAILED!\n";
    print STDERR "Could not set user/group to $uid:$gid: $!\n";
    $ret++;
    next;
}
$perms = $entry->{'perms'};
unless (chmod oct($perms), $file) {
    print "FAILED!\n";
    print STDERR "Could not set permissions to $perms: $!\n";
    $ret++;
    next;
}
```

```
    # Now, move the file to its new destination
    unless (move $file, $entry->{'dest'}) {
        print "FAILED!\n";
        print STDERR "Could not move $file to $entry->{'dest'}: $!\n";
        $ret++;
        next;
    }
    print "Done!\n";
}

exit $ret;
```

Hopefully there are enough comments in that script for you to get a good understanding of its operation. All it does is use wget to retrieve the data and then it parses manifest.html into an array of hashes. Each of these hashes is then processed as one file. If there are any errors, this script aborts its processing of the current file and proceeds to the next file.

One shortcoming of this script is that it fails if any of the destination directories are not found; this is because it assumes that all the files already exist and are just being replaced with new files. You could automatically create the new directories, but what permissions would you use? The best option, if you need it, is to extend this system to include directories in the manifest file.

### 7.10.3.3  *Being Aware of Security Concerns*

There are several security issues that must be considered if you were to use this system.

First of all, a knowledgeable attacker could hijack your server's IP address or DNS entry and distribute his own files to your systems. Since the client systems have no way of identifying the proper server, they install these files without concern.

Without access control on the web server, anybody can download any of the files from the server. In some cases this might not be a problem, but in other cases it might provide somebody with proprietary data or helpful information for potential attackers of your systems.

Even with access control, the data is transmitted unencrypted and could potentially be intercepted by a third party. Again, this may or may not be a concern in your situation.

If you need to use HTTP and also need encryption, security, and server validation, you could probably come up with a custom solution using HTTP over Secure Socket Layer (SSL) (a.k.a. HTTPS). Perl, for example, has the module Net::HTTPS that uses the OpenSSL package to perform encrypted data transfers. This, combined with password authentication on the server, would at least significantly reduce the chances of somebody intercepting the password or data.

### 7.10.3.3.1 *Adding Access Control*

Access control, particularly both password- and host-based, is much better than nothing. If you are inside of a private, switched, network then this can provide pretty good security.

Access control can use a password and/or the incoming IP address for validation. Assuming you are using Apache, the following can be placed in your httpd.conf:

```
<Directory />
    AuthUserFile /etc/htpasswd
    AuthType Basic
    AuthName "Configuration Access"
    require valid-user

    order deny,allow
    allow from 192.168.0.0/255.255.0.0
    allow from 127.0.0.1
    deny from all

    # Must pass both password and source-host checks
    Satisfy all
</Directory>
```

This directive would enable authentication for every file on this particular web server. The directory in the Directory tag could be changed to only reflect the directory you are using for your purposes.

Any host requesting files must first be coming from an internal IP address (192.168.X.X in this example) or from the localhost address (127.0.0.1). It must also provide a valid username and password found in the /etc/htpasswd file. To create a new htpasswd file and add the first username and password, you can use this command:

```
# htpasswd -c /etc/htpasswd sysadmin
New password:
Re-type new password:
Adding password for user sysadmin
```

You now have created an account sysadmin with your chosen password. Now any client coming from the correct IP address *and* providing the correct username and password will have access to any web content on the system.

The clients would have to expand their HTTP URL to include this username and password. Here is an example:

```
lftpget "http://sysadmin:PASSWORD@server.mydomain.com/$file"
```

Remember that you are now storing the password in plaintext on the client system, so the script should usually not be readable by anybody but root. Don't forget that the password is transmitted in (almost) clear text over the network as well.

## 7.11 RPM

You can use The Red Hat Package Manager (RPM) to distribute files to other systems. RPM is especially useful if your systems are running a Linux distribution that uses the RPM format for its installation routine and update process. Extra applications can, for example, be added directly to the system installation data. You can also install and upgrade the files using the same tools that are used to install operating system updates and other applications on the system.

When it comes to distributing data, RPMs are nice because they bundle everything into one file, or package. This package includes the package information—including description, version, and dependencies—along with the actual files and their locations and permissions. Once the package is built, you can transfer it to your systems using any number of methods. Regardless of where the package was built or how it was transferred to the system, it can be managed and installed in the same way.

RPM is discussed in more detail in section 8.5.1.

# CHAPTER 8

# Packages and Patches

IT WOULD BE A perfect world if every system you were responsible for ran the same operating system with the same versions of all software. You could have one development system and one test system. The development system is where you could play with new and updated software until everything worked just how you liked.

You could then package and deploy the software to your test system. You could use any of the options discussed in Chapter 7 to do this distribution: a network filesystem, rsync, or even CVS. You will often find that you have forgotten something in this process—something you did on your development system that you neglected to properly record. You may make mistakes in your packaging and deployment (such as leaving out some files) that can be corrected on the test system.

After you are sure everything works fine on the test system, you can deploy the software to all your other systems. Assuming you have no fires to put out, you are done and can repeat the whole process for the next change.

Believe it or not, there are people who have lives just this simple. They have a large number of identical systems and they have taken the time to automate their data distribution. These are usually people running large computing clusters (i.e., Beowulf clusters) or high-demand modular systems (such as large web sites).

For the rest of us, life is a bit more complicated. We might have different operating systems and/or different versions of the same operating system all being used at the same time. We might be responsible for systems we can't directly access—systems in another facility that are managed by other administrators, for example.

Some companies provide turnkey systems or network appliances. These are sold as a hardware and software bundle. Network appliances run some operating system that is partially or completely hidden from the user. If there are bugs or security problems with these systems, the company that sold the system needs to be able to provide updates for it with little or no effort by the end user.

A flexible and powerful upgrade and/or patch system is useful even in the simplest example (all identical systems). As the number and variety of systems increases, the benefits of this type of system increases. An upgrade/patch system is even more beneficial when you have little or no direct control over the systems that need updating.

This chapter covers patches and then packages. I will introduce commonly used existing solutions and then we will create custom methods as appropriate.

## 8.1 Packages vs. Patches

Almost every UNIX variant has some sort of package and/or patch system. The reason should be fairly obvious. An operating system vendor has the most complex update requirements of all. A typical vendor has no direct access to any systems, numerous versions are deployed at any given time, and system stability and security ranges from important to mission critical.

In my experience, the average commercial UNIX system uses both patches and packages. The patch system is usually used to update the base operating system (the kernel, system libraries, etc.). The package system, on the other hand, is primarily used to add extra utilities and applications. Some or all of the base operating system may belong to packages, but it really depends on the specific operating system. The patch and packaging systems are sometimes completely separate and independent.

The open-source operating systems (such as Linux and FreeBSD) usually have package systems as well. Their package systems, naturally, provide distribution methods for the source code as well as the binary packages themselves. In some cases (like FreeBSD's Ports system), packages are always compiled from the source when you install them. On most Linux systems, however, precompiled binaries are often used because they are quick and convenient (although the source is available separately).

Most Linux systems are installed purely from packages. This means that every file that comes with the operating system is part of a package. There are a lot of nice benefits to this sort of system that I cover later in this chapter. Consistency is obviously one big advantage. Everything from the system's kernel to interactive shells to web browsers are (or at least should be) managed by one unified packaging system.

Any system that does not have a patch system typically uses its package management system for any system updates. If there is a bug in the bash shell, for example, a new complete package for the bash shell is released. That package can be used to install bash on a system that has never had it installed before. The very same package can also be used to upgrade a system with an older version of the bash package already installed. Having one package that can be used for both upgrades and new installs is very useful in most circumstances.

One obvious disadvantage of this system is its inefficiency. If there is only one problem with one file in a package, the entire package still needs to be rereleased and transferred to each system, and the old package needs to be replaced with the new one. In reality, however, network bandwidth and processor usage are not at a premium on most systems. This is especially true if it is updated during non-peak use periods (i.e., during the night).

A patch system can usually distribute only the changes that need to be made to existing files (and any new files, if need be). Patch systems usually group changes to one or more files into a single patch file. Each patch file fixes one particular bug or adds one particular enhancement. Although this is clearly more efficient, patch systems can be more complex than a packaging system. Although you can log when a patch is installed, it is difficult (if not impossible) to verify that the patch has actually been installed properly. This is because other patches may be installed later that make other changes to the same files. This is also the reason why patches must usually be installed in a certain order. You usually can't skip a few patches and then successfully install a new patch.

Perhaps the biggest problem with patches is that it is often difficult, if not impossible, to remove a patch from your system. It can also be difficult to determine what changes the patch made to your system. With a package management system (like RPM), you can simply remove the newer package and reinstall the older one. You can also quickly determine which file(s) are part of either version of the package.

---

 **NOTE**    There have been some recent attempts to build a patching system on top of packaging systems. This type of system would combine the efficiency of a patching system with the verification abilities of a packaging system. I don't know of any systems of this type that are in common use quite yet, but I think it is a very good idea and could become very useful if implemented properly.

---

## 8.2 What Should I Use?

Like all of the topics covered in this book, there is no one solution that is best for everybody. You will, in most cases, need to use whatever system is provided by your operating system vendor to apply updates to the operating system itself. If all of your systems run the same operating system and the operating system updates come in packages, then that packaging system might very well be your best choice for all of your packaging needs.

If you have several UNIX variants in your network, you will probably be forced to use several different systems to apply operating system updates. In this case, however, you should probably decide on a single system to be used for your other software installation needs. Hopefully at least one of the operating systems on your network already uses a packaging system for its operating system updates that can also work on your other systems. It usually cannot be used for operating system updates on the other systems, but it will at least allow you to install additional software on all of your systems with a consistent packaging system.

There are two very popular packaging systems that can be installed and used on a wide variety of UNIX systems: the Red Hat Package Manager (RPM) and the Debian (deb) package formats. These package formats were originally created for use on Linux systems, but it is very common for large sites with mixed UNIX variants to install and use one of these packaging systems on all of their systems. Although their names may appear to tie them to one specific Linux distribution, they both compile and operate on all Linux systems and many different UNIX variants. RPM, in particular, has a huge user base and plenty of online support.

You may not need to use packages at all. You already have to use each operating systems' unique method for installing operating system patches. Many of the techniques in Chapter 7 can be used to distribute additional applications to your various systems. If you have direct access and direct control to all of the systems, that may be your best option. If, however, you have a large number of systems (regardless of their types), you should definitely consider using a packaging system to distribute all of your applications.

## 8.3 How to Begin

Unfortunately, most people are not in a position to start everything from scratch. These people have systems that may have some patches installed and some patches that need to be installed. In addition, they may have some software that was installed as packages and other software that was done manually. Consequently, software may be in special directories or even mixed in with the system binaries.

One good approach is to gradually replace existing systems with new ones. If you do this one system at a time, you can avoid any significant additional hardware investment. Simply replace one system, and then use that hardware for the next new system. Each of these new systems should be installed from scratch using your new automation system. They should be configured automatically. Extra software and patches should be installed using the methods in this chapter and in Chapter 7.

One advantage of a gradual approach is that you tend to learn everything each system does. If you are entering a new environment, this can be overwhelming. Replacing the system forces you to analyze the system closely. If you miss something, the users are sure to let you know, and you still have the old system around to use as a guide. You obviously want to try to avoid breaking things—especially when the system is mission critical—but it is one way to get the job done.

As you migrate systems, you should find out if each service provided is still necessary. If it is, you should perform a security audit on that service. You should also scrutinize each program that has been added to the existing system. Do you still need it? Does it present any security risks? Does it need to be upgraded or changed in some other way?

Some systems you are already using may be very difficult to replace. If this is the case, you need to migrate the system without starting over. Start doing things the new way as soon as possible. When you install or upgrade software, don't follow the old bad practices. Some things might take a while to migrate, but the system(s) should eventually come around.

## 8.4 Updating Systems with Patches

Almost all modern operating systems have some sort of update facility. In some cases, the vendor releases new versions of certain packages as necessary. In other cases, the vendor releases patch files that may or may not be related to the package management system (if there is one).

These update methods are, unfortunately, usually completely different among the UNIX variants and even among Linux distributions. I'll risk being wrong and make a guess that Sun's Solaris is the most common UNIX operating system in use today with a patching system. Because of this assumption, I will use this system as an example in this section.

It is important to mention that there are two types of "patch files." One type is usually generated by the diff program and specifies changes in one or more files. These patch files can later be applied with the patch command. The other type of patch files, and the type I discuss in this section, are archive files (such as tar files) that contain metadata, scripts, new files, and so on. These tar files may include regular patch files as well.

### 8.4.1 Understanding and Applying Solaris Patches

Sun Microsystems releases updates to its Solaris operating system using patches. Each patch contains updates to one or more packages. Each patch may require other patches, which is where the complications begin. If you download just one patch from Sun's support site (http://sunsolve.sun.com), it is likely that you will also need to download another patch that is required by the first. This can go on for a while and can be very frustrating. For this reason, Sun also releases patch bundles from time to time that include groups of patches that should be installed on all systems. This is fine for many people, but if you have a large number of systems and want to be able to install new patches quickly, you need a better system.

Anybody who has worked with Solaris patches knows that applying patches can take quite some time. Patch bundles may take several hours per system and manually following dependencies can take even longer. This reason alone makes the Solaris patch system a good candidate for automation. In this section, I present a system to partially automate the patch application process.

This is not a complete patch automation system, but it can serve as a good starting point. Sun even has its own patch management software (Patch Pro) that may take care of everything for you. If you have specific needs or are using other patching systems, a custom solution based on this example would be nice to have.

### 8.4.1.1 Background Information

Here is a brief summary of the Solaris patch system for readers who may not be familiar with the specifics.

Every patch has a unique number, such as 109326-09. You usually download the patch in a zip file such as 109326-09.zip. This can be unzipped using the unzip command, which creates a 109326-09 directory. This directory contains one directory for each package this patch modifies (such as SUNWhea). In each of these directories is a file called pkginfo that contains information related to that particular portion of the patch.

Each patch may require one or more other patches. This information can be found in the following line in the pkginfo file:

```
SUNW_REQUIRES=108528-04 108979-09 109877-02 109883-02
```

You install a patch using the patchadd command and you specify the directory of an unzipped patch file as its argument. A list of currently installed patches can be obtained by running patchadd -p, as shown here:

```
# patchadd -p

Patch: 109087-01 Obsoletes: Requires: Incompatibles: Packages: JSat8xw
Patch: 111232-01 Obsoletes: Requires: Incompatibles: Packages: SUNWcsu
Patch: 111234-01 Obsoletes: Requires: Incompatibles: Packages: SUNWcsu
Patch: 111111-01 Obsoletes: Requires: Incompatibles: Packages: SUNWesu

...
```

The number following the hyphen in a patch ID is its "release." If a patch requires patch 109087-01, then 109087-02 is also adequate, since it is simply a newer release of the same patch.

### 8.4.1.2 The Solaris Patch Files

The scripts designed in this section assume a certain directory structure already exists. You need to manually create and organize this directory. Under the base directory, you need to create one directory for each version of the operating system (as reported by uname -r). Within each directory, place every patch released for that version of the operating system. Make sure these patches have been extracted and that you have removed the original zip files.

```
solaris_patches/
|-- 5.7/
|    |-- 108935-03/
|    `-- 108985-04/
|-- 5.8/
|    |-- 103735-03/
|    `-- 108735-01/
`-- 5.9/
     `-- 103725-02/
```

Obviously, this initial setup could take a good amount of effort. After that, manually adding new patches should be relatively easy. There are certainly some options for automating this part of the process, but going into them would be more involved than is appropriate for this example. However, there is a small Perl script called get_patches that you can use to retrieve the actual patches (http://www.ohrberg.org/getpatches.html).

This directory of system patches is a perfect candidate to be shared using a network filesystem. It is not critical for system operation, it contains a large amount of data, and each patch is only applied once per system, so the data is rarely accessed.

This example assumes all of your Solaris systems are of a compatible architecture (i.e., either sparc or x86). It would require another level in the directory structure, as well as changes to the script, to support multiple architectures.

### 8.4.1.3  Designing an Automatic Patching Script

In this section, we will create one script to automate patch installation. This script can be run manually as we need it or automatically from cron. It starts by retrieving the list of currently installed patches. The script then determines which patches have not been applied and displays this information. If the --apply command-line option is specified, the script applies any needed patches, following dependencies as necessary. In either case, the exit value is the number of patches that still need to be installed.

The script has to store (internally) several lists of patches: those that are installed, those that are available, and those that have dependencies. The function StoreEntry takes two parameters: a reference (pointer) to a hash table and a patch ID (such as 109087-01). This function splits the ID into the patch (109087) and the release (01). It adds a node named 109087 to the hash table and stores the release in that node. If the node already exists and the release of the new entry is greater than the existing entry, the higher release is stored. This allows us to look up any patch by its name and find the newest release.

### 8.4.1.4 The Automatic Patching Script

In order to better explain the script, I display it here in several sections. These sections should be combined, in the given order, to form a single Perl program, named something like autopatch.pl. Here is the beginning of the script:

---

 **NOTE** You can find the code samples for this chapter in the Downloads section of the Apress web site (http://www.apress.com).

---

```perl
#!/usr/bin/perl -w
use strict;

my $PatchDir = "/mnt/patches";

# Determine the current Solaris release
my $Release = `uname -r`;
chomp($Release);

my (%Installed, %Available);
```

This portion of the code is fairly simple. The base directory containing patches is stored in the $PatchDir variable. The uname command is used to determine the release level of the operating system. Two hashes are also defined: one to hold the list of installed patches (%Installed) and one to host the list of available patches (%Available).

The next portion of code is the function StoreEntry:

```perl
sub StoreEntry ($$) {
    my ($hashref, $id) = @_;
    my $patch = $id;
    my $release = $id;
    $patch =~ s/-\d+$//;
    $release =~ s/^\d+-//;
    if ($hashref->{$patch}) {
        # Already exists... compare releases
```

```
        if ($release > $hashref->{$patch}) {
            $hashref->{$patch} = $release;
        }
    } else {
        # Doesn't exist yet
        $hashref->{$patch} = $release;
    }
}
```

As described in the design section, this function will first split the patch ID into the patch name and patch release (using the hyphen as the separator). It will then add the patch to the hash if it doesn't exist. If it does exist, and the new release is newer than the existing release, the release will be updated.

Here is the first portion of the InstallPatch function. It takes one parameter—the name of the patch. It then re-creates the patch ID by looking up the release in the %Available hash. It also defines $PatchLocation, which contains the base directory of the patch. This function is a little odd (for a Perl program) because it returns 0 on success (meaning no packages remaining) and 1 on failure (meaning one package remaining).

```perl
sub InstallPatch {
    my ($patch) = @_;
    my $id = "$patch-$Available{$patch}";
    my $PatchLocation = "$PatchDir/$Release/$id";
    print " Installing $id...\n";
```

Next, the function needs to check for any dependencies the patch may require. It has to look through each package directory contained within the patch directory for all pkginfo files. It has to look through each of those files for any dependencies.

```perl
    # Check for dependencies
    my %deps;
    unless (opendir(PATCHDIR, $PatchLocation)) {
        print STDERR " Could not open $PatchLocation: $!\n";
        return 1;
    }
    while (my $pkg = readdir(PATCHDIR)) {
        next if ($pkg =~ /^\./);
        next unless (-d "$PatchLocation/$pkg");
        unless (open(PKGINFO, "$PatchLocation/$pkg/pkginfo")) {
            print STDERR
                " Could not open $PatchLocation/$pkg/pkginfo: $!\n";
            return 1;
        }
```

```
        while (my $line = <PKGINFO>) {
            if ($line =~ s/^SUNW_REQUIRES\s*=\s*//) {
                chomp($line);
                if ($line) {
                    # Yes, there are dependencies after the = sign
                    foreach (split /\s+/, $line) {
                        StoreEntry(\%deps, $_);
                    }
                }
            }
        }
        close(PKGINFO);
    }
    closedir(PATCHDIR);
```

Any line that begins with SUNW_REQUIRES= and contains text after the equal sign is considered a dependency list. Everything after the equal sign is split on whitespace into tokens. Each token is considered one required patch.

Now that the dependency list has been generated and stored in the local hash %deps, the dependencies need to be checked and followed:

```
# See if we have these dependencies
foreach my $dep (keys %deps) {
    if ($Installed{$dep} and ($Installed{$dep} >= $deps{$dep})) {
        # Patch already installed... good!
    } elsif ($Available{$dep} and
        ($Available{$dep} >= $deps{$dep})) {
        # Patch available... install
        print " Installing Dependency: $dep-$Available{$dep}\n";
        unless (InstallPatch($dep) == 0) {
            # Delete failed patch from available list
            delete $Available{$dep};
            return 1;
        }
    } else {
        # Patch not available...
        print STDERR " Dependency $dep not found\n";
        return 1;
    }
}
```

Assuming all required patches were already satisfied or installed successfully, the function finally installs the new patch:

```perl
    if (system("patchadd $PatchLocation") == 0) {
       print "   Patch $id Installed!\n";
       StoreEntry(\%Installed, "$id");
       return 0;
    } else {
       print STDERR "   Patch $id FAILED!\n";
       return 1;
    }
}
```

That is the end of the InstallPatch function. The script continues with the following main code to check for the --apply argument:

```perl
# Apply is true if first arg is --apply
my $Apply = ($ARGV[0] and ($ARGV[0] eq '--apply'));
```

The script must now retrieve the list of currently installed patches and store that list in %Installed. This is done by running patchadd -p and looking for lines beginning with Patch:.

The actual patch ID is marked within the regular expression with parentheses and is then stored as $1.

```perl
# Get list of installed patches
foreach my $line (`patchadd -p`) {
if ($line =~ /^Patch:\s+([\d-]+)/) {
StoreEntry(\%Installed, $1);
   }
}
```

Now, the script needs a list of all available patches for this operating system release. It only considers directories that do not begin with a period (because those would be hidden directories such as . and ..).

```perl
# Get list of available patches
opendir(DIR, "$PatchDir/$Release") or
   die "Could not open directory: $PatchDir/$Release: $!\n";
while (my $entry = readdir(DIR)) {
   next if ($entry =~ /^\./);
   next unless (-d "$PatchDir/$Release/$entry");
   StoreEntry(\%Available, $entry);
}
closedir(DIR);
```

Now, the script reports and possibly installs any new patches. This happens for completely new patches or newer releases of existing patches. The patches are installed and the results are tallied. The exit code is the number of patches remaining to be installed. An exit code of 0 means all patches are installed at this time.

```perl
# Determine which patches need to be installed
my $ret = 0;
foreach my $patch (keys %Available) {
    # Skip if this patch has already failed
    next unless defined($Available{$patch});
    unless ($Installed{$patch} and
        ($Installed{$patch} >= $Available{$patch})) {
        print "Need to install: $patch-$Available{$patch}\n";
        if ($Apply) {
            $ret += InstallPatch($patch);
        } else {
            $ret++;
        }
    }
}
exit $ret;
```

Whether you run this script manually or automatically, you should check the exit code. A code of 0 means no patches need to be applied. Any other exit code means patches need to be applied. You either need to use the --apply switch or, if you did, you need to examine the output for errors in the patching process. For cron, you could save the output to a file and email the file to yourself if the exit code is non-zero. Here is an example script that could execute this script from cron:

```bash
#!/bin/bash

FILE="/root/tmp/autopatch.out"

if ! /usr/local/sbin/autopatch --apply >$FILE 2>&1 ; then
    mail -s "AutoPatch Failures ($? Failed)" root <$FILE
fi

rm -f $FILE
```

Note that the temporary file is created in a temporary directory under root's home directory. Assuming this directory is only writable by root, users cannot exploit any race conditions in this script.

## 8.4.2 Custom Patches

If your network largely consists of a single operating system that provides a native patching system, you should probably try to use that patching system for all of your patching needs. Information that tells you how to create your own patches with that system may be available. There might even be a way to get that patching system to work on other operating systems.

If you are looking for a patching system that will work across a variety of systems, I'm afraid you are out of luck. There just aren't any generic patching systems out there (well, at least not any that I can find). A nice, powerful, open-source, and portable patching system would be something nice to have available in the system administration toolbox. If I wasn't so partial to packaging systems, I might even write such a system myself.

Well, writing such a system is not what I plan to do in this chapter. I will provide a simple example that could be pretty useful and could even be expanded into something very useful. It will not support verification or even patch reversal, but it will be simple and efficient. It will also be easy to create patches for this system. Most patch systems are pretty useless if it is so difficult to create patches that the whole system is bypassed.

### 8.4.2.1 The Patch Design

I want this system to be more powerful than the patch command, because I want to be able to group several related changes into one single "patch file." I also want it to be simple to create and install these patches—much simpler than the more sophisticated patching systems that come with many operating systems (if I wanted a complex patching system I would just use one of those other systems).

Each patch will be a single file with an extension mypatch. The file is really just a simple tar file with an unusual extension. All patch files will be given a symbolic name that identifies the patch contained within. They will all be placed in one directory, such as /usr/local/patches/.

Each tar file should contain the following executable files. They will usually be shell scripts, but they could also be Perl or even compiled programs. There may be (and usually will be) other files in the archive. These files can be referenced by any of the required scripts.

check: This script determines if the patch should be installed on this system. This script can check things such as the operating system, its version, the presence of certain installed software, and so on. This script allows all of your patches to be stored in one directory, yet only the appropriate patches are installed on each system.

**apply:** This script is executed to actually install the patch. It also can try to apply any other required patches before it installs the current patch. When installing the current patch, other files in the patch file might be copied onto the system. Patch files (the ones created with diff) might be applied to the system (using patch). Permissions may be changed. In fact, any shell commands could be executed by this script as necessary to apply the patch.

**verify:** This script will verify that the patch is properly installed on this system. Although this script could perform checksums on the installed files, in this example it will simply verify that the files exist.

**remove:** This script will remove the patch.

Each patch could also have a desc to contain a patch description for informational and management purposes. A command, called mypatch, will be created to install (and list installed) patches. This command will keep data in a directory such as /var/lib/mypatch/. The data files contained within this directory will be as follows:

**installed:** This is the list of patches that have been installed on this system.

**not_needed:** This is a list of patches that have already said they do not need to be applied to this system. This significantly increases performance because the check script in each patch will only need to be run once per system.

### 8.4.2.2  Example Patch

First I will start with an example patch file. This patch will install version 2 of the bash shell on a Linux (x86 processor) or Solaris (Sparc processor) system. This patch will not remove any current shells, but it could do so in its apply script if necessary. This example patch will only include a few important files so the patch is not too complex. You could include many other man pages with this patch to provide a complete installation of the shell.

Here is a list of files we want installed on each system:

- /bin/bash2

- /usr/share/man/man1/bash2.1.gz (or /usr/man/man1/bash2.1.gz)

- /usr/share/info/bash2.info.gz (or /usr/info/bash2.info.gz)

The info and man pages have two possible locations because some (usually older) Linux distributions still use /usr/man/ and /usr/info/ for these types of files. This is one benefit of patches as opposed to packages. Most packaging systems have fixed file locations so that you would have to create separate packages for every type of system. With a patch system, however, the files can be dynamically placed wherever appropriate for the current system. This is why I can create one patch for multiple architectures and operating systems. Ideally the patch would contain a binary for each type of system on your network.

Although you could build scripts to automate the patch creation process, for the purposes of this example, I am going to manually create the patch file. This only involves placing some files in a directory and using the `tar` command to create the patch file.

So, first I create an empty directory and the required files. Here's the patch's description (place in the `desc` file):

```
Installs version 2 of the <application>bash</application> shell on the following
systems:
   Linux: x86
   Solaris: sparc
```

Well, that was easy, now I'll write the `check` script. This check does not have to check to see if the patch has already been applied, because the patch system itself maintains this information. This script only checks to see if this patch *should* be applied on this system. So, for this patch, I will only return true if the system is of the appropriate architecture and is running a supported operating system.

For a patch that implemented security fixes, this script should also check to see if the system is vulnerable or not. You might, for example, have a security fix for the wu-ftpd FTP server. If the system is not running an FTP server, the patch does not need to be applied at all. The following `check` script returns an exit code of 0 if the patch should be applied on this system.

```bash
#!/bin/bash

case `uname -s` in
   Linux)
      case `uname -m` in
         i?86)
            exit 0
            ;;
         *)
            exit 1
            ;;
      esac
      ;;
   Solaris)
```

```
            case `uname -m` in
               sparc)
                  exit 0
                  ;;
               *)
                  exit 1
                  ;;
            esac
            ;;
      *)
         exit 1
         ;;
esac
```

This script first checks for an appropriate operating system (uname -s) and then checks for an appropriate architecture (uname -m). On Linux systems, an architecture of i?86 is accepted, which would match i386, i586, and so on. In this example, it is assumed that the Linux bash binary is compiled for the i386 and will run on any later processors. Although this practice is fairly typical, you should be able to get better performance with a binary compiled for each specific architecture. In this case you could have the apply script (shown next) choose among several binaries for Linux.

The apply script installs the patch on a system. It assumes that all of the patch's files are in the current directory. This script simply copies files to the appropriate locations and sets their permissions. It uses the install_file command, which will be defined before the script runs (see the next section). It also adds this shell to the official shells listing in /etc/shells. As you can see, you could pretty much do whatever you wanted to within this script—which makes complex patches easy to make. Here is the apply script:

```
#!/bin/bash

# Exit immediately on an error
set -e

# Install appropriate executable
install_file bash2.`uname -s` /bin/bash2 0755

# Install the man page
if [ -d "/usr/share/man" ] ; then
    install_file bash2.1.gz /usr/share/man/man1/bash2.1.gz 0644
```

```
else
    install_file bash2.1.gz /usr/man/man1/bash2.1.gz 0644
fi


# Install the info page
if [ -d "/usr/share/info" ] ; then
    install_file bash2.info.gz /usr/share/info/bash2.info.gz 0644
else
    install_file bash2.info.gz /usr/info/bash2.info.gz 0644
fi


# Add an entry to /etc/shells...
if ! grep -q '^/bin/bash2$' /etc/shells ; then
    echo "/bin/bash2" >> /etc/shells
fi


exit 0
```

The set -e command causes the script to immediately exit on any error. This allows me to not check every command for an error, which makes the script much cleaner. I also need to create a simple patch removal script, called remove:

```
#!/bin/bash


rm -f /bin/bash2
rm -f /usr/share/man/man1/bash2.1.gz
rm -f /usr/man/man1/bash2.1.gz
rm -f /usr/share/info/bash2.info.gz
rm -f /usr/info/bash2.info.gz


# Remove entry from /etc/shells
grep -v '^/bin/bash2$' /etc/shells > /etc/shells.new && {
    mv /etc/shells.new /etc/shells
    chmod a+r /etc/shells
}


exit 0
```

Finally, we have a very simple verification script, named verify. This script could do a variety of verification tasks, such as file checksums and even operational tests. In our example, however, we will simply verify that each file is installed and has the correct permissions. We will also check the /etc/shells file for a /bin/bash2 entry. This script uses the verify_file function that will already be defined by the main patching script (described in next section):

```
#!/bin/bash

# Exit immediately on an error
set -e

# Check the executable
verify_file /bin/bash2 0755

# Check the man page
if [ -d "/usr/share/man" ] ; then
    verify_file /usr/share/man/man1/bash2.1.gz 0644
else
    verify_file /usr/man/man1/bash2.1.gz 0644
fi

# Install the info page
if [ -d "/usr/share/info" ] ; then
    verify_file /usr/share/info/bash2.info.gz 0644
else
    verify_file /usr/info/bash2.info.gz 0644
fi

# Check for the entry in /etc/shells...
grep -q '^/bin/bash2$' /etc/shells
```

Now that we have all of the required control files, we just have to place the patch payload into the directory. In our case, we need to add the following files:

- bash2.Linux (the bash binary as compiled on a Linux system)

- bash2.Solaris (the bash binary as compiled on a Solaris system)

- bash2.1.gz (the bash man page)

- bash2.info.gz (the bash info page)

Once you have all of the files in the directory, you can create the patch. Change into that directory and run the following:

```
% tar -cf ../bash-2.05a.mypatch *
```

This patch file should be tested and then moved to a common directory, such as /usr/local/patches/. Since each patch can determine if it needs to be installed on each system, all patches for all systems can be placed in the same directory. It is important to note that all patches must remain in this directory until they are no longer needed *and* they are no longer installed on any systems.

As I mentioned earlier, an automated process for building patches could be concocted. But it would be difficult for this patch because it contains binaries from multiple systems. Even if you have to manually create the patch, it is a lot less work than manually implementing the changes on every single machine.

### 8.4.2.3  Using the Custom Patch System

The mypatch script handles all the patching tasks in this custom patch system. It does not handle dependencies at all. Instead, each patch can handle its own dependencies. Since the mypatch command can be called from the apply script, that script should remove any conflicting patches from the system before installing itself. It should also install any dependencies.

To see what patches (in the main patch directory) need to be applied to a system, you can run:

```
% mypatch --check
wu-ftpd-fix: already installed
bash-2.05a: need to install
Installs version 2 of the bash shell on the following systems:
    Linux: x86
    Solaris: sparc
```

You could also specify one or more patch files and/or directories on the command line to use other directories. If you want to install the patches, you can just run this command:

```
# mypatch --apply
Installing bash-2.05a...
Installs version 2 of the bash shell on the following systems:
    Linux: x86
    Solaris: sparc
SUCCESS!
```

You can even remove a patch:

```
# mypatch --remove bash-2.05a
Removing bash-2.05a... Removed.
```

To see what patches are installed, use the --list option:

```
% mypatch --list
bash-2.05a
wu-ftp-fix
```

You can verify that all patches are installed correctly:

```
% mypatch --verify
Verifying bash-2.05a... FAIL!
Verifying wu-ftp-fix... Good.
```

If there are failures, you can fix them by using both the `fix` and `verify` options. This causes any failed patches to be installed again.

```
# mypatch --verify --fix
Verifying bash-2.05a... FAIL!
Installing bash-2.05a...
Installs version 2 of the bash shell on the following systems:
    Linux: x86
    Solaris: sparc
SUCCESS!
Verifying wu-ftp-fix... Good.
```

Since systems change over time, the cache of patches that don't need to be installed on a system might become outdated and incorrect. This cache should be rebuilt during off-peak hours. In fact, most of the update process should be done automatically at night by the cron daemon. Here is an example wrapper script that will take care of any patching needed for a system:

```
mypatch --recheck --apply >/dev/null || {
    echo "There were errors applying patches" >&2
}
mypatch --verify --fix >/dev/null || {
    echo "There were errors verifying and fixing patches" >&2
}
```

### 8.4.2.4  *The mypatch Script*

The mypatch script does all of the dirty work for this process. It is fairly lengthy, but its operation shouldn't be too hard to understand. I will present the script in several portions which can be combined to form the entire script. First, I'll define a couple functions that can be used by the apply and verify scripts:

```
install_file() {
    cp -f $1 $2 || return 1
    chmod $3 $2 || return 1
}
verify_file() {
    [ -f "$1" ] || return 1
    perm=`stat $1 | sed -n 's/^Access: (\([0123456789]*\)\/.*$/\1/p'`
    [ "$2" = "$perm" ]
}
```

The install_file command takes the source filename, the destination filename, and the permissions as arguments. The verify_file command takes only the destination filename (because the file has already been copied) and the expected permissions. It uses the stat command to retrieve information about the file and then the sed command to isolate the file's permissions. These functions should be placed somewhere in the mypatch script. This script should begin with the following:

```
#!/bin/bash

PATCH_DIR="/usr/local/patches"
DATA_DIR="/var/lib/mypatch"

usage() {
    echo "Usage: $0 [--recheck] --apply|--check [file|dir ...]" >&2
    echo "  --recheck: re-check every patch (rebuild cache)" >&2
    echo "  --apply: Apply any applicable patches" >&2
    echo "  --check: Check to see if a patch should be installed" >&2
    echo "Query: [--fix] --list|--verify" >&2
    echo "  --fix: fix any verification problems by re-applying" >&2
    echo "  --list: list the currently installed patches" >&2
    echo "  --verify: verify that installed patches are okay" >&2
    echo "Remove: --remove pkgname" >&2
    exit 1
}

[ "$1" = "--help" ] && usage
mkdir -p "$DATA_DIR/tmp"
```

You shouldn't see anything new so far in this script. The usage function displays the program's usage and exits. Next comes the argument processing:

```
recheck=''; check=''; apply=''; verify=''; list=''; fix=''; remove=''
while [ -n "$1" ] ; do
    case $1 in
        --fix)
            fix=1
            ;;
        --recheck)
            recheck=1
            ;;
        --check)
            check=1
            ;;
        --apply)
            apply=1
            ;;
        --verify)
            verify=1
            ;;
        --list)
            list=1
            ;;
        --remove)
            remove=1
            ;;
        --*)
            echo "Unknown option: $1" >&2
            usage
            ;;
        *)
            break
            ;;
    esac
    shift
done
```

All of the functions should follow the argument processing section, but I'm going to skip to the main portion of the script because it comes next logically. Remember that the functions need to be defined before this section appears in the file:

```
ret=0
if [ -n "$remove" ] ; then
    # We need to remove a package
    remove_patch $1
    ret="$?"
fi
if [ -n "$list" -o -n "$verify" ] ; then
    # We need to loop through all installed patches
    for patch in `cat $DATA_DIR/installed` ; do
        if [ -n "$list" ] ; then
            echo $patch
        else
            verify_patch $patch
            ret="$[$ret+$?]"
        fi
    done
fi
if [ -n "$check" -o -n "$apply" ] ; then
    list="$*"
    [ -z "$list" ] && {
        list=$PATCH_DIR
    }
    for arg in $list ; do
        if [ -d "$arg" ] ; then
            for file in $arg/* ; do
                process_file $file
                ret="$[$ret+$?]"
            done
        elif [ -f "$arg" ] ; then
            process_file $arg
            ret="$[$ret+$?]"
        else
            echo "Not a valid file or directory: $arg"
        fi
    done
fi
exit $ret
```

This is the main code that actually does what has been requested in the command-line arguments. The only strange thing in here is the return variable, ret. This variable is incremented by one (using bash's mathematical operations) for each error. This variable is ultimately used as the exit code of the program.

So, back to the functions used by the main section of this script. Probably the most important is the install_patch function. Here it is:

```
install_patch() {
    name="$(basename $1 .mypatch)"
    echo "Installing $name..."
    tar -xOf $1 desc
    cd $DATA_DIR/tmp
    tar -xf $1
    chmod u+x apply
    export -f install_file
    if ./apply ; then
        rm -rf *
        echo "SUCCESS!"
        if ! grep -q "^$name$" $DATA_DIR/installed 2>/dev/null ; then
            echo "$name" >> $DATA_DIR/installed
        fi
        return 0
    else
        rm -rf *
        echo "FAILURE!"
        return 1
    fi
}
```

The tar command is called twice. The first call, with the -xOf options, cause the desc file to be displayed to the standard output (i.e., the terminal). This is a convenient way to show a patch's description to the user. The second tar command extracts all files. The apply script is then executed and its exit code is checked for a success or failure.

The basename command is used to isolate the patch's name from the filename. This command removes any directories and removes the .mypatch extension, if it is present. The export -f command is used to export the install_file so that it can be used in the apply script.

Next, we have the check_patch function, which determines if a patch needs to be applied to the current system. It uses the cached result, if possible, or it executes the check script in the patch archive.

```
check_patch() {
    name="$(basename $1 .mypatch)"
    if [ -n "$recheck" ] ; then
        grep -v "^$name$" $DATA_DIR/not_needed > \
            $DATA_DIR/not_needed.new
```

```
        mv $DATA_DIR/not_needed.new $DATA_DIR/not_needed
    else
        if grep -q "^$name$" $DATA_DIR/not_needed 2>/dev/null ; then
            return 1
        fi
    fi
    cd $DATA_DIR/tmp
    tar -xf $1 check
    chmod u+x check
    if ./check ; then
        rm -f check
        return 0
    else
        rm -f check
        echo "$name" >> $DATA_DIR/not_needed
        return 1
    fi
}
```

The process_file function is called by the main portion of the script to process each individual patch file. If the patch is not already installed, it is checked. If the check says it needs to be installed, it is installed (if the --apply switch was given).

```
process_file() {
    name="$(basename $1 .mypatch)"
    if grep -q "^$name$" $DATA_DIR/installed 2>/dev/null ; then
        [ -n "$check" ] && echo "$name: already installed"
        return 0
    fi
    if check_patch $1 ; then
        if [ -n "$check" ] ; then
echo "$name: need to install"
            tar -xOf $1 desc
            return 1
        else
            install_patch $1
            return $?
        fi
    else
        [ -n "$check" ] && echo "$name: not needed"
        return 0
    fi
}
```

The removal of a patch is done with one function:

```
remove_patch() {
    echo -n "Removing $1... "
    file="$PATCH_DIR/$1.mypatch"
    if ! grep -q "^$1$" $DATA_DIR/installed 2>/dev/null ; then
        echo "Not installed!" >&2
        return 1
    fi
    [ -r $file ] || {
        echo "Unable to find patch file!" >&2
        return 1
    }
    cd $DATA_DIR/tmp
    tar -xf $file remove
    chmod u+x remove
    if ./remove ; then
        rm -f remove
        echo "Removed."
        grep -v "^$1$" $DATA_DIR/installed > $DATA_DIR/installed.new \
            && mv $DATA_DIR/installed.new $DATA_DIR/installed
        return 0
    else
        rm -f remove
        echo "FAIL!"
        return 1
    fi
}
```

As you can see, this function simply finds the patch file for the named patch and calls the remove file in that patch file. The verify_patch is almost the same:

```
verify_patch() {
    echo -n "Verifying $1... "
    file="$PATCH_DIR/$1.mypatch"
    [ -r $file ] || {
        echo "Unable to verify!" >&2
        return 0
    }
    cd $DATA_DIR/tmp
    tar -xf $file verify
    chmod u+x verify
    export -f verify_file
```

```
   if ./verify ; then
rm -f verify
      echo "Good."
      return 0
   else
      rm -f verify
      echo "FAIL!"
      if [ -n "$fix" ] ; then
         install_patch $file
         return $?
      else
         return 1
      fi
   fi
}
```

And that's about it. With the code presented in this section, you have a complete multiplatform, yet relatively simple, patching system. Enjoy and expand!

## 8.5 Understanding and Installing Packages

Many modern operating systems have some sort of packaging system. If this is the case with your system, this package system is probably used for the initial system installation. If the initial install comes with the bash shell, for example, the actual binary (such as /bin/bash), the man page (such as /usr/man/man1/bash.1), and any other related files will belong to a bash package. The initial installation program installs the bash package instead of creating each individual file separately.

At first glance, this may appear to be a trivial difference. The advantage comes when you don't do a full install of the operating system. If you later want to add the bash application, for example, you can usually manually install the bash package directly from the installation media. This is a lot better (from an organizational standpoint) and a lot less error-prone than manually copying the appropriate files from another system.

System updates, when necessary, can come in many flavors. Your operating system vendor may release completely new versions of a package to address a problem within that package. This new package can then be upgraded with the packaging system just like the original package was installed with the packaging system. Alternatively, your vendor may use a patch system. This patch system may or may not be aware of the packaging system. So, on some operating systems, one patch could contain updates to one or more packages (and maybe a shell script to perform other changes). On other systems, the patch might directly modify files without regard to the underlying packaging system.

Packaging systems are, unfortunately, usually different between each UNIX variant and even the various Linux distributions. The packaging system on most (if not all) commercial UNIX variants will not work on any other system, because the binaries will not be compatible and the source code is not available. The best you can expect from a commercial UNIX packaging system is the ability to create your own packages, but even this process might be very difficult. The vendor probably has tools to help in the package creation process, but these tools are not always distributed to the general public (or even their customers).

The huge benefit of Linux packaging systems is full availability of the source code. This allows you to compile and run the packaging systems on other operating systems. In most cases, the source code is actually designed to compile on a variety of systems, reducing or eliminating any porting efforts on your part. With this amount of portability, along with source availability, it is not surprising that these packaging systems are commonly chosen to be used across a variety of systems. The wide availability of tools and utilities related to these packaging systems should not be surprising either.

If every system you administer runs the same operating system, you should probably use that packaging system to install additional programs. If you can't build custom packages for that packaging system, then you need to use another distribution method to add software (such as a network filesystem).

If your network uses a variety of incompatible operating systems, network filesystems are less useful. This is a perfect opportunity to use a packaging system for software distribution. You should pick the best packaging system and install that system on every machine in your network. You can use that packaging system to install your custom software and other additional applications. The Red Hat Packaging System (RPM) and the Debian Packaging System are both great choices for this situation.

## 8.5.1 Red Hat Package Manager (RPM)

The Red Hat Package Manager (or RPM) is used to install the Red Hat Linux operating system (and many other Linux distributions). You can also use it to remove, add, upgrade, and verify software after the initial installation. If all or most of the systems in your network will be running Linux, it is easy to create your own custom Linux distribution using RPM packages as described in Appendix B.

Even if your network has a mixed set of systems, you can still install the RPM program because it compiles and operates on most operating systems. Once installed, it allows you to install RPM packages on all of those systems. If the packages are not architecture dependent (such as shell scripts, configuration files, and Perl scripts), you can install the same packages everywhere. For binary programs, however, you have to build several RPMs for your different system architectures.

Fortunately, you can usually use the same SPEC file (instructions for building a package) to build binary packages on all of your systems.

This section discusses the features and basic use of the RPM program. Details on building RPM packages are presented in Appendix C. The RPM program is not completely suitable for an automation system except in very controlled environments. If all of your systems are the same, you can use the simple scripts provided in section 8.5.1.3 to fully automate software installation and updates using RPM. In more common environments, you need a wrapper program such as AutoRPM or AutoUpdate. AutoRPM is discussed in section 8.6.

### 8.5.1.1 Basic RPM Concepts

Like any package manager, RPM deals with packages, called RPMs. A package is usually in one of two forms: installed on a system or contained within a file. A file might also be a source RPM (SRPM) that contains all the information (and source code) you need to build a binary RPM.

An example filename for an RPM is apache-1.3.22-6.i386.rpm. The filename provides several pieces of valuable information:

apache: This is the name of the package. It can contain just about any characters, but I would avoid any characters with special meanings in the shell.

1.3.22: This is the version of the actual program being packaged. This value cannot contain the hyphen character.

6: This is the release of the RPM. In most cases, each time an RPM is built with the same version of the underlying software, this release is incremented. This value cannot contain the hyphen character.

i386: This is the architecture of the binaries contained within the package. There are a large number of possibilities because a wide variety of processors are in use today. Also, the architecture noarch indicates that the package does not contain any compiled binaries and can be installed on any system.

Any of the RPM query operations (rpm -q) can be performed on package files or installed packages. The default is to query an installed package (by name), but you can use the -p switch to query a package file.

A source RPM is usually named apache-1.3.22-6.src.rpm. This file contains the source code for the application being packaged, any necessary patches, and the building and packaging instructions used by RPM to build a binary RPM. This information is contained within the SPEC file for the package.

An installed package may have any number of configuration files. These files are treated much differently than normal files for upgrade and removal purposes. A normal file will overwrite any existing file when a package is upgraded, and such a file will be deleted (and not saved) when a package is removed.

Configuration files have a different set of rules. If you remove a package, any configuration files that you modified from the version included with the package (i.e., any you modified after the package was installed) are renamed with the extension .rpmsave instead of being deleted. Even more importantly, if you modify a configuration file and then upgrade to a newer version of the package, your modified configuration file usually remains unchanged. In other words, your custom configuration file will not be clobbered on the upgrade like a regular file would be. The exception to this rule is if the configuration file included with the package changed between the last version and the current version *and* you have modified that file. In this case, your file will be renamed with the extension .rpmsave, or the new file will be created with the extension .rpmnew (depending on what option the package builder used).

## 8.5.1.2 Basic Operations with RPM

If you look at the man page for rpm (or run rpm --help) you see an overwhelming number of command-line options. Fortunately, you do not need most of these for normal operations. This section attempts to show you just the basic operations that are usually done with RPM.

### 8.5.1.2.1 Installing and Removing Packages

The most basic operation you can perform with any package manager is installing a package. But, before you do so, you might want to get some basic information about that package:

```
% rpm -qip sendmail-cf-8.11.6-3.i386.rpm
Name        : sendmail-cf              Relocations: (not relocateable)
Version     : 8.11.6                   Vendor: (none)
Release     : 3                        Build Date: Mon 16 Sep 2002 09:57:04 PM EDT
Install date: (not installed)          Build Host: kaybee.org
Group       : System Environment/Daemons Source RPM: sendmail-8.11.6-3.src.rpm
Size        : 742866                   License: BSD
Summary     : The files needed to reconfigure Sendmail.
Description :
This package includes the configuration files you need to generate the sendmail.cf
file distributed with the sendmail package. You must have the sendmail-cf package
if you ever need to reconfigure and rebuild your sendmail.cf file.
```

The -q option says we want to perform a query, the -i option says we want package information, and the -p option says we are interested in a file (and not an installed RPM). It is also prudent to check for pre-install and post-install scripts unless you already know the package is safe, because these are automatically run during the installation process (unless the --noscripts switch is given during the installation process).

```
% rpm -q --scripts -p sendmail-cf-8.11.6-3.i386.rpm
```

In this case, no scripts are in this package at all. If there were any scripts, they should be examined because they will be run when the package is installed. If the scripts are doing something bad, you should think twice about installing the package (even with the --noscripts option), because the enclosed program could be just as bad or even worse. Finally, we can install the RPM:

```
# rpm -ivh sendmail-cf-8.11.6-3.i386.rpm
Preparing...                ########################################### [100%]
   1:sendmail-cf            ########################################### [100%]
```

If the package is an upgrade to a package already installed, you can use the -U option to specify that you want an upgrade (in lieu of the -i option). You can also use the -U option to install new packages because it either installs or upgrades each package as appropriate. You can erase packages using any of the following commands:

- rpm -e sendmail-cf

- rpm -e sendmail-cf-8.11.6

- rpm -e sendmail-cf-8.11.6-3

Since you can only erase packages that are already installed, the package name must refer to an installed package. An installed package can usually be referred to by its name. Only in the rare case when more than one version of the same package is installed is it necessary to also specify the version and/or release to the rpm -e command.

### 8.5.1.2.2 Query Operations

Once you have a package installed, you can do more than just erase it—you can use the RPM query command to get information about the package. Here are a few examples:

```
% rpm -q apache
apache-1.3.22-6
% rpm -ql apache
/etc/httpd
/etc/httpd/conf
/etc/httpd/conf/access.conf
/usr/sbin/httpd

...
% rpm -qc apache
/etc/httpd/conf/access.conf
/etc/httpd/conf/httpd.conf
/etc/httpd/conf/magic
/etc/httpd/conf/srm.conf
/etc/logrotate.d/apache
/etc/rc.d/init.d/httpd
/var/www/html/index.html
% rpm -qi sendmail-cf
Name        : sendmail-cf      Relocations: (not relocateable)
Version     : 8.11.6           Vendor: (none)

...
```

The first command (just -q) is used to see if a package is installed and, if so, what version. The next command (-ql) shows the files that belong to this package. The third command (-qc) shows only the configuration files for the package, which is very handy when you are trying to configure an unknown program. The fourth command shown, with the options -qi, shows package information just as was shown previously with an uninstalled package. In fact, any of these commands can be used on an uninstalled package with the addition of the -p switch.

Another operation I frequently use involves the -qa options. These options cause rpm to show a listing of all packages installed on the system. You usually want to filter this output with the grep command. Doing this is helpful because the rpm -q apache command only tells you the version of the package with the name apache. However, there may be other related packages, as shown here:

```
% rpm -qa | grep apache
apache-1.3.22-6
apacheconf-0.8.1-1
apache-devel-1.3.22-6
apache-manual-1.3.22-6
```

In fact, you can specify the -a option in lieu of a package name for all of the query commands shown previously. It tells RPM to query all installed packages. So, to see a list of every file owned by every RPM installed on your system, you could run rpm -qal.

Another very useful operation is the `rpm -qf` command. This allows you to determine which package owns a file on your system. If you use this, you might see the file /usr/sbin/rotatelogs and wonder why it is there. You can find out using RPM:

```
% rpm -qf /usr/sbin/rotatelogs
apache-1.3.22-6
```

So, you now know that the file is owned by the apache package. You would, of course, still need to figure out what the command actually does—but at least you have a good starting point.

### 8.5.1.2.3  Package Verification

RPM provides some very useful verification tools. First of all, you can verify the signature of a package (particularly useful before installation):

```
% rpm --checksig autorpm-3.0.1-1.noarch.rpm
autorpm-3.0.1-1.noarch.rpm: pgp md5 OK
```

This package passes its md5 checksum, which means it wasn't accidentally corrupted or modified after the build process. It also passes the Pretty Good Privacy (PGP) check, which means it hasn't been touched since the person with the appropriate private key signed it. However, unless you have the proper PGP or GnuPG (GNU Privacy Guard) public keys, you will not be able to verify the actual signature. The md5 checksum is still useful; you can use it to verify that an accidental change (i.e., corruption during transfer) did not occur. Here is a package signed with a private key that I do not have a matching public key for:

```
% rpm --checksig bind-utils-9.2.1-0.71.1.i386.rpm
bind-utils-9.2.1-0.71.1.i386.rpm: md5 (GPG) NOT OK (MISSING KEYS: GPG#DB42A60E)
```

Another nice feature is the ability to verify installed packages. You can run `rpm -Va` to verify all installed packages, but this can take quite a while. It is, however, not a bad idea to run this every so often (maybe a daily or weekly cron job) and store the results in CVS so that changes to the system will be logged (you could see what files an intruder modified, for example—assuming they didn't modify the RPM database). If you have packages on a read-only medium, such as a CD-ROM or a read-only network filesystem, you could use those packages to verify a system. Assuming you also run the rpm command from that medium, the attacker cannot hide changes to files owned by these packages from you. You can simply run something like this: /mnt/cdrom/rpm -V -p /mnt/cdrom/rpm/*.rpm.

You can also verify an itemized list of packages, which is much quicker than verifying all packages on your system. Here is an example:

```
% rpm -V sendmail
.......T c /etc/aliases
..5....T c /etc/mail/access
.M...... g /etc/mail/access.db
..5....T   /usr/sbin/sendmail
```

The first entry tells us that /etc/aliases is a configuration file (the c) whose mtime (modification time) is different than its installation time (the T). But, since that is the only problem, it was probably edited and saved by somebody, yet no actual changes were made.

The next entry, /etc/mail/access, shows us that somebody definitely modified that file. Its modification time is wrong and its md5 checksum is wrong (the 5), but this is also a configuration file that I remember changing, so that is fine.

The /etc/mail/access.db file is a ghost file (listed in the package, but not actually installed) that is generated from the access file. The letter M says the permissions on the file are not completely correct, which is not surprising because it was created after installation.

The final entry is one that really scares me. Fortunately, I made up that entry for this example. If you come across this entry, though, you should definitely be scared. It says that the binary /usr/sbin/sendmail has been modified. This may be because somebody installed a new version of sendmail using another method besides RPM (which is not a good idea when using RPM—they should have at least removed the RPM first). If this isn't the case, then it probably means an attacker has entered your system and has replaced this program, possibly to intercept all mail, or as a backdoor for later reentry.

A quick and fairly accurate way to check the binaries on your system for any unauthorized changes is the following:

```
% rpm -Va | egrep '/s?bin'
```

Hopefully, this command does not return any matches (or at least not any significant matches) on your system. Full information, including the meanings of the other fields, can be found in the rpm man page.

### 8.5.1.2.4 Source RPMs

A source RPM contains all the information you need to build a package, all in one convenient file. RPM provides a command-line option, --rebuild, to build binary RPMs from a source RPM:

```
# rpmbuild --rebuild sendmail-8.11.6-3.src.rpm
Installing sendmail-8.11.6-3.src.rpm
Executing(%prep): /bin/sh -e /var/tmp/rpm-tmp.99648
...
Wrote: /usr/src/redhat/RPMS/i386/sendmail-8.11.6-3.i386.rpm
Wrote: /usr/src/redhat/RPMS/i386/sendmail-doc-8.11.6-3.i386.rpm
Wrote: /usr/src/redhat/RPMS/i386/sendmail-cf-8.11.6-3.i386.rpm
...
```

First, the source RPM is installed, which means the source and any patches are installed in (usually) /usr/src/redhat/SOURCES/ and the SPEC file is installed in /usr/src/redhat/SPECS/. Next, the binary RPMs are built, and then the source files are removed. The binary RPMs are placed in /usr/src/redhat/RPMS/arch/ where arch is the build architecture of the packages.

If you want to view and/or modify the source files, you can simply install the source RPM manually by doing rpm -i sendmail-8.11.6-3.src.rpm. You can modify the source files and/or the SPEC file (/usr/src/redhat/SPECS/sendmail.spec), and then build the source and binary RPMs with the command rpmbuild -ba /usr/src/redhat/SPECS/sendmail.spec.

You will find more information on creating, modifying, and building RPMs in Appendix C. In particular, section C.1 shows you how to set up a build environment so it lets you build most RPMs as regular, non-privileged users.

### 8.5.1.3  Simple Automation

The concepts discussed in this section assume that all systems in your environment are generally the same. It is assumed that all systems were installed with any packages they needed from the base operating system. The scripts in this section only add new software to systems (presumably software that did not come with the operating system) and update any existing software. For a more powerful and robust system, you need to use a wrapper program such as AutoRPM as discussed later in section 8.6.

To use this simple update system, you must first make sure that all of the operating system's base packages are installed on all systems. So, your web servers should already have Apache installed and your mail servers should already have imap installed. You can do this manually when you install the system, or you can do it with a package bundle script as discussed next.

### 8.5.1.3.1  Package Bundles

You can use a simple script to add package bundles to a system based on its
"responsibilities." Each system is responsible for performing one or more tasks
and/or fulfilling one or more rolls. Each of these tasks and rolls are defined as a
responsibility, and each system can have any number of responsibilities.

As a start, you could create the file /etc/responsibilities that contains one
responsibility per line, and each responsibility would have a directory under
/usr/local/packages/bundles/. You could then place the line web in the
responsibilities file for your web servers and the line mail for mail servers.
Any system can have any number of these responsibilities.

### 8.5.1.3.1.1  Creating Bundles

When using package bundles, the tough part is manually creating the package
bundles under the /usr/local/packages/ directory. The only easy way to do this is
to use a staging server. On this server, you can install all the packages the responsibility and any required dependencies need. Once the packages are installed,
simply place all of those package files into the /usr/local/packages/bundles/web/
directory (for example) along with their dependencies. If all of your systems are
nearly identical, your staging server should always start from this state, which
requires you to remove any packages from the previous bundle building process. If
this is not practical, you could also use the following script to determine exactly
which packages a currently installed package needs:

```
#!/bin/bash

for installed in "$@" ; do
    for require in `rpm -q --requires "$installed"` ; do
        pkg=`rpm -q --whatprovides "$require" 2>/dev/null`
        if [[ $pkg != "no package provides "* ]] ; then
            echo "$pkg"
        fi
    done
done | sort | uniq
```

This script loops once for each package name specified on the command
line (such as apache or sendmail). The rpm -q --requires command is used to
determine the requirements for each package. For each of these dependencies,
the rpm -q --whatprovides command is used to determine which package provides
that dependency. Unfortunately, at least with the version of RPM I am using
(4.0.4), any dependencies not found are returned on stdout (not stderr) as no

package provides xxx. This is why the [[ $pkg != "no package provides "* ]]
sequence is used to ignore any entries that match that string.

Any dependencies not found are assumed not to be important and/or a
result of spaces within a single dependency listing. For example, the dependency
bash >= 2.0 is split into three tokens. The first token is provided by the bash
package and is found properly by the rpm -q --whatprovides command. The other
tokens (>=and 2.0) are not found, which is fine, because we can assume that RPM
has made sure the proper version is installed. The output of the outside loop, which
lists every package required by the packages specified on the command line, has
its duplicates removed with the | sort | uniq sequence.

If a set of base packages is definitely on every system, any of those packages
listed as a dependency could be ignored and not placed in the bundle directory.

### 8.5.1.3.1.2 *Installing Bundles*

Installing the appropriate bundles on a system is easy. This following script installs
every package from every appropriate bundle if the package is not already installed.
It also upgrades any packages as necessary.

```
#!/bin/bash

BUNDLE_DIR="/usr/local/packages/bundles"

list=''
for resp in `cat /etc/responsibilities` ; do
   if [ -d "$BUNDLE_DIR/$resp" ] ; then
      echo "Installing bundle $resp... "
      for pkg in "$BUNDLE_DIR/$resp/"*.rpm ; do
         name=`rpm -q --queryformat '%{name}' -p $pkg`
         if ! rpm -q "$name" >/dev/null ; then
            list="$list $pkg"
         fi
      done
      [ -n "$list" ] && rpm -ivh $list
      # Now, use the -F option to upgrade any packages as necessary
      rpm -Fvh "$BUNDLE_DIR/$resp/"*.rpm
      echo "Done."
   fi
done
```

Since a system-wide responsibility list might be used for more things than
package installation, a bundle directory is not required to exist for any given
responsibility. If the directory does exist, each package in the directory is processed.

The package's name is determined using the rpm -q --queryformat '%{name}' command. The --queryformat option to the query command (-q) identifies the fields to include in the output as well as the output format. The -p option tells RPM to process a package file instead of an installed package.

The package's name is then given to the rpm -q command to determine if the same package is already installed. This command normally displays the full version of the specified package, but all you care about is the exit value, so you hide the output. If the package is not installed, you add the file to the list. You must build the list first so that you can install all the packages at once. Any one package might depend on another package, but if all the packages are installed together, any dependencies are resolved by other packages being installed (well, assuming the bundle contained all necessary dependencies, as it should). The -ivh options tell RPM to install new packages (-i), with verbose output (-v) and hashmarks to show installation progress (-h).

Finally, the script uses RPM's -F option and specifies the complete list of all RPMs in the bundle. The "freshen" option tells RPM to only upgrade RPMs that are already installed. There are some situations, however, where one of the new packages depends on an upgraded version of an installed package. In this case, the new package fails because it is being installed separately from the updated packages. A second try might fix the problem, unless they depend on each other. This next solution is very similar, but it builds a complete list of packages (both new and updated) before it installs any of them. It will break if packages in the bundle are older than packages already installed. As long as you make sure this doesn't happen, this script will work flawlessly:

```
#!/bin/bash

BUNDLE_DIR="/usr/local/packages/bundles"

list=''
for resp in `cat /etc/responsibilities` ; do
    if [ -d "$BUNDLE_DIR/$resp" ] ; then
        echo "Installing bundle $resp... "
        for pkg in "$BUNDLE_DIR/$resp/"* ; do
            name=`rpm -q --queryformat '%{name}' -p $pkg`
            installed=`rpm -q "$name" >/dev/null`
            if [ $? -eq 0 ] ; then
                # Is instaled, see if it is a different version
                if [ "$installed" != "$(rpm -q -p $pkg)" ] ; then
                    # Different versions... assume an upgrade
                    list="$list $pkg"
                fi
```

```
      else
          # Not installed
          list="$list $pkg"
      fi
  done
  [ -n "$list" ] && rpm -Uvh $list
  echo "Done."
  fi
done
```

You can run either script on a regular basis to install any necessary packages. You can add new and upgraded packages to bundles as you need them. Here is what either script looks like when I run it on my mail server (with two packages needing installation):

```
# install_bundles
Installing bundle mail...
Preparing...                ########################################### [100%]
   1:sendmail               ########################################### [100%]
   2:sendmail-cf            ########################################### [100%]
Done.
```

### 8.5.1.3.2 *Performing Simple System Updates*

The hard part is over. Each system has all required packages installed. Most of them were probably installed during the system installation; others may have been installed as package bundles. If you want custom packages on every system, you can have an all bundle, or you can add the packages to the actual distribution (if you have a custom distribution).

If you have a custom distribution, the actual distribution can have updated RPMs applied to it on a regular basis. You could, for example, replace the openssh-3.0p1 packages with openssh-3.1p1 packages when necessary. Any new systems would have the newer version installed from the start. Any older systems would have to upgrade to the newer version using an upgrade script.

If you don't have a custom distribution, you probably still have updates. At the very least, your operating system vendor probably releases bug fixes and security updates. You also might want to add your own updated packages to this list of updates. All of these updates should be stored in one directory. The following script installs any updated RPMs, whether they are merged in with the distribution itself or contained in a separate directory.

```
#!/bin/bash

cd /usr/local/distributions/custom/RedHat/RPMS
# -or-
#cd /usr/local/packages/updates

rpm -Fvh *.rpm
```

That's it. As you can see, once you have the proper packages installed, applying updates is easy. You will, however, run into problems if the updated packages require dependencies the original packages did not need. Since the -F option will *only* install newer versions of packages that are already installed, even if the newly required packages are also in the directory, they will not be installed. RPM is a low-level package manager and does not perform any dependency resolution by itself. The bundle script in the previous section handles most of these situations, or you can use AutoRPM as described in section 8.6, to handle your package upgrade needs.

### 8.5.1.4  RPM on Other Systems

Just like most package managers, when you install RPM on a nonnative system (such as other Linux distributions and most commercial UNIX variants) you must compile the program, create some configuration files, and initialize the package database.

You can download RPM from ftp://ftp.rpm.org/pub/rpm/dist. You can also find the source for the popt command-line processing library, which RPM needs. You may also need to download gettext from ftp://ftp.gnu.org/gnu/gettext. If you don't want to compile RPM yourself, you can also find links to precompiled versions at http://www.rpm.org/platforms/.

First install gettext, then popt, and finally RPM. Start by unzipping the source with gunzip and extracting the contents with tar -xf. All three programs can be compiled with default options by running ./configure and make from within its base directory. This assumes, of course, that you have the make command and a C compiler on your system. If you do not, you'll first have to install gmake and gcc, also from GNU. After compilation, each program can be installed by running make install. By default, all of these programs are installed in the /usr/local/ directory.

Once you have everything installed on one system, you can use any of the methods described in this or the previous chapter to distribute RPM to all of your systems. On each system, you need to create the data directory specified at compile time (such as /var/lib/rpm/) and run rpm --initdb to initialize the RPM database; once this is done, you are ready to go.

Just installing RPM doesn't do much for you. You also, of course, need actual packages that you can install on your systems. If packages don't already exist for your specific operating system, you can download any source RPM for that package (you can find plenty of source RPMs at http://www.rpmfind.net and try rebuilding it on one of your systems (with rpmbuild --rebuild program-XX-X.src.rpm).

If there are failures, you will have to install the source RPM and modify the SPEC file as needed to fix the build process. This is discussed in Appendix C.

Many packages also have dependencies on packages (like bash) and files (such as /bin/sh). This isn't a problem on an RPM-based system because your system will pretty much always have this dependency listed within the database. On a non-RPM system, however, you still almost certainly have this dependency, but RPM does not know about it because any files installed manually or by the original operating system install are not in its database.

One option is to always use the --nodeps option when you are installing RPMs. You would obviously have to worry about dependencies in some other manner, though. You could also build a virtual package that contains all dependencies provided by your underlying operating system. RPM comes with a script called vpkg-provides2.sh that can help you build this package, but this script (and its helper script u_pkg.sh) may need to be extended to work on your system.

### 8.5.1.4.1 *Installation Locations*

Most RPM packages install files directly in the /usr/ or even the root (/) directory. This may be contrary to the standard practice in your environment—installing all extra software in /usr/local/, or /opt/, or some other special directory. The reason for this is that most RPMs are built for RPM-based systems. These systems are fully installed with RPMs, so there is no real difference between extra RPMs and the base system RPMs.

Because RPM provides powerful query and removal operations, this may not be an issue. Even if a package places ten files in /usr/bin/, you can quickly remove them when you need to by removing the package. It could, however, allow an RPM package to overwrite a file being used by the operating system that is not known to the packaging system.

To solve this problem, you could only install relocatable packages and place them in a directory such as /usr/local/. To determine that a package is relocatable, perform a rpm -qip on the package and look for a Relocations field. The value shown is the default root directory. You can override this when you are installing by specifying rpm -i --relocate OLDPATH=NEWPATH or, even simpler, rpm -i --prefix NEWPATH.

If a package is not relocatable, you have to install the source RPM and modify it to install within the directory of your choice. Relocating each package upon installation can make automation difficult, unfortunately. It is best if each package is installed in the correct location by default, which means, for each package, you either need to live with its installation location or modify the package itself.

You could also build a ghost package that lists all important system files. This would prevent any future package from overwriting these files. You could use the `find` command to build a file listing and create a very simple RPM (like the aforementioned `vpkg-provides2.sh` command does) with a huge file listing. Each file would be preceded with the `%ghost` directive, so the files aren't actually included in the package (it would be a very big package if they were). You could then install this package on your system, and then all of your base system files would be owned by this package, and could not be replaced by future RPMs.

---

 **WARNING**  If you ever want to remove a ghost package, you had better use the `--justdb` option. Although ghost files are not installed when the package is installed, they will be deleted when the package is removed. Ghost files are supposed to be log files and other automatically created files, so, if you removed this package normally, it would effectively delete most of your operating system!

---

## 8.5.2 Debian Packages

From a user's perspective, both Debian and RPM packages are very similar. They offer pretty much the same features and both provide similar command-line functionality. Many end-users prefer Debian packages because of the powerful (yet user-friendly) wrapper programs like `dselect`, `tasksel`, and `apt-get`.

Debian packages also completely separate the software installation from the software configuration. When a package is installed, its files are installed, and then it is configured. If many packages are installed together, they are all installed and then all configured. For some packages, the configuration step is interactive. Although this is great for users, it is not so great for automation. Fortunately, most interactive configurations use debconf for the user interaction, which can be configured to operate noninteractively (by running `dpkg-reconfigure debconf`). A package can always be configured interactively at a later time by running `dpkg-reconfigure` on the package.

Debian package archives are generally maintained by the Debian organization through approved package maintainers. The packages are stored in specific directory structures, accessible via FTP and HTTP, that include index files to aid in package processing by remote systems. This setup makes finding and installing packages and their dependencies relatively easy, and it makes tools like `apt-get` possible.

Anybody can create a Debian package without making it part of the official distribution. The package can always be installed manually (or though scripts) using the underlying packaging tool dpkg. You could even set up your own FTP or HTTP package archive that can be accessed from a properly configured apt-get.

Although I don't personally like the Debian build process as much as RPM's, Debian packages do have certain advantages. The biggest advantage is the reliability and widespread use of the Advanced Packaging Tool APT along with the carefully maintained package archives. APT makes it very easy to find and install new packages (with apt-get) and even automatically resolve most dependencies. Debian packages also have greater control over dependencies. In addition to being able to require needed packages, Debian packages can also recommend and suggest other packages that the user may find useful.

In my experience, Debian packages are not as common as RPM packages. There are a variety of contributing factors to this lower popularity. The most likely reason is that the Debian package format has not been around as long as RPM. For these reasons, and because RPM seems to be more widely supported, it is the main packaging system used in examples in this book. Many, if not all, of the concepts discussed with rpm can also be done with dpkg, so the same topics will not be rehashed within this section.

### 8.5.2.1  Basic Use of Debian Packages

Just like with RPM, if you have a Debian package file, you can get some information about the package before installation:

```
% dpkg-deb --info cscope_15.3-1_i386.deb
new debian package, version 2.0.
 size 104934 bytes: control archive= 1658 bytes.
      72 bytes,     2 lines        conffiles
     584 bytes,    16 lines        control
    2085 bytes,    28 lines        md5sums
     249 bytes,     8 lines    *   postinst       #!/bin/sh
     190 bytes,     6 lines    *   prerm          #!/bin/sh
 Package: cscope
 Version: 15.3-1
 Section: devel
 Priority: optional
 Architecture: i386
 Depends: libc6 (>= 2.2.4-4), libncurses5 (>= 5.2.20010310-1)
 Suggests: cbrowser
 Installed-Size: 416
 Maintainer: Anthony Fok <foka@debian.org>
```

```
Description: Interactively examine a C program source
 cscope is an interactive, screen-oriented tool that allows the user to

browse through C source files for specified elements of code.
 .
 Open-Sourced by: The Santa Cruz Operation, Inc. (SCO)
      Maintainer: Petr Sorfa <petr@users.sourceforge.net>
       Home Page: http://cscope.sourceforge.net/
```

We can see that there is a post-installation script (postinst) and a pre-unin-stallation script (prerm). There is not, however, an easy way to see these scripts, apart from extracting the package control files with dpkg-deb --control. Installing a package is quite easy, however:

```
# dpkg -i cscope_15.3-1_i386.deb
Selecting previously deselected package cscope.
(Reading database ... 48510 files and directories currently installed.)
Unpacking cscope (from cscope_15.3-1_i386.deb) ...
Setting up cscope (15.3-1) ...
```

Unlike RPM, upgrades are done using the same command-line option (-i). To remove a package, just use the dpkg -r command:

```
# dpkg -r cscope
(Reading database ... 48545 files and directories currently installed.)
Removing cscope ...
```

This command, however, does not remove any configuration files. To remove configuration files, you must use the --purge option:

```
# dpkg --purge cscope
 (Reading database ... 48545 files and directories currently installed.)
Removing cscope ...
Purging configuration files for cscope ...
```

Listing packages is where dpkg is much different than rpm. The dpkg -l allows you to specify a pattern when listing packages as follows:

```
% dpkg -l '*bash*'
Desired=Unknown/Install/Remove/Purge/Hold
| Status=Not/Installed/Config-files/Unpacked/Failed-config/Half-installed
|/ Err?=(none)/Hold/Reinst-required/X=both-problems (Status,Err: uppercase=bad)
||/ Name           Version       Description
```

```
+++-==============-==============-==========================================
[[78 characters long!lc]]
ii  bash           2.05a-11       The GNU Bourne Again SHell
pn  bash-builtins  <none>         (no description available)
un  bash-completio <none>         (no description available)
pn  bash-doc       <none>         (no description available)
pn  dotfile-bash   <none>         (no description available)\
```

Users of RPM and other package managers may be surprised at this point. This is not a simple listing of the packages installed. This listing includes both installed packages and packages known to the packaging system, yet not installed. The status of each package is also shown and, as you can see, there are a variety of possible status codes for each package, apart from just installed and not installed. To see a list of files belonging to an installed package, you can run this command:

```
% dpkg -L cscope
...
/usr/bin/cscope
...
```

You can also determine which package provides a specific file by running dpkg --search. You actually specify a search string, which could be a complete or partial filename. Here is an example:

```
% dpkg --search /usr/bin/passwd
passwd: /usr/bin/passwd
```

There is one thing in particular that is easier to do with Debian packages than RPMs—extracting files from a package without actually doing an install. You can use the dpkg-deb -X command to extract the files into a directory, or even dpkg-deb --fsys-tarfile to create a tarball directly from the package.

### 8.5.2.2  Building Debian Packages

Debian packages do not have source packages in the same sense as source RPMs. Instead, if you download the source with apt-get, you get a description file, an original tar file, and usually a patch file. The patch file might make changes to the original source, but it will usually add the debian directory within the source tree. This directory contains a variety of files used for building and installing a binary package. Rebuilding a package from source is not as easy as with RPM. A variety of methods and tools are available for building your own packages. Although there is not a single standard technique for package builds, the conventions discussed within this section are the most common.

To build a binary package from a set of source files, you must get the source files. The description file (with extension .dsc) identifies the other source files you need to build the binary package. You can get all of these files as follows:

```
% apt-get source cscope
Reading Package Lists... Done
Building Dependency Tree... Done
Need to get 202kB of source archives.
Get:1 ftp://ftp.us.debian.org stable/main cscope 15.3-1 (dsc) [624B]
Get:2 ftp://ftp.us.debian.org stable/main cscope 15.3-1 (tar) [197kB]
Get:3 ftp://ftp.us.debian.org stable/main cscope 15.3-1 (diff) [5205B]
Fetched 202kB in 2s (74.1kB/s)
dpkg-source: extracting cscope in cscope-15.3
```

In this case, three files were downloaded: the description file, the original source, and a diff file. apt-get was also nice enough to extract the source into the cscope-15.3 directory and apply the patch. If you downloaded the files in some other manner, you can execute dpkg-source -x on the description file to extract and patch the source into a new directory.

To build a binary package, simply change into this new directory and run debian/rules binary. The program is compiled, based on the commands in the rules makefile, and a binary package is created. The package is placed in the directory above the source directory from which you executed the debian/rules binary command. You now have a fully usable binary package that can be installed on your systems. You may need to install the debhelper package, compilers, and other development tools to complete this process.

Creating your own package is, naturally, a bit more difficult. I try to provide a simple introduction that you can use as a starting point when you build your own packages. I am assuming that the Debian build files cannot be added to the original source (i.e., that you are not maintaining the actual source). If you are maintaining the source code, the patch file will not be necessary, because you can make the changes directly in the original source.

You definitely need to make sure a few packages are installed on your system. You need make, fakeroot, cpio, file, debmake, dpkg-dev, devscripts, and patch. You also may need to install compilers and other development tools such as gcc, cpp, and binutils.

Now, extract the original source into a new directory based on the package name and version. If you were packaging Logwatch, for example, you would want to extract its source into a directory named logwatch-3.3. Go into this directory and run deb-make and answer the questions. Once this command is completed, you may need to make a variety of changes:

- Edit debian/control and modify and add any necessary information.

- Edit debian/copyright.

- Edit debian/rules (may not be necessary if the program uses a standard makefile in its base directory with a default target to compile and an install target to install files).

- Edit original makefile (again, may not be necessary if the program uses a standard makefile in its base directory with an install target that accepts a DESTDIR argument). The important thing is to make sure the program's build process only installs files into the debian/tmp/ directory (within the source tree) and not the actual filesystem.

- Create debian/config to add any configuration tasks to be done after installation.

- Create debian/postinst to add any post-installation tasks.

Once everything is done, simply run debuild (only one b) from the base directory. If everything works, the binary package will be created (one directory up from the program's base directory). If there is a problem, usually with the build process, modify the debian/rules file and/or the original makefile, and rerun debuild.

### 8.5.2.3 Advanced Packaging Tool

The Advanced Packaging Tool (apt) system allows you to quickly and easily install packages on a system. It retrieves the packages (and any dependencies) from one or more sources. These sources must first be listed in /etc/apt/sources.list. This file can be created with apt-setup or from within dselect.

Note that, although apt and its most popular command (apt-get) are integral parts to Debian GNU/Linux, they can also be used to install RPMs, assuming a proper RPM repository has been created (Conectiva Linux ported apt so that it could work with RPM packages). If you want to use RPM packages but want the power of apt-get, this is an option you should consider. You can also check out Apt-rpm at http://apt4rpm.sourceforge.net to install RPMs using apt.

A package source may be on the local filesystem or might be accessed over a network using the HTTP or FTP protocols. It may contain binary packages or sources. The main Debian packages can be found at ftp://ftp.debian.org/debian and are also available from many mirror sites. You can also create your own package source on your own network (or even a local source) as described later in this section.

Many people love Debian just because apt is easy to use. To upgrade all packages on your system to the latest versions (usually the latest stable versions, depending on what sources you have listed), you can simply do the following:

```
# apt-get update
Hit http://http.us.debian.org stable/main Packages
Hit http://http.us.debian.org stable/main Release
Hit http://http.us.debian.org stable/contrib Packages
Hit http://http.us.debian.org stable/contrib Release
Hit http://http.us.debian.org stable/non-free Packages
Hit http://http.us.debian.org stable/non-free Release
Reading Package Lists... Done
Building Dependency Tree... Done

# apt-get upgrade
Reading Package Lists... Done
Building Dependency Tree... Done
0 packages upgraded, 0 newly installed, 0 to remove and 0  not upgraded.
```

You can also install any package by name and apt-get will follow dependencies if it can:

```
# apt-get install kpackage
Reading Package Lists... Done
Building Dependency Tree... Done
The following extra packages will be installed:
  rpm
The following NEW packages will be installed:
  kpackage rpm
0 packages upgraded, 2 newly installed, 0 to remove and 0  not upgraded.
Need to get 724kB of archives. After unpacking 2736kB will be used.
Do you want to continue? [Y/n] <userinput>y</userinput>
Get:1 http://http.us.debian.org stable/main rpm 4.0.3-4 [545kB]
Get:2 http://http.us.debian.org stable/main kpackage 4:2.2.2-7 [180kB]
Fetched 724kB in 8s (81.6kB/s)
Selecting previously deselected package rpm.
(Reading database ... 49454 files and directories currently installed.)
Unpacking rpm (from .../archives/rpm_4.0.3-4_i386.deb) ...
Selecting previously deselected package kpackage.
Unpacking kpackage (from .../kpackage_4%3a2.2.2-7_i386.deb) ...
Setting up rpm (4.0.3-4) ...

Setting up kpackage (2.2.2-7) ...
```

Here, I just installed the kpackage application that apparently requires rpm to be installed on the system as well. So, apt-get downloaded and installed both programs. This process did require me to answer one question. It could be made fully automatic by including the --yes option to apt-get. Eliminating user interaction is obviously very important when automatically installing packages to avoid all user interaction.

Because of the automatic dependency resolution, you can easily install package bundles using apt-get, assuming the packages and their dependencies are in the official Debian sources or are available in a local source. Some people even create special packages that contain no files and only have dependencies. You can install these virtual packages to cause apt to install the dependencies. You could create a virtual package called dev that, when installed, would cause a variety of development tools to be installed on the system.

```bash
#!/bin/bash

LIST_DIR="/usr/local/etc/pkglists"

list=''
for resp in `cat /etc/responsibilities` ; do
    echo "Installing packages for responsibility $resp... "
    if [ -f "$LIST_DIR/$resp" ] ; then
        for pkg in `cat $LIST_DIR/$resp` ; do
            echo "Installing package $pkg... "
            apt-get --yes install $pkg
            echo "Done with package $pkg."
        done
    fi
    echo "Done with responsibility $resp."
done
```

For each responsibility, this script reads a list of packages and each package is installed. Dependencies do not need to be listed because apt-get follows those dependencies automatically—assuming they are found.

Creating your own source that apt can access is very easy, at least in the simplest case. If you can place all of your Debian packages into one directory that is available via HTTP, FTP, or via the local filesystem, then you can use this command to create the necessary Packages.gz file:

```
%dpkg-scanpackages . /dev/null | gzip > Packages.gz
 ** Packages in archive but missing from override file: **
  cscope

Wrote 1 entries to output Packages file.
```

You must run this from within the directory that contains the Debian packages. The second argument to dpkg-scanpackages is the override file that specifies how packages are organized in your custom distribution. Unless you are actually creating a distribution, you don't really need an override file. This will, however, cause dselect to show the packages as "Unclassified without a section."

Once your archive is set up, just include the proper URL in /etc/apt/sources.list:

```
deb file:/usr/local/debian ./
```

The file URL in the example can be replaced with a valid HTTP or FTP URL depending on your situation. Remember that any number of sources may be listed in this file, so you would usually want to leave the official sources listed as well.

## 8.5.3 Slackware Packages

Unless you have been using Linux for a while, you might not have heard of Slackware. Slackware was one of the earliest Linux distributions and is still around today. Slackware has, for one reason or another, been largely eclipsed by the more popular distributions such as Red Hat, Debian, SuSE, and so on.

You may be wondering what this has to do with packaging systems. Well, I was trying to come up with a simple packaging system that could operate on any system. Although I would normally recommend using RPM or Debian packages, these other systems might be too complex for some situations. So, I started to design a system that would provide some basic features of a package management system but without all the complexity. After a basic design began to take form, I realized it was very similar to what I remembered from Slackware. So, I looked around and found that the Slackware package management system already does what I was looking for.

Slackware provides tools for installing, upgrading, removing, and building Slackware packages. Each tool is a Bourne Shell script that should work on just about any UNIX system. Some paths might need to be tweaked and programs added, but that should be relatively easy. There is also the pkgtool command that provides a curses-based interface to the package management system. This is also a Bourne Shell script and uses the dialog program for its graphical interface.

So, if you just aren't ready for the complexities of RPM or Debian packages, visit ftp://ftp.slackware.com/pub/slackware/slackware-current/source/a/pkgtools and download all the files in that directory. You will receive the packaging system and its man pages. You could then port these scripts (as necessary) to work on your collection of operating systems.

### 8.5.3.1  Understanding Slackware Packages

A Slackware package is simply a gzipped tar archive with an extension of .tgz. This means utility scripts could effortlessly extract information from the packages. This also means that you could modify existing packages manually using just the tar program.

Within this tar file, the ./install/ directory contains files used by the packaging system. The package description is contained in the file slack-desc, and the installation script is contained in the file doinst.sh. There also may be one or two scripts in the ./var/log/setup/ directory. Everything else in the package file will be directly installed on the system when the package is installed. Here is the directory structure from an example package:

```
.
|-- install/
|   |-- doinst.sh
|   `-- slack-desc
`-- usr/
    `-- sbin/
        `-- myprogram
```

In this example, the only real file in the package is ./usr/sbin/myprogram, which will be installed in /usr/sbin/myprogram when you install the package. This package also contains a package installation script (./install/doinst.sh). This script should perform any actions necessary to complete the package installation. You should write this script with basic Bourne Shell commands. Remember that the script will be executed after the package files are extracted in their final locations.

You can manually extract and re-create any package using only the tar command. This approach allows you to determine exactly what the package contains, and it can even allow you to quickly modify the package to your liking before you install it. If you wish to manually extract the contents of a package (using tar xzvvf package.tgz), you should do so from within an empty directory.

This example package does not have a configuration script. You can add a configuration script to the package, and you must name it ./var/log/setup/setup.mypackage. You should be able to execute this script numerous times without problems. On any given execution, it should make sure the package is properly configured. During the installation process, this script executes after the doinst.sh package, and it may execute again if the user requests it. Unlike the doinst.sh script, this script can interact with the user.

The final special shell script that may be contained in a package is ./var/log/setup/setup.onlyonce.mypackage. This script only executes once, just like doinst.sh, but it can interact with the user, like setup.mypackage.

### 8.5.3.2 Using Slackware Package Tools

You can use the installpkg -warn command, to see what installing a package on your system accomplishes:

```
# installpkg -warn bash-2.05b-i386-1.tgz
#### Scanning the contents of bash-2.05b-i386-1.tgz...
The following locations will be completely WIPED OUT to allow symbolic
links to be made. (We're talking 'rm -rf') These locations may be files,
or entire directories. Be sure you've backed up anything at these
locations that you want to save before you install this package:
usr/bin/bash
The following files will be overwritten when installing this package.
Be sure they aren't important before you install this package:
-rwxr-xr-x root/bin      628664 2002-08-26 20:22:14 bin/bash2.new
...
-rw-r--r-- root/root      64807 2002-08-26 20:22:13 usr/man/man1/bash.1.gz [[73
characters long]]
-rw-r--r-- root/root      93937 2002-08-26 20:22:13 usr/info/bash.info.gz
-rw-r--r-- root/root        389 2002-08-26 20:22:14 install/doinst.sh
-rw-r--r-- root/root        965 2002-08-26 20:22:14 install/slack-desc
```

To install a package, use the installpkg command and specify the filename of the package. You can also specify a different installation directory or "root" (other than /) with the -root option. Here is a package installation:

```
# installpkg bash-2.05b-i386-1.tgz
Installing package bash-2.05b-i386-1...
PACKAGE DESCRIPTION:
bash: bash (sh-compatible shell)
bash:
bash: The GNU Bourne-Again SHell.  Bash is a sh-compatible command
bash: interpreter that executes commands read from the standard input or
bash: from a file.  Bash also incorporates useful features from the Korn
bash: and C shells (ksh and csh). Bash is ultimately intended to be a
bash: conformant implementation of the IEEE Posix Shell and Tools
bash: specification (IEEE Working Group 1003.2).
bash:
```

```
bash: Bash must be present for the system to boot properly.
bash:
Executing install script for bash-2.05b-i386-1...
```

You can upgrade a package that is already installed to a newer version with the upgradepkg command. You just specify the filename like you do with the installpkg command. A package can be removed with the removepkg command. You simply specify the package to be removed, such as removepkg bash or removepkg bash-2.05b-i386-1. There are a few switches that may interest you:

**-warn:** Generates a report to the standard output about which files and directories would be removed but does not actually remove the package.

**-preserve:** If specified, the complete package subtree is reconstructed in /tmp/preserved_packages/packagename/.

**-copy:** Constructs a copy of the package under /tmp/preserved_packages/packagename/, but doesn't remove it.

To create your own package, you should start with an empty directory and copy all the files you need into that directory. The files need to be placed in the in the proper subdirectories such as the ./install/ directory for scripts and the desired destination directory for other files. You can also create any desired installation scripts such as install/doinst.sh. Then, from within that directory, you run the makepkg command, as follows:

```
% makepkg mypackage.tgz

Slackware package maker, version 2.0.

Searching for symbolic links:

No symbolic links were found, so we won't make an installation script.
You can make your own later in ./install/doinst.sh and rebuild the
package if you like.

This next step is optional--you can set the directories in your package
to some sane permissions. If any of the directories in your package have
special permissions, then DO NOT reset them here!

Would you like to reset all directory permissions to 755 (drwxr-xr-x) and
directory ownerships to root.root ([y]es, [n]o)? n
```

```
Creating tar file mypackage.tar...

./
./usr/
./usr/sbin/
./usr/sbin/myscript
./install/
./install/doinst.sh
./install/slack-desc
tar: ./mypackage.tar: file is the archive; not dumped

Gzipping mypackage.tar...

Renaming mypackage.tar.gz to mypackage.tgz...

Package creation complete.
```

To modify an existing package, first extract the package contents. You can do this with the tar command directly, or with the explodepkg utility. Remember to do this from within an empty directory.

```
% explodepkg bash-2.05b-i386-1.tgz
Exploding package ../bash-2.05b-i386-1.tgz in current directory:
./
bin/
bin/bash2.new
...
usr/man/man1/bash.1.gz
usr/info/
usr/info/bash.info.gz
install/
install/doinst.sh
install/slack-desc

An installation script was detected in ./install/doinst.sh, but
was not executed.
```

Once you have extracted the package, you can modify it as necessary and then re-create the package with the makepkg command as previously described.

# 8.6 Automatic Package Installations with AutoRPM

An automatic package and retrieval system was part of Debian GNU/Linux from the early days. The underlying package manager is dpkg, whereas both dselect and later apt provide automatic installation of packages.

Red Hat Linux and its RPM package manager are both much older than Debian Linux and did not, for a while at least, have any automatic updating facilities. However, Red Hat did (and still does) regularly and promptly release security and bug fixes for its operating systems.

This lack of an automatic update system prompted me to write a little script that I believe was called autoupdate sometime in 1997. This was a bash script that applied official Red Hat updates to a system, and that's about it. It turned out to be much more popular than I anticipated and soon grew to be too complex for its original design. This prompted me to start writing AutoRPM, also in 1997, which was my first experience with Perl. From the start, AutoRPM was designed to be very flexible and to allow you to do just about anything you wanted with a set of RPMs.

Unfortunately, I did not maintain AutoRPM for a period of time while I was involved in other projects, and therefore, it became outdated. Fortunately, Gerald Teschl wrote a new Perl program called AutoUpdate. This program took a different approach to the problem and added automatic dependency resolution—a feature badly needed and missing from AutoRPM.

Around the same time, Red Hat came out with up2date, a program that automatically applies official updates on a Red Hat Linux system. I believe this first shipped with Red Hat Linux 7.0. This program works very well and handles dependencies automatically, can update the kernel, and so on. The software is free and works well if you only have a few systems and/or each user takes care of their own systems.

If you subscribe to the Red Hat Network (RHN) (`http://rhn.redhat.com`), you can manage your systems, organize them into groups, and apply updates all from a web interface. Red Hat also offers a proxy that can cache the updates locally as well as an entire "RHN-in-a-box" so that you can manage everything locally and, presumably, add your own packages to the process. Although I have never used the system, it sounds very useful, and it is something you might want to consider if you have a large number of Red Hat Linux systems and have the available funds.

In addition, Mandrake Linux (based on Red Hat Linux) has a program called urpmi that is supposed to be an `apt-get` for RPMs. Ximian, which is an open-source desktop, has a program called Red Carpet that is a graphical package management system. I haven't used either of these systems, but urpmi in particular might be useful for managing a range of systems.

Recently, I have been continuing my work on AutoRPM because I feel that it still has benefits that AutoUpdate does not offer. I think AutoRPM is more flexible and easier to configure. It now supports dependency resolution and provides a powerful command-line interface that can be used when manual intervention is required.

That said, currently AutoUpdate still has more reliable dependency resolution. It also supports HTTP, HTTPS, and SFTP RPM sources (AutoRPM currently only supports FTP and file-based sources). AutoRPM also requires a configuration file for just about anything you want to do with it, while AutoUpdate can be fully configured on the command line. Both AutoUpdate and AutoRPM can be configured to use a client/server approach where official Red Hat updates are downloaded to a local repository, possibly right into your custom distribution, and then other systems can update themselves from the local source.

AutoRPM does provide some powerful automation features. For instance, you can create pools of FTP sites and allow AutoRPM to automatically score and rank those sites so that it uses the best site available. AutoRPM also lets you downgrade to older RPMs and even delete packages (if you want to) so that you can make an exact replica of a system. Also, AutoRPM can operate without downloading any packages until they need to be installed. You may find this characteristic useful if you don't want to store any updated packages locally. Finally, AutoRPM allows you to use regular expressions and/or external lists to determine which packages should be included and excluded. Basically this means that an external program can first determine which software should be installed on the system (using whatever logic necessary) and then AutoRPM will do the dirty work.

It's really impossible to be impartial when you have written one of the programs being compared. Personally, I still think AutoRPM provides some useful features not available in any other package management tools that can be very useful when you are automating system administration. If I didn't think this, I would no longer be developing the program! So, I would recommend that you take a look at both programs and decide which will work best in your situation. In my opinion, if you just want to automatically install some new packages and some upgraded packages to all of your systems, both programs work about as well. If you want to install different sets of packages on different systems and/or do exact installs onto systems, AutoRPM has features that just can't be found elsewhere.

## 8.6.1  Basic AutoRPM Setup

At the time of this writing, the most current version of AutoRPM is 3.2.2. The newest version can always be downloaded from ftp://ftp.autorpm.org.

AutoRPM is not much more than a Perl script with some support files. AutoRPM depends on a few pathnames; these pathnames have defaults in the actual code, but they can be overridden with the following configuration options:

- /etc/autorpm.d: This directory can be copied directly out of the tar file (or, if you install the RPM, it will already be populated). Most notably, this directory contains the pool directory (pools/) and the default configuration file (autorpm.conf).

- /var/spool/autorpm: This is where packages are cached and other dynamic data is stored. Most notably, this directory contains the settings file that stores program settings (can be modified with the interactive set command), install.log (installation logs), interactive.queue (packages waiting to be installed interactively), and auto-ignore (packages that have been permanently ignored). The command-line option --tempdir can set this location to another location.

- /var/run/autorpm.pid: This is a lock file containing a process ID that AutoRPM uses to make sure that only one copy of AutoRPM is running at any given time. A different file can be specified with the --pidfile option, if necessary.

AutoRPM accepts a series of commands. You can specify a command on the command line, or you can enter it during an interactive session. Zero or more commands can be specified on the command line—you enter interactive mode by not specifying any commands at all.

The most useful command is the auto command. With no arguments, this command reads and executes the default configuration file (/etc/autorpm.d/autorpm.conf). You can also specify an alternate configuration file, if you need one. Here are a variety of commands that all perform the same tasks:

```
autorpm auto
autorpm --tempdir ~/autorpm --pidfile ~/autorpm.pid auto
autorpm "auto autorpm.conf"
autorpm "auto /etc/autorpm.d/autorpm.conf"
autorpm "set debug on" auto
/etc/autorpm.d/autorpm.conf"
autorpm "set debug on" auto
```

As you can see, you must specify any command-line *options* (to the program itself) before you specify any command-line *commands* (to be executed by the program). If a command has one or more options, they need to be separated by spaces, which means the command and its options need to be enclosed by quotes (so AutoRPM knows where the start of the next command is).

To see a list of command-line options, run `autorpm --help`. To see a list of commands, run `autorpm help`. To see help information for a specific command, run `autorpm "help command-name"`. To see a list of settings, run `autorpm set`. You can modify settings interactively or on the command line by using the command `set setting_name value`.

## 8.6.2 Working in Interactive Mode

Interactive mode allows you to manually process files and directories. In the interactive mode, you can install all packages from a directory, for example. You can also view and edit program settings. None of this really has to do with automation, so I'll let you play with these features on your own.

Hopefully you will find the interactive mode useful when you are learning and testing AutoRPM. If all goes well, you shouldn't have to use it much more after that. If, at any time, AutoRPM has any trouble installing an RPM (unresolvable dependencies, conflicts, etc.), it will be placed in the interactive queue. After this happens, you can enter interactive mode and use the `ls` command to see the list of packages that are in the interactive queue. You can use the `rm` command to remove packages and you can use the `install` command to install packages (after you have addressed any problems that were found). Here is an example of a package that is being manually installed in the interactive queue:

```
# autorpm

  1 RPM(s) waiting to be installed/updated/removed Interactively

AutoRPM@kaybee.org> ls
[New    ] php-snmp-4.1.2-7.2.4
AutoRPM@kaybee.org> info php-snmp-4.1.2-7.2.4
            --= php-snmp =--
Type         : New (no version installed)
Architecture : i386

AutoRPM@kaybee.org> install php-snmp-4.1.2-7.2.4/
   Installing Packages...
   Downloading php-snmp-4.1.2-7.2.4... (24 KB)... ###
Done.
Preparing...              ######################################## [100%] [[78
characters]]
   1:php-snmp              ######################################## [100%] [[78
characters]]
     Package php-snmp-4.1.2-7.2.4 Installed
       Deleted /var/spool/autorpm/php-snmp-4.1.2-7.2.4.i386.rpm
```

It is important to remember that if you remove a package from the interactive queue, that exact version of that package will be ignored indefinitely. To un-ignore the package, you have to remove its entry from the `auto-ignore` file. This function prevents unwanted or failed packages from showing up in the interactive queue every time the `auto` command is run.

Since the interactive mode is most useful for interactive upgrades, I will not spend any more time talking about its features. If you do use the interactive mode, however, be sure to read the tips and install the Perl module `Term::ReadLine::Gnu`. This provides command-line editing, command history, and very powerful tab completion within AutoRPM.

## 8.6.3  Understanding FTP Pool Files

A pool file is simply a listing of various sources for the same group of packages. AutoRPM variables can be present in the pool files. Since AutoRPM variables are really just environment variables, you can also use environment variables as substitutions in the pool file. Here is an example pool file (a portion of `/etc/autorpm.d/pools/redhat-updates`:

```
ftp://ftp.rpmfind.net/linux/redhat/updates/${RHVersion}/${Lang}/os
ftp://updates.redhat.com/${RHVersion}/${Lang}/os
```

In all of the example configuration files presented in the coming section, the AutoRPM variables `RHVersion` and `Lang` are already defined before AutoRPM processes an FTP pool. So, these variables can be placed within the pool files and will expand to the proper values when necessary.

## 8.6.4  Example Configuration Files

The rest of the discussion on AutoRPM focuses on its configuration files and provides some examples for different situations. Just about any automation you want done with AutoRPM will require a configuration file. Remember that these files can be located anywhere on the system and can be executed by running `autorpm "auto configfile"`.

### 8.6.4.1  Simple System Upgrades

The configuration file I introduce in this section is pretty close to the default configuration supplied with AutoRPM, and it is intended for use on a small number of systems. When you use this configuration file, each system will download and automatically apply any official updates. AutoRPM will only download packages as needed, but this will occur on each system separately. Any of the other programs mentioned earlier in this section can do this same task, but often through different methods. Here is the configuration file:

```
1   Eval_Var("RHVersion",
2   "sed 's/\(Red Hat Linux \)\?release \([^ ]*\) (.*)/\2/' /etc/redhat-release");
    [[78 characters]]
3
4   Set_Var("Arch", "i686|i586|i386|noarch");
5   Set_Var("Lang", "en");
6
7   Report_Queues_To("root");
8
9   ftppool ("redhat-updates") {
10      Recursive(Yes);
11      Regex_Dir_Accept("${Arch}");
12
13      Regex_Ignore("^kernel-");
14
15      action (updated) {
16         PGP_Require(Yes);
17         Install(Auto);
18         Auto_Follow_Deps(Yes);
19      }
20
21      action (new) {
22         Install(Interactive);
23      }
24   }
```

**Line 1:** This command sets RHVersion based on the /etc/redhat-release file.

**Line 4:** These two lines provide information about the system. The architecture list itemizes all acceptable architectures.

**Line 7:** This is the email address to which reports regarding the installation queues should be sent. There are two installation queues: the auto queue automatically installs files, and the interactive queue contains files that could be installed interactively. The AutoRPM report will show what the auto queue did and how many packages remain in the interactive queue.

**Line 10:** This tells AutoRPM to process the remote directories recursively. The Regex_Dir_Accept command is then used to limit which directories can be entered, since only directories of the appropriate architecture should be processed.

**Line 13:** This directs AutoRPM to ignore any packages beginning with kernel-. I have never auto-updated the kernel—doing so may or may not work, but it will definitely require a reboot to take effect in any case. I don't upgrade the kernel automatically to be safe.

**Line 15:** This is an action block for any updated RPMs (i.e., a local version of the package is older). Every command in this block applies to every updated RPM. For each update, the Pretty Good Privacy (PGP) or GNU Privacy Guard (GPG) signature is checked. If this check succeeds, the package is marked for automatic installation. Dependencies are followed automatically, if necessary.

**Line 21:** This is an action block for any new RPMs (i.e., no local version of the package exists). The only action in this particular block is to mark the package for interactive installation, which causes it to be placed into the interactive queue.

A package is only downloaded if it needs to be installed (so, normally only upgrades will be downloaded). New RPMs are placed in the interactive queue for two reasons. The first is to give the user a chance to install the package if they decide they want to install it. The second is that, currently, the dependency resolution code only looks in the interactive queue to resolve dependencies. It is not uncommon for an upgraded version of a package to require new packages that are placed in the update directory as well. This setup allows the dependencies to be properly resolved.

AutoRPM can be executed in the following way to prevent the interactive queue from slowly filling up with a list of new packages:

```
autorpm auto
autorpm "rm !update"
```

The packages are there for dependency resolution purposes but are then removed (and ignored from then on). This could still cause a problem if an updated package requires a new package that was placed in the directory earlier and not installed. If this is something that might happen (not too likely), you could always just let the interactive queue slowly fill up with new RPMs to provide flawless dependency resolution. Leaving RPMs in the interactive queue does not hurt anything.

### 8.6.4.2 Caching Updates Locally

The following script downloads all official updates into a local directory. Since the Compare_To_Dir command is specified, the local packages in that directory are used in the comparison instead of installed files (the default). Neither updated nor new packages are installed, but both are stored in the local directory. Any old versions of packages are deleted. If the source has multiple architectures for the same package, the "best" architecture is kept. The definition of "best" is the highest architecture that runs on the system currently executing AutoRPM. This could be a problem if other systems on your network have lower processors. The All_Arch command, discussed later in this section, can help with that problem. Here is the configuration file:

```
Set_Var("Arch", "i686|i586|i386|noarch");
Set_Var("RHVersion", "7.2");
Set_Var("Lang", "en");

Set_Var("Path", "/usr/local/updates/");

ftppool ("redhat-updates") {
    Compare_To_Dir("${Path}/${Version}");
    Recursive(Yes);
    Regex_Dir_Accept("${Arch}");
    Delete_Old_Version(Yes);

    action (updated) {
        Install(No);
        Store("${Path}/${Version}");
    }

    action (new) {
        Install(No);
        Store("${Path}/${Version}");
    }
}
```

If you want to cache the updates for more than one version of Red Hat Linux, you could remove the Version variable from the mirror script shown and call that script numerous times with different values for Version:

```
Set_Var("RHVersion", "7.1");
Config_File("mirror-updates.conf");
Set_Var("RHVersion", "7.2");
Config_File("mirror-updates.conf");
```

Or, since AutoRPM variables are really just environment variables, you could do this:

```
#!/bin/bash

for ver in 7.1 7.2 ; do
   export RHVersion="$ver"
   autorpm "auto mirror-updates.conf"
done
```

Note that the updates on the remote FTP site are stored in different directories based on the package's architecture. When transferred to the local system, however, the packages are stored in one directory. This is fine for most situations, but you could use the Recursive_Compare_To_Dir and Recursive_Store commands to create an exact mirror.

If you have a custom Linux distribution, all of your packages will be in one directory. You may have multiple copies of the same package but with different architectures (such as glibc). This allows the installation program to choose the best architecture for the installation system. In this case, all you have to do is add the All_Arch(yes) command to the source block. With this command, if you start out with two local architectures for a given package, you will always end up with two local architectures.

When updating a custom Linux distribution, you will probably not want to add all new packages automatically. You could take out the Store command for new packages, but you would have to manually add new packages if any are required for dependencies.

### 8.6.4.3 Updating Systems from Previously-Downloaded Package Cache

Clients can quickly install updated RPMs from the local cache:

```
Set_Var("Path", "/usr/local/updates/");
Directory ("${Path}/${RHVersion}") {
   action (updated) {
      Install(Auto);
      PGP_Require(Yes);
      Auto_Follow_Deps(Yes);
   }
   action (new) {
      Install(Interactive);
   }
}
```

You can also have a special directory that contains packages that should be added to all systems:

```
Set_Var("InstallPath", "/usr/local/updates/all");
Directory ("${InstallPath}") {
    action (updated) {
        Install (Auto);
        Auto_Follow_Deps(Yes);
    }
    action (new) {
        Install (Auto);
        Auto_Follow_Deps(Yes);
    }
}
```

The cron script that is packaged with AutoRPM should be used directly or at least as an example. It uses the `--delay` option to cause AutoRPM to delay for up to two hours before it actually checks for updates. This will really reduce the load on your update server when the updates are occurring. Here is that script, with some comments trimmed out:

```
#!/bin/bash

# Start AutoRPM and tell it to wait up to 2 hours before actually
# looking for updates (backgrounds the process to avoid delaying
# other cron jobs)
/usr/sbin/autorpm --notty "auto --delay=7200" &
```

### 8.6.4.4 *Precise Package Installation*

The following configuration file causes a system to make itself an exact copy of the specified directory of RPMs. What this means is that packages will be added, upgraded, downgraded, or even removed to make the set of installed packages on the system exactly the same as the source directory.

This can obviously be very dangerous. Any manually installed packages will be removed. If some or all the packages in the source directory are removed, the system will subsequently remove all of its packages. For this reason, you should create an `autorpm.remove.exclude` file that lists packages (by name) that should never be removed. Here is an example:

```
rpm
popt
lilo
glibc
kernel
mktemp
autorpm
fileutils
textutils
perl-libnet
```

With the exclusion file in place, you can try the following configuration file. Note that, as if automatically removing packages is not dangerous enough, I threw in the --nodeps option to be used when removing packages. When automatically deleting files without regard to dependencies, you must really make sure the directory being used as the guide has every necessary RPM listed. Here is the example configuration file:

```
Set_Var("Source", "/usr/local/distribution/RedHat/RPMS");

Remove_Packages(Yes, "--nodeps");
Remove_Exclude("/usr/local/etc/autorpm.remove.exclude");

Directory ("${Source}") {
    action (updated) {
        Install(Auto);
        Auto_Follow_Deps(Yes);
    }
    action (new) {
        Install(Auto);
        Auto_Follow_Deps(Yes);
    }
    action (old) {
        Downgrade(Yes);
    }
}
```

### 8.6.4.5  Advanced Uses of AutoRPM

I have not mentioned many options you can use in the AutoRPM configuration file—see the man page for autorpm.conf for more information on these. Some of the options I have not yet discussed include a variety of reporting options and package include/exclude options. If you have your own logs and/or reporting system, remember that you can also parse the /var/spool/autorpm/install.log file, which records all installs, upgrades, and even removals.

### 8.6.4.5.1 Install Only Needed RPMs

One thing you can do with AutoRPM is specify a list of packages you want installed. This listing can be generated by an external program, stored in a temporary file, and then provided to AutoRPM with the Accept_List command. Say that you have a list of responsibilities for the current system. You then have a file for each responsibility that defines which packages you need for that responsibility. You could use the following Perl script to create the include list:

```perl
#!/usr/bin/perl -w
use strict;

my $GroupFile = "/etc/responsibilities";
my $GroupDir = "/usr/local/etc/groups";
my $RPMDir = "/usr/local/distribution/RedHat/RPMS";

my %AllRPMs;
my %PkgsByGroup;
my %AllGroups;
my %MyGroups;

sub ReadGroup {
    my ($group) = @_;
    my $file;
    my $line;
    my @ret;
    open($file, "$GroupDir/$group") or
        die "Could not open $GroupDir/$group: $!\n";
    while ($line = <$file>) {
        chomp($line);
        $line =~ s/^\s+//;
        $line =~ s/\s+$//;
        if ($line =~ s/^\@\s*(.+)$/$1/) {
            # Including another group
            push @ret, ReadGroup($line);
        } else {
            push @ret, $line;
        }
    }
}
```

```perl
      close($file);
      return (@ret);
   }


   # Retrieve list of all RPMs
   my $rpm;
   foreach $rpm (`rpm -qp --queryformat="%{NAME}\n" $RPMDir/*.rpm`) {
      chomp($rpm);
      $AllRPMs{$rpm}++;
   }


   # Read in list of group RPMs
   my $file;
   opendir(GROUPDIR, $GroupDir) or die "Could not access directory $GroupDir: $!\n";
   while ($file = readdir(GROUPDIR)) {
      next if $file =~ /^\./;
      foreach $rpm (ReadGroup($file)) {
         $AllGroups{$rpm}++;
         $PkgsByGroup{$file}{$rpm}++;
      }
   }
   closedir(GROUPDIR);


   # Determine the RPMs from the groups we are in
   my $group;
   open (GROUPS, $GroupFile) or die "Could not open $GroupFile: $!\n";
   while ($group = <GROUPS>) {
      chomp($group);
      if ($PkgsByGroup{$group}) {
         foreach $rpm (keys %{$PkgsByGroup{$group}}) {
            $MyGroups{$rpm}++;
         }
      } else {
         print STDERR "WARNING: Unknown group: $group\n";
      }
   }
   close (GROUPS);


   unless (keys %MyGroups) {
      die "No responsibilities defined!\n";
   }
```

```
# Now, output RPM listing
foreach $rpm (keys %AllRPMs) {
    if ($AllGroups{$rpm}) {
        if ($MyGroups{$rpm}) {
            print "$rpm\n";
        }
    } else {
        print "$rpm\n";
    }
}
```

The script is a bit complicated, but all it does is output a list of needed package names. Any package in the distribution, but not listed in any group file, is listed; packages within our group files are, obviously, listed; but any package that is in a group file not associated with one of our responsibilities is not listed. You would need to use the script like this:

```
#!/bin/bash

if build_rpm_list > /var/spool/autorpm/packages.include ; then
    autorpm "auto exact_copy.conf"
fi
```

Here we are assuming that the configuration file exact_copy.conf has the following line within the source block:

```
Accept_List("/var/spool/autorpm/packages.include");
```

As an example, let's say that one of the responsibilities a system can have is web. The group file for web (/usr/local/etc/groups/web) contains one line: apache. Assuming this is the only group file, all packages will be installed on all systems, unless they do not have the web responsibility listed, in which case the apache package will not be installed.

The group files may also include other group files by starting a line with @, followed by a space, followed by the other group's name.

## 8.6.5  AutoRPM Triggers

Triggers are a new feature in AutoRPM versions 3.2 and later. They basically tell AutoRPM to execute arbitrary external programs/scripts when certain packages are installed, upgraded, downgraded, or have a failure. Using triggers is simple:

```
Directory ("${Source}") {
   action (updated) {
      Install(Auto);
      Auto_Follow_Deps(Yes);
      Trigger("kernel", "/etc/autorpm.d/triggers/run_lilo.sh");
   }
}
```

This says that if the `kernel` package is upgraded, the script
`/etc/autorpm.d/triggers/run_lilo.sh` should be executed. This is the most obvious
use for triggers, because you want to make sure `lilo` is executed to update your
system's boot sector when the kernel is upgraded. The script can be as simple
as this:

```
#!/bin/bash

lilo >/dev/null || {
   echo "ERROR: Execution of LILO failed after kernel upgrade!" >&2
   exit 1
}
```

Since this is such a new feature, I don't have any other example triggers, but
I can provide you with a place to start. You might consider using triggers when you
are upgrading important software. If you are upgrading Apache on your web server,
for example, your trigger could make sure the configuration files are correct and
restart the web server. You can also use regular expressions in your trigger definitions:

```
Regex_Trigger("^mod_", "/etc/autorpm.d/triggers/apache_module.sh");
```

This runs the specified trigger any time an Apache module is installed, upgraded,
and so on. We are assuming that any packages whose name begins with the string
`mod_` is an Apache module, which is a pretty good assumption in my experience.
The trigger script also has some information passed to it on the command line.
The first argument is the package that was installed, upgraded, downgraded, or
experienced an installation failure. It will contain the package name, version, and
release (such as `kernel-2.4.9-6`). The next argument is INSTALLED, UPGRADED,
DOWNGRADED, or FAILED. The third and final argument is only present when an
upgrade or downgrade occurred and is the name, version, and release of the
version of the package that used to be installed.

## 8.7 Cross-Platform Packaging with OpenPKG

Almost everybody likes package managers. They allow you to quickly and consistently install software on multiple systems. Most people would like to use the same package manager on all of their systems, but there are usually a variety of problems associated with this, as discussed in "RPM on Other Systems".

This is where the relatively young OpenPKG project becomes useful. You can download the base program in either binary or source form and install it on just about any UNIX system. It creates a new directory hierarchy under /cw/. This directory is completely independent from the underlying operating system. Within this tree, a customized version of RPM is installed. This package manager lets you build, install, and execute programs completely within this isolated directory. This allows you to manage the operating system itself using any means desired, yet it still gives you the ability to install custom software almost automatically on almost any system.

Although OpenPKG uses the RPM package manager, the team has made enough modifications to the packaging system that you will need special packages. The SPEC files for these packages (again, slightly different than standard RPM SPEC files) are carefully constructed to build on a wide variety of systems and to be fully relocatable (so that they can be installed under the OpenPKG tree).

Several operating system versions are officially supported by OpenPKG, but many others will usually work as well. If a platform is supported, you can compile and/or install the base software on the system without modification. In addition, for each official release, binary versions of all packages are built and tested for all of these platforms. If you want the newest code (i.e., from a pending release) or binaries for unsupported systems, however, you will have to build from the source packages. The current version, at the time of this writing, is OpenPKG 1.1, which provides 274 official packages for the following official platforms:

- FreeBSD 4

- Red Hat Linux 7.X

- Debian GNU/Linux 2 and 3

- Sun Solaris 8 and 9

OpenPKG claims to work on most other modern UNIX variants, including Tru64, HP-UX, OpenBSD, and NetBSD. You would, of course, always have to compile your own binary packages from the provided source packages. I have not personally verified all of these platforms, but I would guess that it is worth a try if you are using these platforms.

## 8.7.1  Installing OpenPKG

Before you can install other packages, you must first install the openpkg package. This would be pretty difficult, except that the OpenPKG team has provided a convenient source file that can be easily compiled on your system (assuming you have a C compiler). Use your favorite FTP client to connect to ftp://ftp.openpkg.org/current/SRC and download openpkg*.src.sh. Then execute the following command:

```
# sh openpkg-1.1.0-1.1.0.src.sh --prefix=/cw
(tons of output not shown)
# sh openpkg-1.1.0-1.1.0.arch-os-cw.sh
openpkg-20020909-20020909.sparc64-solaris2.8-cw.sh: installing into /cw... [[74
characters long]]
openpkg-20020909-20020909.sparc64-solaris2.8-cw.sh: installation done.
```

Even on a quick system, the first command will take a while. After the compilation is complete, you will have a binary OpenPKG package that you can install on any similar systems using only the Bourne Shell (sh). The name will reflect its version as well as the system it is built on. I just built the latest version on a Solaris system and ended up with the file openpkg-20020909-20020909.sparc64-solaris2.8-cw.sh.

If you don't have a compiler, or if you don't want to build the package yourself, you can download a binary package of the latest stable release by going to ftp://ftp.openpkg.org/release/1.1/BIN/ (obviously release 1.1 will not always be the most current stable release). This package can be installed by executing it with the sh command just as shown in the previous example.

When it is installed, OpenPKG touches only three areas of the base system:

- Several special accounts are added to the system. These accounts are used for various tasks within OpenPKG. No further accounts will be created for any other installed packages (they will all use these accounts). The accounts are the cw management account, the cw-r restricted account, and the cw-n non-privileged account.

- Several entries are added to the system crontab (usually /etc/crontab). These entries all call the /cw/etc/rc script that actually runs any cron jobs necessary for any installed packages.

- A file is added to your system startup script directory (such as /etc/init.d/ as well as any necessary symbolic links). This file just executes /cw/etc/rc, which actually takes care of starting and stopping any programs that have been installed with OpenPKG.

## 8.7.2  Installing Packages with OpenPKG

OK, you now have OpenPKG installed—hopefully it went as smoothly as it did for me. The first thing you should do now is set up your shell environment to work with the new directory structure. Execute this command (which could be placed in your login script, such as ~/.bash_profile):

```
% eval `/cw/etc/rc --eval all env`
```

OK, now you can run the rpm command to manage packages within the /cw/ directory. If your base operating system has RPM installed as well, do not confuse the two commands, because they are not the same, nor are they compatible. You should still use your system's rpm command (usually /usr/bin/rpm) to add or upgrade packages within your base operating system.

To install a new package with OpenPKG, you usually want to download the appropriate source RPM, compile it into a binary RPM, and then install that binary RPM on one or more similar systems. If you want to use a package from a stable release on a officially supported system, you could also just download the binary package directly and skip the compilation process. This obviously does not allow you to make any custom changes, however.

To compile a new package from source, you start by using your favorite FTP client to download the source package. If you don't have a favorite FTP client, I highly recommend lftp. For this example, I use my not-so-favorite FTP client to download this much better FTP client:

```
# ftp ftp.openpkg.org
Connected to master.openpkg.org.
220 ftp.openpkg.org OpenPKG Anonymous FTP Server (ProFTPD) ready.
Name (ftp.openpkg.org:kirk): ftp
331 Anonymous login ok, send your complete email address as your password.
...
ftp> cd current
ftp> cd SRC
ftp> binary
200 Type set to I.
ftp> mget lftp*
mget lftp-2.6.2-20020910.src.rpm? y
200 PORT command successful
150 Opening BINARY mode data connection for lftp-2.6.2-20020910.src.rpm (1136266 bytes)
226 Transfer complete.
local: lftp-2.6.2-20020910.src.rpm remote: lftp-2.6.2-20020910.src.rpm
1136266 bytes received in 7.7 seconds (143.64 Kbytes/s)
```

OK, now you need to build the binary package from the source package. Here is the easy method:

```
#  rpm --rebuild lftp-2.6.2-20020910.src.rpm
#  cd /cw/RPM/PKG/
#  rpm -i lftp-2.6.2-20020910.sparc64-solaris2.8-cw.rpm
```

It may complain that you are missing a compiler and/or the make program. In that case, just download and install binary packages for gcc and make and try the build again.

If you know the full URL, you can skip the manual download completely:

```
#  rpm --rebuild ftp://ftp.openpkg.org/current/SRC/lftp-2.6.2-20020910.src.rpm
#  cd /cw/RPM/PKG/
#  rpm -i lftp-2.6.2-20020910.sparc64-solaris2.8-cw.rpm
```

You can also install binary RPMs by specifying the URL. Remember that the build process can take a while and produces a lot of output I have not bothered to show in these examples.

Also, remember that all packages install completely within the OpenPKG directory tree and do not touch your system. Just about everything discussed in "Red Hat Package Manager (RPM)" can be done with the OpenPKG version of RPM. You can perform query, verification, and package removal operations just as you can with the normal RPM.

## 8.7.3  Modifying Packages

You can modify existing OpenPKG packages and build your own packages as you need them. Although OpenPKG SPEC files are not quite the same as normal RPM SPEC files, the information in Appendix C should still provide enough information with which to build your own packages. You could also use other existing packages as templates or references as well as the information provided on the OpenPKG web site at http://www.openpkg.org.

If you want to modify a package before you build a binary RPM, simply install the source package:

```
#  rpm -i ftp://ftp.openpkg.org/current/SRC/lftp-2.6.2-20020910.src.rpm
```

A new directory, in this case called lftp, is created under /cw/RPM/SRC/, and it contains the SPEC file and all source files for the package. The creation of a separate directory for the sources of each package is different, but better (in my opinion) than what the standard RPM does. The SPEC file will be called lftp.spec for this particular program. You can modify this file (and any of the source files) and build the binary package as follows:

```
# rpmbuild -bb lftp.spec
```

This builds only a binary RPM. A source and binary RPM will be built if you use -ba instead of -bb. Either way, the resulting package files will be placed in /cw/RPM/PKG/.

Some packages also provide compile-time options that you can set without modifying the SPEC file. These are listed at the top of the SPEC file or even in the information block contained within the source RPM. Here are some compile-time options for the apache package, for example:

```
$ rpm -qip apache-1.3.26-20020918.src.rpm
Name:    apache                     Source RPM:   (none)
Version: 1.3.26                     Packager:     The OpenPKG Project
...

   Options (additional modules I):
   --define 'with_mod_dav          no' \
   --define 'with_mod_layout       no' \
   --define 'with_mod_macro        no' \
   --define 'with_mod_perl         no' \
   --define 'with_mod_php          no' \
...
```

These options can be set in any of the following ways:

```
#  rpm --rebuild apache-1.3.26-20020918.src.rpm --define "with_mod_perl=yes"
#  rpmbuild -bb apache.spec --define "with_mod_perl=yes"
```

# CHAPTER 9

# System Maintenance and Changes

ANY TYPE OF SYSTEM needs maintenance—especially operating systems. In addition, assuming your systems actually do something, you will need to make regular changes. We have discussed many system changes and maintenance tasks in previous chapters such as system configuration and upgrades. This chapter covers topics we have not yet covered (or have not covered completely).

Common system maintenance falls into several categories:

**Log files:** All systems produce some log files. Busy systems create quite a large amount of logs. They may be spread throughout the system in several directories, or (if you are lucky) isolated in one directory such as /var/log/. Although many systems take care of their own log files, some applications do not. Rotating and trimming these log files is an important task, but it is easy to neglect.

**Synchronizing time:** This task sounds pretty simple, but it is often neglected and can cause problems, especially when you are using network filesystems.

**Removing files:** Temporary files can build up in a system's temporary directories; your operating system may take care of these for you. Temporary files and other unneeded files can also build up in your user's home directories or corporate public directories; your operating system will not take care of those for you. Finding and removing temporary files that are no longer needed will help keep your systems clean.

**System updates:** Your systems will ultimately need security and bug fixes. Your operating system might provide a native automated system for applying these fixes. If it does not, Chapter 8 provides a variety of possible solutions.

You may only make changes to your systems every few months. It is more likely, however, that you will need to make changes much more often. You might find yourself implementing a broad range of changes:

**Managing users:** Many operating systems provide a simple `adduser` or `useradd` command. These commands may set up a simple home directory for the user, but they usually don't support remote home directories, additional passwords (such as a Samba account/password), specialized directory structures, mail aliases, and other items that may be required by your specific circumstances. In a company, every time a person leaves, their account must be deleted, and every time a person is hired, a new account must be made. In a large company, these tasks can become quite common—and quite tedious.

**Adding/removing software:** Adding new software is one of the more common changes made by system administrators. Removing software is something administrators also do, although usually much less often. Sometimes, new programs can be installed once and shared as discussed in Chapter 7. Other times, a packaging system can be used as described in Chapter 8.

**Configuration changes:** Whenever you find a problem with your systems, you must make configuration changes to one or more machines. If you make a network change, all of your systems must be modified. Automatic configuration of your systems is fully discussed in Chapter 6.

**Adding/removing systems:** In some cases, you will need to modify some or all of your existing systems when a new system is added. This may be as simple as adding an entry to the `/etc/hosts` file on all systems, or adding a DNS entry to your DNS servers. It may also involve adding the new system to permission tables for network filesystems such as `/etc/exports` or the NIS/NIS+ `netgroups` file. These situations are discussed in Chapter 4.

**Adding drives/moving data:** This is a common task that is really impossible to automate. First of all, it usually includes physical tasks that are tough to automate until you get your robotic system administration assistant. Secondly, each situation is usually different. Thirdly, the whole process is completely dependent on your hardware and operating systems. Since this is covered in most standard system administration books, I will not discuss it here.

Looking through the list, you will notice that I already covered most of these tasks earlier in this book. Some of the remaining tasks may be completely or partially handled by your operating system. However, there are always situations in which you must handle them yourself, so this chapter will provide examples for these miscellaneous tasks.

# 9.1 Synchronizing Time

If you are running distributed applications, the time on the various systems may be critical. When using networked filesystems (such as NFS), you will have problems if the time on the client is not close to the time on the server (some files will have access and modification times in the future when they are written by a system with a clock set in the future, causing problems with applications that rely on these timestamps to make decisions). Other network protocols such as NIS+ also depend on relatively synchronized system clocks.

## 9.1.1   Setting the Time Zone

The first thing you must do is make sure the time zone on your systems is correct. The time zone is important because time synchronization usually uses Coordinated Universal Time (UTC), which is not the time you are used to seeing on your system. How you set the time zone is, unfortunately, completely system dependent. Here are some pointers for some popular systems:

**Red Hat Linux**: /etc/sysconfig/clock (or run timeconfig)

**Debian GNU/Linux**: /etc/timezone

**Solaris**: /etc/TIMEZONE (symbolic link to /etc/default/init)

**AIX**: /etc/environment and /etc/profile

**FreeBSD**: /etc/localtime

**HP-UX**: /etc/TIMEZONE

**Tru64**: /etc/svid3_tz (or run timezone)

## 9.1.2   Synchronizing Your Clocks

On most systems, you have two ways to synchronize time. One involves using the rdate or ntpdate commands to synchronize your clocks on a regular basis (hourly or daily from a cron job). The other option involves running a Network Time Protocol (NTP) time daemon (called xntpd on some systems and ntpd on others).

### 9.1.2.1  The rdate Command

Most UNIX variants come with the rdate command. This command can quickly synchronize a system's clock to a well-known timeserver using the RFC 868 protocol. Here is an example on a Linux system:

```
% rdate -s time.nist.gov
```

Although used in this example, the -s switch is not standard and should not be used on most systems (on Solaris, for example, the command rdate time.nist.gov would accomplish the same task). The server specified here (time.nist.gov) is run by the National Institute of Standards and Technology (NIST) Laboratories in Boulder, Colorado. You can find plenty of other public timeservers using some quick web searches.

You can set up your own server easily since most versions of inetd internally support this protocol. The protocol is not very accurate (i.e., the times might be off by a few milliseconds), but it is more than suitable for most situations. You would need to run this command from cron on a regular basis (usually at least once per day, or even hourly).

### 9.1.2.2  Using the Network Time Protocol

NTP has gone though several revisions and has several associated Request For Comments (RFCs are published Internet standards documents). It provides very accurate system time updates (to the millisecond). NTP is usually used with a daemon that continuously updates the system clock and may also provide services to other clients. The software is included by default on many systems and can be installed on most others.

If you like the simplicity of the rdate command but would rather use NTP, you can simply pick an appropriate server and use the ntpdate the same way you use rdate as mentioned in the previous section. This is the easiest, but least accurate and efficient, method of using NTP on a system.

The NTP software suite allows for much more advanced uses that are beyond the scope of this book. The daemon (either ntpd or xntpd) can determine the time from a variety of sources including one or more remote systems or a local device such as a GPS. The same daemon can allow other clients to synchronize their clocks from the system. It also continuously monitors any time drift present in the internal clock, and then regularly updates the clock, accounting for known drift, even if time servers are not currently available. This also reduces the chance of the system clock having sudden significant jumps in time. Quite a bit of information about the NTP protocol can be found at http://www.ntp.org.

One thing to keep in mind—NTP will not update the system clock unless it is pretty close to the server's time. For this reason, you should use rdate or ntpdate to get the time pretty close first, and then start your NTP daemon. You might want to perform this rdate every time the system boots to make sure it starts out with a fairly accurate value.

### 9.1.3  Updating the Hardware Clock

On some systems (such as x86-based systems running Linux), an updated time within the operating system kernel only lasts until the next reboot. On these types of systems, you should set your hardware clock whenever you set the time. Alternatively, setting the hardware clock once per day from cron would be adequate. Implementing one of these methods prevents the system from booting with the incorrect time.

I can't profess to know the details of all hardware platforms and operating systems. The only system I have personally experienced this on is x86-based Linux. On these systems, the command /sbin/hwclock --systohc synchronizes the date as it is stored in the kernel into the hardware BIOS.

Alternatively, you could execute your time synchronization command during system startup as well as on a regular basis so that your system always starts with the correct time.

## 9.2 Managing Accounts

For a small number of systems, the standard account management tools provided with your operating system are usually adequate. If you have automounted home directories, use data synchronization systems like NIS or NIS+, or use alternate authentication systems, things are a bit more complicated.

In this section, I develop a system for adding and removing users that is flexible and component based. I develop some example components, but you can create many more for your specific situation. In some ways, the script developed throughout this section is similar to the scripts I used to add and remove systems in Chapter 4. Here, I use a slightly different approach. Both approaches have their benefits and drawbacks, and therefore, I want to illustrate both within this book.

The scripts I develop in this section only support adding and removing users. You can modify these scripts manually or through additional scripts. Since only one aspect of a user is typically modified at any given time, a separate script for modifying each aspect would be appropriate. You can easily make modification scripts by using the code from the add/remove components provided in this section.

If an error occurs when you are adding a user, the script will abort, possibly leaving incomplete changes behind. In this case, you should remove the user and then add them again (once you have fixed the problem). The user removal script will tolerate errors because it is created to remove both complete and incomplete user accounts. If you want to, you can undo any steps you have completed when you encounter an error while adding a user; this makes it so you never leave partially added users. This approach is fairly complicated, however, and this level of complexity is not necessary in most situations. You could also have the add user script call the remove user script automatically when an error occurs. Personally, I like to have the option of examining the problem before I decide how I want to handle it.

## 9.2.1 Designing Account Management Scripts

Here I create one script that can add and delete users. I use symbolic links to provide two names for the script. This allows the script to behave differently depending on what name was used to execute it.

Setting this up is easy. Just place the main script (to be discussed later) in a directory such as /usr/local/sbin/ and name it adduser. Then change into that directory and create a symbolic link to the script named deluser (ln -s adduser deluser).

This script first checks to see if a username was specified as the first argument. If none was, it prompts the user to enter a username. The main script then verifies that the username contains valid characters. If a user is being deleted, it makes sure the user already exists. If a user is being added, it makes sure that the user does *not* already exist.

Any internal data the script uses is stored in /usr/local/var/prepare_system/. The script also uses a variety of other scripts located in the directory /usr/local/lib/usertool/. Within this helper directory is a data/ directory that contains scripts executed to generate data about the user.

The data flow throughout the script is as follows. When adding a new user, the administrator is prompted to enter new data, which is later stored in the appropriate locations. When a user is being deleted, the script automatically retrieves information from the appropriate locations. Any script can also output data that cause variables to be set in the main script. This allows other scripts to use this data without having to read it from files.

Next, you will execute all scripts within /usr/local/lib/usertool/mod/. These scripts can use any of the data retrieval scripts generated. They should modify any system files necessary to add or remove the specified user.

This modular design is very flexible and is perfect for this type of script. Every environment requires you to perform different actions when you are adding a user.

If more information is needed, you can add a new script in the data/ directory. If you need to make new modifications, you can throw an additional script into the mod/ directory.

I am assuming that you will run this script on your master account system. If you are using NIS, this would be your master NIS server. You could obviously (and will probably need to) modify this script to fit your needs. If more than one user will run this script, you should also add some locking code as described in section 4.3.

## 9.2.2 Laying Out the Account Management Configuration File

This script has a central configuration file in which you may set environment variables to be used by the main script or any of the component scripts. Here is an example configuration file that will definitely need to be modified for your system.

 **NOTE** You can find the code samples for this chapter in the Downloads section of the Apress web site (http://www.apress.com).

```
component_dir='/usr/local/lib/usertool/'
data_dir='/usr/local/var/usertool/'
skel_dir='/usr/local/etc/skel'
passwd_file='/etc/passwd'
yp_passwd_file='/etc/passwd.yp'
group_file='/etc/group'
yp_group_file='/etc/group.yp'
shadow_file='/etc/shadow'
shell_file='/etc/shells'
min_uid=500
max_uid=32000
default_groups='public'
optional_groups='dev cvs web'
home_dirs='/export/home server2:/export/home server3:/export/home'
use_ssh=1
show_space=1
automount_dir=/home
automount_file=/etc/auto.home
alias_file='/etc/aliases'
```

The precise meaning of these various settings should become obvious as you read through the following code, but here is a brief summary:

component_dir: The directory that contains the component script directories (mod/ and data/).

data_dir: A directory in which the scripts can store special data.

skel_dir: The directory that contains a skeleton home directory structure such as default login scripts.

passwd_file: The system password file.

yp_passwd_file: Optional password file that contains YP/NIS accounts. If specified, new accounts will be added here.

group_file: The system group file.

yp_group_file: Optional group file that contains YP/NIS accounts. If specified, new groups will be added here.

shadow_file: The file where account passwords should be placed, if applicable on your system.

shell_file: File that contains a listing of valid shell locations.

min_uid: The minimum user ID that can be allocated for a new user.

max_uid: The maximum user ID to be allocated to new users.

default_groups: A space-delimited list of groups in which all new users should be placed.

optional_groups: A space-delimited list of groups that a new user can optionally be placed into (at the discretion of the person adding the account).

home_dirs: A space-delimited list of directories containing home directories. Each entry may be preceded by a hostname and a colon to specify a remote host.

use_ssh: When set to 1, the script uses SSH (as opposed to NFS) to access home directories on remote systems. This has no effect if only local home directories are specified.

show_space: This determines whether or not the available space is shown when the user add script is listing home directories. If there are a large number of remote home directories, this can be quite inefficient.

automount_dir: The directory on which automounted home directories are mounted for each user. Leave this empty if you are not using automounted home directories.

automount_file: The file in which entries are placed for automounted home directories. Leave this empty if not applicable.

> `alias_file`: The file in which the script should place mail aliases for user accounts.

## 9.2.3 Account Management Helper Functions

You should place these helper functions near the top of the main script. They will be used by the main script and/or any of the component scripts. For this reason, each function is exported with the `export -f` command.

The first of these account management functions is the `getvalue` function. This function takes a mandatory first parameter that contains a message to be displayed to the user. The second parameter is optional and contains a default value. If no default is specified, the function loops until a value is entered. This function interacts with the user using `stdin` and `stderr`. It outputs the final value on `stdout`. This allows the function to be executed in the following manner:

```
username=`getvalue 'Enter the username'`
```

This causes the environment variable $username to be set to the value entered by the user. Here is the function:

```
# Args: message [default_value]
getvalue() {
    value=''
    echo >&2
    while [ -z "$value" ] ; do
       if [ -n "$2" ] ; then
          echo -n "$1 [$2]: " >&2
          read -e value
          if [ -z "$value" ] ; then
             value="$2"
          fi
       else
          echo -n "$1: " >&2
          read -e value
       fi
    done
    echo >&2
    # Return the value on STDOUT
    echo "$value"
}
export -f getvalue
```

Component scripts use the next function, onlyaction, to exit (successfully) if the action is not the specified action.

```
onlyaction() {
    [ "$action" == "$1" ] || {
        echo 'true;'
        exit 0
    }
}
export -f onlyaction
```

Another useful function is one that can remove a line from a file. It's not too complicated, but it eliminates a lot of redundant code. Note that the permissions on the original file are preserved because you can use the `cp -p` command to create the new file with the same permissions as the original. You can then move the new file over the original, but you only do this once you know that there were no errors generating the new file. The move operation is as close to an atomic operation as you get in a shell script, so even if the power goes out during the process, you will probably be okay.

```
#!/bin/bash

# Args: pattern file
remove_line() {
    cp -p "$2" "$2.new" && \
    egrep -v "$1" "$2" &gt; "$2.new" && \
        mv "$2.new" "$2"
}
export -f remove_line
```

Finally, you come across the usual `die` command. This function is not appropriate for the data-gathering scripts, because their exit code is not important (remember, they must write out the command `false` on `stdout` to indicate failure). You can, however, call this command from the main script and all of the modification scripts.

```
die() {
    echo >&2
    echo "$*" >&2
    echo >&2
    exit 1
}
export -f die
```

## 9.2.4 Account Management Main Script

The main script is not too complicated since most of the hard work is taken care of by the component scripts, which I discuss in the next sections. This script (and most of the following component scripts) uses the configuration variables defined in section 9.2.2. It starts out the same as many other scripts within this book:

```
#!/bin/bash

set -a
source /usr/local/etc/usertool.conf

usage() {
   echo "Usage: $0 [username]" 2>/dev/null
   exit 99;
}
[ "$1" == "--help" ] && usage
```

The first thing you should do is mark all variables for export with the set -a command. Although every variable does not need to be exported, most of them do, and marking them like this eliminates the need to use the export command on each variable. Once you have done this, source the configuration file (whose variables are automatically exported). Then define the usage function and check for a parameter of --help which, if present, causes the program to display that usage information. Next, determine and verify the username:

```
username="$1"
if [ -z "$username" ] ; then
   username=`getvalue 'Enter the username'`
fi
# Make sure the username contains only valid characters
if ! echo "$username" | egrep -q '^[0-9a-zA-Z_-]+$' ; then
   die "Invalid username: $username"
fi
```

As you can see, the first thing I did here was check to see if the username was specified as the first argument. If it wasn't, the script used the getvalue function I described in the previous section to request the username from the administrator. Then the script checks the username to make sure it contains only valid characters. Your system(s) may allow more or less flexibility in usernames, but this should be appropriate for most systems.

Next, the script does one of two things depending on how it was called. The script starts by setting the $action variable to the name that was used to execute the program. This is determined by reading the $0 variable and using the basename command to strip off the pathname, if any. Then the script checks this value and acts accordingly:

```
action=$(basename $0)
if [ "$action" == "adduser" ] ; then
    # Make sure the username is not already in use
    if grep -q "^$username$" "$data_dir/userlist" >2/dev/null ; then
        die "User already exists: $username"
    fi
    # Record the new username
    echo "$username" >> "$data_dir/userlist"
elif [ "$action" == "deluser" ] ; then
    # Make sure the username exists
    if ! grep -q "^$username$" "$data_dir/userlist" 2>/dev/null ; then
        die "User does not exist: $username"
    fi
else
    die "Unknown action: $action"
fi
```

Now make sure the username does exist (when removing a user) or does not exist (when adding a user). The username is also stored in the userlist in the data directory. You should perform this check first thing because, if you encounter any errors in the component scripts, this means that the user was only partially installed and should be removed before being added again. The script will not, however, remove a user that is not in the list. The next function is a helper function for this main script:

```
# Returns all scripts from a directory
get_scripts() {
    for script in $1/* ; do
        # Go to next file if this is a directory
        [ -d $script ] && continue
        # Go to next file if this is not executable
        [ -x $script ] || continue
        # Good, return this script on STDOUT
        echo $script
    done
}
```

This function processes the directory specified as the first argument and returns any executable files that are not directories. This is used by the next section of the script:

```
# Now, execute all data-gathering scripts
for script in `get_scripts $component_dir/data` ; do
    # Execute this script, execute its output, abort on failure
    eval `$script` || die "$script returned error"
done
```

This block of code executes each of the data retrieval scripts. Anything printed on stdout in the component script executes. This allows the component script to set variables by sending the string name=value; on stdout. Each script must also output either true; or false; as the last line of output to indicate its exit status. The scripts can, of course, interact with the user via stderr and stdin. The next section of code also uses the get_scripts:

```
# Now, execute all modification scripts
for script in `get_scripts $component_dir/mod` ; do
    # Execute this script, execute its output, abort on failure
    $script || die "$script returned error"
done
```

This section of code executes the component scripts that make the actual modifications to the system. These scripts can do anything they want, as long as they return a zero exit code on success. Finally, you have to clean up a bit (for instance, you need to register that a user has been removed—if, indeed, that is what you did).

```
if [ "$action" == "deluser" ] ; then
    # Remove the username from the user list
    remove_line "^$username$" "$data_dir/userlist"
fi

echo
echo "Action $action for $username has been completed"
echo

exit 0
```

You might want to record the username and their user ID in a "deleted users" file for future reference. This would be quite easy to add to the script at this point.

## 9.2.5 Account Management Data Components

These scripts do not have to be written in any specific language. They could be C executables or Perl scripts. They must simply output valid Bourne Shell commands on stdout with the last command indicating its exit status. You must place all of the following scripts in the data/ component directory. Their names are not important since they can be executed in any order. However, if you add scripts that need to be executed before other scripts, you need to name them appropriately. The usual thing to do is precede the filename by a number, such as 00first.sh and 99last.sh.

### 9.2.5.1 Allocating UID/GID

For this example, I am assuming that the master system has system-specific users and groups as well as NIS (a.k.a. YP) user and group files. If any of these configuration items are empty, the files will be ignored (so, if you only use one or the other, you could just define one or the other). The assumption in this script is that each user has their own default group in which the user ID and group ID are equal. This assumption is not necessary, but it makes user management simpler and doesn't make this script much more complicated.

```perl
#!/usr/bin/perl -w
use strict;

# Only need to allocate a UID/GID if adding a new user
if ($ENV{'action'} ne 'adduser') {
    print "true;";
    exit 0;
}

my @IDs;
my @files = (
    $ENV{'passwd_file'},
    $ENV{'yp_passwd_file'},
    $ENV{'group_file'},
    $ENV{'yp_group_file'}
);

foreach my $file (@files) {
    next unless $file;
    unless (open (FILE, $file)) {
        print STDERR "Can't open $file: $!\n";
        print "false;\n";
        exit 1;
    }
```

```
    while (my $line = <FILE>) {
        if ($line =~ (/^[^:]+:[^:]*:(\d+):/)) {
            $IDs[$1] = 1;
        }
    }
    close (FILE);
}

for (my $i = $ENV{'min_uid'}; $i <= $ENV{'max_uid'}; $i++) {
    if ($IDs[$i]) {
        print STDERR "\nAllocated UID/GID: $i\n\n";
        print "newid=$i;";
        print "true;";
        exit 0;
    }
}

print STDERR
    "Out of UIDs (min=$ENV{'min_uid'}, max=$ENV{'max_uid'})\n";
print "false;";
exit 1;
```

This script simply sets the index in an array for each user and group ID in use in any of the account files specified (both NIS and regular files). It then looks through the list and returns the first ID available. The new user/group ID is returned in the $newid variable.

### 9.2.5.2  Requesting a Full Username

This script simply asks for the user's full username, but only if a user is being added. Nothing too exciting here:

```
#!/bin/bash

onlyaction 'adduser'
fullname=`getvalue "Enter full name for $username"`
echo "fullname='$fullname';"
echo 'true;'
exit 0
```

This script requires the user's full name which is returned in the $fullname variable.

### 9.2.5.3 *Selecting a Shell*

This script uses the file specified in $shell_file and prompts the user to select from a list of shells.

```
#!/bin/bash

onlyaction 'adduser'

echo "Select a shell:" >&2
select shell in `sort $shell_file` ; do
   [ -n "$shell" ] && break
done

echo >&2
echo "shell='$shell';"
echo 'true;'
exit 0
```

The selected shell is returned in the $shell variable.

### 9.2.5.4 *Allocating Extra Groups*

This script sets the $extragroups variable. It always contains the space-delimited list of group names specified in the $default_groups setting in the configuration file. If there are any groups listed in $optional_groups, the user is prompted to choose one or more of these optional groups. All of the optional groups chosen are also listed in the $extragroups output variable.

```
#!/bin/bash

onlyaction 'adduser'

export PS3="Enter group ('q' to quit): "
extragroups=''
[ -n "$optional_groups" ] && {
   echo "Select one or more extra groups:" >&2
   select group in $optional_groups ; do
     [ -z "$group" ] && break
     extragroups="$extragroups $group"
   done
}
```

```
echo >&2
echo "extragroups='$extragroups $default_groups';"
echo 'true;'
exit 0
```

### 9.2.5.5 Determining the Home Directory

If you are deleting an account, only the beginning of this script is executed. It simply uses the eval to determine the home directory of the user. Assuming the username is kirk, the eval echo ~$username command is converted to eval echo ~kirk, which is then evaluated, which causes the user's home directory to be printed on stdout. This user's home directory is then stored in the variable $homedir for the benefit of the deletion scripts which are executed later. Here is the first part of this script:

```
#!/bin/bash

if [ "$action" == "deluser" ] ; then
    echo "homedir='$(eval echo ~$username)';"
    echo 'true;'
    exit 0
fi
```

If you are adding a user, the script continues past that block of code. The next block of code is fairly complex and I am hesitant to include it in this example. However, it is a good example of the large amount of information that can be made available to a systems administrator. In this case, the script determines the amount of free space on every available home directory. Each home directory is listed in the space-delimited configuration variable $home_dirs. Local directories begin with a /; remote home directories are of the form host:/path. If the configuration variable $use_ssh is set, you access all remote home directories via SSH. Remember that the directories listed should be the base directories where home directories are placed. For example, if /export/home1/ is listed and the user kirk is added, the home directory /export/home1/kirk/ would be created as this user's home directory. Here is that block of code:

```
dirlist=''
if [ "$show_space" == "1" ] ; then
    # Determine available space on each drive
    for entry in $home_dirs ; do
        space=`
```

```
            if echo "$entry" | grep -q ':' ; then
                host=$(echo "$entry" | sed 's/:.*$//')
                dir=$(echo "$entry" | sed 's/^.*://')
                if [ "$use_ssh" == "1" ] ; then
                    if ! ssh -T $host "df -m $dir" ; then
                        echo "WARNING: Could not access $dir on $host" >&2
                    fi
                else
                    if ! mount -t nfs "$host:$dir" /mnt/tmp ; then
                        echo "WARNING: Could not mount $dir from $host" >&2
                    fi
                    df -m /mnt/tmp
                    umount /mnt/tmp
                fi
            else
                # Local directory
                df -m $entry
            fi 2>/dev/null | awk '/^\// {print $4}'

        [ -z "$space" ] && {
            space='??'
        }
        if [ -z "$dirlist" ] ; then
            dirlist="$entry ($space MB avail)"
        else
            dirlist="$dirlist|$entry ($space MB avail)"
        fi
    done
else
    # Just display the drives
    dirlist=`echo "$home_dirs" | sed 's/ /|/g'`
fi
```

Like I said, this code is a bit scary. All it really does is build a list of home directories, separated by the pipe (|) character. If the $show_space configuration variable is set, the space available in each directory is determined. Since there are three different access methods for a directory that might be used, all three of them are enclosed in the multiline backtick substitution. Within these backticks, the df -m command is run on the directory—either locally on an NFS-mounted filesystem, or over SSH. Note that the -m option to df causes the available space to be shown in megabytes which is a GNU extension and thus may not be supported on your system. If it is not, you can use the -k option to show the space in kilobytes instead. Here is the raw output from the df command:

```
% df -m /
Filesystem          1M-blocks      Used Available Use% Mounted on
/dev/sda2               4161       3808       311  93% /
```

If the home directory is a remote directory (if it contains a colon), it is split into the host and directory portions. Then, either SSH or NFS is used to access that filesystem and run the `df` command. The complete output of the `if` statement is sent through the `awk` command. This allows you to use only one `awk` command to process the output in all three cases. The `awk` command only processes lines beginning with a / (i.e., not the header line) and isolates the fourth column. This is finally set in the `$space` command and represents the space available on that partition.

The rest of the script is easy in comparison:

```
homedir=''
IFS="|"
while [ -z "$homedir" ] ; do
    select homedir in $dirlist ; do
        if [ -n "$homedir" ] ; then
            homedir=`echo "$homedir" | sed 's/ (.*$//'`
            break
        fi
    done
done
unset IFS

echo >&2
echo "homedir='$homedir';"
echo 'true;'
exit 0
```

The `$IFS` variable is set to | to allow the `select` command to tokenize the list of directories using this character. Using | as the delimiter allows for spaces within the list items. This is important since every list item contains spaces (which separate the directory from the space available). The user is forced to make a selection, and once they do, anything after a space is removed (i.e., the description of the space available). Finally, the `$IFS` variable is unset, which causes it to return to its default value.

### 9.2.5.6 Choosing Mail Aliases

This script simply allows the user to enter zero or more mail aliases for the new account. They are stored and returned in the variable `$aliases`.

```
#!/bin/bash

onlyaction 'adduser'

aliases=''
echo >&2
while true ; do
    echo -n "Enter mail alias [leave blank when done]: " >&2
    read -e value
    if [ -n "$value" ] ; then
        aliases="$aliases $value"
    else
        echo >&2
        break
    fi
done
echo >&2

echo "aliases='$aliases';"
echo 'true;'
exit 0
```

## 9.2.6  The Modification Components

These components have no output restrictions. They can use both stdout and
stderr freely. They simply should exit with a zero status on success, and non-zero
on failure. These scripts should actually make any necessary modifications to add
or delete an account. Each of these scripts can be named whatever you would like,
but the order does matter in most cases. So, you could precede each script name
with a number so that their alphabetical ordering equals the order in which they
are presented.

### 9.2.6.1  The Basic Account Setup Script

This script adds (or removes) the basic account entries in the password and group
files. First, it determines which files to use (NIS/YP, if possible), then it either
removes or adds entries to each of these files as necessary.

```
#!/bin/bash

# Determine which password & group files
pwfile="$yp_passwd_file"
[ -z "$pwfile" ] && {
    pwfile="$passwd_file"
}
gfile="$yp_group_file"
[ -z "$gfile" ] && {
    gfile="$group_file"
}

if [ "$action" == "deluser" ] ; then
    echo "Removing entry from $pwfile..."
    remove_line "^$username:" "$pwfile"

    echo "Removing entry from $gfile..."
    remove_line "^$username:" "$gfile"

    [ -n "$shadow_file" ] && {
        echo "Removing entry from $shadow_file..."
        remove_line "^$username:" "$shadow_file"
    }

else

    # Determine home directory (either automounted or not)
    if [ -z "$automount_dir" ] ; then
        home="$automount_dir/$username"
    else
        home="$homedir"
    fi

    echo "Creating entry in $pwfile..."
    echo "$username:*:$newid:$newid:$fullname:$home:$shell" \
        >> $pwfile

    echo "Creating entry in $gfile..."
    echo "$username:*:$newid:$username" >> $gfile
```

```
    # Create shadow entry, if applicable
    [ -n "$shadow_file" ] && {
        # Creation of the shadow entry is OS-dependent
        echo "Creating entry in $shadow_file..."
        echo "$username:*::::::" >> $shadow_file
    }

fi

exit 0
```

Note that the exact format of these files, particularly the shadow file (if used), can differ from one operating system to another.

### 9.2.6.2 The Extra Groups Script

This script, again, determines the proper group file to be used. If the user is being deleted, they are removed from any groups in which they are listed. The sed command that does this contains three separate expressions. The first removes the user if they are the first name listed within a group; the next removes the user if they are the only user listed for that group; and the last removes any other entries (i.e., not the first and not the only) for the user who may exist.

```
#!/bin/bash

# Determine group file
gfile="$yp_group_file"
[ -z "$gfile" ] && {
    gfile="$group_file"
}

if [ "$action" == "deluser" ] ; then
    echo "Removing $username from all groups"
    cp -p "$gfile" "$gfile.new"
    sed -e "s/:$username,/:/" \
        -e "s/:$username$/:/" \
        -e "s/,$username//" \
        "$gfile" > "$gfile.new" && \
            mv "$gfile.new" "$gfile"

else
```

```
      [ -n "$extragroups" ] && {
        for group in $extragroups ; do
          if grep -q "^$group:" "$gfile" ; then
            echo "Adding $username to group $group"
            cp -p "$gfile" "$gfile.new"
            if sed -e "s/^$group:.*[^:]$/&,$username/" \
                   -e "s/^$group:.*:$/&$username/" \
                   "$gfile" > "$gfile.new" ; then
              mv "$gfile.new" "$gfile"
            else
              die "Could not add $username to group $group"
            fi
          else
            # Doesn't exist yet, find ID and create entry
            echo "Creating new group $group for $username"
            eval `$component_dir/data/getuid.pl` || \
              die "Could not allocate ID for new group $group"
            echo "$group:*:$newid:$username" >> $gfile
          fi
        done
      }

fi

exit 0
```

When you are adding a user, each group listed in $extragroups (as set by one of the data gathering scripts) is processed by the script. If the group doesn't exist, the script adds it with the new user as a member. If it already exists, the user is added to the existing member list. This sed command must have two expressions: one that adds a user to a group in most cases, and a second that handles the special case of an empty group.

### 9.2.6.3 Adding and Removing from Automount Files

This script is really pretty simple. It just adds or removes an entry for the user in the automount file. This is only done if the configuration variable $automount_file is set.

```
#!/bin/bash

[ -n "$automount_file" ] && {
    if [ "$action" == "deluser" ] ; then
        echo "Removing entry from $automount_file..."
        remove_line "^$username" "$automount_file"
    else
        if echo "$homedir" | grep -q ':' ; then
            echo "Adding entry to $automount_file..."
            echo "$username $homedir:$username" >> $automount_file
        fi
    fi
}
```

### 9.2.6.4  The NIS Update Script

This script is very simple, but it is not very flexible. If you are using NIS/YP
(assumed to be the case if $yp_passwd_file is defined), it will distribute the changes
made so far. This is important because some of the remaining scripts assume that
the user already exists. You can expand this script to use any number of distribution
schemes to distribute the new account data files.

```
#!/bin/bash

if [ -n "$yp_passwd_file" ] ; then
    cd /var/yp
    make
fi
```

### 9.2.6.5  The Home Directory Creation Script

The home directory script uses the $homedir variable and creates a new directory
for this user under that directory. The script then copies the skeleton home directory
(as specified in the $skel_dir) over to create the new directory. The ownership on
the directory then changes to that of the new user. You can do all of this locally over
NFS, or you can use SSH. When you are deleting a user, their home directory is
renamed to start with deleted-. You can then clean it up later using the script
discussed in section 9.2.7.

```bash
#!/bin/bash

if echo "$homedir" | grep -q ':' ; then
    host=$(echo "$homedir" | sed 's/:.*$//')
    dir=$(echo "$homedir" | sed 's/^.*://')
    if [ "$use_ssh" == "1" ] ; then
        if [ "$action" == "deluser" ] ; then
            ssh -T $host "mv $dir/$username $dir/deleted-$username"
        else
            ssh -T $host "cp -r $skel_dir $dir/$username" && \
            ssh -T $host "chown -R $username.$username $dir/$username" \
                || die "Could not create $dir on $host via SSH"
        fi
    else
        if ! mount -t nfs "$host:$dir" /mnt/tmp ; then
            die "Could not mount $dir from $host"
        fi
        if [ "$action" == "deluser" ] ; then
            mv /mnt/tmp/$username /mnt/tmp/deleted-$username
        else
            cp -r "$skel_dir" "/mnt/tmp/$username" && \
            chown -R $username.$username "/mnt/tmp/$username" || \
                die "Could not create home directory in $dir on $host"
        fi
        umount /mnt/tmp
    fi
else
    # Local directory
    if [ "$action" == "deluser" ] ; then
        mv $homedir/$username $homedir/deleted-$username
    else
        cp -r $skel_dir $homedir/$username && \
        chown -R $username.$username $homedir/$username || \
            die "Could not create home directory in $homedir"
    fi
fi

exit 0
```

### 9.2.6.6 The Mail Aliases Script

This script assumes the $fullname variable is in the form Firstname Lastname. It then
creates a mail alias (in the file defined in $alias_file of the form Firstname.Lastname

by replacing the space in the username with a period. Then it creates any additional mail aliases listed in the $aliases variable. All of these are created using the add_alias function, which adds a single line to the aliases file. If a user is being removed, any mail aliases pointing to that user are deleted.

```
#!/bin/bash

add_alias() {
    echo "Adding mail alias for $username: $1"
    echo "$1: $username" >> "$alias_file"
}

if [ "$action" == "deluser" ] ; then

    cp -p "$alias_file" "$alias_file.new"
    sed "/: *$username$/d" "$alias_file" > "$alias_file.new" && \
        mv "$alias_file.new" "$alias_file"

else

    # Always add first.last alias
    add_alias `echo "$fullname" | sed 's/ /./g'`
    for alias in $aliases ; do
        add_alias "$alias"
    done

fi
```

### 9.2.6.7  Setting the Passwords

Finally, after everything else is done, you can set the passwords. This particular script sets the account password and a Samba password. You can set other passwords as is appropriate in your environment. Theoretically, you could ask for a password in a data-gathering script and then set a variety passwords to that single value. The problem is that password programs usually do not allow you to specify the password on the command line or through stdin. There are ways around this—changing the password programs, fooling programs into taking your password on stdin, or doing your own password encryption and insertion—but, unless you have more than two passwords to set, I don't think it is worth that much effort.

This script uses the yppasswd command, if appropriate. Otherwise, it uses the standard passwd command. It then calls smbpasswd to add a new entry (with a password).

```
#!/bin/bash

onlyaction 'adduser'

echo
echo "Setting account password..."
if [ -n "$yp_passwd_file" ] ; then
    yppasswd $username
else
    passwd $username
fi

echo
echo "Setting Samba password..."
smbpasswd -a $username

exit 0
```

## 9.2.7 Deleted User Cleanup

Since users' home directories are not actually deleted, you need a script to go through and delete them permanently at a later time. All "deleted" home directories are renamed with the prefix deleted-. This script checks each home directory (remote and local) and deletes any that have not been touched in over 30 days.

In this case, the main script calls a function and sends the commands to be executed into that function via stdin. The function then executes the commands as appropriate. Here is the main part of the script:

```
#!/bin/bash

source /usr/local/etc/usertool.conf

for hostdir in $home_dirs ; do
    dir=$(echo "$hostdir" | sed 's/^.*:///')
    if [ "$use_ssh" != "1" ] ; then
        dir="/mnt/tmp"
    fi
    echo "Checking $hostdir..."
    dohost $hostdir << __EOF__
```

```
for entry in `find $dir -type d -name 'deleted-*' -mtime +30 -print`
do
    rm -rf \$entry;
done

__EOF__
done

exit 0
```

For each home directory, this loop first determines which directory should be checked. If the access is to be done via NFS, the directory is overridden to /mnt/tmp/. The dohost is then called with some commands passed in via stdin. For those of you who are not already familiar with this, what you see is a "here document." Everything on the lines after << __EOF__ is redirected through stdin. The string __EOF__ is arbitrary, but it must not appear in the text, because the next occurrence of this string at the beginning of a line marks the end of the block of text.

These commands use the find command to find and delete any old home directories. You want to look only for directories that begin with deleted- and haven't been modified in 30 days. Note that a backslash must be used for the $entry variable because you want it to be substituted during the loop processing and not before.

```
dohost() {
    if echo "$1" | grep -q ':' ; then
        host=$(echo "$1" | sed 's/:.*$//')
        if [ "$use_ssh" == "1" ] ; then
            ssh -T $host "bash -"
        else
            dir=$(echo "$hostdir" | sed 's/^.*:://')
            if ! mount -t nfs "$host:$dir" /mnt/tmp ; then
                die "Could not mount $dir from $host"
            fi
            bash -
            umount /mnt/tmp
        fi
    else
        bash -
    fi
}
```

This function executes the bash shell and tells it to execute commands coming from `stdin` (indicated by the hyphen). It may execute the shell via SSH or it may execute it after mounting an NFS directory.

## 9.3 Maintaining Log Files

Almost any computer system has log files. Fortunately, many of these systems have a facility in place that rotates or trims these log files. Sometimes, a specific application can even rotate or manage its log files internally.

That having been said, there are many reasons why you, as an administrator, might need to be concerned with log files. For instance, if your system does not rotate its own logs, you will have to set up your own log rotation system. Likewise, you may have applications (custom or third party) on your system that have continuously growing log files and do not manage these logs in any way. If you are lucky, the log rotation facility provided with your system can be extended to handle additional log files. If it can't, you may have to add a custom rotation system just to handle any extra log files on your system.

If you do have to add a new rotation system, you may want to use that system for all of your log rotation needs. Doing so can simplify your life and add more power and flexibility to your log rotation possibilities. A custom rotation system can also be applied to multiple platforms and can support the exact style of log rotation you require.

Fortunately, there are several log rotation programs available that you can deploy on almost any system. I will present a few of the more popular ones in this section. If you are already using (or are thinking about using) GNU cfengine, it can also take care of log rotations for you, thus eliminating the need for an additional program.

### 9.3.1 Red Hat's logrotate

Red Hat has a log rotation system called logrotate. It has shipped with Red Hat Linux for as long as I can remember and has slowly evolved over the years. It is written in C and can be directly compiled on or easily ported to almost any system. Its source can be found at `ftp://ftp.redhat.com/pub/redhat/linux/code/logrotate/`.

The program is simple enough. The actual executable is typically installed as `/usr/sbin/logrotate`. The main configuration file is usually `/etc/logrotate.conf` (but you can specify any file on the command line). The program also maintains the data file `/var/lib/logrotate.status` (which can also be specified on the command line with the `-s` option).

On Red Hat Linux, logrotate is set to execute once per day through the cron daemon. You can specify any number of configuration files on the command line, but only /etc/logrotate.conf is specified in the cron job. That configuration file contains global settings and includes the directory /etc/logrotate.d/, which causes the configuration files in that directory to be read as well. This directory can contain any number of files, usually one file per application or set of log files.

Here is the main portion of Red Hat's default /etc/logrotate.conf:

```
# rotate log files weekly
weekly

# keep 4 weeks worth of backlogs
rotate 4

# create new (empty) log files after rotating old ones
create

# uncomment this if you want your log files compressed
#compress

# RPM packages drop log rotation information into this directory
include /etc/logrotate.d
```

These global options tell logrotate to rotate each log file once per week and to keep four rotated files. logrotate will create a new empty file once the rotation has taken place and can optionally compress the rotated files. Finally, the include directive is used to include additional configuration files from the /etc/logrotate.d/ directory. The rest of this file follows:

```
/var/log/wtmp {
    monthly
    create 0664 root utmp
    rotate 1
}
```

This block of code rotates the file /var/log/wtmp. Everything within the braces applies to this file only. In this case, the global weekly rotation setting is changed to monthly and the rotation limit is reduced to one. Once the file has been rotated, it is replaced with an empty file with permissions of 0664, an owner of root, and a group of utmp.

There are actually about 40 commands you can use within the configuration files. These commands allow you to rotate files based on their size, mail the log entries, and execute pre and post rotate scripts. They are all discussed in the man page provided with the program. I am not going to discuss all of these commands in this section, but I will provide one more example that is a bit more complicated:

```
/var/log/samba/*.log {
    notifempty
    missingok
    sharedscripts
    copytruncate
    postrotate
      /bin/kill -HUP `cat /var/run/samba/smbd.pid \
      /var/run/samba/nmbd.pid 2> /dev/null` 2> /dev/null || true
    endscript
}
```

This configuration file is placed in the /etc/logrotate.d/ directory and is part of the Samba package. The first thing you should notice is that a wildcard is used in the log file specification. This helps make the configuration files much less complex. A file will not be rotated if it is empty (notifempty). If no files are found, Logwatch will not complain (missingok). Any scripts within this block are run once after all files have been rotated (sharedscripts) and not after each individual rotation. Finally, when the files are rotated, they are copied to a new filename and then the original file is truncated (copytruncate).

This example also has a postrotate script. This script sends the HUP signal to the two Samba processes after the rotation has taken place. As is the case with many daemons, this signal causes them to close and reopen any log files. If this is not done, they will keep writing to the log file after it has been truncated, causing file corruption.

For more information on the commands available within the logrotate configuration files, see the man page provided with the program.

## 9.3.2 Rotating Logs with Spinlogs

The Spinlogs program is a very simple, yet useful, file rotation script that can run on just about any system. Its only requirement, apart from the standard UNIX commands such as egrep, mv, and cp, is the Korn shell (ksh).

You can download Spinlogs from http://isle.wumpus.org/cgi-bin/pikie?SpinLogs. Its archive contains the shell script, a sample configuration file, and its license file (the "Artistic License"). Here is an example configuration file:

```
# log_filename    owner:group mode num size time flags pid_file signal
#                       |        |    |   |    |    |       |       |
/var/log/messages root:root   0600 14  *         D    Z
```

This simply says to rotate `/var/log/messages` every time the program is executed (because no maximum size is specified). The meanings for each field are as follows:

`log_filename`: The file to be rotated, surprisingly enough. No wildcards are allowed.

`owner:group`: The ownership to be applied to the rotated log files as well as the new blank log file.

`mode`: The permissions for the rotated and original log files.

`num`: How many rotated log files to keep. In this case, if the program is being run daily, two weeks worth of logs will be stored. If the program was run hourly, you'd only have 14 hours of log archives.

`size`: The maximum size of a file, in kilobytes. A file will only be rotated if it is larger than this limit. If set to *, the file will always be rotated.

`time`: This is only here to maintain the same file format as the FreeBSD's newsyslog log rotation utility. The Spinlogs program does not support time-based rotations.

`flags`: This field can contain any number of the following flags:

D: Do not create an empty log file in its place after rotation.

Z: Use this flag to compress files after rotation.

0: Don't compress the `.0` rotated log (the most recent archive).

B: This says the log file is binary and a rotation message should not be placed in the file.

`pid_file`: If specified, this file should contain a PID for a program to signal after the rotation has completed.

`signal`: This is the signal to be sent to the process (such as `HUP`).

Once you have created your configuration file, you should run the `spinlogs` command on a regular basis (usually daily) from your system's cron daemon. A typical invocation would be:

```
% /usr/local/sbin/spinlogs \ -c /usr/local/etc/spinlogs.conf \
-p /var/run/syslogd.pid
```

This specifies a configuration file of `/usr/local/etc/spinlogs.conf` and identifies `/var/run/syslogd.pid` as the file that contains the process ID for the syslog program. The `HUP` signal will be sent to this process ID after Spinlogs has completed execution.

### 9.3.3  Log Rotation with cfengine

If you have read the discussions of GNU cfengine thus far (particularly section 6.4), you should realize that cfengine can do just about anything on your systems automatically. When it comes to log rotation, it can get the job done just about as well as any other program, and it can do so on any of your systems.

Unfortunately, the section of cfengine that can perform these rotations—the `disable` section—is not exactly obvious. The `disable` section can be placed in `cfagent.conf` along with the rest of your configuration directives. Like many other sections, the `disable` section was originally created to delete or rename unwanted files, but it is flexible enough to handle other tasks, such as log rotation.

Like many log rotation systems, you can rotate based on time or file size, and you can store as many rotated files as you desire. This first example will cause cfengine to rotate your web server's access log every Sunday:

```
disable:
  Sunday::
      /var/log/httpd/access_log rotate=52
```

The Sunday class will only be defined on Sundays, so the rotation will only take place on that day. The `rotate` argument specifies that (at most) 52 rotated files should be present. Here, since the rotation is performed once per week, one year's worth of logs will be stored (52 weeks). One problem with this section is that it assumes `cfagent` is only executed one time on each Sunday. If it is executed more than once, the rotation will be performed multiple times for that week (and some rotated files will contain less than a day's worth of data).

Another (perhaps better) option is to rotate based on the log file's size. Here is another example:

```
disable:
  /var/log/httpd/access_log size=>100mb rotate=4
```

This only keeps four previous log files, and the rotation only takes place if the file is greater than 100Mb. It is important to remember that, if you run `cfagent` only once per day, the file will only be rotated at most once per day. The rotated file can, however, be much larger than 100Mb if your daily traffic is significant. Even if the file grows to one gigabyte in a day, it will only be rotated the next time `cfagent` executes.

You can also perform certain actions (like sending the HUP signal to a daemon) by defining a class when a rotation occurs. For example:

```
disable:
    /var/log/httpd/access_log size=>100mb rotate=4 define=http_rotated

processes:
  http_rotated::
      "httpd" signal=hup
```

Whenever the log file is rotated, the http_rotated class is defined. Then, in the processes section, the HUP signal is sent to all httpd processes only if this class is defined.


# 9.4 Removing Files

You are about to read an entire section on removing files. Yes, I hope you already know all about the rm command by now. But, as you may have guessed, this section goes beyond simple file deletion and talks about *automating* the removal of files.

Files tend to collect in many places on UNIX systems. The first place that comes to mind is the /tmp/ directory (and, on some systems, the /var/tmp/ directory). Many users (including myself) are guilty of throwing all kinds of things in these directories that usually don't get deleted when we are finished. A simple solution for these directories is to delete files that have not been accessed for a specified period of time (maybe a day, maybe a month).

Another area where files constantly grow are users' home directories. This is a case where a simple access time-based removal process is not appropriate (I see some files in my home directory that have not been touched for six years, yet I would be quite upset if they were deleted). If you have a "share" or another common data directory that many people access over Samba or NFS, this directory also tend to grow indefinitely.

Ever-growing files, particularly temporary files, have been a problem ever since magnetic storage was invented. For this reason, there are a number of options you can use to solve these problems.


## 9.4.1 *Custom Drive Cleaning*

In this section, I present a couple of quick file removal solutions using basic UNIX commands. The first can be used to clean out temporary directories and uses only the find command. The next example is a fairly simple shell script that can clean up users' home directories.

### 9.4.1.1  Cleaning Temporary Directories

You can use the find command to quickly remove old files under a directory. You should first see what files will be deleted to make sure you aren't deleting anything important. You can run this command to see files that have not been accessed within the previous week:

```
# find /tmp -atime +7 -type f -print
```

You can then use the -exec command to remove these files:

```
# find /tmp -atime +7 -type f -exec rm -f {} \;
```

The -exec option can be quite overwhelming at first glance. This option specifies a command to be run for each matching file. Take a look at the -exec option in the preceding example, which ends with four special characters. Every time the command is executed, the two-character {} sequence is replaced with one of the matched files. The \; sequence ends the string of commands to be executed. The backslash is required to prevent the shell from interpreting the semicolon, as the find expects a semicolon to end the command sequence that is to be executed.

Once old files have been removed, you can then run a command to remove empty directories (this command requires GNU's version of the find command):

```
# find /tmp -type d -empty -exec rmdir {} \;
```

You can place these commands into a shell script that you can run daily using the cron daemon.

### 9.4.1.2  Cleaning Home Directories

You have to be much more careful when cleaning users' home directories. The following is a simple script that warns users via email about files that will be deleted, and then it deletes the files at a later time:

```
#!/bin/bash

TMPDIR=~/tmp
WARNTIME=30
RMTIME=60
SIZE="500k"
USERS=`awk -F: '{if ($3 >= 500) print $1}' /etc/passwd`
```

```
# Find files to warn about
for user in $USERS ; do
   homedir=`eval echo ~$user`
   find $homedir -atime +$WARNTIME -type f -size $SIZE -print \
      > $TMPDIR/$user
   [ -s "$TMPDIR/$user" ] && {
      # Some files were found
      mail -s 'SCHEDULED FOR DELETION!!' "$user" < "$TMPDIR/$user"
   }
   rm -f "$TMPDIR/$user"
done

# Now, delete any files that are old enough
find $homedir -atime +$RMTIME -type f -size $SIZE -exec rm -f {} \;
```

Take a look at this code; there are a few settings at the top. First of all, the temporary directory should *not* be set to /tmp/ because predictable filenames are used (and would present a possible local security exploit). Second, the directory must only be writable by root. After that, the $WARNTIME variable specifies that the user will be warned about files that have not been accessed for 30 days, and the $RMTIME variable specifies that files will be deleted when they have not been accessed in 60 days. Next, we have $SIZE, which limits the file deletions to files larger than 500 kilobytes. Finally, the $USERS variable is set to include all users on the system with user IDs greater than 500. This assignment directly accesses /etc/passwd and may have to be changed in your environment.

The script then uses the find command to find files to warn the user about. The output is placed in a temporary file and is then mailed to the user if the file is non-empty (checked with the -s switch). Once this is taken care of, any files older than the deletion threshold are removed with the find command.

This script can be run from cron on a regular basis. It should only be run once per week (or less often) because most users will not want to receive a daily email about files that may be deleted in 30 days. Users would soon ignore these types of emails.

### 9.4.2  Red Hat's tmpwatch

Again, I find that Red Hat has created a simple yet effective program that is packaged with their version of Linux, yet can be used on a variety of systems. Its usage is very simple:

```
# tmpwatch 168 /tmp
```

This command removes any files under the /tmp/ directory that have not been accessed in 168 hours (one week). It also removes any directories that are empty after these files are removed. Obviously you would want to run this, from cron, on all appropriate directories every day or so.

A few command-line options are described in the provided man page. One that you might find useful for testing purposes is the -t switch, which shows what would have been done, but makes no changes to the filesystem:

```
# tmpwatch -t 168 /tmp removing directory /tmp/ssh-XXqyfOhY
removing directory /tmp/orbit-kirk
removing directory /tmp/.wine-kirk/server-306-bfOde
removing directory /tmp/.wine-kirk
removing directory /tmp/.sawfish-kirk
```

This command is generally only useful for real temporary directories—not home directories and the like.

## 9.4.3  Removing Files with cfengine

Once again, GNU cfengine can help you keep the drives on your system relatively clean. It can quickly clean out the /tmp/ directory and remove most core files as follows:

```
tidy:

    any::

        /tmp/    pat=*              R=inf   age=7   rmdirs=true
```

As usual, this tidy section would be placed in cfagent.conf or a file included by this file. The filesystem is recursed up to three directories deep while it is looking for core files. All files under /tmp/ that have not been accessed in seven days are also deleted.

Assuming you have cfengine configured to quickly access users' home directories as discussed in in section 7.7, you can easily clean up users' home directories. Here are a few examples:

```
tidy:
    AllHomeServers::
        # Remove all core files
        home      pattern=core   r=inf   age=0
        # Remove emacs-style backup files after 7 days
        home      pattern=*~     r=inf   age=7
        # Remove CVS backup files after 30 days
        home      pattern=.#*    r=inf   age=30
```

This set of commands only runs on systems that are part of the `AllHomeServers` class. It performs some basic cleanup of your users' home directories. If your users use a web browser like Netscape, you can help keep their local cache directory relatively trim:

```
tidy:
    AllHomeServers::
        home/.netscape/cache pattern=* r=inf age=7
```

You can also remove big files like this:

```
tidy:
    AllHomeServers::
        home pattern=* r=inf age=60 size=>500kb
```

Each person will obviously set up this section differently based on their users, their available disk space, their company policy, and so on. But, it should be clear that you will find cfengine to be very useful when you are attempting to clean up your users' files which, if left untamed, will continue to grow indefinitely.

# CHAPTER 10

# System Monitoring

PERHAPS THE EASIEST and most simple method of system monitoring is the "user method." You read email and catch up on current events until a user reports a problem, which you promptly fix—or so you hope. Unfortunately, your users may grow tired of being used as one of your automation tools. Or the users may be customers, in which case your company would expect a more professional monitoring system.

Ironically, the more automated your systems management becomes, the more automated your monitoring system must be. With a good automation system, you might not personally use a service or log in to a system for months at a time. A system could have a failed drive in a RAID array, or a shortage of disk space for the users' home directories, or a web server that has stopped running for some unknown reason. Without automation, you might have noticed the lack of disk space while you were manually adding a new account on the system, but now it may go unnoticed until it becomes a real problem.

With a good monitoring system, you can indeed catch up on your emails while you wait for a problem to be reported. The difference is that your system should notice problems more reliably, and report them more quickly, than any user ever could. In the best case scenario, your system can alert you to potential problems before they become critical, or even repair the situation automatically.

With that having been said, you will still need to make some decisions and interpret the reports (otherwise you will have automated yourself out of a job!). If you get a report that a new version of Apache was installed on a system last night, you need to decide if that should have happened. Did you want it to be upgraded, or did somebody else do it? If it was somebody else, is it something that should have been done?

This chapter discusses the three most important aspects of system monitoring. The system and its hardware must be checked for space shortages, drive failures, excessive system load, and so on. The log files must be checked for anomalous entries and any indications of security problems. Finally, the actual services running on the system need to be checked to make sure they are running and operating properly.

Keep in mind that the discussion in this chapter is far from comprehensive. I discuss the most basic and common things that you should monitor. As always, the amount and types of things you monitor depends on your situation.

I also only discuss what I feel are the best or most popular tools being used today. There are many other tools available—including a wide variety of commercial applications. If you are designing a large monitoring system, please do additional research on tools that are not covered in this book.

## 10.1 General System Monitoring

There are many little things that you should monitor on a system. Unfortunately, the items that should be checked and the methods you use to check them differ from system to system. You may want to check your RAID arrays, for example, to make sure that all drives are operating properly—that is, of course, only if you actually have RAID arrays. Your operating system's kernel might report on drive failures, but the format of such a log entry varies from system to system.

Because of this rich variety of possible problems, the first thing that you will learn how to create within this section is a flexible reporting utility that you can use to log and report various significant system events.

### 10.1.1 Creating a General Reporting Facility

I find it very convenient to have a unified reporting system for all of my monitoring scripts. If I need to make changes to how events are reported (such as establishing a new alert email address, sending messages to pagers, etc.), I can simply modify that one script and none of my actual monitoring scripts will be affected.

The nice thing is that creating such a system is much easier than it may sound. In a minute, you will see a Perl script that provides unified reporting functionality. It takes two command-line arguments. The first is the level or severity of the event (such as WARNING or CRITICAL). The second argument is the subject of the message (such as "disk failure").

For ultimate flexibility, this program can take lines in through stdin. If the --stdin argument is specified, each line is included in the report. One nice thing about the --stdin option is that no report is generated if no lines are sent in. So, if you use this option, and you want a report, you should make sure at least one line comes in through stdin. If you do not use the --stdin argument, you must make the subject fully descriptive because it will be the only information included in the report.

The first portion of the script contains its configuration items and my usual usage function:

**NOTE**   You can find the code samples for this chapter in the Downloads section of the Apress web site (http://www.apress.com).

```perl
#!/usr/bin/perl -w
use strict;

# Configuration items
my $MailThreshold = 'WARNING';
my $LogFile = '/var/log/event.log';
my $Email = 'alert@company.com';

# Available log levels
my %Levels = (
    'INFO'  => 1,
    'WARNING' => 2,
    'ERROR' => 3,
    'CRITICAL' => 4
);

sub usage () {
    print STDERR "Usage: $0 [--stdin] <level> <subject>\n";
    print STDERR "Levels: ";
    foreach (keys %Levels) {
        print STDERR "$_ ";
    }
    print STDERR "\n";
    exit 1;
}
```

The $MailThreshold variable specifies the minimum level required to mail a report. If a report's indicated level is equal to or greater than (more severe than) this level, it will be mailed to the address specified in the $Email variable. Finally, all events will be logged in the file $LogFile, whether they are mailed or not.

Next, the script performs basic initialization tasks such as checking its arguments, determining the system's short hostname (by stripping the domain name off of the full hostname, if necessary), and storing a properly formatted date for logging purposes. This is all relatively basic stuff:

```perl
# Check and store parameters
my $stdin = 0;
if ($ARGV[0] eq '--stdin') {
    shift @ARGV;
    $stdin = 1;
}
usage() unless ($#ARGV == 1);
usage() if ($ARGV[0] eq '--help');
my ($level, $subject) = @ARGV;
$level = uc($level);
usage() unless ($Levels{$level});

# Determine system's hostname (first portion only)
my $hostname = `hostname`;
chomp($hostname);
$hostname =~ s/\..*$//;
# Store formatted date string
my $date = localtime;
```

Now we get to the real meat of the program which is still pretty simple. First the script opens the log file in append mode. The rest of this section of the script only applies if the --stdin switch is *not* used.

In this case, a subject-only email is sent if the log level is above the mail threshold. The log entry is also added to the log file.

```perl
open (LOG, ">>$LogFile");
unless ($stdin) {
    if ($Levels{$level} >= $Levels{$MailThreshold}) {
        system ("mail -s '[$level] $hostname: $subject' '$Email'");
    }
    print LOG "$date $hostname [$level] $subject";
    close(LOG);
    exit 0;
}
```

The remainder of the script only applies if the --stdin argument *is* given on the command line. Each line on stdin is appended to the already open log file. The lines are also stored in an array (keep this in mind—you don't want to send a million lines into this program). The mail command will only be executed if the threshold is met *and* there were actually lines sent in on stdin. This feature is here to allow us to pipe output right into the script yet only generate a report if something was actually sent into it.

```
my @lines;
while (my $line = <STDIN>) {
   push @lines, $line;
   print LOG "$date $hostname [$level] $subject: $line";
}
close(LOG);
if ((@lines) and $Levels{$level} >= $Levels{$MailThreshold}) {
   open (MAIL, "| mail -s '[$level] $hostname: $subject' '$Email'");
   foreach (@lines) {
      print MAIL $_;
   }
   close(MAIL);
}
exit 0;
```

This script can be used in several different ways. The first way is to send a "subject-only" report:

```
/usr/local/sbin/report INFO 'Test report' </dev/null
```

Since the --stdin switch is not present, only the subject is included in the log entry. You can also do something like this (I will make this report more meaningful later):

```
df | /usr/local/sbin/report --stdin INFO 'Available drive space'
```

When run, the available disk space on every mounted drive is logged, one drive at a time.

Since this was only done at the INFO level, it is something you may want to do every day, if only to log trends in your available disk space. Likewise, if you wanted to keep a log of your system's load average on an hourly basis, just run this command every hour:

```
uptime | /usr/local/sbin/report --stdin INFO 'System load'
```

As you can see, this reporting facility can be used for logging informational items as well as reporting problems and failures. You could modify the script to use the syslog facility instead of, or in addition to, its own log file. I would recommend doing this if you are using a log host (a central system that receives and stores log entries from all of your systems through syslog).

## 10.1.2 Monitoring System Load

In the previous section, you saw how simple it is to log the system load every hour. What I want to show you now is how to expand on this idea and send a WARNING level report if the system load rises above 1.0. First, take a look at the output of the uptime command on my system:

```
% uptime
 10:18am  up  1:16,  1 user,  load average: 0.29, 0.20, 0.18
```

You should only care about the 15-minute load average (the last number), which is the tenth field within this output. The awk command can help you with this situation:

```
#!/bin/bash

uptime | awk '{if ($10 > 1.00) print "15-min average: " $10}' | \
    /usr/local/sbin/report --stdin WARNING 'High Load Average'
```

In this case, the awk command only prints something if the tenth field is numerically greater than 1.00. If it does print something, it only prints the tenth field (preceded by the text 15-min average:). The custom report command only logs anything if there is input on stdin, so, a report will be generated only if the 15-minute load average is above 1.00.

This script could be run every hour (or even more often) from your cron daemon.

## 10.1.3 Watching Available Disk Space

Next, I would like to show you how to report on any drives that are too full. One problem is that many systems have CD-ROM drives that are always completely full. Other systems have special virtual filesystems that do not represent real devices. As a result, this script only checks for the types of filesystems specified in the $types variable, which are separated by the pipe character (|). Also, the $cutoff variable determines how full a drive must be (in percent) before a report is generated. Here is the script:

```
#!/bin/bash

types="ext2|ext3|ufs|vfat"
cutoff="90"
```

```
for drive in `mount | awk "/type ($types)/ {print \\\$1}"` ; do
   df "$drive" | awk -v "cutoff=$cutoff" '/^\// {
      gsub(/%$/, "", $5);
      if ($5 > cutoff)
         print "Drive " $1 " (" $6 ") is " $5 "% Full"
      }'
done | /usr/local/sbin/report --stdin WARNING 'Drives almost full'
```

This is the most complex use of awk so far in this book. First, I use it to determine which partitions are of the appropriate type by parsing the output of the mount command:

```
% mount
/dev/hda3 on / type ext3 (rw)
none on /proc type proc (rw)
usbdevfs on /proc/bus/usb type usbdevfs (rw)
...
```

Then we run the df command on each partition that matched one of the filesystem types specified. Here is example output from the df command:

```
% df /dev/hda3
Filesystem          1K-blocks      Used Available Use% Mounted on
/dev/hda3            19510368  16685792   2824576  86% /data
```

Since this output contains a lot of information and the spacing is variable, I again use the awk command to process this output. I set the awk variable cutoff to be equal to our environment variable $cutoff using the -v command-line option. The awk program first matches only lines beginning with a slash (since I specified a pattern of /^\//) because I don't want to parse the header line. It then uses its gsub function to remove the percent character from the end of the fifth column (so 86% becomes 86). This number is then checked by the remainder of the awk code to see if it is greater than cutoff (90). If it is, an output line is generated that provides the partition (the first column), the mount point (the sixth column), and the percentage of drive space used (the fifth column).

A script like this requires very little system resources and could be run hourly from your cron daemon, but it should at least be run once per day.

## 10.1.4  Monitoring System Services

Every system has certain processes that should be running at all times. If, at any time, these are not running, you should have a script start them and notify you of the problem. This is especially true for a service such as sshd because it may be the only way you can access the system. You should also watch any important services running on the system, such as a mail, DNS, or web server.

Checking to see that a certain service is running is easy (note that your system may require different command-line switches to generate the same output with the ps command):

```
% ps ax -o '%c %P' | grep 'sshd'
sshd                    1
sshd                    12599
sshd                    12599
sshd                    12599
sshd                    12599
sshd                    12599
sshd                    12599
sshd_checker            1
```

The first column is the process name, whereas the second column is its parent's process ID. Many daemons spawn multiple child processes; these child processes may continue to run, even if the parent process is dead. For the current discussion, you are interested only in the parent process—that is, the process with a parent process ID of 1:

```
% ps ax -o '%c %P' | grep 'sshd' | grep '1$'
sshd                    1
sshd_checker            1
```

Here, you can see that I found the appropriate parent sshd process, but you also see an sshd_checker daemon (which I made up). This illustrates an important point: you need to make sure you match the exact process you are looking for. You can use awk to take care of all of this work:

```
% ps ax -o '%c %P' | awk '{if (($2 == 1) && ($1 == "sshd")) print $0}'
sshd                    1
```

You can use this knowledge to build a simple script that monitors services. You can use a configuration file (/usr/local/etc/services.conf) as follows (this one is for a Linux system that uses System V init scripts):

```
syslogd|/etc/rc.d/init.d/syslog restart
sshd|/etc/rc.d/init.d/sshd restart
httpd|/etc/rc.d/init.d/httpd restart
named|/etc/rc.d/init.d/named restart
atd|
```

The left side of each line is the program name that you see in the ps output (which is not always what you expect). The right side is the command that the script should execute if the service is down. The script will restart all of these services if they are down except for atd, which has no restart command specified. Here is a script that uses this configuration file to monitor your services:

```
#!/bin/bash

SLEEP=30    #seconds

while true ; do
    cat /usr/local/etc/services.conf | while read line ; do
        match=`echo "$line" | sed 's/|.*$//'`
        cmd=`echo "$line" | sed 's/^.*|//'`
        ps ax -o '%c %P' | awk -v "process=$match" \
            '{if (($1 == process) && ($2 == 1)) exit 1}' && {
            # Process not found!
            /usr/local/sbin/report ERROR "Process $match not running"
            [ -n "$cmd" ] && {
                $cmd && {
                    /usr/local/sbin/report INFO \
                        "Process $match was restarted ($cmd)"
                }
            }
        }
    done
    sleep $SLEEP
done
```

This style of script should be fairly familiar to you by now. I go through each line of the configuration file and check the specified process. I use awk's -v switch to set the awk variable process to the name of the process I am are trying to find. I then have awk check both the process name and parent process ID fields. If awk finds the process, it exits with a code of 1 (which normally would be an error, but I am using to indicate success here). If awk exits with a code of 0 (the default, which will be used if no lines are found), the script takes the appropriate actions.

For many services, you can actually test them to make sure they are operating properly. This is better than just checking for a running process, because a process can be running yet be in an unresponsive state. You can run the following script on a web server, which checks the specified URL every 30 seconds. The URL must be accessible by the system running the script and it must contain the string HTML. wget is used to perform the HTTP request:

```
#!/bin/bash

SLEEP=30      #seconds
TIMEOUT=10 #seconds
URL='http://localhost/index.html'
MATCH='<HTML>'

while true ; do
    wget -q -O - -T=$TIMEOUT --tries=1 "$URL" | grep -q "$MATCH" || {
        /usr/local/sbin/report ERROR "Web server not responding"
        /etc/rc.d/init.d/httpd restart && {
            /usr/local/sbin/report INFO "Web server restarted"
        }
    }
    sleep $SLEEP
done
```

You can also use GNU cfengine to monitor and restart processes (this was illustrated in section 6.4.2.2). cfengine does this very well and is particularly convenient if you are already using it for other tasks.

## 10.1.5  Watching for Package Changes

This script assumes you are using RPM for your package management, but it could easily be modified to work with other package systems. It runs the rpm -qa command, which provides a listing of currently installed packages. It then compares this listing to the previous listing using the diff command, which will produce this type of output:

```
< removedpackage-1.1
< upgradedpackage-1.0
> upgradedpackage-1.1
```

You can use the sed command to make the output from diff more friendly. It changes any lines beginning with < to indicate that a package has been removed, and it modifies any lines beginning with > to show that a package has been added. It ignores any other lines. Note that a package upgrade is reported as a removal of the old version and an addition of the new version.

```
#!/bin/bash

TMPDIR="$HOME/tmp"

rpm -qa | sort > $TMPDIR/packages.curr

if [ -r $TMPDIR/packages.last ] ; then
    diff $TMPDIR/packages.last $TMPDIR/packages.curr | \
      sed -n -e 's/^</Removed/p' -e 's/^>/Added/p' | \
      /usr/local/sbin/report --stdin INFO 'Packages changed'
fi

mv $TMPDIR/packages.curr $TMPDIR/packages.last
```

Here is an example of the log entries that would be created:

```
Wed Jan 8 19:43:56 2003 kaybee [INFO] Packages changed: Removed removedpackage-1.0
Wed Jan 8 19:43:56 2003 kaybee [INFO] Packages changed: Removed upgradedpackage-1.0
Wed Jan 8 19:43:56 2003 kaybee [INFO] Packages changed: Added upgradedpackage-1.0
```

By making this script a little more complicated, you can create a script that works on a variety of systems. Note that, unlike the script I just discussed, the following version has RPM display only the package names (no version or release), which makes the report consistent on all three systems (because the Solaris and Debian package listings do not include the version). However, after you make the changes to the script, it will no longer report package upgrades—only additions and removals. Here is the script:

```
#!/bin/bash

TMPDIR="$HOME/tmp"

if [ `uname -s` == 'SunOS' ] ; then
    # Solaris
    pkginfo | awk '{print $2}'
elif [ -x /usr/bin/dpkg ] ; then
    # Debian GNU/Linux
    dpkg -l | grep '^ii ' | awk '{print $2}'
elif [ -x /bin/rpm ] ; then
    # Red Hat Linux (or other RPM-based system)
    rpm -qa --qf '%{name}\n'
fi | sort > $TMPDIR/packages.curr
```

```
if [ -r $TMPDIR/packages.last ] ; then
    diff $TMPDIR/packages.last $TMPDIR/packages.curr | \
        sed -n -e 's/^</Removed/p' -e 's/^>/Added/p'  | \
        /usr/local/sbin/report --stdin INFO 'Packages changed'
fi

mv $TMPDIR/packages.curr $TMPDIR/packages.last
```

You could add other systems that are present in your environment simply by expanding this if statement.

---

 **NOTE**   These package monitoring scripts are fairly resource intensive and shouldn't be run any more frequently than once every day.

---

## 10.1.6 Drive Failures

Drive failures are important things to watch for on your systems. Sometimes a drive just goes and you have no warning. Other times, however, the kernel creates some log entries that indicate a drive problem. These warnings can give you time to replace the drive before it fails completely, and they can prevent, or at least reduce, data loss.

If you are using RAID1 or RAID5, checking for drive failures is even more important. If one of the drives fails in these types of RAID arrays, the data is just as vulnerable as if you weren't using RAID at all (RAID protects data by using redundant disks which are no longer redundant once they have failed). The data is probably too important to be exposed to this type of risk because you are storing it on RAID drives in the first place. From this you see that the benefit of RAID (the system keeps operating after a drive failure, and without data loss) can also be its biggest problem (you may never know a drive failed).

Unfortunately, drive failures look different on every operating system. RAID failures can also be different depending on the type of RAID being used (software RAID, and the various types of hardware RAID controllers). You may also find it difficult to know what to look for if you have not yet had a drive failure. For RAID systems, unplugging one of the drives will tell you. But for other drive failures, you may have to ask around to get some example log entries for your system.

Here are some example log entries from a Linux system using software RAID5:

```
May 28 14:19:24 hostname kernel: Device 08:41 not ready.
May 28 14:19:24 hostname kernel: I/O error: dev 08:41, sector 98566248
May 28 14:19:24 hostname kernel: raid5: Disk failure on sde1, disabling device. \
                        Operation continuing on 2 devices
```

The first log entry probably represents a drive failure, but there may be other cases in which this message is generated. The second entry indicates a specific sector with a problem, and it is almost certainly an indication of a drive problem. The third entry clearly indicates a disk failure, but it would only appear in the logs when you are using software RAID.

Here is a simple script that will report any of these failures:

```
#!/bin/bash

# Check for any drive failures
egrep 'I/O error: dev .+, sector' /var/log/messages | \
   /usr/local/sbin/report --stdin CRITICAL 'Drives failure'

# Check for any RAID failures
egrep 'raid.*Disk failure on' /var/log/messages | \
   /usr/local/sbin/report --stdin CRITICAL 'RAID drive failure'
```

It should be obvious that you will need to modify this script to support your operating system(s), but it does show you how this reporting facility can be very helpful with catching serious problems, possibly before they get any worse. This script imposes a moderate system load because it has to look through the entire system log each time it executes. You should run it at least once a day, but you could run it more often if your systems can take it.

You should also consider the smartmontools project for your Linux systems. It allows you to actively monitor your drives by watching for erroneous values coming from the Self-Monitoring, Analysis and Reporting Technology (S.M.A.R.T.) system that is included in most modern ATA and SCSI drives. You can find information about this project at http://smartmontools.sourceforge.net.

## 10.2 Monitoring System Logs

There are really two ways to handle the logs generated by multiple systems. One method is to have each system store its own log files; this is what most people do unless they have a large number of systems. Even then, some people prefer to keep each system's logs separate and not rely on a log host.

The other option is a log host. This is one system that collects the logs from other systems and stores them all in one place. The standard UNIX syslog facility allows log entries to be forwarded to other hosts (instead of, or in addition to, being stored locally). This is easy to set up by modifying your system's default `/etc/syslog.conf`:

```
*.info;mail.none;authpriv.none;cron.none /var/log/messages
*.info;mail.none;authpriv.none;cron.none @loghost
```

Assuming the first line was already in your configuration file, adding the second line will cause the log entries to also go to the specified host. The destination log host must, of course, have the syslog daemon (`syslogd`) running and accepting external connections in order to receive these log entries.

You can configure log hosts to only allow incoming log entries and no other network connections. This provides very good security since a person would have to have physical access to enter the system and modify log entries (or they would have to find a vulnerability in the `syslogd` daemon). Compared to logs stored on each system individually, this approach provides excellent security. Also, since all logging over the network is done with the User Datagram Protocol (UDP), problems with the log host and/or the network will not adversely affect the client systems' operation.

Another benefit of using a log host is that it is easier to correlate log entries from several hosts. If this is your intention, you must be sure the systems' clocks are synchronized (as discussed in Section 9.1).

Even if you have one system, chances are you do not look at your logs enough; if you have several systems, it is even less likely. If you have a secure log host that requires you to physically walk to the system to review logs, you may only do so after a security breach occurs.

This is where automated log monitoring becomes important. Systems produce tons of log entries, but most of them are not usually very useful. They may be useful when you are tracking down a specific problem or a security breach, but they are of no interest to you on a daily basis. Some entries, however, are more important. An automated log monitoring system can process your log files and summarize their contents and/or report only the specific entries that require your attention. This processing can be done daily on each system, or even on a log host that can send emails out (even if you can't get into the system remotely).

There are two popular programs used widely for log analysis—Logwatch and swatch. These programs are sufficiently different enough that only one will be best for your needs. If you have only a few specific entries you are interested in, you can also write your own program (just like in section 10.1.6).

## 10.2.1  Log Monitoring with Logwatch

Again, I must start out with a disclaimer on this one. Logwatch is my program—I may be a bit biased, so keep that in mind. That being said, there really aren't any other noncommercial programs like it.

Logwatch checks your logs and produces a summary of the information in a much easier to read form. It is far from perfect, but it performs very well on most systems. It can be downloaded from http://www.logwatch.org. It is also included as part of Red Hat Linux as of version 7.0. New versions of Logwatch are released all the time, so I would advise you to use the newest version available (version 4.2 or higher) when you try out the examples in this section.

Logwatch is installed in one directory, such as /etc/log.d/. Its main script is found in /etc/log.d/scripts/logwatch.pl, but a symbolic link to this script is typically created in /usr/local/sbin/ or another system bin directory. Although you can run it on the command line, it usually runs from the system's cron daemon every night.

### 10.2.1.1  Overall Design

Logwatch was designed from the start to be very flexible and extensible. It works on logfile groups; each group might represent one single log file or a collection of related log files. Each logfile group may also have archives that can be processed when the --archives command-line option is used. Each logfile group is defined in a configuration file located in /etc/log.d/conf/logfiles/. Consider the messages logfile group as an example. It represents the file /var/log/messages as well as the archives /var/log/messages.* and /var/log/messages.*.gz.

Once a logfile group has been defined, any number of services can filter and report on the contents of these logfiles. In fact, any service can parse any number of logfile groups. The dhcpd service, for example, uses the messages logfile group and processes all lines for the service dhcpd. Each service is defined within a file in /etc/log.d/conf/services/ and must also have a filter script in /etc/log.d/scripts/services/ that does the actual log filtering and reporting.

The complete list of services supported is too long to list here and grows all the time. To see what services are supported in your version of Logwatch, simply look in the /etc/log.d/conf/services/ directory. Don't worry if you don't use most of the services. If your system does not have the service, it will not produce any output in the reports.

One important thing to mention—all Logwatch configuration files are case insensitive (love it or hate it). If you need to preserve case, you must enclose the item in double quotes.

## 10.2.1.2  Creating the Main logwatch.conf

When you run it with no command-line options, Logwatch uses its default configuration in /etc/log.d/conf/logwatch.conf. Here are the default values found in this file (with the comments removed for enhanced readability):

```
LogDir = /var/log
MailTo = root
Print = No
UseMkTemp = Yes
Range = yesterday
Detail = Low
Mailer = /bin/mail
Service = All
```

Let's take a look at these options:

**LogDir:** This is the default directory where most of your system's logs are placed. Log files are not restricted to this directory, however.

**MailTo:** The email address to which the Logwatch reports should be mailed.

**Print:** If set to Yes, the reports will be printed to stdout instead of mailed.

**UseMkTemp:** Assuming your mktemp command supports the -d (directory) option, you will want to use this command.

**Range:** The only values currently supported for this parameter are All, Today, and Yesterday. Since you usually run Logwatch just after midnight every day, the default of Yesterday is probably fine.

**Detail:** The level of detail that should be included in the reports. Low indicates that only security concerns and indications of problems should be reported. Med says to also include information and summaries that may be of interest to you. High causes Logwatch to summarize almost everything and produces quite verbose reports.

**Mailer:** The location of your system's command-line mailer command, such as /bin/mail.

**Service:** Any number of Service lines may be present. The All value indicates that all services should be included in the report. You can remove individual services by using the - symbol before its name (such as -pam_pwdb). If the All value is not used, then each service you want included must be individually listed.

### 10.2.1.3  Using Command-Line Options

As I mentioned in the previous section, you usually run Logwatch daily using the system's cron daemon. However, plenty of command-line options allow you to run Logwatch however you desire without modifying the configuration file. The most useful command-line arguments are as follows:

--**detail level:** Can override the detail level in logwatch.conf to any of the values (Low, Med, or High).

--**service name:** Can be specified multiple times. If this is specified, it overrides any services specified in logwatch.conf with the services listed here.

--**print:** Causes the report to be printed to stdout.

--**mailto address:** Mails the report to address.

--**archives:** Includes archived log entries in the processing (this usually significantly increases run time).

--**save filename:** Saves the report to the specified filename instead of mailing or printing it.

--**range period:** Overrides the range to Yesterday, Today, or All.

--**hostname value:** Sets the hostname to be used in the reports. In addition, if HostLimit is set in the main configuration file, only logs from this host will be processed (see the next section).

In most cases, these command-line arguments are used more for testing purposes than anything else. They can be useful, however, when you are running Logwatch multiple times on the same system, as described in the next section.

### 10.2.1.4  Running Logwatch on a Log Host

If you have one system that is your log host, it will contain log entries for many systems, sometimes mixed in with its own log files. You can use Logwatch on this type of system, but it may require a little more work. If all of the log entries from all of the hosts are mixed in with the log host's own log entries and you don't mind receiving one large report (combining data from all systems together), then everything will work as is.

Chances are, however, that this won't work for you. If you use special log files or multiple log files where there is normally one (i.e., what normally goes into /var/log/messages may go into multiple files), you need to edit the appropriate logfile group's configuration file found in /etc/log.d/conf/logfiles/. You can specify as many log files per group as is necessary for your system.

Generating a separate report on each system can be done a couple of ways. One way is to separate the logs from each system into separate files. You can then run Logwatch once per set of files by changing the `LogDir` setting on each run.

The better way is to use the `HostLimit` option and the `--hostname` command-line option. If you set `HostLimit` to `Yes` in `logwatch.conf`, the report only contains information from this system's log entries. When you combined this with the `--hostname` command-line option that allows you to override the hostname, you can run Logwatch once per host and generate one report per host. Here is an example script that supports any number of hosts and a separate email address for each host:

```
#!/bin/bash

HOSTS='
    host1|admin1@someplace.com
    host2|admin2@someplace.com
    host3|admin3@someplace.com
'

for entry in $HOSTS ; do
    host=`echo "$entry" | sed 's/|.*$//'`
    email=`echo "$entry" | sed 's/^.*|//'`
    logwatch --mailto "$email" --hostname "$host"
done
```

## 10.2.1.5  Writing Your Own Filter

If you have special log entries you are interested in, or if you have services on your system that are not supported, you can add a new service to Logwatch with relative ease. If you think you have created a filter that will be useful to others, please send it in to be included in the distribution (if you can).

### 10.2.1.5.1 Creating a New Logfile Group

If you are processing logs from a logfile not yet supported, you first need to create a new logfile group. Assuming you are making a filter for the `example` program, you would create the file `/etc/log.d/conf/example.conf` with the following contents:

```
LogFile = /var/log/example/example.log
```

You can explore other available options (like specifying archives) by looking through existing logfile groups. If the logfile is in the standard syslog-style format, you can use some shared scripts to do some of the work for you:

```
LogFile = /var/log/example/example.log
*OnlyHost
*ApplyStdDate
```

You can find these two scripts in the /etc/log.d/scripts/shared/ directory. The first filters out any log entries for other hosts (only if HostLimit is set as discussed in the previous section). The second filters out any entries that do not fall into the specified date range.

Again, these filters only work on some log files. If your log has a special format, you may have to do this work yourself (but you can use these shared scripts as examples). Every logfile group can have an optional directory under /etc/log.d/scripts/logfiles/. Any scripts within that directory will be applied to the logfile during the filter process.

If your example logfile was not in the standard format, you could create the directory /etc/log.d/scripts/logfiles/example/ and place a script in there. That script should take log entries on stdin and send any log entries it wants to keep on stdout. The date range being used will be stored in the $LOGWATCH_DATE_RANGE environment variable. These filters can be written in any language, but are usually written in Perl.

### 10.2.1.5.2 Creating a New Service

Once you have created your logfile group (or decided to use an existing logfile group), you can create your own service. You begin by creating a configuration file in /etc/log.d/conf/services/. I'm going to assume that you are using the standard messages logfile group for this example. Here is an example configuration file (/etc/log.d/conf/services/example.conf):

```
Title = "Example"
LogFile = messages
*OnlyService = example
*RemoveHeaders
```

Here I set the title of the service to Example (to displayed in the report output). I requested the messages logfile group and two shared scripts. The first script ignores all log entries that do not pertain to the service example. The second removes the headers (the date, the hostname, and the service) from a standard syslog-style log.

These scripts are executed after any scripts specified in the logfile group but before the filter for your service.

Once you have created the configuration file for your service, you *must* create your main service processing script. This goes in /etc/log.d/scripts/services/ and must be named according to the name of your configuration file. Since my configuration file was example.conf, my script will be /etc/log.d/scripts/services/example.

This script takes the filtered log entries in on stdin. If there is nothing to report, it should produce no output. If you do not generate output, Logwatch will not include a section for your script in the report. If no services generate output, no report will be sent (so the administrator does not receive emails without any interesting information in them).

If there are things to report, your script should organize the data into a clear and concise form and send that out on stdout. When your script does generate output, Logwatch will surround it with section dividers with your service's title.

This script can be written in any language, although most of the time such scripts are written in Perl. The current detail level is stored in the $LOGWATCH_DETAIL_LEVEL environment variable. A value of 0 indicates low detail, 5 indicates medium detail, and 10 indicates high detail. If you want to create your own detail levels, you can; just use numbers instead of the strings in the configuration file and command-line arguments. Other variables are defined as well, as illustrated in this example service script:

```
#!/bin/bash
# This nice script shows you the lines you will process and report.
# First it displays the standard environment variables, then it
# takes STDIN and dumps it right back out to STDOUT.

# These are the standard environment variables.
echo "Date Range: $LOGWATCH_DATE_RANGE"
echo "Detail Level: $LOGWATCH_DETAIL_LEVEL"
echo "Temp Dir: $LOGWATCH_TEMP_DIR"
echo "Debug Level: $LOGWATCH_DEBUG"

# Now take STDIN and dump it to STDOUT
cat
```

This script is a good place to start because it shows you exactly what the log entries coming into your script will look like. Your real service filter will vary depending on what you are trying to do, but there are plenty of existing services you can use as references.

### 10.2.1.5.3 Simple Example Service Filter

Although not really a "service," the filter I am about to show you tells me how many times my Linux system booted, if any. Looking in my /var/log/messages log, I see this line:

```
Nov 10 21:18:50 kirk-laptop kernel: Initializing CPU#0
```

This line seems as if it would only happen on startup, so if I simply count this line, I can determine the number of startups for this system. First, I'll create /etc/log.d/conf/services/startups.conf:

```
Title = "System Startup"
LogFile = messages
*OnlyService = kernel
*RemoveHeaders
```

Remember that the messages logfile group has already taken care of the date/time filtering for me. So I simply have requested all lines from the "kernel" service and removed the headers. Ultimately, I'm looking for the line Initializing CPU#0 on stdin. Here is my filter:

```perl
#!/usr/bin/perl -w
use strict;

unless ($ENV{'LOGWATCH_DETAIL_LEVEL'} > 0) {
   # Don't report system boots at lowest detail level
   exit 0;
}

my $startups = 0;
while (my $line = <STDIN>) {
   if ($line eq 'Initializing CPU#0') {
      $startups++;
   }
}

if ($startups > 0) {
   print "System started: $startups Time(s)\n";
}
```

As you can see, these scripts can be quite simple. If you look through the services included in the Logwatch distribution, however, you will find some that are quite complicated. It just depends on how thorough you want your script to be and how complicated the logs being processed are.

This boot count script will not produce any output unless at least one startup occurred. This is important, because I don't want to receive a report every day telling me that some server that has been running for two years straight did not reboot yesterday.

This script could be made more complicated by detecting startup messages from a wide variety of operating systems. I'll definitely leave that one as an exercise for you—when you are done, send it to me and I can include it in the official distribution.

## 10.2.2  Real-Time Log Monitoring with swatch

Like Logwatch, swatch monitors system logs. That is about where their similarities end. Whereas Logwatch reports on what occurred the day before, swatch monitors the logs in real time and takes appropriate actions as defined in its configuration file. Starting it is very simple:

```
swatch
```

This is actually the same thing as running the following:

```
swatch --config-file=~/.swatchrc --tail-file=/var/log/syslog
```

Or, if /var/log/messages exists on your system, you would run this:

```
swatch --config-file=~/.swatchrc --tail-file=/var/log/messages
```

Using these options, you can watch different logfiles, each with different configuration files. Keep in mind that, without these options, the default configuration file (~/.swatchrc) will be used.

Instead of the --tail-file option, you can use --examine or --read-pipe. The --examine command does one pass through a file and exits. The --read-pipe command causes swatch to execute the specified command and monitor its output. These options allow you to use swatch offline (such as in a cron job) or to monitor the output of a running program.

This may seem a bit too simple so far—this is because we still have to create a configuration file before anything exciting will happen. The two basic commands found in this file are watchfor and ignore. As you might expect, these commands either watch for or ignore certain lines within the log text. After any watchfor command, you can specify one or more actions that should take place when the line is found. Here is an example:

```
ignore /bogus/
watchfor /ALERT/
   echo
   bell
```

This configuration file causes swatch to first ignore any lines containing the regular expression (just a word in this case) bogus. It then looks for any lines containing the regular expression (again, just a word in this case) ALERT. If it finds such a line, it sends the line out on stdout and sounds the terminal's bell. Here are some more actions that can be very useful:

**echo:** This command causes the matching line to display on stdout. It can take an optional argument such as blink or red to change its appearance when it is printed.

**bell:** Sounds the terminal's bell/beep.

**exec:** Executes the command specified in its first argument. The command should be enclosed in double quotes. You can use the special variables $0 or $* to pass the matched line to the command, or the variables $1, $2, and so on, to include tokens from the matched line.

**mail:** By default, sends the matched lines to the user running the command by email. Can also specify different addresses and/or a subject as follows: mail addresses=alert@company.com,subject=ALERT.

**pipe:** Executes the command specified in its first argument and pipes the matched lines into the command.

**write:** Uses the write command to send matched lines to the user specified in its first argument (users can be separated by colons).

**throttle:** This command has one required argument—the number of hours, minutes, and seconds that must elapse between events for this log entry. For example, this could be used to prevent an email from being sent out every second. The command throttle 1:00:00 would cause all of the actions for the specific pattern being watched for to only execute once per hour at the most.

In the discussions of Logwatch, I created an example custom filter that looked for system restarts and reported how many there were the day before. You can do this in real-time with swatch using the following configuration file (placed in ~/.swatchrc):

```
watchfor /Initializing CPU#0/
   echo
   bell
   mail addresses=alert@company.com,subject="System Restarted"
```

Obviously this script would not be too useful when monitoring a system's own logfiles—if the system has just booted, swatch is probably not yet running. You can, however, use something like this on your log host (if you have one) to notify you of system startups in real time.

## 10.3 Monitoring Network Services

It has probably happened to us all—the system seems fine, the logs are fine, yet the system isn't doing what it is supposed to be doing. A web server with good disks, a low system load, and no errors in the logs is still not very useful if the actual web server software is not running and operating properly.

The most basic form of network monitoring is the simple ping. When you successfully ping a system, you know that there are no major network problems between the two systems. You also know that the kernel on the remote system is at least partially operational because it is responding to your ping.

Although a good first step, pings are not a great way to remotely monitor a system. Even if a system responds to pings, it could be completely out of virtual memory, the kernel could be in a bad state, or there could be other problems that cause the system to not operate properly.

The next best thing is port monitoring. If you use TCP to connect to port 80 on a system, it means that the kernel is even more functional (at least its TCP/IP stack is functioning) and that the web server is running and listening on the port. Depending on the server, a successful connection might even mean that memory is available (because many servers fork a new process or at least allocate memory for each connection).

Everything above and beyond port monitoring is necessarily application specific. For web servers, you can actually request a page from the server and examine its contents (you are usually looking for a known string). For a database you can connect and perform a simple query.

You can, in fact, do fully functional remote testing of pretty much any service because, by definition, a network service performs some task for remote clients. Therefore, you can connect to any service and have it perform a task for you, allowing you to verify that it performed the task properly.

The bigger a site gets, the more complicated tasks can become. Monitoring is definitely no exception. If an NFS system goes down, do you want 500 systems to send you an email that says they have a problem? You would probably prefer to receive only one message telling you specifically that the NFS server is down. The simple solution might be to have one system monitor the NFS server and that's it. But what if only one client has an NFS problem? You'd want to be notified about that too.

Somebody might probe the machines on your site over the Internet. If they probe one system, you probably want to be notified. If they probe 1000 systems, you probably want to be notified also, but just *once*. The best solution is to have a centralized database that gathers reports from systems and consolidates them as necessary. There are no off-the-shelf solutions of this type freely available at this time, but I'm pretty sure some commercial options are available to you.

In this section, I first provide a simple custom system monitoring solution if you are looking for minimal functionality with minimal effort. I then cover NetSaint and Mon—both popular open-source network monitoring solutions that are quite powerful, but can also be a bit complicated.

## 10.3.1 Custom Monitoring and Automatic Repairs

There are times when you want to perform a simple monitoring task and it is not practical to use existing monitoring tools. These tools often provide much more power than you need, and using these tools can result in unnecessary complexity.

My favorite example is a *network appliance.* This is usually a self-contained system with little or no outside administration. It may not even have much of an administrator at all. It might be a DSL router purchased by an average consumer and shoved behind their computer desk to be forgotten forever (unless, of course, it stops working).

This section provides a couple of examples that give you ideas for your own scripts. These are, by their nature, fairly specific. If you wanted a general system for monitoring systems you would just use NetSaint or Mon. You should note, however, that both of these existing programs use many external helper scripts. These could easily be used as part of your custom monitoring script.

Remember that you should have these commands notify somebody (if appropriate) when they take corrective action. The reason is that these commands fix the symptom of the problem, but not the source. You still need to know that there is a problem (and how often it occurs), because these scripts work best when they never actually have to repair anything. Notification can be as simple as the following:

```
mail -s 'web server restarted' support@company.com </dev/null
```

### 10.3.1.1 Checking for a Process

Whether you like it or not, processes just die sometimes. No program is perfect. In this section, I create a simple script, perhaps run by cron hourly, that verifies that a process is running. If it is not running, the script starts it again. You can use the output from the ps command to determine if a process is running (remember that the output of this command can be very system dependent):

```
% ps ax
  PID TTY      STAT    TIME COMMAND
    1 ?        S       1:46 init
20288 ?        S       0:06 /usr/sbin/httpd -DHAVE_PROXY...
...
```

Given this output, you can use awk to isolate the last (fifth) column and see if it matches the program you are checking. Here is the code:

```bash
#!/bin/bash


process="/usr/sbin/httpd"
start="service httpd restart"

ps ax | awk '{print $5}' | grep -q "^$process$" || {
    # Apparently not running, so start the process
    eval "$start"
    exit $?
}

exit 0
```

This script has two parameters that are set at the top of the script. The first is the name of the program to verify (as shown in the ps output). This must match the entire first token of the command name but can also contain regular expressions (any supported by grep). The second parameter is the command to execute when the program is found to not be running. In the previous example, you are checking to make sure the web server is running. In many network appliances, the web server provides the only interface to the system, so it is important that it is running.

A similar, but more powerful script is provided in section 10.1.4.

### 10.3.1.2  Checking a Port

Another useful test you can conduct involves making sure that something is listening on a certain port on your local system. Again, you could use this to further test that your web server is running and operating properly. You can use the netstat -l command to see what ports are being listened to:

```
% netstat -ln
Active Internet connections (only servers)
Proto Recv-Q Send-Q Local Address          Foreign Address        State
tcp       0      0 0.0.0.0:80             0.0.0.0:*              LISTEN
tcp       0      0 0.0.0.0:6000           0.0.0.0:*              LISTEN
tcp       0      0 0.0.0.0:22             0.0.0.0:*              LISTEN
...
```

Again, you can use awk to isolate the fourth column for all lines of protocol tcp:

```
% netstat -ln | awk '/^tcp/ {print $4}'
0.0.0.0:80
0.0.0.0:6000
0.0.0.0:22
...
```

Now you can use this to check the specified port:

```
#!/bin/bash

port="80"
restart="service httpd restart"

netstat -ln | awk '/^tcp/ {print $4}' | grep -q ":$port$" || {
    # Apparently not listening, so run restart command
    eval "$restart"
    exit $?
}

exit 0
```

### 10.3.1.3  Checking a Web Server

The more a test can verify, the better. The previous scripts could check to make sure a web server is running and to make sure it is listening on a port. None of this, however, verifies that it is operating correctly (or at all). The following script actually performs an HTTP GET request for the specified URL and searches for the specified string in the resulting page. If the page is not retrieved or if the string is not found, the service is restarted.

```
#!/bin/bash

URL="http://localhost/netsaint/index.html"
TIMEOUT=10 #(seconds)
MATCH="<HTML>"
restart="service httpd restart"

wget -q -O - -T=$TIMEOUT --tries=1 "$URL" | grep -q "$MATCH" || {
    # Something is wrong, so restart
    eval "$restart"
    exit $?
}

exit 0
```

## 10.3.2  NetSaint (a.k.a. Nagios)

NetSaint is a very structured, flexible, easy to use network and system monitoring package. The official homepage for the NetSaint project is http://www.netsaint.org. The latest version as of this writing is 0.0.7 (don't ask me why the version number is so low—the program is very reliable and robust). There is also an official set of plugins for NetSaint and, although you can find others and even create your own, these plugins are necessary for normal operation.

 **NOTE**  According to the authors, version 0.0.7 will be the final release of NetSaint. It is now being developed with a new name (Nagios). As of this writing, Nagios is still in its infancy, so it is not covered explicitly in this chapter (but it is pretty similar to NetSaint). I have seen Nagios in use, however, and it looks nice, so it is an option you may want to explore. You can find more information on Nagios at http://www.nagios.org.

The primary interface to the network and system status is through a web server that must be running on your system. Apache is the most common web server to use with NetSaint, but others could work as well. The web interface is very useful for quickly determining the status of all of your systems and your network. It provides all the information you could desire in a nice, organized format.

That having been said, this book does not discuss the web interface, because it is pretty much self-explanatory. You will want to use it, of course, but the actual configuration of NetSaint will be the topic of this section. The active notifications (email and pager) as well as the event handlers provided by NetSaint are of particular importance for automation purposes.

### 10.3.2.1 Basic Organization

NetSaint is configured through a series of definitions. Most definitions refer to other existing definitions. A good place to start are the command definitions, usually found in the command.cfg file included with the plugins distribution. These command definitions create commands that you can use to check various items on your systems or network. These commands can execute valid shell commands, but generally they call the appropriate NetSaint plugin.

In addition to host and service check commands, you usually define notification commands. These are typically found in the hosts.cfg file. They notify contacts via email or pager of problems and other events that occur.

You may also define optional event handlers. These are very powerful feature that allows you to proactively fix problems (especially service problems) before they become critical. The event handlers alone make NetSaint an active automation tool in addition to a useful and powerful monitoring system.

The remainder of the definitions involve contacts, hosts, and services. These are usually found in the hosts.cfg file. The first basic definitions within this file are the time period declarations. The standard time periods defined are 24x7 (24 hours per day, 7 days per week), workhours (9 to 5, Monday through Friday), nonworkhours (everything that is not included in workhours), and none (represents no time period at all).

Another basic definition within this file is the host. Each host has a name, an alias, an address, and a basic host check command (which determines if the host is up). You can also set certain notification levels for each host (i.e., should the contacts be notified when the host is down or unreachable?). Once some hosts are defined, you can group them into host groups. Each host group has a name, an alias, a contact group (to be discussed later), and a list of member hosts.

Contacts are another basic definition. Each contact has certain available hours as well as notification thresholds (i.e., some contacts should only be notified when there is an error, others should be notified about warnings). The notification methods are defined for each contact and usually involve email and/or pager notification. Just as with hosts, contacts can be organized into contact groups. Each group has a name, an alias, and a list of contacts who are members.

The final, and perhaps most important, definitions almost always found in this file are the service declarations—since services are ultimately what you care about. Each host may have any number of services defined. Each service has a check command defined (usually one of the plugins) as well as a variety of contact information of who to notify when there are problems with the service.

### 10.3.2.2  *NetSaint Configuration*

The configuration for NetSaint starts with the netsaint.cfg file (usually
/etc/netsaint/netsaint.cfg). This command usually includes other configuration
files (using the cfg_file directive) such as the file shosts.cfg and command.cfg. You
can, of course, split your configuration into as many files as you desire, or you can
combine it all into one file. This is just the standard configuration.

From version 0.0.6 on, NetSaint can be configured to allow distributed monitoring. You can also configure notification escalation for both hosts and services.
Starting in version 0.0.7, NetSaint can also track performance data in addition to
simple up/down checks. Service dependencies are added and can be used to
control complicated series of status checks. Since these are fairly new and generally
advanced topics, I will not discuss them in this book. Be sure to look into them if
they are something you feel you could use. The documentation provided with Net-
Saint discusses these features very well.

#### 10.3.2.2.1 *Basic Program Configuration*

There are quite a number of configuration options found in netsaint.cfg. These
include the logfile location, the logging levels, global timeouts, temporary file
locations, and other program settings. There are plenty of options in this file and
I will not discuss them here because the file is well documented and pretty much
self-explanatory. I find the defaults to be fine for most cases, but this is where you
can change them if you so desire.

#### 10.3.2.2.2 *Command Declarations*

All commands in NetSaint are declared using the command declaration statement.
There are, however, several different types of commands. When I say different,
I mean that they are used differently (and behave differently), but are still defined
the same. Here are the types that I will discuss:

- Host checks

- Service checks

- Host notifications

- Service notifications

- Host event handlers

- Service event handlers

You can use a wide variety of macros within these command declarations. Some macros are valid for all types of commands, but others are only valid in certain types of commands. There is a nice macro availability matrix available in the NetSaint documentation (the macros.html file in the documentation directory), so I only discuss the ones we actually use in the book. See the documentation for additional macros that are available.

### 10.3.2.2.2.1 Host Check

Let's start out with the most common host check command, which uses the check_ping plugin:

```
command[check-host-alive]=/usr/lib/netsaint/plugins/check_ping \
 -H $HOSTADDRESS$ -w 5000,100% -c 5000,100% -p 1
```

First, you can see that plugins are really separate programs that are accessed using these command declarations. Obviously your plugins don't have to be in this exact location. There is one macro in this declaration—the $HOSTADDRESS$ macro expands to the address of the host (surprisingly enough). The next argument (-w) specifies the warning threshold. In this case, the value is 5000,100%, which means a warning should be triggered if the round trip ping time is greater than 5 seconds (5000ms) or if the packet loss is 100 percent. The value for the critical threshold (-c) is set to the same thing, because the host check just wants to quickly check to see if the host is up. The final argument (-p 1) says to send only one packet.

### 10.3.2.2.2.2 Service Checks

Now I will define another ping test, but this one is to be used as a service check. This means that I want to be more accurate and generate a warning if necessary (instead of only an okay/failure like the check-host-alive command did). Here it is:

```
command[check_ping]=/usr/lib/netsaint/plugins/check_ping \
 -H $HOSTADDRESS$ -w $ARG1$ -c $ARG2$
```

In this case, you expect the service declaration to provide arguments for the warning and critical thresholds. The macros $ARG1 and $ARG2 expand to the value of these arguments.

Another service check I will define is a very simple HTTP status check:

```
command[check_http]=/usr/lib/netsaint/plugins/check_http \
 -H $HOSTADDRESS$ -I $HOSTADDRESS$
```

Note that you can extend this to include response-time thresholds and strings to be searched for in the content, and even to perform a POST request instead of the default GET request. How you use these features depends on your specific setup, so I will stick with this simple version.

### 10.3.2.2.2.3 Host Notification

This is a notification command that sends an email when there is a problem with a host:

```
command[host-notify-by-email]=/usr/bin/printf \
    "***** NetSaint *****\n\nNotification Type: $NOTIFICATIONTYPE$\n \
    Host: $HOSTNAME$\nState: $HOSTSTATE$\nAddress: $HOSTADDRESS$\n \
    Info: $OUTPUT$\n\nDate/Time: $DATETIME$\n" | /bin/mail \
    -s 'Host $HOSTSTATE$ alert for $HOSTNAME$!' $CONTACTEMAIL$
```

Although lengthy, this command declaration simply sends an email with a subject including the host's current state and its hostname to the contact email address (will be executed once for each contact). The body of the message will include more detail, including the actual output of the service check command ($OUTPUT$).

Creating a pager notification is very similar:

```
command[host-notify-by-epager]=/usr/bin/printf "Host '$HOSTALIAS$' is \
    $HOSTSTATE$\nInfo: $OUTPUT$\nTime: $DATETIME$" | /bin/mail -s \
    '$NOTIFICATIONTYPE$ alert - Host $HOSTNAME$ is $HOSTSTATE$' $CONTACTPAGER$
```

In this case, of course, $CONTACTPAGER$ is used instead of $CONTACTEMAIL$ as the destination email address. Note that the message is a bit more brief for easier reading on a pager.

### 10.3.2.2.2.4 Service Notification

Almost identical to host notification, these events notify you about a failure of a specific service on a specific host. Here is an email notification:

```
command[notify-by-email]=/usr/bin/printf '***** NetSaint *****\n\n \
    Notification Type: $NOTIFICATIONTYPE$\n\nService: $SERVICEDESC$\n \
    Host: $HOSTALIAS$\nAddress: $HOSTADDRESS$\nState: $SERVICESTATE$\n\n \
    Date/Time: $DATETIME$\n\nAdditional Info:\n\n$OUTPUT$' | /bin/mail \
    -s '** $NOTIFICATIONTYPE$ alert - $HOSTALIAS$/$SERVICEDESC$ is \
    $SERVICESTATE$ **' $CONTACTEMAIL$
```

It should be clear that you can customize this message any way you would like. More macros are available to provide more data, or you can cut information out that you do not care about. I will not bore you with a service notification by pager, because it would be repetitive (you saw the differences in the previous section).

### 10.3.2.2.2.5 Host Event Handler

A host event handler allows certain activities to be performed when the state of a host changes. If you have some sort of ability to perform a remote hard reset of a system, this would be the place to do it. Maybe you have wired up a siren in the middle of your office that can go off when a host is down. In most cases, host events cannot repair the problem, but you may find other uses for them. Here is a simple example:

```
command[reboot_host]=/usr/local/sbin/reboot_host \
    $HOSTSTATE$ $STATETYPE$ $HOSTATTEMPT$
```

The first macro expands to the current state of the host. The possible values are OK, WARNING, UNKNOWN, and CRITICAL.

The next macro expands to the type of state the host is in: either SOFT or HARD. If the host has a warning or is in a critical state but the specified number of retries have not yet been performed, it will be in a SOFT state. Once the retry count has been met, the state becomes HARD. If a host's state is OK, the state is equal to the state of the problem from which the host has recovered.

The final value indicates the host check attempt number (when in a SOFT warning or critical state).

### 10.3.2.2.2.6 Service Event Handler

Service event handlers can be more useful to the average person. They allow you to repair or restart services that are failing their status tests. The obvious example is a script that can restart a web server that is having problems:

```
command[restart-httpd]=/usr/local/sbin/restart-httpd \
    $SERVICESTATE$ $STATETYPE$ $SERVICEATTEMPT$ $HOSTADDRESS$
```

This isn't of much use without a script that actually performs the restart (when necessary). Here is an example:

```bash
#!/bin/bash
# Set this to the number of failed checks that can occur before
# a restart should be attempted (usually one less than retry count)
failcount=2

# Store arguments
state="$1"
statetype="$2"
attempts="$3"
host="$4"

[ "$state" != "CRITICAL" ] && {
    # Exit if not in a critical state
    exit 0
}

if [ "$statetype" == "SOFT" ] ; then
    # Service has failed at least one test
    [ "$attempts" == "$failcount" ] && {
        ssh "root@$host" 'service httpd restart'
    }
else
    # Service has failed all status tests!
    # We should have restarted it before this happened.
    # We probably did, and it probably didn't fix the problem...
    # But, we can try one more time just for the fun of it.
    ssh "root@$host" 'service httpd restart'
fi

exit 0
```

As you will see in the service declarations, a check has to fail a defined number of times before it is marked as officially down (a hard state). If it has failed once, but not enough times to be *hard down*, it is in a *soft down* state. This script tries to restart the service right before it enters this hard failure state (which is when notifications are sent). It also tries to restart it if it has fully failed (enters a hard failure state). Note that the script assumes it has passwordless SSH access to the remote host.

### *10.3.2.2.3 Host Declarations*

Here is a basic host declaration:

```
host[linux_web1]=Linux Web Server 1;192.168.100.1;;check-host-alive \
;10;480;24x7;1;1;1;
```

This declares a host with a name of linux_web1. After the equal sign is a list of parameters, separated by semicolons. Their meanings are as follows:

1. An alias (long name or description) for the host (Linux Web Server 1, in this case).

2. The address for the host (an IP address is preferable; in this example, it is 192.168.100.1).

3. This field (empty in this example) lists any parent hosts for this host. A parent host is any host (such as a switch, router, multihomed host, or managed hub) between the system running NetSaint and the host being defined. This allows NetSaint to build a physical hierarchy of your hosts.

4. This is the command to be used to check if the system is up (must be a defined host check command). In this case, we are using the check-host-alive command as defined in the previous section.

5. This field (10 in the example) is the number of times the host needs to fail the status check before it is reported as down or unreachable.

6. This value (480) is the notification interval, in minutes, for reporting that the host is down. In this case, a second notification will be sent 8 hours (480 divided by 60) after the first if the host is still down.

7. The name of the time period (24x7, in this case) during which notifications for this host should be sent out (if it is down or unreachable).

8. The value of 1 means that the contacts should be notified when the host recovers.

9. The value of 1 means that the contacts should be notified when the host is down.

10. This value of 1 means that the contacts should be notified when the host is unreachable.

11. The final field (following the last semicolon) is blank in this example. If a value is specified, it should be the name of a defined event handler command to be executed when a change in the host's status is detected. You must create your own event handlers using the command declaration.

### 10.3.2.2.4 Host Group Declarations

Host groups are very simple, which you will probably appreciate after reading through all of the parameters necessary for host definitions. Here is an example host group declaration:

```
hostgroup[linux_web]=Linux Web Servers;linux-web-admins;linux_web1,linux_web2
```

This declaration has created a host group named linux_web, which contains two hosts (linux_web1 and linux_web2). Any notifications related to either of these hosts is sent to the members of the notification group linux-web-admins.

### 10.3.2.2.5 Contact Declarations

A contact is simply a person or other contact point. Problem reports and other notifications (for hosts and services) can be sent to contacts. Contacts can also be organized into groups (as shown in the next section). You define a contact as follows:

```
contact[kirk]=Kirk Bauer;24x7;24x7;1;1;0;1;1;0;notify-by-email; \
host-notify-by-email;kirk@localhost.localdomain;
```

This command defines a contact named kirk. Like the rest of the declarations, there are several arguments separated by semicolons. Remember that the final semicolon means the final argument is empty. The meanings of these arguments are as follows:

1. Like all declarations, the first argument is a description (or alias) for the contact (Kirk Bauer, in this case).

2. The name of a time period during which service notifications can be sent to this contact (24x7).

3. The name of a time period during which host notifications can be sent to this contact (24x7, again).

4. If set to 1, the contact will be notified when a service recovers.

5. If set to 1, the contact will be notified when a service is in a critical state.

6. If set to 1, the contact will be notified when a service is in a warning state.

7. If set to 1, the contact will be notified when a host recovers from a down state. In this example, it is set to 0 so no notifications will be sent out for host recoveries.

8. If set to 1, the contact will be notified when a host is down.

9. If set to 1, the contact will be notified when a host is not reachable.

10. One or more defined commands (separated by commas) that should be used to notify the contact of service related events. (notify-by-email, in this case)

11. One or more defined commands (separated by commas) that should be used to notify the contact of host related events (host-notify-by-email, in this case).

12. An email address for the contact (kirk@localhost.localdomain).

13. A pager number or email address (as required by the pager notification command, if defined). In this example, no pager number is given.

### 10.3.2.2.6 *Contact Group Declarations*

Contact group declarations are about as simple as they get. There is the name, the description, and the comma-delimited list of members (their contact names). Here is an example:

```
contactgroup[linux-admins]=Linux Administrators;kirk,moshe,nick
```

Contact groups are used to define who should be contacted for issues with each host group.

### 10.3.2.2.7 *Service Declarations*

Service declarations are used to specify which services on which systems should be monitored. They also specify the method of monitoring, who gets the reports, and other various settings. As you can imagine, these declarations require quite a number of parameters. One difference between service declarations and all other declarations is that the name in the brackets is the host on which the service is running (while in all other cases this is the name of the declared item). Here are two example service declarations (which would be repeated for each web server):

```
service[linux_web1]=PING;0;24x7;3;5;1;linux-web-admins;240;24x7;1;1;0;; \
    check_ping!100.0,20%!500.0,60%
service[linux_web1]=HTTP;0;24x7;3;2;1;linux-web-admins;240;24x7;1;1;1;; \
    check_http
```

These are two services that are to be checked on the host linux_web1. The first declaration, with the description PING, checks the host's basic networking functionality by pinging the host and measuring the response rate and the number of packets lost. The second declaration, with the description HTTP, performs a simple responsiveness check of the web server running on the host. There are many parameters in these declarations, with the following meanings:

1. As usual, the first argument is the arbitrary description (or "alias") for the service (PING and HTTP in this example).

2. If the second argument is set to 1, the service is considered volatile. If a service is volatile, a notification occurs every time the service check fails. Most services should not be marked as volatile.

3. This specifies the time period during which the service should be checked (24x7 in this example).

4. This is the number of times the check should be retried (on failure) before the service is considered down (or in a warning state). This is set to 3 for both services in this example.

5. This is the number of minutes that should elapse between normal checks of the service (5 and 2).

6. This is the number of minutes NetSaint should allow to pass between retries (1).

7. This is the contact group that should be notified of any issues with this service, and changes in the state of this service. This is set to linux-web-admins in this example.

8. The 240 is the notification interval. After the service is in a warning or critical state for this number of minutes, the contacts will be renotified.

9. This time period specifies when notifications for this service can be sent out.

10. Contacts will be notified when the service recovers if this field is set to 1.

11. Contacts will be notified when the service is at a critical level if this field is set to 1.

12. Contacts will be notified when the service is in a warning state if this field is set to 1.

13. If specified, this is an event handler that will be executed when the state of the service changes.

14. The command to be used to perform the actual service status check.

## 10.3.2.3  Writing Your Own Plugins

Writing your own plugin can be simple—at least if the test you are trying to perform is simple. A NetSaint plugin can be written in any language. The official plugins are written in C, but I find it much easier to write personal or custom plugins in bash or Perl. If you want the plugin to be part of the official distribution, of course, you should stick with C.

I would like to write a generic plugin as an example, but all of the generic plugins that come to mind are already included in the official plugin distribution. So, as a very contrived example, I will create a plugin that checks for the presence of a certain file (passed in as its only parameter). The file must also be a regular file and contain some data.

A plugin should always produce exactly one line of output on stdout. It should be relatively short (less than 80 characters or so). It must exit with an appropriate exit value as explained in the following table.

*Table 10-1. NetSaint Plugin Return Codes*

| Exit Code | Status Label | Description |
|---|---|---|
| -1 | Unknown | An internal error occurred in the plugin or the check could not be performed for some reason. |
| 0 | OK | The service status check was successful. |
| 1 | Warning | The service appears to be working, but there is some problem or potential problem that may require attention. |
| 2 | Critical | The service is not running or is not operating properly. Immediate attention is required. |

Now that the ground rules have been set, here is the simple and contrived plugin written in the bash shell:

```
#!/bin/bash

file="$1"

[ -z "$file" ] && {
    echo "No file specified!"
    exit -1    # UNKNOWN
}

if [ -f "$file" ] ; then
    if [ -s "$file" ] ; then
        # Everything is fine
        echo "File $file OK."
        exit 0
    else
        # Warn if the file is empty
        echo "File $file is empty."
        exit 1
    fi
else
    # Error if not a normal file
    echo "$file not a regular file."
    exit 2
fi
```

A script like this might be used by external programs to communicate with NetSaint through a special file. The logic of the script could be reversed, and if the file exists, it would be assumed to contain some kind of error message. If the file did not exist, it would be assumed that nothing is wrong.

### 10.3.3   Mon

Mon is similar in many ways to NetSaint. It allows you to define host groups, check services on those hosts, and alert certain contacts upon service failures. Although it does not provide as thorough of a web interface, Mon does use a client-server model and comes with both text- and web-based client interfaces.

NetSaint is more modern and more flexible and can provide a complete monitoring solution for a relatively complex network right out of the box. Mon, on the other hand, is less complicated to configure—in part because of its smaller feature set. Its text client would also be a great way to use Mon as part of a larger custom monitoring system. If you really wanted to, you could even have your custom system communicate with Mon directly over its network interface.

At its heart, Mon is simply a scheduler. You plug in monitor scripts and corresponding upalert/downalert scripts to make it a monitoring system. This is very useful for advanced and custom systems since you can craft it into exactly what you need.

You can download Mon from `http://www.kernel.org/software/mon/`. You will also need to download and install the fping program as well as several Perl modules as explained in the Mon installation instructions. This chapter was written using Mon version `0.99.2`.

### 10.3.3.1   Simple Configuration of Mon

Here is a very simple sample configuration file, usually created as `/etc/mon/mon.cf`. It only checks the local system for ping responses. This is a test that should never fail, but it is a good place to start.

```
cfbasedir = /etc/mon
alertdir = /usr/local/lib/mon/alert.d
mondir = /usr/local/lib/mon/mon.d

hostgroup test 127.0.0.1

watch test
   service ping
      interval 1m
         monitor fping.monitor
```

The first three lines are usually necessary to identify the directories that contain the configuration files, the alert scripts, and the monitor scripts, respectively. These will not be included in any additional examples because I assume that you already have them (if necessary).

Next a hostgroup named test is defined. A hostgroup can contain any number of systems (separated by whitespace). Each system is identified by either a hostname or IP address. In this case, our test group contains only the local system (127.0.0.1).

Once a group of hosts has been defined, they can be watched. In this example, the "ping" service is monitored once every minute using the fping.monitor monitoring script. This script uses the fping program to send ICMP pings to the host.

This book will not discuss user authentication through the Mon application. All of the examples in this section require only read access, which is open to anybody with the default security configuration. In many cases, this is too permissive, so you may want to password protect even read-only access to your Mon daemon.

### 10.3.3.2  Checking Status

Assuming your configuration file is named /etc/mon/mon.cf and the specified directories within that file exist, you can run Mon by simply executing the mon command. Once the program is running, you can use moncmd to see that your local system is responding to pings (usually a good thing):

```
% moncmd -s localhost list successes
group=test service=ping opstatus=7 last_opstatus=7 exitval=undef
timer=22 last_success=0 last_trap=0 last_check= ack=0 ackcomment=''
alerts_sent=0 depstatus=0 depend='' monitor='fping.monitor'
last_summary='' last_detail='' interval=60
220 list successes completed
```

As you can see, this text client provides output that is easy to parse with external scripts. The command list successes is only one of many commands that can be executed through moncmd. A full list can be obtained as follows:

```
% moncmd -h

usage: moncmd [-a] [-l login] [-s host] [-p port] [-f file] commands

Valid commands are:
    quit
    reset [stopped]
    term
```

```
list group "groupname"
list disabled
list alerthist
list failurehist
list successes
list failures
list opstatus
list pids
list watch
stop
start
loadstate
savestate
set "group" "service" "variable" "value"
get "group" "service" "variable"
disable service "group" "service"
disable host "host" ["host"...]
disable watch "watch"
enable service "group" "service"
enable host "host" ["host"...]
enable watch "watch"
```

### 10.3.3.3  Sending Alerts

Like NetSaint, Mon can send alerts to specified contacts when there is a service failure. Here is an extension of the previous example provided:

```
watch test
    service ping
        interval 1m
            monitor fping.monitor
                period wd {Mon-Fri} hr {9am-5pm}
                    alertevery 1h
                    alertafter 2 10m
                    alert mail.alert somebody@company.com
```

In this case, the contact somebody@company.com will be notified if the ping fails. They will be notified every hour until the service stops failing the status check. They will only be notified after there have been two failures in a ten minute period (alert after 2 10m). Finally, they will only be alerted during "normal" working hours (Monday through Friday, 9AM until 5PM).

### 10.3.3.4  Real-World Example

Here is a configuration file that actually monitors a couple of web servers. The servers will be checked every five minutes for both proper ping and HTTP responses. Note that the HTTP service depends on the ping service. This prevents the contact(s) from receiving reports from both services during a network outage.

```
hostgroup webservers www1 www2 www3

watch webservers
    service ping
        interval 2m
            monitor fping.monitor
    service http
        interval 5m
            monitor http.monitor
                depend SELF:ping
                period wd {Mon-Fri} hr {9am-5pm}
                    # Daytime support
                    alertevery 1h
                    alertafter 2 10m
                    alert mail.alert somebody@company.com
                period wd {Sun-Sat}
                    # 24-hour support
                    alertevery 1h
                    alertafter 3 20m
                    alert mail.alert support@company.com
```

In this case, there is one daytime support person who gets reports fairly quickly (after 2 failures in 10 minutes). There is also a 24-hour support email address that receives alerts at any time, but only after 3 failures in 20 minutes.

Many more monitoring scripts are included with Mon. There are also other alert scripts, including ones that support pagers, one that can write to a file, and so on.

### 10.3.3.5  Creating a Custom Monitoring Script

Creating a custom monitoring script that can be used by Mon is easy. It can be written in any language and is placed in the mon.d/ directory. Here is a simple bash shell script that you can extend to perform your own service checks:

```
#!/bin/bash

custom_check() {
    # Perform your custom check here
    # The host is passed in as $1
    # Return 0 on success, 1 on failure
    return 0
}

failed=''
for host in "$@" ; do
    custom_check "$host" || {
        failed="$failed $host"
    }
done

[ -n "$failed" ] && {
    echo "$failed"
    exit 1
}

exit 0
```

This script takes any number of hosts as arguments. It checks each host in series. Any hosts that fail are printed on stdout. A non-zero exit code indicates that there were failures.

Since all of the hostnames are passed in at once, you could theoretically check all of the hosts simultaneously. This would be much quicker, but whether or not it is worth the effort is up to you. If it is time consuming to check a specific service, performing that check in parallel across multiple systems makes a big difference.

# CHAPTER 11

# Improving System
# Security

GOOD ADMINISTRATORS SHOULD be conscious of security in everything they do. Hopefully, you have seen this in practice throughout this book. The scripts I have presented, for example, do not use predictable temporary filenames in a public directory such as /tmp/. This is because I know that this practice almost always opens up a potential avenue for attack. I hope that you take this and other security precautions seriously as you automate your systems.

Although important, the security of your scripts is not the topic of this chapter. Instead, this chapter discusses some automated security procedures that can help you make your systems more secure. The scripts and examples in this chapter are not, however, a replacement for a security-conscious administrator. This is because security is broken by people, not machines. At this point in human history, it is relatively easy for a person to outsmart a machine. This includes any security automation you may put in place, regardless of how elegant the solution might be.

The quickest and easiest way to enhance your network security is to reduce the number of network services your system provides. Most operating systems come with a wide range of network services; some operating systems enable these services by default. Simply disabling the services you don't need goes a long way toward improving system security. Some examples of how to quickly do this with GNU cfengine can be found in section 11.1.4. In fact, cfengine can take care of many security-related tasks for you. For this reason, it will be discussed first.

Setting up a properly configured corporate firewall is a great idea, but that does not mean that it is impenetrable. Not only might it not operate correctly, but your users may not be perfect or even trustworthy. If your system can run system-level firewalling software, that software can be used to add an additional layer of security. Creating a good firewall on every system is a tedious task when done by hand, but the scripts you'll learn about in this chapter can make that job easier.

Another layer of system security is file monitoring. Watching for suspicious changes on your filesystem won't usually stop an attack, but your monitoring of files will alert you after the fact, which could possibly prevent further network compromises. cfengine can monitor your systems' files pretty well, but if you are looking for more power and flexibility, check out the popular Tripwire, which can monitor just about any properties of any files. Tripwire is discussed in detail in section 11.3.

---

 **NOTE**  As you might guess, I can't provide a comprehensive security guide in just one chapter. What I can do, however, is recommend the book *Practical UNIX & Internet Security* by Simson Garfinkel, Alan Schwartz, and Gene Spafford (O'Reilly and Associates, 2003).

---

## 11.1 System Security with GNU cfengine

GNU cfengine can improve system security in many ways. First, it allows you to automatically configure systems in a consistent manner. The cfengine configuration is general enough that you can quickly apply your changes to other hosts in the same or different classes, even to systems that haven't been installed yet. This means that if you correct a security problem on your Linux systems through cfengine, and then later install a new Linux system, the security problem will be fixed there as well (if necessary). These, and other basic principles surrounding cfengine, are discussed in section 6.4.

Some other ways cfengine can help with system security are illustrated within the following sections. Just be aware that this is far from a comprehensive list. Your own systems will almost certainly have more areas where you can use cfengine to enhance their security. You probably run applications like web and FTP servers that can be serious security problems if not properly configured. I can't cover all of these situations, but a good security book will tell you what to configure, and cfengine can do the actual configuration for you.

### 11.1.1 *Performing Basic File Checks*

GNU cfengine automatically performs certain security checks on any files and directories mentioned within the files section. First of all, it reports and logs any files that are setuid or setgid root (a file will not be reported more than once, though). Executable setuid and setgid files cause the programs to run as a specific user (such as root) regardless of who actually executes the command. This can obviously be a very powerful yet frequently dangerous capability.

In addition, when processing the files, tidy, and copy sections, cfengine identifies suspicious files. You can control this behavior with the following settings:

**NOTE** You can find the code samples for this chapter in the Downloads section of the Apress web site (http://www.apress.com).

```
control:
    NonAlphaNumFiles = ( on )
    FileExtensions = ( o a c gif jpg html ) # etc
    SuspiciousNames = ( .mo lrk3 lkr3 )
```

The first setting causes cfengine to report and disable any completely nonalpha-numeric files it finds. The second setting (FileExtensions) includes a list of standard file extensions. If cfengine finds directories with these extensions, it reports them, since users can try to hide directories by creating them with a standard filename extension.

The third item (SuspiciousNames) identifies files that should cause a warning if they are found.

## 11.1.2 The disable Section

You can use cfengine to disable a variety of files and programs on your system (if they exist). When executables and any other files are disabled, they are renamed with a .cf-disabled extension and their permissions are set to 0400. Here are a few examples:

```
disable:
    any::
        /root/.rhosts
        /etc/hosts.equiv

    solaris::
        # Some versions provide a local root exploit
        /usr/bin/eject
```

The first section disables the files /root/.rhosts and /etc/hosts.equiv on all systems (class any) because using these files is often considered a security risk.

The next section "fixes" a very old security problem with Solaris. It's not likely that your systems would be vulnerable to this specific problem. If you do have a system that is this old, the better option is to apply the appropriate patch. You could then create your own class that would indicate if this patch had been applied. If it had not, you would disable the file.

Another option is to just disable this binary on all systems and then create a symbolic link to your own safe binary:

```
links:
    solaris||linux::
        /usr/bin/eject ->! /usr/local/bin/safe_eject
```

The ->! sequence forces the symbolic link to be created, even if it means replacing an existing file.

## 11.1.3  The files Section

You can use cfengine to make sure the permissions on important system files are correct. Here is an example that sets the permissions on the system account files:

```
files:
    /etc/passwd mode=644 owner=root group=root action=fixall
    /etc/shadow mode=600 owner=root group=root action=fixall
    /etc/group mode=644 owner=root group=root action=fixall
```

You can also use cfengine to monitor binary files on your system. Like any other file, the permissions of a binary file can be checked and any problems can be fixed. For binaries, particularly those of the setuid root variety, this can be a very useful feature. You can also use cfengine to provide some Tripwire functionality—you can use it to monitor the md5 checksum of a file. Here is an example:

```
files:
    /bin/mount mode=4555 owner=root group=root action=fixall checksum=md5
```

On many systems, the /bin/mount program is setuid root. This allows normal users to mount specific drives without superuser privileges. The parameters given in this example tell cfengine to check the permissions on this binary (and all others that are setuid root) and to record its checksum in a database.

If the checksum does change, you will be notified every time cfagent runs. This will continue until you execute cfagent with the following setting in the control section:

```
control:
    ChecksumUpdates = ( on )
```

This setting will cause all stored file checksums to be updated to their current values. You can also have cfengine find and eliminate any setuid root files that you do not specifically list:

```
filters:
   { root_owned_files
      Owner:     "root"
      Result:    "Owner"
   }


files:
   /
      filter=root_owned_files
      mode=u-s      # no SUID bit may be set
      recurse=inf
      action=fixall
      inform=true
      # And the full paths of files that *should* be SUID
      ignore=/proc
      ignore=/bin/ping
      ignore=/usr/bin/su
      ignore=/usr/bin/passwd
      ignore=/usr/bin/at
      ignore=/usr/bin/crontab
      ignore=/usr/bin/rsh
      ignore=/usr/sbin/traceroute
```

All I do here is recurse through the entire filesystem and disable the setuid bit for all files owned by root. I use the ignore option to exclude files that I *do* want setuid root. You can also ignore directories (/proc/ in this case) with this directive. Be sure to use full pathnames—although you could use ignore=ping instead of ignore=/bin/ping, the shorter version would inadvertently ignore the file /home/hackeduser/.hidden/my_fake_ping.

Note that this example is by no means comprehensive. If you were to place this in an active cfagent.conf it could very well mess up your system. The reason is that every operating system has different programs that must be setuid root in order to operate properly. This sample listing is not really appropriate for any operating system. You would have to use the cfengine classes to specify a different ignore list for each type of operating system you are using. You can quickly find the setuid root files on your system with the following command:

```
# find / -perm +4000 -user root
/usr/bin/chage
/usr/bin/gpasswd
/usr/bin/chfn
/usr/bin/chsh
/usr/bin/newgrp
/usr/bin/at
/usr/bin/passwd
/usr/bin/sudo
/usr/bin/crontab
...
```

You can look through the output of this command and decide which of the programs found should be left setuid root. Making these decisions is beyond the scope of this book, but your operating system vendor should probably be able to provide a basic list of important ones.

## 11.1.4  Controlling Network Services

The first thing you should do on every system is disable all unnecessary processes—particularly those that accept connections over the network. You will probably need to leave at least some services running. You can restrict access to these using TCP wrappers, as described in this section.

### 11.1.4.1  Disabling inetd Services

You can quickly disable services launched from inetd using cfengine. For instance, say you wanted to disable the "r" services (rsh, rlogin, etc.):

```
editfiles:
  { /etc/inetd.conf
    HashCommentLinesContaining "rshd"
    HashCommentLinesContaining "rlogind"
    HashCommentLinesContaining "rwall"
    DefineClasses "modified_inetd"
  }
```

Since the "r" services actually listen on a socket using the system's inetd, I simply commented out the appropriate entries in the inetd configuration file (/etc/inetd.conf on some systems, /etc/inet/inetd.conf on others). I also requested that the class modified_inetd be defined—but only if a change was made. This class, when defined, can be used to send the HUP signal to inetd so that it will reread its configuration:

```
processes:
  modified_inetd::
    "inetd" signal=hup
```

### 11.1.4.2  Disabling Daemons

A good number of processes will probably run on your systems by default. You will find that you do not need some of them, and some of *those* are listening on a port for remote connections. Disabling these processes requires two steps.

First, you need to make sure that the processes in question are not running. This is easy to do with cfengine. For example, say that you do not use NFS on your systems—NFS uses several processes that you may want to kill:

```
processes:
  "nfsd"              signal=kill
  "rpc.statd"         signal=kill
  "rpc.rquotad"       signal=kill
  "rpc.mountd"        signal=kill
```

Every time cfagent runs, it kills these processes if they are running. Keep in mind that some of these processes might be used for other reasons, so be careful what processes you kill.

This is a step in the right direction, but these processes may still start at boot time. So, we need to take it a step further and prevent these processes from starting during the next system boot. Enabling and disabling daemons at system startup is a very system-specific task, but I can provide a few examples.

On a Red Hat Linux system, for example, I could do this:

```
shellcommands:
  "/sbin/chkconfig nfs off"
```

Or, I could remove the appropriate SysV-style symlink directly:

```
disable:
  /etc/rc.d/rc3.d/S60nfs
```

Finally, I could remove the init script completely to make sure it cannot be (easily) started by anybody:

```
disable:
    /etc/rc.d/init.d/nfs
```

If your system does not use SysV-style init scripts, you will have to consult another source to find out how to disable certain services. Since cfengine can run arbitrary commands, it shouldn't be hard to automate. Even if you do have SysV-style init scripts, the directories and filenames will probably be different than the ones in these examples.

### 11.1.4.3 TCP Wrappers

You will always want some network services to remain active. If any of these services are executed by inetd, it is a good idea to use TCP wrappers. TCP wrappers is a program (usually named `tcpd` or `in.tcpd`) that can be executed by inetd. It performs some checks on the network connection, applies any access control rules, and ultimately launches the necessary program.

Your systems may or may not have TCP wrappers installed, and it may or may not be configured properly for its use. If TCP wrappers is not installed, you need to install it first using the methods in Chapter 8. It could also be installed through cfengine by copying the files from one server to another.

Once the TCP wrappers program is actually installed (in a location like `/usr/sbin/tcpd`), you need to make sure your systems use it. A system without TCP wrappers enabled would have a `/etc/inetd.conf` with entries like this (your file location and entry format may vary):

```
ftp stream tcp6 nowait root /usr/sbin/in.ftpd in.ftpd
telnet stream tcp6 nowait root /usr/sbin/in.telnetd in.telnetd
```

To activate TCP wrappers, you want to modify these entries to call the `tcpd` program as follows:

```
ftp stream tcp6 nowait root /usr/sbin/tcpd in.ftpd
telnet stream tcp6 nowait root /usr/sbin/tcpd in.telnetd
```

You can do this using the `editfiles` section:

```
editfiles:
    { /etc/inetd.conf
      ReplaceAll "/usr/sbin/in.ftpd" With "/usr/sbin/tcpd"
      ReplaceAll "/usr/sbin/in.telnetd" With "/usr/sbin/tcpd"
      DefineClasses "modified_inetd"
    }
```

This will cause your system to use TCP wrappers for both the FTP and Telnet services. Don't forget to send the HUP signal to inetd:

```
processes:
  modified_inetd::
    "inetd" signal=hup
```

Simply enabling TCP wrappers enhances the security of the selected network services. You can gain additional benefits by restricting access to these services using /etc/hosts.allow and /etc/hosts.deny. A properly configured corporate firewall, a system-level firewall, if possible (as described in the next section), and TCP wrappers with access control enabled provide three tiers of protection for your network services. It may seem like overkill, but when you can do all of this automatically, there really is little reason not to be overly cautious. Any one of these security devices could fail or be misconfigured, but probably not all three.

## 11.2 Configuring System-Level Firewalls

Configuring a firewall is very tedious because a firewall configuration may have thousands of entries. Many elements (such as remote and local IP addresses, ports, etc.) must be set exactly right for each entry. Although doable, configuring your firewall manually is generally a risky and frustrating task.

Several operating systems, particularly of the open-source variety (Linux and FreeBSD) offer firewall support directly in their kernel. This has prompted many people to use these systems (albeit very stripped down versions of them) as their firewall. Many other people also use these facilities to create a virtual firewall on each host since it is so easy to do. Fortunately, these operating systems also generally include Perl and bash, which means you can script these firewall configurations without even installing additional software. Once you have written your own automatic firewall configuration scripts, it would be a shame not to apply a firewall to every supported system.

We have reached a point, again, where I must choose a specific technology to use in my examples. The one I see used the most is iptables, which is a fairly recent replacement for ipchains. It is available on Linux systems starting with the 2.4 kernel. It consists of a kernel module as well as the utility program iptables. This command allows you to set and view the system's firewall configuration.

Since the firewall configuration is stored in the running kernel, it needs to be reentered each time the system boots. For this reason, any sane administrator will create a shell script to perform this configuration whenever necessary. You should have this script run whenever the system boots, but you can also run it whenever a change in the system's firewall configuration is necessary. Instead of manually making a change, the script is modified and then reexecuted. This makes the change permanent and reduces the chance of mistakes.

When you have more than one system, a simple script is not the best solution. Instead, I usually create a generic script that operates on a high-level configuration file. Since, in many cases, each system needs a slightly different configuration, you can create a separate configuration file for each system. The generic script can then use a certain set of default values in addition to the configuration file specific to the local system.

I present a script in this section that provides a fairly basic firewall configuration for Linux systems. It uses a set of configuration files to determine each system in an appropriate manner. Keep in mind that this script should be executed before any network interfaces become active; this prevents the firewall from being ineffective for any period of time, no matter how small. The interfaces used in the scripts don't actually need to be present when the firewall rules are entered into the kernel.

## 11.2.1  Firewall Configuration Files

The script in this chapter expects the firewall configuration files to be located in a common directory, such as /usr/local/etc/firewall/. You can distribute this directory using any of the methods discussed in .

The first file needed is the global configuration, stored in global.conf. Here is an example:

```
trusted_hosts="192.168.0.0/255.255.0.0 1.2.3.4"
trusted_tcp="22"
```

In this file, a set of trusted hosts is defined. These are listed (separated by spaces) in the variable $trusted_hosts. Each entry may also contain a netmask to specify a range of hosts. The first entry in this example causes all hosts in the 192.168 network to be trusted; this would presumably be your internal, private network—depending on your situation, this might be a bit too broad. Additionally, the host 1.2.3.4 is listed as a single trusted host.

Next is the variable $trusted_tcp. This also contains a space-delimited list. Each item in this list is a port to which connections can be made from trusted hosts. In this case, only SSH access (port22) is allowed from trusted hosts. Of course, trusted hosts can also access publicly available ports.

In addition to this global configuration file (which you will probably want to expand), you need one configuration file for each host that needs a firewall enabled.

You may not want to copy all configuration files to all systems. If an attacker gains access to one system, they may be able to use the other system's firewall configuration files to help them continue their attack on your network. If you use GNU cfengine to distribute these configuration files, copying only certain files to certain systems should be relatively easy.

In any case, here is an example configuration file. It should be named `host.conf`, where `host` is the host's short hostname.

```
iface="eth0"
in_tcp="80 443"
```

Again, this example is very simple. You will almost certainly need to expand this configuration file, as well as the script that uses it. In this case, I identify `eth0` as the system's external network interface. I also specify that both ports `80` and `443` should be open to incoming connections from all hosts. This host would presumably be running a web server and accepting both HTTP and HTTPS connections.

## 11.2.2  Firewall Configuration Script

Here is a nice generic script that you can use to create a simple firewall on each of your systems. It is great for single systems with only one network interface. You would have to expand it to support systems with multiple interfaces that perform routing tasks (such as a network firewall system).

The script does allow a user or program to initiate any type of connection out to other systems. This policy may be too lax for your environment, but in most cases, it is okay. The important thing is that the firewall prevents unwanted incoming connections to your system. It would also be very easy to expand this script to allow specific incoming UDP traffic.

First, the script must determine its hostname and read the appropriate configuration files. The host's configuration file specifies the name of the external interface in the `$iface` variable. The script uses that variable to determine the system's IP address.

```
#!/bin/bash
confdir=/usr/local/etc/firewall

thishost=`hostname | cut -d'.' -f1`

[ -r "$confdir/$thishost.conf" ] || {
    # Exit if no configuration file for this host exists
    echo "No firewall configuration for host: $thishost"
    exit 0
}
```

```
source $confdir/global.conf
source $confdir/$thishost.conf

# Determine this system's external IP address
IPADDR=`ifconfig $iface | awk '/inet addr/ {print $2}' | cut -d: -f2`
```

Next, commands are issues that clear all current rules, chains, and counters. The kernel is told to drop all packets by default. Packets claiming that they are from the local system, yet coming in on the network interface, are also dropped:

```
# Flush all chains, delete user-defined chains, and clear counters
iptables -F ; iptables -X ; iptables -Z

# We want to drop all packets by default
iptables -P INPUT DROP
iptables -P FORWARD DROP
iptables -P OUTPUT DROP

# Do not allow spoofed packets (external packets with our IP)
iptables -A INPUT -i $iface -s $IPADDR -j DROP
# Don't allow external packets coming from the loopback net
iptables -A INPUT -i $iface -d 127.0.0.1/8 -j DROP
```

Now, these commands tell the kernel to allow some basic packets through the firewall—all traffic on the local loopback interface is allowed and limited ICMP traffic is also allowed. Most importantly, both TCP and UDP connections initiated from the system are allowed through the firewall:

```
# Now, allow all traffic on the loopback interface
iptables -A INPUT  -i lo -j ACCEPT
iptables -A OUTPUT -o lo -j ACCEPT

# Allow certain ICMP packets
iptables -A INPUT  -i $iface -p icmp -m state \
   --state ESTABLISHED,RELATED     -j ACCEPT
iptables -A OUTPUT -o $iface -p icmp -m state \
   --state NEW,ESTABLISHED,RELATED -j ACCEPT

# Allow any connections initiated from this system
iptables -A OUTPUT -o $iface -p tcp -m state \
   --state NEW,ESTABLISHED -j ACCEPT
iptables -A INPUT  -i $iface -p tcp -m state \
   --state ESTABLISHED     -j ACCEPT
```

```
iptables -A OUTPUT -o $iface -p udp -m state \
   --state NEW,ESTABLISHED -j ACCEPT
iptables -A INPUT  -i $iface -p udp -m state \
   --state ESTABLISHED      -j ACCEPT
```

Now comes a set of nested loops. The commands inside this loop allow incoming connections to be initiated from each trusted host to each specified port:

```
# Now, allow traffic from trusted hosts
for trusted in $trusted_hosts ; do
   for service in $trusted_tcp ; do
      echo "Allowing $service TCP traffic from $trusted"
      iptables -A INPUT -i $iface -p tcp -s $trusted -d $IPADDR \
         --dport $service -m state --state NEW,ESTABLISHED -j ACCEPT
   done
done
```

Finally, we instruct the kernel to allow incoming traffic from all hosts to connect to specified ports:

```
# Allow traffic to select ports from anywhere
for service in $in_tcp ; do
   echo "Allowing all incoming $service TCP traffic"
   iptables -A INPUT -i $iface -p tcp -d $IPADDR --dport $service \
      -m state --state NEW,ESTABLISHED -j ACCEPT
done
```

## 11.2.3  Groups of Systems

You could modify the previous script to configure groups of identical systems. The original script sources a host-specific configuration file:

```
thishost=`hostname | cut -d'.' -f1`

[ -r "$confdir/$thishost.conf" ] || {
   # Exit if no configuration file for this host exists
   echo "No firewall configuration for host: $thishost"
   exit 0
}

source $confdir/global.conf
source $confdir/$thishost.conf
```

You could have the host first load the global configuration, then load its group's configuration, and finally load a host-specific file, if present, as shown here:

```
source $confdir/global.conf

host_dir='/usr/local/etc/hosts/'
thishost=`hostname | cut -d'.' -f1`

# Load configuration for our group(s)
for group in $host_dir/* ; do
    grep -q "^$thishost$" "$group"&& {
        # This host is part of this group, so load group config
        config="$confdir/$(basename $group).conf"
        [ -r "$config" ] && source $config
    }
done

[ -r "$confdir/$thishost.conf" ] && \
    source $confdir/$thishost.conf
```

This allows you to have a global configuration, configuration options for each group of hosts, and even host-specific settings if necessary.

## 11.3 Watching Files with Tripwire

Tripwire is a program that has gone through many changes in its life. Currently, it is a commercial product (http://www.tripwire.com) as well as an open-source program (http://www.tripwire.org)—but only for the Linux operating system.

The program I discuss and use within this section is the open-source version 2.3 for Linux. If you aren't using Linux, the commercial product does provide binaries for many other systems as well as nice management tools. Purchasing the commercial version is something to consider if your budget allows for such an expense.

If Tripwire will not fulfill your needs, you can consider using the Advanced Intrusion Detection Environment (AIDE), which is a completely free "drop-in replacement" for Tripwire. You can download this software and find more information about it at http://www.cs.tut.fi/~rammer/aide.html.

Another similar, but newer (and hence less popular), program is Osiris. This is fully open source, so it may be a better solution if you have a mixed environment and don't want to spend money on the commercial version of Tripwire. Osiris can be found at http://osiris.shmoo.com.

A final alternative to consider is samhain. One thing nice about this program is that it can run as a daemon so that it can check your system more frequently. It also supports a client/server model so that you can consolidate security reports from your various systems. It also has a nice web interface called Beltane. You can find more information at http://la-samhna.de/samhain/.

At this point, you may be asking, "What does Tripwire do?" It monitors the files on your system for changes. This may sound like a simple enough task, but Tripwire does it very well and very securely. It can check a wide variety of file attributes and store these attributes in a database that is encrypted with a private key. This makes it extremely difficult (practically impossible) for an attacker to install backdoors or cover their tracks after they intrude into your system.

Of course, the fact that you must enter a passphrase every time you want to reconfigure Tripwire or update its database might seem to preclude the program from your automation suite. This is an example of where security and automation do not go hand in hand. You may have to give up some automation to enhance your systems' security. Using Tripwire is, however, still much easier than checking the files yourself!

## 11.3.1 Installing Tripwire

Tripwire comes with a nice installation script. It installs the tripwire binary as well as some configuration files, and it keys in /etc/tripwire/. You can find the actual program configuration in /etc/tripwire/tw.cfg, but if you look at this file, you will discover that it is encrypted. This is for security reasons—the file is created from a plain-text file that can be deleted afterward. The default plain-text version can be found in /etc/tripwire/twcfg.txt.

The default configuration is usually correct, but the plain-text version can be modified if necessary. If you modify this configuration, you must then use the command twadmin --create-cfgfile /etc/tripwire/twcfg.txt to import the new configuration file. Whether you modify the configuration or not, the plain-text file should be deleted to enhance system security. The encrypted configuration file can be displayed using the command twadmin --print-cfgfile (using your passphrase, of course).

## 11.3.2 Generating a Tripwire Policy File

The meat of Tripwire's configuration is its policy file. Once that has been created (or the default one has been modified), you are ready to start using Tripwire. The security policy is stored in /etc/tripwire/tw.pol. Again, this file is an encrypted

version of the actual text-based policies, which can be found in
`/etc/tripwire/twpol.txt`.

If you modify this file, you must re-create the encrypted version by running
the command `tripwire --update-policy /etc/tripwire/twpol.txt`. It will ask for
your passphrase and create a new encrypted policy file. You should then remove
the text-based version to enhance system security (you can always retrieve the text
again by running `twadmin --print-polfile` and entering your passphrase). Once
you have updated the policy file, you have to reinitialize your database by running
`tripwire --init`.

Alternatively, if your database already exists, you can try running
`tripwire --update-policy /etc/tripwire/twpol.txt` to both import the new policy
and update the database. This is a great option if you change the policy after you
are already using Tripwire, but I do not always have success with this approach.

### 11.3.2.1  Understanding File Properties

Tripwire can check many aspects of your system's files and directories. Each of
these checks is represented by a single letter in the policy files, each of which can
be enabled or disabled on a per-file basis. Here they are:

- `a`: Access timestamp (last time the file was accessed)

- `b`:  Number of blocks allocated to the file

- `c`:  Timestamp of the inode (when the file was created or modified)

- `d`:  ID of the device on which the inode is located

- `g`: The group ownership

- `i`:  The actual inode number

- `l`: File growing in size

- `m`: Modification timestamp (last time the file was modified)

- `p`:  Permission and mode bits

- `r`: Device pointed to (for device files)

- `s`:  File's size

- `t`:  File's type

- `u`:  The user ownership

- `C`:  CRC-32 hash of file contents

- `H`:  Haval hash of file contents

- `M`:  md5 hash of file contents

- `S`:  SHA hash of file contents

When preceded by a + (or nothing), a particular letter indicates that the particular check should be performed. When preceded by a -, the letter means that the check should not be performed.

### 11.3.2.2 Setting Variables

Variables are set in the following manner:

```
MYHOME = /home/kirk;
```

You can access variables by using a substitution string such as $(MYHOME). You can substitute variables anywhere you desire in the policy file. A very common technique involves creating a variable that performs certain checks on a file. You can then use this variable in many places to make the policy file cleaner. Here is an example:

```
SEC_SUID = $(IgnoreNone)-SHa;
```

You can now use the variable SEC_SUID when checking setuid binaries. All properties will be checked except for S, H, and a. The IgnoreNone variable is a predefined internal variable in Tripwire. Here is the complete list of these variables:

**Device:** Should be used for device files, named pipes, and other files that should not actually be opened by Tripwire. Expands to the property string +pinugtsdbmCM-rlacSH.

**Dynamic:** Is appropriate for user directories and frequently changing files. Represents the string +pinugtd-srlbamcCMSH.

**Growing:** Useful for files that should only grow larger but not change in other ways. Expands to +pinugtdl-srbamcCMSH.

**IgnoreAll:** Used to ignore certain files. Tripwire does not check any properties and only reports a problem if the file is missing. Expands to -pinugtsdrlbamcCMSH.

**IgnoreNone:** Checks every single property, as would be expected. Expands to the string +pinugtsdrbamcCMSH-l.

**ReadOnly:** Generally used to mark files that are publicly readable but tend not to change. Expands to +pinugtsdbmCM-rlacSH.

Remember that you can use these variables as a starting point and then add or remove additional properties as you deem necessary. This was illustrated in the previous definition of the SEC_SUID variable.

### 11.3.2.3  Defining a Tripwire Rule

Defining a rule is simple. With an appropriate rule, Tripwire can monitor any file on your system in any way you desire. As an example, consider a common file for an attacker to modify --/bin/login. This program can be replaced with a version that logs the users' passwords to be used by the attacker at some future time. This file is a good example of a file that should be strictly monitored:

```
/bin/login -> +pinugtsdrbmcCM-l;
```

Looking up each of these letters in the listing provided in the previous section is tedious. This is why it is better to write the rule this way:

```
/bin/login -> $(IgnoreNone)-SHa;
```

Now you can quickly determine that all properties of this file will be checked except for an SHA hash, a Haval hash, and the file's last access time. Why should those hashes be ignored? You must remember that Tripwire still performs and stores the md5 and CRC32 checksums. An attacker would be hard-pressed to modify the file without changing either of these checksums (it is virtually impossible). Disabling the other two checksums makes the file checks much quicker with virtually no decrease in security.

Using this rule, Tripwire will not check the file's access time either. This file's access time will virtually always change since it will be updated each time the binary is executed (in this case, each time a user logs in). It is a very special circumstance when you would want to monitor the access time of a file—so rare, I can't even think of an example!

If a directory is specified on the left-hand side of a rule, it will be processed by Tripwire. Everything under the directory will also be processed. You can limit this recursion by adding the option (recurse = x) after the properties to check, where x is the maximum number of levels the recursion should follow. If it is set to zero, no recursion occurs (only the base directory is processed).

Even if a directory is recursively processed, you can specify rules for specific files or directories under that directory. Say that you never expect your /etc/hosts file to change, but you expect other files under /etc/ to occasionally change. You could do this:

```
/etc          -> $(Dynamic);
/etc/hosts    -> $(ReadOnly);
```

It is important to remember that a file should not be directly listed twice. This would create an error because Tripwire would not know how to process that particular file.

You can also exclude specific files as follows:

```
/etc            -> $(Dynamic);
!/etc/passwd-;
```

This causes Tripwire to completely ignore the backup file /etc/passwd-. Here are a few more examples rules:

```
# Changing configuration file
/etc/passwd -> $(Dynamic);
# Read-only binaries
/usr/bin -> $(ReadOnly) (recurse = 1);
# Watch this setuid binary more closely
/usr/bin/gpasswd -> $(IgnoreNone)-SHa;
# Watch the permissions on these directories
/home -> +tpug (recurse = 0);
/etc -> +tpug (recurse = 0);
/tmp -> +tpug (recurse = 0);
```

### 11.3.2.4  Rule Attributes

You can place rules into groups to improve the readability of the reports and the organization of the policy file. These groups can be assigned names, severities, and contact email addresses. Here is an example:

```
# Read-only binaries
(
    rulename = "User binaries",
    severity = 75,
    recurse = 1,
    emailto = "alert@domain.com;root@host.domain.com"
)
{
    /bin -> $(ReadOnly);
    /usr/bin -> $(ReadOnly);
    # Watch this setuid binary more closely
    /usr/bin/gpasswd -> $(IgnoreNone)-SHa;
    /usr/local/bin -> $(ReadOnly);
}
```

All of the rules in this block will be reported together under the section "User binaries." The severity can be an arbitrary number from zero to one million. When checking your system with Tripwire, you can specify a minimum threshold for the rules that should be checked. This allows you to quickly check only the most important files on your system in a crisis. You could also do a quick check on a daily basis and a full check on a weekly basis.

The `recurse` attribute specifies that all directories in this group will only be recursed one level deep (the directories themselves and their direct contents). Finally, the `emailto` attribute specifies one or more email addresses. If there are problems within this group, and the `--email-report` option is used when you run `tripwire --check`, Tripwire will send an email to these addresses indicating the problems.

You can also specify these attributes on a per-file basis, as shown in the previous section with the `recurse` option. As an example, the following rule:

```
/some/file -> +abcd (severity = 50, emailto=alert@domain.com);
```

is exactly the same as this rule:

```
(
    severity = 50,
    emailto=alert@domain.com
)
{
    /some/file -> +abcd;
}
```

You can even have attributes on rules within a block of rules with attributes, as follows:

```
(
    severity = 50,
    emailto=alert@domain.com
)
{
    /some/file -> +abcd;
    /some/directory -> +abcd (recurse = 1);
}
```

## 11.3.3  Using Tripwire

Before you can use Tripwire, you need to create the database. Assuming your policy file is in place, you can run the following:

```
# tripwire --init
Please enter your local passphrase:
Parsing policy file: /etc/tripwire/tw.pol
Generating the database...
*** Processing Unix File System ***
Wrote database file: /var/lib/tripwire/kirk-laptop.twd
The database was successfully generated.
```

Once the database has been generated (a process which, as you can see, requires your passphrase), you can run Tripwire on a regular basis to check your system. It is preferable that you place your `tripwire` binary on a read-only filesystem. If you don't, and an attacker replaces this program with a hacked version, you may never know that anything happened—to Tripwire or to any other files on your system. Alternatively, you could periodically perform a checksum on the Tripwire binary from a remote system to verify that it has not been modified. This practice is not perfect, but it does provide an additional layer of security.

In most situations, the command `tripwire --check` should be run every night or every week using your cron daemon. When executed, Tripwire generates a report on `stdout` summarizing the results. Here is an example:

```
# tripwire --check
Parsing policy file: /etc/tripwire/tw.pol
*** Processing Unix File System ***
Performing integrity check...
Wrote report file: /var/lib/tripwire/report/kirk-laptop-20021208-210935.twr


Tripwire(R) 2.3.0 Integrity Check Report

Report generated by:        root
Report created on:          Sun Dec  8 21:09:35 2002
Database last updated on:   Never


===============================================================================
Report Summary:
===============================================================================


Host name:              kirk-laptop
Host IP address:        127.0.0.1
Host ID:                None
Policy file used:       /etc/tripwire/tw.pol
Configuration file used: /etc/tripwire/tw.cfg
Database file used:     /var/lib/tripwire/kirk-laptop.twd
Command line used:      tripwire --check
```

```
================================================================================
Rule Summary:
================================================================================


--------------------------------------------------------------------------------
 Section: Unix File System
--------------------------------------------------------------------------------


    Rule Name                   Severity Level   Added   Removed  Modified
    ---------                   --------------   -----   -------  --------
    Invariant Directories       66               0       0        0
    Temporary directories       33               0       0        0
    Tripwire Data Files         100              0       0        0
    Critical devices            100              0       0        0
    Tripwire Binaries           100              0       0        0
    Libraries                   66               0       0        0
    System Information Programs 100              0       0        0
    Application Information Programs
                                100              0       0        0
    Shell Related Programs      100              0       0        0
    (/sbin/getkey)
    Critical system boot files  100              0       0        0
    Critical configuration files 100             0       0        0
    System boot changes         100              0       0        0
    OS executables and libraries 100             0       0        0
    Security Control            100              0       0        0
    Login Scripts               100              0       0        0
    Shell Binaries              100              0       0        0
    Root config files           100              0       0        0

 Total objects scanned:   20328
 Total violations found:  0


================================================================================
Object Summary:
================================================================================


--------------------------------------------------------------------------------
 # Section: Unix File System
--------------------------------------------------------------------------------


No violations.
```

```
===============================================================================
Error Report:
===============================================================================


No Errors


-------------------------------------------------------------------------------
*** End of report ***


Tripwire 2.3 Portions copyright 2000 Tripwire, Inc. Tripwire is a registered
trademark of Tripwire, Inc. This software comes with ABSOLUTELY NO WARRANTY;
for details use --version. This is free software which may be redistributed
or modified only under certain conditions; see COPYING for details.
All rights reserved.
Integrity check complete.
```

This report can be mailed to an administrator or simply saved for future reference. An even better solution would be to mail the report only when Tripwire exits with a non-zero exit code. Here is an example:

```bash
#!/bin/bash


file="/usr/local/var/tw_reports/$(date +'%m-%d-%y')"
tripwire --check > $file || {
   mail -s "$(hostname): Tripwire errors" < $file
}
```

If you do receive a report with errors, you need to either fix the errors or update the database. If a file has been modified or its permissions have been changed, you need to determine if this should have happened. If another administrator made the change, then you need to update the database. If an attacker made the change, you need to repair the problem, and scrutinize the entire system for other changes (and to determine, and correct, the method of entry).

I like to update the database using the command `tripwire --check --interactive`. This checks your system and then executes your favorite editor with a file which allows you to update any number of entries in the database.

CHAPTER 12

# Backing Up and Restoring Data

BACKING UP DATA is one of those tasks that is easy to put off—until it is too late. You only have to do that once (or twice for the more stubborn among us) before you learn your lesson and begin backing up data regularly.

You accomplish two things when you set up a regular backup system: you minimize the loss of data if a disk drive fails, and you provide a method for recovering files that users may accidentally delete. I have seen too many people configure a system with RAID1 or RAID5 and think that they are completely covered. True, you should be fine if a hard drive fails, but what happens when a user (or a program that is misbehaving) unintentionally deletes a file?

Some people have the opposite problem. They have a good backup system, but the data is not stored on RAID drives. If a drive fails, they may lose a day's worth of work. If it is just yourself, that may not be too big of a problem (although I really hate it when I lose any work at all), but if your company employs 100 developers, how much is a day of their work worth? Somewhere around $50,000 in Silicon Valley and $25,000 anywhere else in the US? You can get a couple of 18GB SCSI drives and a hardware RAID controller for around $1,000 these days. Sounds like a good investment to me—for your most important data at the very least.

Now let's get back to data backups. Choices for backup hardware run the gamut, from floppy disks to multiterabyte robotic tape systems that occupy a few hundred square feet. Backup software is no different; you can use tar or purchase a multimillion dollar software suite. The most important thing to remember is that any backup system, regardless of its complexity and cost, is useless unless you are able to actually restore data on demand.

This chapter provides an introduction to some popular, freely available tools and uses them to build some simple custom solutions. For a more detailed discussion of backing up and restoring data, check out *UNIX Backup and Recovery* by W. Curtis Preston and Gigi Estabrook (O'Reilly and Associates, 1999).

If you have a large number of systems with a large amount of data, exploring the commercial options available is a good idea. I find that the big advantage of commercial backup software is the availability of quality client software for many different operating systems. This software can often allow everybody from the mainframe administrator to the Windows user in the Marketing department to easily back up and even restore data.

But you won't usually need commercial software. Even with tape changers that can cost well over $100,000, it is often possible to control the hardware from the UNIX shell and write data to the tapes using tar. You might not have as nice of an interface (particularly for restoring data), but you could save a lot of money. As with many of the topics in this book, you will need to pick the best solution for your situation. That's why they pay you the big bucks!

## 12.1 Determining Your Backup Policies

You must decide which files to include in your backup process. This can be a difficult decision and, in a business environment, it can have serious repercussions. If you back up too much data, the cost of your backup system can be enormous; it could possibly be so big that it could cause you to make unneeded cuts in other areas. If you don't back up enough, important data might be lost—and possibly your job as well.

It is easy to just back up your entire system (being sure to exclude NFS mounts and special filesystems such as /proc/), but often that is overkill. If your entire system drive is lost, you will most likely have to install the base operating system before you can recover any data. Having these system files on the backup tape is just about useless.

So, to reduce your backup costs (in hardware, network and system load, and time) you should usually only back up important files. Here I have shamelessly copied the handy list from Chapter 7, which itemizes the types of data you might want to share between systems. Amazingly enough, this is the same data you generally want to back up; if it is important enough to share, it is usually important enough to back up.

**Shared applications:** Common applications that can be used on several systems. The /usr/local/ or /opt/ directories are often shared between systems and contain additional applications that did not come with the operating system.

**User data:** The users' home directories that contain all of their data and personal files.

**Application data:** In distributed computing environments, application data is often shared between systems. A cluster of web servers, for example, will usually need to share the same content.

**System information:** System information includes account information (users, groups, passwords), mail aliases, host listings, and so on.

Only you know where all your data is stored—or at least you had better figure it out before you create your backup system. I can't list every piece of data you may need to back up, but I can provide some guidelines:

**Important system data:** Don't forget important system data, such as the files in /etc/ and sometimes /var/. If these are generated automatically, they may only need to be backed up on the master system.

**Added software:** Include any software installed on the system that was not included in the original operating system. Hopefully, you have installed all of these in /opt/ or /usr/local/ to make backing them up easy. Or, you may have all of the programs on a central fileserver, which makes backups even easier. If you used a packaging system, be sure to save the packages that have been installed and include them in your backup process.

**Application configuration and data:** Consider what services are running on each system. If a system is running a DNS server, be sure to include the zone files. If it is running a web server, back up the web content and maybe even the access logs (which may or may not be important to you).

**Development resources:** If you have CVS repositories, bug databases, knowledge bases, and other development tools that store important data, you should be sure to include them in your backups.

**Administration tools:** Don't forget to include all of your system automation scripts and tools in the backup process.

**Databases:** If you have data stored in one or more databases, definitely include their data, but be sure to back it up properly. In many cases, you would need to shut the database down or perform a data dump in order to properly back up a database's contents. Some database software can export data suitable for backup, though, and some backup software can back up a database while it is running.

**User data:** Finally, the users of your systems generally appreciate their personal data being included in the backups.

If you have one big fileserver, that machine may be the perfect system to perform the backups, copying data from other systems as necessary. If your network bandwidth is at a premium, you may want to perform disk-based backups on each individual system (automatically, of course). If you do perform backups over the network (as many people do), it is generally not a good idea to use network filesystems for this task. Utilities such as rsync and rdiff-backup can perform backups with significantly less network load.

The other thing to consider is what timeframe your backups should cover. If you use a tape backup system and have only one tape, you would have to replace the data on the tape every day. If it takes somebody a few days to realize they deleted a file, they are out of luck.

Of course, if all of your data can fit onto only one tape, the solution is easy—just buy a bunch of tapes. But if you have a large amount of data it can become much more complicated. Personally, at home, I use a separate disk drive for my backups and keep one week's worth of backups. If it takes me more than a week to realize I made a mistake, then I am out of luck.

## 12.2 Backing Up Data with cfengine

If you have read most of the book up to this point, you will know that I think GNU cfengine is great. Once you get it installed and running, it can do just about anything, including backing up your data. If you do not already know how to use cfengine and are interested in its data backup capabilities, be sure to read section 6.4.

Using cfengine just for data backup is probably not the best course of action; I present plenty of easier solutions throughout this chapter. If you are already using cfengine, however, expanding it to handle system backups is quick and easy, but there are limitations. I'm afraid to say that cfengine can't do something, because I'm bound to be proven wrong, but I haven't yet found a way to perform incremental backups with cfengine.

### 12.2.1 Using cfengine to Perform Local Backups

As a start, you can use cfengine to make complete copies of files and directories. The nice thing is that cfengine can make perfect copies—including special files, symbolic links, and directories. It also preserves the files' ownership and permissions. Here is a basic configuration that you would place in `cfagent.conf` (or add to your existing `copy` section if you already have one):

```
copy:
    /etc dest=/usr/local/backup/etc purge=true r=inf
```

This causes every host on your network to make a perfect, recursive copy of their `/etc/` directory into `/usr/local/backup/`. The `purge=true` option causes the copy operation to delete any files in the destination directory that no longer exist in the source directory.

That copy procedure happens every time `cfagent` is executed, which is usually too often. You can limit this to once per day:

```
copy:
   Hr03.OnTheHour::
      /etc dest=/usr/local/backup/etc purge=true r=inf
```

Now the copy only happens if `cfagent` is run at exactly `03:00` every day. I am assuming here that you run `cfagent` every hour, on the hour. If you don't, you should adjust the time classes in the examples accordingly.

The problem with this example is that each day's backup overwrites the backup of the previous day. This gives you less than 24 hours to catch any problems that may occur within a system's `/etc/` directory. Never fear, I can enhance this system to keep one week's worth of backups:

```
control:
   day_of_week = ( ExecResult(/bin/date +%a) )
```

```
copy:
   Hr03.OnTheHour::
      /etc dest=/usr/local/backup/${day_of_week}/etc
         purge=true r=inf
```

Now you will always have seven days worth of backups, in the directories `/usr/local/backup/Mon/etc/`, `/usr/local/backup/Tue/etc/`, and so on.

## 12.2.2  Excluding Files from Backups

If you want to include or exclude files, you can use three optional parameters within the copy section. The first is the `ignore` parameter. Any number of these may be specified. Each one provides a pattern, and any matching files or directories will be ignored. This is the only way to prevent recursion into specific directories.

Next is the `include` parameter. You can use this to specify an exclusive list of files that should be included in the copy. Any number of `include` parameters may be specified, but specifying even one causes any files that don't match to be excluded by default.

Finally, you have the `exclude` option. Any files matching these patterns are excluded from the copy operation. Here is an example:

```
copy:
   Hr03.OnTheHour::
      /home dest=/usr/local/backup/home purge=true r=inf
         ignore=cache       # Netscape cache directory
         ignore=Cache       # Mozilla cache directory
         exclude=*.mp3      # Huge music files
```

## 12.3 Using rsync to Back Up Data

rsync was previously discussed in section 7.8. Since that chapter was about sharing data, and since backups between systems involves sharing data, it is only natural to consider the same program within this chapter. See this previous discussion of rsync for information on its basic usage and how to configure it to use SSH as its transport layer.

The big advantage of rsync is its speed and efficiency. It can quickly determine which files have been modified and it can be set to only copy the individual files that have actually changed. It can also use a variety of transport methods and it is easy to install on a variety of systems.

rsync can also do incremental backups that keep entire copies of previous versions of files. Although there are more space-efficient methods (such as the method used by rdiff-backup), this method does allow you to quickly examine and recover old versions of files.

### 12.3.1 Basic Backups with rsync

You can perform basic complete backups with rsync just like you saw done with cfengine. Here is an example shell script that can be executed on a daily basis on each of your systems:

```
#!/bin/bash

BACKUP_PATH="backup@backup.mydomain.com:/usr/local/backup"
DIRS="/etc /var /usr/local /home"

weekday=`date +%a`
shorthost=`hostname | sed 's/\..*$//'`

rsync -a --delete $DIRS "$BACKUP_PATH/$shorthost/$weekday"
```

The -a switch places rsync into archive mode, which means all permissions and ownership are preserved. In addition, symbolic links, special files, and directories are also preserved. rsync also operates recursively when in archive mode, so there is no reason to specify the -r option.

The --delete switch causes any files within the destination directory that are not present in the source directory to be deleted. Since the backup directories are based on the day of the week and are reused from week to week, you need this option to prevent your backups from perpetually growing. This also allows you to create a true snapshot of the system.

If you don't have enough disk space to keep multiple days worth of backup for each host, you may need to use the script in section 12.5 or move the data to tapes. If none of this is possible, you might need to keep only one day's worth of backups using this slightly simpler script:

```
#!/bin/bash

BACKUP_PATH="backup@backup.mydomain.com:/usr/local/backup"
DIRS="/etc /var /usr/local /home"

shorthost=`hostname | sed 's/\..*$//'`

rsync -a $DIRS "$BACKUP_PATH/$shorthost"
```

Note that I removed the --delete switch from the second example. This would not delete any files on the backup server, allowing you to retrieve files that were accidentally deleted more than 24 hours ago. It doesn't help with corrupted files, of course, because the corrupted version will be copied to the backup server anyway. You will also need to occasionally wipe out the backup directory (or run the script *with* the --delete switch) to prevent it from growing perpetually.

## 12.3.2 Incremental Backups

You can also perform incremental backups onto a disk drive with rsync. If you want to perform incremental backups with tapes, you need to use other software (such as tar or dump).

Here is a basic incremental backup script:

 **NOTE** You can find the code samples for this chapter in the Downloads section of the Apress web site (http://www.apress.com).

```
#!/bin/bash

BACKUP_SERVER="backup@backup.mydomain.com"
BACKUP_DIR="/usr/local/backup"
DIRS="/etc /var /usr/local /home"
```

```
yesterday=`date +%a -d yesterday`
shorthost=`hostname | sed 's/\..*$//'`
archive_dir="$BACKUP_DIR/$shorthost/$yesterday"

# Clean out existing archive directory (from last week)
mkdir -p /root/.emptydir
rsync --delete -a /root/.emptydir/ "$BACKUP_SERVER:$archive_dir/"
rmdir /root/.emptydir

rsync -a --force --ignore-errors --delete \
   --backup --backup-dir=$archive_dir \
   $DIRS "$BACKUP_SERVER:$BACKUP_DIR/$shorthost/current"
```

This script should be run once per day on each system. It first uses rsync to empty this directory on the remote system. It then mirrors the specified directories into the current/ directory on the backup server. Any files that have been modified or deleted since the last time the script was executed will be copied into the archive directory. If, for example, it is run at 3:00AM on Sunday, the archive directory will be Sat/ (since it is working with files from the previous day).

rsync performs this archiving automatically when you use the --backup and --backup-dir options. Only files that have changed in the source location are copied to the destination directory. If the file already exists, it is copied to the backup directory. Likewise, if a file is to be deleted (because the --delete option was specified), it is copied to the backup directory instead.

What this all means to you is that if you just made a mistake, you can find your files as they were at 3:00AM that morning in the current /directory. If you made the mistake several days ago, you can find the original files in one of the backup directories. Just look in the directory for the appropriate day of the week.

## 12.3.3  Excluding Files

You can exclude certain files when backing up with rsync, which has a very powerful include and exclude system. As a start, you can specify as many --include and --exclude parameters as necessary on the command line. Every file and directory is checked against this list of patterns, in the order they were specified. If a file matches one of the include patterns, it is copied (regardless of the patterns that follow). If a file matches an exclude pattern, is it not copied.

If a pattern begins with a /, it is compared against the beginning of the filename (with its full pathname). If it doesn't begin with a /, it is compared against the actual filename (without a path). The exclude pattern /etc would cause all files under the /etc/ directory to be excluded, whereas the pattern etc would cause any files named etc to be excluded.

If a pattern ends in a /, it can only match a directory. Therefore, the exclude pattern etc/ would also cause the /etc/ directory to be excluded, but it would not affect files named etc. Standard shell wildcards (*, ?, and []) can be used in any of the patterns.

You can also use the --include-from and --exclude-from options to specify files containing inclusions and exclusions. This allows you to build these lists in any way you desire using external programs.

Because rsync has such powerful matching patterns, though, you can get along without an external include/exclude list in most cases. However, there are some cases when rsync's internal logic isn't quite flexible enough. The find command can match on a wide range of criteria. If, for example, you want to exclude all files owned by a certain user, you can do this:

```
find /some/dir -user someuser -print > ~/.exclude.tmp
rsync --exclude-from=~/.exclude.tmp ...
```

## 12.4 Backing Up Data with rdiff-backup

rdiff-backup is an excellent backup program that creates incremental backups onto a disk drive. It can operate over the network and is very efficient (it uses the rsync library, in fact). By default, it performs its operations through SSH, which is something I like.

Just like with our rsync examples in the previous section, the most recent backup is a complete mirror of the source files. The previous versions of the files, however, are maintained by storing reverse diffs of any modified files. Both text and binary files are stored in this fashion, which makes for very efficient usage of disk space.

You must have the rdiff-backup program installed on all systems involved in the backup process—the server(s) and every client. You can obtain the software and find additional documentation at http://rdiff-backup.stanford.edu.

### 12.4.1 Creating Incremental Backups with rdiff-backup

Let's start with a basic script that performs backups of specified directories onto a local backup directory:

```
#!/bin/bash

DIRS="etc home var usr/local"
DEST="/mnt/backup"

cd /
for dir in $DIRS ; do
    rdiff-backup $dir "$DEST/$(basename $dir)"
done
```

You can run this script as often as you like. I would recommend running it once per day. If the data is very important (like a corporate CVS repository), running it once per hour wouldn't be unreasonable.

Modifying this script to back up to a remote system is as simple as changing the $DEST variable. Here is an example:

```
DEST="backup.mydomain.com::/mnt/backup"
```

This causes rdiff-backup to connect to the host backup.mydomain.com via SSH and place the backup in its directory /mnt/backup. Regardless of what system contains the backup data, it will be almost an exact mirror of the source directory. Permissions, special files, hard/soft links, and ownership will all be preserved, if possible.

The backup directory is exactly like the original, except for the additional rdiff-backup-data/ directory. This directory contains the backup logs and, most importantly, the diff files that can be used to generate older versions of files. It is very important that you do not manually change the files in the backup directory in any way. Doing so can permanently damage the backup data, probably preventing the correct recovery of *any* versions of the modified files.

If you are backing up the data to a remote host, you will usually want to use a directory on that system based on your system's hostname. We have done this in previous discussions of backup tools. Here is a simple example:

```
#!/bin/bash

DIRS="etc home var usr/local"
DEST="/mnt/backup"
shorthost=`hostname | sed 's/\..*$//'`

cd /
for dir in $DIRS ; do
    rdiff-backup $dir "$DEST/$shorthost/$(basename $dir)"
done
```

## 12.4.2 Removing Old Backup Data

If left alone, the backup directory perpetually increases in size, unless, of course, the source data is static. For this reason, you will want to clean out the old backup data every week or so. The following script takes care of this for you:

```
#!/bin/bash
DEST="/mnt/backup"


rdiff-backup --remove-older-than 1M $DEST
```

The string 1M is a time specification representing one month. This means that all data relating to files or versions of files more than one month old will be deleted.

Time specifications can be given in other formats as well. You can use the standard "seconds since the epoch," or you can use a string such as 2003-01-06T23:30:45-04:00 (which provides the date, the time, and the local time zone's deviation from Coordinated Universal Time (UTC)). Simpler date-only formats, such as 2003-01-07 and 12/31/2002 are also supported.

The most useful specifications, however, are the relative ones. The letters s, m, h, D, W, M, and Y represent seconds, minutes, hours, days, weeks, months, and years, respectively. You can combine these as necessary; for instance, 1M2D3h specifies one month, two days, and three hours ago.

Sometimes it is nice to be able to remove data only when the backup drive is filling up. Here is a script that is fairly cryptic, not too efficient, but very flexible. You can specify a directory to monitor and a maximum amount of space to be used on that drive. If the drive is too full, this script searches for all backups under that directory created by rdiff-backup. When you run the following script, rdiff-backup removes the oldest increment and repeats the whole process, if necessary. You should run this script regularly from your backup server's cron daemon:

```
#!/bin/bash

# Drive or directory to clean up
prune="/mnt/backup"

# The maximum used space allowed on the drive (percent)
cutoff="80"

# Removes one increment from each rdiff-backup repository until the
# drive falls below the specified cutoff
```

```
    until df "$prune" | awk -v "cutoff=$cutoff" '/^\// {
        gsub(/%$/, "", $5);
        if ($5 > cutoff)
            exit 1
        }' ; do
      # Too full, clean out some old data
      # First, find and store rdiff-backup repositories
      [ -z "$DIRS" ] && {
          for dir in `find $prune -name rdiff-backup-data -type d` ; do
              DIRS="$DIRS $(echo "$dir" | sed 's/\/rdiff-backup-data//')"
          done
      }
      # Now, delete the oldest increment
      for dir in $DIRS ; do
          del=`rdiff-backup -l "$dir" | sed -n \
              's/^ *increments\.\(....-..-.....:..:..-..:..\)\.dir.*/\1/p' \
              | head -n2 | tail -n1`
          echo >&2
          echo "Cleaning $dir..." >&2
          rdiff-backup --remove-older-than "$del" "$dir" >&2 || {
              echo "Only one increment left for $dir (skipping)" >&2
              DIRS=`echo "$DIRS" | sed "s= *$dir *=="`
          }
      done
      # Prevent an infinite loop from occurring
      [ -z "$DIRS" ] && {
          echo >&2
          echo "No rdiff-backup data directories left to prune!" >&2
          exit 1
      }
  done

exit 0
```

This script assumes that your drive is sufficiently large to keep several increments in each repository. At the very least, it keeps all of the current data and the most recent increment. This script is careful to exit if no more data can be removed; otherwise an infinite loop would occur.

## 12.4.3 Restoring Data

Once you have a backup directory, you can quickly display a listing of the *increments* available. An *increment* is some previous date for which exact files are available. Whenever you run `rdiff-backup`, the current mirror is updated and a new increment is created, still allowing you to retrieve the previous set of data. Here is an example listing of increments:

```
% rdiff-backup -l /some/backup/directory
Found 4 increments:
    increments.2003-01-02T23:30:45-04:00.dir   Thu Jan  2 23:30:45 2003
    increments.2003-01-03T23:31:40-04:00.dir   Fri Jan  3 23:31:40 2003
    increments.2003-01-04T23:31:54-04:00.dir   Sat Jan  4 23:31:54 2003
    increments.2003-01-05T23:32:02-04:00.dir   Sun Jan  5 23:32:02 2003
Current mirror: Mon Jan  6 23:32:18 2003
```

There are two ways to restore data from an rdiff-backup archive. One is to look through the data and run `rdiff-backup` on one of the increment files. I'll let you read the `rdiff-backup` man page if you want to try that one. The second method, which is my favorite, is to use the `--restore-as-of(-r)` switch.

Let's assume that the backup archive shown in the previous increment listing was created by the following backup script, executed at around 23:30 every day:

```
rdiff-backup /etc /some/backup/directory
```

Now, assuming it is Tuesday at 16:00, and I want to restore the `/etc/` directory as it was yesterday at this time, I would run the following command:

```
rdiff-backup -r 1D /some/backup/directory /tmp/etc.old
```

Since no backup was performed exactly one day ago, the next oldest increment is used. In this case, that would be the backup performed on Sunday night (`2003-01-05T23:32:02-04:00`). I could also have specified this full date string instead of `1D` as the argument to the `-r` switch.

The exact state of the `/etc/` directory when that backup was performed is now re-created in the local directory `/tmp/etc.old/`. You can then do anything you would like within this temporary directory.

## 12.4.4 Excluding Files When Using rdiff-backup

A wide variety of command-line options allows you to control which files are included in the backup process. Here are the ones more commonly used:

**--exclude** **pattern:** Files matching the pattern should be excluded. Matching directories, and their contents, will be excluded.

**--exclude-device-files:** Causes all device files to be ignored.

**--exclude-filelist** **filename:** All files listed in the file filename are excluded from the backup operation.

**--exclude-filelist-stdin:** A list of files can be sent in through stdin. These files will be excluded.

**--exclude-other-filesystems:** Only files on the same physical filesystem as the base source directory are backed up.

**--exclude-regexp** **regex:** Files matching the regular expression will be excluded. Python-style regular expressions are used. Files within matching directories are processed separately.

**--include** **pattern:** Files matching the pattern should be included. Matching directories, and their contents, will also be included.

**--include-filelist** **filename:** Only files listed in the file filename are included in the backup operation.

**--include-filelist-stdin:** A list of files can be sent in through stdin. Only files found in this list will be part of the backup.

**--include-regexp** **regex:** Files matching the regular expression will be included. Python-style regular expressions are used. Files within matching directories are processed separately.

Regardless of the number of these options specified, each rule is applied to each file. The first rule that matches the file determines its fate. If no rule matches, the default action is to include the file. For instance, let's say that you want to back up the /var/ directory, except for the /var/spool/ directory, but you *do* want /var/spool/mail/. You can do this:

```
rdiff-backup --include /var/spool/mail --exclude /var/spool /var /backup
```

A file pattern (used by the --include and --exclude options) can contain the standard shell globbing characters (*, +, and [ ]). Neither * nor + can match a /; this is important since the full pathname of each file is compared. The special sequence **, however, does match any number of characters, including forward slashes. The pattern can begin with the string ignorecase: to—you guessed it—make the pattern case-insensitive. Be sure to quote these patterns so that the shell doesn't interpret them before rdiff-backup gets a chance at them.

# 12.5 Performing Tape Backups with tar

Although none of the programs discussed so far can operate directly on tapes, the resulting data could be archived onto tapes as necessary. Although this isn't the same as doing real tape backups, it is an available option.

If you want to use tapes, instead of hard drives, on a regular basis to back up your data, you have several choices. The most commonly used programs are dump and tar, which are included on most, if not all, UNIX systems. You can also use the Amanda backup suite or any one of the wide variety of commercial applications available.

Although most versions of tar are similar, there are some differences between the versions on different operating systems. GNU also has its own version of tar, which has many useful enhancements that are not found on other versions.

In this section, I will show you some simple tape backups using GNU tar. This is most useful if you want to just back up a single system onto a tape. You can also use rsync to copy files from a few systems and then use tar to place that data onto a tape.

If you want a more advanced backup system than this, take a look at Amanda and the large selection of commercially available solutions. If none of these fit your needs, you can use the various utilities in this chapter to build your own custom system. Unlike other custom systems that have been discussed in this book, a custom advanced backup solution is just too complicated to be included here.

All of the examples in this section will make the following three assumptions:

- You are backing up the directory /home/. Any other directory, or multiple directories, can be specified in its place with minimal effort.

- Your tape drive is accessed through the device file /dev/st0. If you have a single SCSI tape drive on a Linux system, this will be the correct device file. If not, you will need to use the appropriate device file to match your hardware.

- The script is being executed as root and your current working directory is the root directory (/).

## 12.5.1 Basic Backups Using tar

To create a full backup onto a tape with tar, you can run this command:

```
# tar cvpf /dev/st0 home
home/user1
home/user1/file1
...
```

The c option says that a new archive should be created. The v switch says the files should be displayed as they are added to the archive. The p switch means that all permissions should be preserved, and the f switch means that the archive should be written to a file (/dev/st0, which actually represents your tape drive).

## 12.5.2  Creating Incremental Backups with tar

To create a simple incremental backup, you can use the -N switch provided by GNU tar. This allows you to specify a date and only files that have been created or modified after that date will be included in the archive. Assuming you perform backups every day, this will perform an incremental backup:

```
# tar cpf /dev/st0 -N "$(date -d '1 day ago')" home
```

Like any incremental backup system, you must be sure you save the original full backup until all of the incremental backups are no longer necessary. You might, for example, perform a full backup on Monday and incremental backups on Tuesday through Friday. This would take a set of five tapes. The next week, you could use a different set of five tapes. By alternating these two sets of tapes, you will always have anywhere from one to two weeks worth of backup data.

Here is a script that will perform these backups for you:

```
#!/bin/bash

# Where to place backup log files
LOG_DIR="/usr/local/var/backup_logs"

# Which directories to include in backup
DIRS="home"

# Which output file or tape device to use
DEV="/dev/st0"

today=$(date +%a)
cd /
case $today in
    Mon)
        # Full backup
        tar cvpf $DEV $DIRS
        mt -f $DEV rewind
        mt -f $DEV offline
        ;;
```

```
    Tue|Wed|Thu|Fri)
        # Partial backup
        tar cvpf $DEV -N "$(date -d '1 day ago')" $DIRS
        mt -f $DEV rewind
        mt -f $DEV offline
        ;;
    *)
        # Weekend, do nothing
        ;;
esac > "$LOG_DIR/$today"
```

It only keeps logs for the current week, but you should keep the previous week's tapes intact until the current week has finished. I would just have two sets of five tapes, with each tape labeled Mon, Tue, Wed, Thu, and Fri. Assuming the backup script executes early in the morning every day, you would change the tape every day after the script has run. You would always place the tape in for the next backup day.

The mt command is discussed in the next section.

## 12.5.3  Backing Up to Magnetic Tapes

The discussion of tar up to this point has actually been completely independent of the backup media. It could work just as well on a hard drive as it does on a tape (except that you would need to specify the output filename instead of the tape device).

But backing up to real tapes can present additional challenges. First of all, your backup may need to span multiple tapes. This can be accomplished with the --multi-volume(-M) switch:

```
# tar cpf /dev/st0 -M home
Prepare volume #2 for `/dev/st0' and hit return:
Prepare volume #3 for `/dev/st0' and hit return:
```

You can't use the --gzip (-z) switch to compress the data when spanning tapes. This shouldn't be a problem, however, because it is never a good idea to use compression when backing up onto tapes. One minor error within a compressed archive could destroy a good portion of the data.

If tar has a problem detecting when the end of a tape has been reached, you can use the --tape-length (-L) switch to specify the size of your tapes (in kilobytes):

```
# tar cpf /dev/st0 -M -L 4000000 home
Prepare volume #2 for `/dev/st0' and hit return:
```

We have specified a 4GB tape in this example, but obviously your tape size will vary.

## 12.5.4 Excluding Files When Using tar

You can exclude certain files using the --exclude command-line option. You can repeat this option as needed. Any files whose full pathname contains the exclude pattern are not included in the archive. The pattern may also contain standard file globbing characters. Remember that when you are using tar, all paths are relative to the starting directory (/ in our examples). Here is an illustration:

```
# tar cpf /dev/st0 --exclude home/someuser home
```

Every file matching the pattern home/someuser will be excluded. This includes the directory /home/someuser/ and every file inside. Note that the exclude pattern does not start with a / because the directory specified on the command line (home) did not begin with a forward-slash.

You can also use the option --exclude-from to specify a file containing a fixed exclusion list. You can even specify - as the exclusion filename to accept the exclusion list on stdin. Here is an example:

```
# find home -size +1000k -print | \
tar cpf /dev/st0 --exclude-from - home
```

This archives all files under /home/ except for any files that are greater than 1000 kilobytes in size (one megabyte). Note that the first parameter of the find command (home) is the same as the last parameter of the tar command (home). If the search path for the find command was /home, the exclusion file list generated would not match any of the entries in the tar archive and would not cause any files to be excluded.

## 12.5.5 Restoring Data from tar Archives

Unless you have extremely bad luck, restoring data is not usually a candidate for automation. Even in a medium-sized company, restoring data from backups is not a regular task in my experience. This is good, because restoring data from tape archives created with tar can be pretty slow.

When restoring data, whether or not you used incremental backups, you first need to decide the point in time in the past when the proper data was present. You then can select the appropriate tape based on this time and extract the file(s) from that tape.

If you need to see what files are contained in an archive, you can use the t switch. Note that this will require you to read the entire archive, which can be pretty slow if the archive is stored on a tape:

```
# tar tvf /dev/st0
home/user1
home/user1/file1
...
```

You can extract the entire archive into the current directory:

```
# tar xvpf /dev/st0
home/user1
home/user1/file1
...
```

You can also extract only certain files or directories. Here we can retrieve one user's entire home directory:

```
# tar xvpf /dev/st0 home/user1
home/user1
home/user1/file1
...
```

or, we can retrieve just one file:

```
# tar xvpf /dev/st0 home/user1/file1
home/user1/file1
```

Note that the entire archive may need to be processed even when you are extracting only one file. Again, this can be pretty slow on a tape drive.

## 12.6 The Amanda Backup Suite

Amanda stands for Advanced Maryland Automatic Network Disk Archiver. It is an excellent backup suite—especially considering it is freely available. Amanda provides a backup server as well as backup clients for multiple platforms. The server can accept multiple simultaneous backup streams, use local disk drives as a cache, and write to tape archives. It even supports some tape library systems.

As much as I would like to discuss this great backup suite, a program of this magnitude can be fairly complicated to install and configure. There are too many unique situations to provide any kind of generic solution. A full introduction to such a serious backup system is beyond the scope of this book.

The Amanda homepage can be found at `http://www.amanda.org`. There you can find information about the system as well as the actual program, downloadable in source form. If you are in the market for a commercial data backup system, you should definitely take a look at Amanda to see if it can meet your needs at a much lower price.

The book *UNIX Backup and Recovery* by W. Curtis Preston and Gigi Estabrook (O'Reilly and Associates, 1999) provides an entire chapter on Amanda. If you want to consider or use Amanda, take a look at this book. It also presents a much more thorough discussion of all aspects of data backup than was possible within this chapter. In my opinion this book is a must for anybody implementing or using a large-scale backup system.

# CHAPTER 13

# User Interfaces

So, YOU HAVE WRITTEN SCRIPTS—tons of them. With these scripts you can create new accounts, configure new systems, manage your corporate DNS configuration, and much more. If you are the only administrator, you may very well be done. Congratulations! Just sit back and watch your systems run, and deal with any problems as they arise.

If you are part of a team of administrators, however, you may want to clean things up a bit. Providing a convenient and consistent user interface to your scripts can be very beneficial. A good interface can make your automation system much easier to use. This is particularly important when you have other administrators (and even regular users) that are not as proficient with UNIX as you are. You can empower others by creating a friendly front-end for your automation tools; it will make them happier, and minimize the amount of work you personally must do.

If you move on one day and somebody else takes over, a user interface, such as a central web interface, really reduces their learning curve. A good user interface also helps when you hire another administrator in the future.

These are all great reasons to create a user interface, of course, but my favorite reason is that it keeps me from forgetting what my automation system can do and how I should actually use it. At a small company, a few months may go by without a new employee. Without a user interface, I may have to find my scripts and learn how to use them again. Other times my systems run so well for so long that I forget what it is like to do anything at all!

This chapter discusses both text- and web-based user interfaces. Since up to this point, everything in the book has been console-based, web interfaces will be the focus in this chapter. Not only that, but often using the Web is the best way to provide system administration access. Just about any computer in the world with Internet access will have a web browser, and web browsers are available for virtually any operating system. This makes your web-based administration system highly accessible, which is always a good thing (assuming you have proper access restrictions to prevent unwanted accesses).

A good web interface allows you to configure basic system settings, execute specific commands, and perform simple system monitoring. I will present these basic capabilities in this chapter, but the interface can be expanded to include additional functionality as required in your environment.

## 13.1 Web-Based Administration with Webmin

Webmin is a wonderful program that deserves special mention here. In a nutshell, Webmin is a simple web server that provides a web-based front-end to UNIX system administration. Its primary purpose is to provide an easy interface to most aspects of a system's configuration. It allows you to configure network settings, manage user accounts, install and remove software, configure system services, and perform many other administration and configuration tasks.

These tasks are made possible through a variety of modules or plugins. The main distribution of Webmin comes with around one hundred of these modules. Many of these modules perform specific system administration tasks or configure specific applications. Most of the modules will work on any UNIX system. You can also find additional modules on the Internet that add functionality you cannot find in the base distribution. You can even write your own modules using Perl.

Webmin is primarily designed to run on one system and manage that single system. This doesn't mean that you can't use it to automate the administration of several systems, however. You can often use Webmin to fill in any gaps in your custom system.

You may have one mail server, one DNS server, and one web server on your network. You may use the methods discussed in Chapter 6 to perform the basic configuration on these systems, but you may not want to automate the configuration of the mail, DNS, and web servers. No two machines run the same servers, so the return on any investment in automation tools can be quite small. Instead, you could use Webmin to provide an easy interface you could use to configure these services.

You would probably want to remove any modules that handle tasks that are taken care of in other ways. You may use GNU cfengine to configure the network settings on all of your systems, for example. In this case, you may want to disable the Network Configuration module to avoid any conflicts between the two systems.

As another example, you may have a cluster of 100 web servers all automatically configured. One system is the master server and contains the master configuration file for your web server. This file is automatically distributed to your other systems whenever it is modified (again, possibly using cfengine). You could still run Webmin on this master server and use its Apache Webserver module to view and modify your master web server configuration file. I find this particularly useful when I am creating complicated configuration files—especially for programs I'm not too familiar with.

There are even a few Webmin modules that are directly applicable to automating system administration. One module (Custom Commands) allows you to make arbitrary commands you can execute from the web interface. You can use this to trigger certain automation tasks (such as system reconfiguration).

The `Cluster Webmin Servers` module allows one Webmin server to interact with and configure Webmin on other servers. This module can be combined with `Cluster Users and Groups` to manage users and groups across multiple systems. You can also use the `Cluster Software Packages` module to install software packages on multiple systems. Software in the RPM, Debian, or Solaris package formats can be installed on Linux and Solaris systems through this module.

You could even use Webmin for your entire web interface to your automation system by writing a custom module. I definitely suggest that you research this course of action if you already plan to use Webmin for other tasks on your systems.

It may surprise you, after all this praise, that Webmin will not be covered in this book. This is because it is not an automation tool except in the certain situations that I have just described. I hope I have given you a rough idea about what Webmin can do for you. You just have to decide if any of these abilities will help you in your situation.

## 13.2 Creating the Underlying Working Scripts

Most of the scripts presented up to this point in the book could be considered underlying scripts to be used from within a user interface. These underlying scripts are the actual commands that make changes to your systems. For all of your automation tasks, it is a good idea to do the dirty work with command-line programs. They may be bash or Perl scripts, as long as they do not require direct user interaction.

If a command-line program can be completely controlled via command-line arguments and/or sending text into `stdin`, it can be used in any way imaginable. You can run it manually. You can run it from a text-based user interface. You can run it from a web page. You can also run it from a remote system using an access protocol such as SSH.

If the command will definitely be run manually, taking data on `stdin` may be the best option. Any text you want displayed interactively can be sent out on `stderr` and anything that would need to be parsed by another program can be sent out on `stdout`. Here is a simple example:

---

**NOTE**   You can find the code samples for this chapter in the Downloads section of the Apress web site (`http://www.apress.com`).

---

```
#!/bin/bash

echo -n "Enter username to add: " >&2
read new_user
echo -n "Enter full name: " >&2
read full_name

# ... create user ...

echo "New account successfully created!" >&2
echo "New UserID: $new_uid"
```

If you run this program interactively, you see the following:

```
Enter username to add: kirk
Enter full name: Kirk Bauer
New account successfully created!
New UserID: 1001
```

This script is pretty simple to use as it stands, but you may want to execute it from a web interface. Or, you may want to write a wrapper script that adds large numbers of users automatically. This script can be executed noninteractively as follows:

```
#!/bin/bash
echo -e 'kirk\nKirk Bauer' | my_adduser 2>/dev/null
```

In this case, I use the echo command to send the two needed pieces of information into stdin. The -e switch tells echo to allow escape sequences within the string—the \n for a carriage return in our case. This option is available on the GNU version of echo but is not recognized in many other versions. Fortunately, in this case, we are using the version of echo that is built into the bash shell, so it doesn't really matter. Just keep this in mind if you changed the command to /bin/echo because you would then be calling your operating system's version of the command.

We direct stderr to /dev/null because we don't care about it. All that remains is stdout, which we could parse to retrieve the UserID. If you executed the previous script, you would see only the following:

```
New UserID: 1001
```

Another way to send data into such a script is to use a *here document*. Here documents are documents that are inserted directly into a shell script file. Here is an example:

```
#!/bin/bash

my_adduser 2>/dev/null << __END__
kirk
Kirk Bauer
__END__
```

In this example, we only have the two pieces of data necessary to add a new account. These could easily be passed in as parameters to make the script even easier to use from within other scripts. It can make it more difficult to use interactively, though. This is especially true if your script has twenty questions to ask instead of just two. Here is the same script using parameters:

```
#!/bin/bash

usage() {
    echo "Usage: $0 [username] [full name]" 2>/dev/null
    exit 99;
}
[ "$1" == "--help" ] && usage
[ $# -ne 2 ] && usage
new_user="$1"
full_name="$2"

# ... create user ...

echo "New account successfully created!" >&2
echo "New UserID: $new_uid"
```

Notice that I have included a usage function in this example. If you are going to require certain command-line arguments, it is imperative that you provide usage instructions. Even with only two arguments, you can easily forget what arguments you need and in what order you should specify them. You should display the usage information if there are any errors parsing the command line (such as missing arguments) or if a standard parameter (such as --help) is given. This allows a person to determine how to use any command without any prior knowledge (except, of course, that they can use the --help parameter).

As one final option, you can set up your scripts so that they can accept command-line arguments, and if these arguments are not provided, the script can prompt the user. This allows the script to be run in a friendly manner interactively on the shell yet still be easy to use from within shell scripts.

```
#!/bin/bash

usage() {
    echo "Usage: $0 [username] [full name]" 2>/dev/null
    exit 99;
}
[ "$1" == "--help" ] && usage
new_user="$1"
full_name="$2"

[ -n "$new_user" ] || {
    echo -n "Enter username to add: " >&2
    read new_user
}

[ -n "$full_name" ] || {
    echo -n "Enter full name: " >&2
    read full_name
}

# ... create user ...

echo "New account successfully created!" >&2
echo "New UserID: $new_uid"
```

## 13.3 Executing Commands as root

Doing anything as root is a dangerous endeavor. You can quickly ruin an entire system and any data stored within it. For this reason, along with a variety of security concerns, you should avoid doing things as root whenever possible. When you must use the root account, you should be very careful for this very reason.

When talking about system administration, quite a number of tasks must be done as root traditionally. Rebooting the system, for example, cannot usually be done as a normal user. Modifying the system configuration also tends to require root access.

If you have a script that needs to modify a specific set of system files, your first inclination may be to run the script as root. This is a quick solution that always works, but it may present security risks. The script can do much more damage running as root if it operates incorrectly.

Fortunately, when crafting your own system administration automation tools, you can resolve this problem in a safe manner. Instead of running the script as root, consider changing the permissions on the specific files so that they are writable by the user who will run the script. Or, if a group of users will run the script, create a group with all of the users as members, and make the files writable by that group.

This is particularly important when you create user interfaces for your scripts to allow them to be executed by a variety of users. The users usually only have normal user accounts and they may login to a special administration account that only provides them with a limited menu of operations that are allowed. Even more common, today, is a web interface that allows certain commands to be executed. Almost any web interface will be running as a special user, such as nobody or www. This user will definitely not have any superuser privileges, so they will definitely need carefully crafted commands to perform any system tasks.

## 13.3.1  Executing Commands with setuid Wrappers

With all of that having been said, there are some things that certainly must be done as root. Rebooting the system and restarting system processes are the most common examples. If you have executables that perform these tasks, they can be made setuid root so that a normal user can run them. But if the command is a shell script, this is not allowed for security reasons.

If you have scripts like this, consider using the best solution—Sudo. It is definitely the safest way to allow normal users to execute privileged commands. You can configure it (with the NOPASSWD option) to allow certain commands to be executed by specific users without asking them for a password. You can also specify who the command will be run as, which means you can run commands as root or any other user.

An introduction to Sudo was given in section 1.6.1. If you are already using it, then by all means, use it for this purpose as well (and ignore the C program given in this section). The only reason I can think of that you would want to avoid using it is if you want a drop-in web interface that doesn't modify the system. Having to modify /etc/sudoers might be unacceptable. Or, maybe you don't have Sudo on the system(s) that will need to execute commands as root and you would rather install one simple program.

If you decide not to use Sudo, here is a compiled wrapper program (written in C) that can be very useful:

```
#include <stdio.h>

#define WEB_UID 99

int main (int argc, char *argv[]) {
   char *command[5];
   char *basename;

   // Make sure this user is authorized
   if (getuid() != WEB_UID) {
      fprintf(stderr, "You are not authorized.\n");
      return 1;
   }

   // Initialize command items with NULLs
   memset(command, 0, sizeof(command));

   // Determine the basename for this program
   if ((basename = strrchr(argv[0], '/'))) {
      // Basename starts after the last forward-slash in path
      basename++;
   } else {
      basename=argv[0];
   }

   // Using the basename, decide which command to execute
   if (!strcmp(basename, "reboot")) {
      command[0] = "/sbin/reboot";
   } else if (!strcmp(basename, "restart_dhcpd")) {
      command[0] = "/etc/rc.d/init.d/dhcpd";
      command[1] = "restart";
   } else {
      fprintf(stderr, "%s: Unknown invocation.\n", basename);
      return 1;
   }

   // Execute command as root
   setuid(geteuid());
   setgid(getegid());
   execv(command[0], command);
   return 0;
}
```

Even without knowing the details of the C language, you should be able to use and modify this program.

First of all, this program will abort execution if it is not run by the web user, as defined in the WEB_UID constant at the top of the program. This is useful if you want to ensure that the program is only run through the web interface. Since your web server runs as a specific user, the program just presented will allow that one user to execute these specific commands as root. This prevents other users that may have accounts on the system from running the program. It is assumed that you have access controls on the web interface so that only the desired people can cause these commands to be executed.

Next, the program determines its base name, which allows the one program to perform a variety of itemized tasks. The specific task it performs depends on the name you use to execute the program. You can execute one program with different names by creating symbolic links to the program with the specified names. For example, the symbolic link reboot, if linked to this binary, would cause the system to reboot when an authorized user executed it.

Before you can use this script, you must set it up appropriately. First, you need to compile it with your system's C compiler. Here is an example with the GNU C compiler (gcc), which assumes that you have placed the program in the file wrapper.c:

```
# gcc -o wrapper wrapper.c
```

Next, you need to set the ownership and permissions properly:

```
# chown root wrapper
# chmod 4755 wrapper
```

Finally, you need to create the appropriate symbolic links:

```
# ln -s wrapper reboot
# ln -s wrapper restart_dhcpd
```

Obviously you can add as many additional commands as you require. Only allowing very specific commands to be executed with fixed arguments makes the script much safer than any kind of generic setuid wrapper.

Note that this wrapper program is not as safe as Sudo, particularly for executing shell scripts. The reason you can't usually make a shell script setuid root is that a malicious user can use a wide variety of environment variables to take advantage of the script. However, even with a binary program, certain environment variables control the loading of dynamic libraries that may cause problems. Sudo checks and sanitizes all of these environment variables, but the simple wrapper script given here does not. If you have users with nonprivileged accounts on the system that may exploit these security problems, you really have no choice but to use Sudo.

## 13.4 Designing and Using Common Data Files

Regardless of what you are doing with your automation system, what software you are using, and what operating systems it runs on, all data should be stored in a format that can be easily read in any programming language. At the very least, this means using text files, because reading binary data is difficult in some languages, and nearly impossible in shell scripts.

Most system administration is done with shell scripts and Perl. Since Perl can read and process any text file with ease, I always focus on making any data files easy to read in shell scripts.

There are two main types of data you will find yourself reading or writing. The first type is made up of actual system settings, and the second type is made up of configuration files that define how your user interface should operate.

### 13.4.1 *Common File Format for Storing Settings*

You can represent just about any system setting by a name/value pair. The value might be a number, a string, or a list of values. Name/value pairs are also quite easy to read and write in any environment. I always use a format that can be directly used by the bash shell (actually, this format can be directly read by every shell I have ever used). Here is an example:

```
ip_addr='192.168.2.3'
netmask='255.255.0.0'
dns_servers='192.168.0.2 192.168.0.3'
```

There are certain restrictions (as imposed by the bash shell) on the variable names, but they should be easy to control. When the value is enclosed in single quotes as shown, it can contain any character—except for single quotes. In order to avoid a corrupt configuration file, you cannot allow single quotes to be contained in the values. If you don't want this restriction, you can use outer double quotes if there are single quotes present in the value, but then you must escape any double quotes, dollar signs, or backslashes within the string.

When you are manually creating a file that contains shell variables, it is easy to try and use shell substitution. You need to avoid this, of course, if the file will be read by other programs (such as ones written in Perl) that will not process the file the same way a shell would. In addition, if a user will be modifying the values through the web or another user interface, they may be confused by the presence of any variable substitutions.

### 13.4.1.1 Reading in bash

Reading this type of file from bash is easy. You just source the configuration file. Here is an example:

```
source /usr/local/etc/system.conf
```

### 13.4.1.2 Writing in bash

This type of configuration file is easy to write in bash. One method involves creating the file from scratch, like so:

```
FILE="/usr/local/etc/system.conf"

add_value() {
    eval echo "$1=\""'\${$1}'"\"" >> $FILE
}

# Empty the file
>$FILE

# Create entire file
add_value ip_addr
add_value netmask
add_value dns_servers
```

The add_value function expects one parameter. This is the name of a variable that may or may not have a defined value. So, if the environment variable $ip_addr is not defined, the following line will be added to the specified configuration file:

```
ip_addr=''
```

But, if $ip_addr contains the value 192.168.1.1, that value will be used in the file:

```
ip_addr='192.168.1.1'
```

You could also create a function that will work with a non-empty file. It can remove the variable from the current configuration file (if it is there), and then re-add the variable with the new value:

```
FILE="/usr/local/etc/system.conf"

set_value() {
    grep -v "^$1=" $FILE > $FILE.tmp
    mv $FILE.tmp $FILE
    eval echo "$1=\"'"'\${$1}'"'\"" >> $FILE
}


# Update just the IP address
set_value ip_addr
```

Remember that the value may not contain a single-quote character (').


### 13.4.1.3  Reading in Perl

It is also pretty easy to read this type of file in Perl. Here is a function that can read
any configuration file of this format; it returns a reference to a hash table containing
the name/value pairs.

```
sub read_file ($) {
    my ($file) = @_;
    my %ret;
    open(FILE, $file) or return undef;
    while (my $line = <FILE>) {
        chomp($line);
        next if ($line =~ /^\s*$/); # skip blank lines
        next if ($line =~ /^\s*#/); # skip comments

        # Split into name and value
        my ($name, $value) = split('=', $line, 2);
        next unless ($name and $value);

        # Remove single-quotes
        $value =~ s/^'//;
        $value =~ s/'$//;

        # Store value
        $ret{$name} = $value;
    }
    close(FILE);
    return \%ret;
}
```

You can access the values as follows:

```
my $data = read_file('/usr/local/etc/system.conf');
print "IP Address: $data->{'ip_addr'}\n";
```

### 13.4.1.4  Writing in Perl

Writing this type of file in Perl is easier than writing it in bash. Here is a function that writes the entire file out using the hash reference passed into the function:

```
sub write_file ($$) {
    my ($file, $data_ref) = @_;
    open(FILE, ">$file") or return 0;
    foreach my $name (keys %{$data_ref}) {
        print FILE "$name='$data_ref->{$name}'\n";
    }
    close(FILE);
    return 1;
}
```

## 13.4.2  Defining Interface Specifications

When I create a user interface, I like to make sure it is flexible and expandable. Although I could just hard-code the exact functionality I need at the moment, it is better in the long term to define the interface using a configuration file (as much as possible).

There are really an infinite number of options for such a configuration file. I like to place one item on each line, where each item can have any number of name/value pairs. These are separated by the pipe character (|). Here is an example:

```
|variable=item1|type=integer|default=0|desc=Sample Item 1
|variable=item2|type=string|default=|desc=Sample Item 2
```

As you can see, each line represents one item. Each line has any number of name/value pairs in the form |name=value.

### 13.4.2.1  Reading in bash

When reading this type of file in a shell script, it is difficult to store it all in memory like we will do in Perl in the next section. This is not usually a problem, however, because a typical program just loops through one entry at a time. In this bash example, I define the function get_value that will return the value for a named parameter on the current line.

```
FILE='/usr/local/etc/system.conf'
get_value() {
   echo "$1" | sed "s/.*|$2=\([^|]*\).*/\1/"
}

cat "$FILE" | while read line ; do
   echo "Variable: $(get_value "$line" variable)"
   echo " Type: $(get_value "$line" type)"
   echo " Default: $(get_value "$line" default)"
   echo " Description: $(get_value "$line" desc)"
done
```

If executed, this example simply shows all of the entries and the specified value for each named parameter. Remember that everything within the while loop is executed in a subshell, so variables set in there will not propagate to any code outside of the loop.

### 13.4.2.2  Reading in Perl

Since memory is rarely at a premium these days, and since this type of configuration file is almost always very small, I find it much easier to just read the whole thing into memory and work with it there. This is fairly simple to do in Perl, of course:

```
sub read_pipe_file ($) {
   my ($file) = @_;
   my (@ret, $entry);
   open(FILE, $file) or return undef;
   while (my $line = <FILE>) {
      chomp($line);
      next if ($line =~ /^\s*$/); # skip blank lines
      next if ($line =~ /^\s*#/); # skip comments

      # Now retrieve name/values for current line
      $entry = ();
      while ($line =~ s/^\|([^=|]+)=([^|]*)//) {
         $entry->{$1} = $2;
      }
```

```
        push @ret, $entry;
    }
    close(FILE);
    return (@ret);
}
```

This function reads a file and returns an array of references. Each of these references represents one line (or entry) in the configuration file. These are references to hashes that contain the various name/value pairs that belong to the entry. Note that the order of the lines is preserved, but not the order of the name/value pairs.

Using the function is easy. Here is a small snippet of code that you can use to test this function (it just displays all of the name/value pairs from the file):

```
#!/usr/bin/perl -w
use strict;

foreach my $entry (read_pipe_file '/tmp/test.conf') {
    foreach (keys %{$entry}) {
        print "$_: $entry->{$_}\n";
    }
}
```

## 13.5 Text-Based Interface

Assuming your scripts follow the guidelines presented in section 13.2, you already have a basic text interface. Such an interface is all you really need for intermediate and advanced administrators.

When it comes to novices, however, remember that it is not easy for them to learn a system that is made up of a set of disparate shell scripts—they have to remember the names of the scripts, what they do, and how to run them. Instead, consider creating an interactive system that will make configuration changes and execute commands. This will give novice administrators a great place to start. If you are creating a system that will be administered directly by your customers, an easy-to-use text interface makes a nice addition to the almost mandatory web interface.

Text-based interfaces are nice because, thanks to the way UNIX works, they can be accessed in a variety of ways. It may be through a serial console, over telnet, or using SSH. Some web interfaces even allow you to run console programs from the Web.

I like to write a main program that provides a menu interface to all of the available system administration scripts. This program can then be set as the shell for a special administration account. If this user logs in, whether on the console, via SSH, or through a serial terminal, they are immediately placed into the menu system.

You can even have several special accounts, each with different menu systems (or a single menu system that shows different options based on the account used).

---

 **CAUTION** If you do not want the users to have full access to the system, and you think they may intentionally try to gain such access, you need to be very careful setting up this type of system. Just remember that, when a script accepts arbitrary input from the user, the user may be able to enter special characters that will cause arbitrary commands to be executed on the system. If this is a real concern, you may want to use something besides a shell script for this type of activity. You can create a much safer menu interface using Perl, for example.

---

## 13.5.1  Menu Interface

Creating a simple menu interface is easy. You can start with a configuration file that lists each choice on the menu and what command should be executed when that choice is selected:

```
|item=Change Your Password|cmd=/usr/bin/passwd
|item=Configure System|cmd=/usr/local/sbin/configure
|item=Restart DHCP Server|cmd=/usr/local/sbin/restart_dhcpd
|item=Reboot System|cmd=/usr/local/sbin/reboot
```

Once you have created the configuration file, you can use a script like the following to produce a menu interface:

```
#!/bin/bash

FILE='/usr/local/etc/mainmenu.conf'

get_value() {
    echo "$1" | sed "s/.*|$2=\(([^|]*\).*/\1/"
}

IFS='
'
```

```
select resp in \
   `cat "$FILE" | while read line ; do
      get_value "$line" item
   done`
do
   # Check for q or Q to exit
   case "$REPLY" in
      [qQ])
         break
         ;;
   esac
   # Execute command
   cat "$FILE" | while read line ; do
      [ `get_value "$line" item` == "$resp" ] && {
         eval `get_value "$line" cmd`
      }
   done
done
```

The select command does the hard part for you. You just have to tell it what options you want displayed, and then take the appropriate action based on the option selected. Note that the special $IFS variable is set to the newline character to allow for spaces in the menu selections.

One way you can expand this script is to provide a method the user can use to enter parameters for certain commands. When an appropriate command is selected, the script could ask for the required parameters, and then execute the command as specified. This is something I would do in Perl, however, because it would be pretty complicated to parse such a complicated configuration file in a shell script.

## 13.5.2  *Configuring Your Text-Based Interface*

A robust configuration interface that you execute on any terminal can be very useful. Again, a configuration file is used to control the behavior of the script, which makes the behavior easy to change. You can even modify this script to accept the configuration filename as a parameter, which allows you to use the same script to configure different areas of the system simply by specifying different configuration files. The format of this configuration file is explained in the next section.

### 13.5.2.1 Input Configuration File Format

Here is a sample configuration file that you could use to configure the network settings of a system. In this example, it would be called /usr/local/etc/config.in. Note that an optional default value can be given for each setting.

```
|var=IP_ADDRESS|default=|desc=The primary IP address
|var=NETMASK|default=255.255.255.0|desc=The netmask
|var=GATEWAY|default=192.168.1.1|desc=The default router
|var=DNS|default=192.168.1.1|desc=The domain name server
```

The configuration script reads this configuration file and prompts the user for values. These values are then stored in the output configuration file. After storing the values, you would presumably have a shell script that uses the resulting configuration file to make the actual system-level configuration changes. Methods you can actually use to configure the system are discussed in Chapter 6. This script just reads the values from the user and stores them in a sample name/value configuration file.

### 13.5.2.2 The Configuration Script

Here is how the script begins:

```
#!/bin/bash

CONFIG_IN="/usr/local/etc/config.in"
CONFIG_OUT="/usr/local/var/config.out"

get_value() {
    echo "$1" | sed "s/.*|$2=\([^|]*\).*/\1/"
}
```

Nothing new here. You are going to use the same get_value function you used in the previous example. You'll define the input configuration file (previously shown) as well as the desired output file to be created with the values entered by the user. You could change those lines to take these files in as two arguments to the script:

```
CONFIG_IN="$1"
CONFIG_OUT="$2"
```

In either case, you need a function to check the value the user entered:

```
check_value() {
    var="$(get_value "$1" var)"
    default="$(get_value "$1" default)"
    case "$2" in
        *"'"*)
            echo " ** Single quotes (') are not allowed! **"
            ;;
        '')
            if eval [ -z "\"\${$var:-$default}\"" ]; then
                echo " ** Please enter a value (no default available) **"
            else
                eval echo "$var=\"'\${$var:-$default}'\"" >&2
                return 0
            fi
            ;;
        *)
            echo "$var='$2'" >&2
            return 0
            ;;
    esac
    return 1
}
```

This function takes two parameters: the current line from the input configuration file, and the new value entered by the user. It first checks to make sure there are no single quotes in the value because those are not allowed in our name/value pair output file as discussed in section 13.4.

Next, if the value entered by the user is empty, the function uses the default value. If the output configuration file already exists, the function uses the value in that file as the default. Otherwise, the default value specified in the incoming configuration file is used.

If everything is okay, the appropriate line that should be placed in the output configuration file is printed on stderr and the function returns with an exit code of 0. If there are any problems, the function prints an error message on stdout and an exit code of 1 is returned.

Finally, here is the main loop of the program:

```
# First, read existing values, if any
source $CONFIG_OUT 2>/dev/null

while read line <&3 ; do
    case "$line" in
        \#*|"")
            # Skip comments and blank lines
            continue
            ;;
    esac
    # Found a valid line, retrieve data, and store parameters
    var="$(get_value "$line" var)"
    default="$(get_value "$line" default)"
    [ -z "$var" ] && continue
    # Now request and store all settings
    while true ; do
        echo "$var: $(get_value "$line" desc)"
        eval echo -n \
            "\"Enter a value for $var [\${$var:-$default}]: \""
        read input
        echo
        check_value "$line" "$input" && break
        echo
    done
done 3<$CONFIG_IN 2>$CONFIG_OUT.$$
mv -f $CONFIG_OUT.$$ $CONFIG_OUT
```

Note that the existing output file (if any) is sourced first. This allows the script to use the existing values as the default values, making it easy for a user to go through and change only some values on a system that has already been configured. Next, this program shows each line of the input configuration file. These lines are sent into the loop on file descriptor 3 since all the normal file descriptors are being used for other purposes.

Then, for each item specified in the input configuration file, the variable is displayed and its description is given. The user is prompted to enter a new value and shown the default or current value, if any. If the check_value function returns success, the outer loop proceeds to the next input line. Otherwise, the user is prompted for the same value again.

The contents of the output file comes from the check_value function, which sends the actual text to be written out on stderr. The main loop then redirects this output into a temporary output file. Once the program exits properly (meaning it was not aborted), the temporary output file is renamed into its permanent position.

## 13.5.2.3  Example Script Execution

Here is an example run of the program:

```
IP_ADDRESS: The primary IP address for this system
Enter a value for IP_ADDRESS []: 192.168.10.10

NETMASK: The netmask for this system
Enter a value for NETMASK [255.255.255.0]:

GATEWAY: The default router for this system
Enter a value for GATEWAY [192.168.1.1]: 192.168.10.1

DNS: The domain name server for this system
Enter a value for DNS [192.168.1.1]:
```

No default value was available for the first variable (IP_ADDRESS). The defaults were accepted for the other values except for the GATEWAY. After this execution, the output file (/usr/local/var/config.out) contains the following:

```
IP_ADDRESS='192.168.10.10'
NETMASK='255.255.255.0'
GATEWAY='192.168.10.1'
DNS='192.168.1.1'
```

## 13.5.2.4  Extended Data Checking

You can add additional checks on the values entered by the user. In the input configuration file, you can add a new field called datatype. You can then extend the check_value function to verify that the data entered by the user is of the appropriate data type:

```
check_value() {
    var="$(get_value "$1" var)"
    default="$(get_value "$1" default)"
    case "$2" in
      *"'"*)
        echo " ** Single quotes (') are not allowed! **"
        ;;
      '')
          if eval [ -z "\"\${$var:-$default}\"" ]; then
              echo " ** Please enter a value (no default available) **"
```

```
        else
            eval echo "$var=\"'\${$var:-$default}'\"" >&2
            return 0
        fi
        ;;
    *)
        if check_data_type "$2" "$(get_value "$1" datatype)" ; then
            echo "$var='$2'" >&2
            return 0
        else
            echo " ** Invalid value entered! **"
        fi
        ;;
    esac
    return 1
}
```

Then you need to create the check_data_type function:

```
# $1 is the value entered by the user
# $2 is the expected datatype
check_data_type() {
    case $2 in
        integer)
            echo "$1" | egrep -q '^[0123456789]+$'
            ;;
        network_address)
            echo "$1" | \
                egrep -q \
                    '^[0123456789]{1,3}\.[0123456789]{1,3}\.
                    [0123456789]{1,3}\.[0123456789]{1,3}$'
            ;;
        directory)
            test -d "$1"
            ;;
        file)
            test -f "$1"
            ;;
        *)
            # Unsupported datatype, return true
            true
            ;;
    esac
    return $?
}
```

As you can see, you can quickly add more data types as you need them. In the example in this section, the network_address type would be used for every variable. This data type could be checked more thoroughly, but this at least provides a basic sanity check for network addresses.

The file and directory data types can be used to make sure the value entered is an *existing* file or directory, respectively. The integer datatype should be self-explanatory.

## 13.6 Creating a Web-Based Interface

You really can't go wrong with a web interface in today's world. With a web interface, your automation system can be accessed from just about any computer, running any operating system, anywhere in the world.

A web interface also makes your system much more user friendly. Assuming it is designed well, a new administrator (or just about anybody) can quickly learn how to do the usual tasks on your systems. This is great when you need to train a new employee, have somebody help out with the easy tasks, or leave somebody in charge when you are on vacation.

System administration is a very "behind-the-scenes" activity. It is especially easy to forget that administration takes any effort at all when things are automated and everything works well. A glitzy web interface can make the whole experience more fulfilling. More importantly, it can help others (your boss maybe?) see what you have accomplished.

Another major use of web interfaces is on network appliances. These are systems that are nicely packaged and shipped off to a customer who may know little or nothing about UNIX. Your product may be a Linux-based consumer DSL router or a set of high-performance, clusterable web servers. A web interface is a must for these types of devices because it is often the only interface available to the users (i.e., customers).

For the rest of this chapter, I assume you have the skills to install and configure a web server that can run your web interface. I also assume that you have a basic knowledge of HTML. If you do not, there are a wide variety of books available on the subject. A good place to start is *HTML for the World Wide Web with XHTML and CSS: Visual QuickStart Guide, Fifth Edition* by Elizabeth Castro (Peachpit Press, 2002). Other books cover JavaScript, Dynamic HTML, and graphics design, all of which can help you make your web interface look even nicer.

## 13.6.1  *Organizing Your Web Interface*

The extent of your web interface will really depend on the extent of your automation system. Assuming you or other experienced administrators will still have access to the system(s), the web interface doesn't have to include every piece of functionality—just the more commonly used ones. A program such as Webmin can also be used to provide a web interface for any gaps in your automation system; it can provide a quick interface to any aspect of system administration.

You may want to provide a wide range of functionality in your interface. System monitoring is important—from a basic overall status to the health of each service. The web interface should also allow system configuration such as network settings; it can also allow the configuration of the services being run on the system. In addition, the web interface should almost certainly provide the ability to execute certain commands (such as rebooting the system, restarting services, etc.).

There are really two approaches you can take with a system administration web interface. In the first, you create one interface on each system. If you will be shipping individual systems out to customers, this is a must. If you only have a few systems that are significantly different, then the web interface on each system will provide the necessary functionality required by each system.

If you have a large number of systems, particularly when the systems are very similar (web clusters, Beowulf clusters, etc.), then you will probably prefer the second option: creating a central web interface. This interface can show the overall status of all of your systems. It can also allow you to change settings on all of the systems as a group. It can even provide an interface for adding or removing systems from the cluster.

A hybrid approach of these two options is also common. In such an approach, one central interface provides a listing of systems and their status. This interface provides central management functionality, but it also provides a link for each system. This link takes the user to the web interface for that specific system. This hybrid approach allows each machine to be administered separately (if necessary), but it also provides the convenience of a central web interface for system management.

## 13.6.2  *Introduction to Mason*

Considering how popular the World Wide Web is these days, the variety of options a web developer has available for their use should not come as a surprise. First of all, you can use the good old Common Gateway Interface (CGI). When you use CGI, you can write a program in absolutely any language (well, any language that can print to stdout and read environment variables), yet still operate with pretty much any web server. If a specific language is important to you, then I would suggest using CGI for your scripts (or any native web scripting environment provided by that language).

The next "step up" is server-parsed HTML. These types of files are simply HTML files with special embedded commands that the web server recognizes. You can use these to insert the page's last modification time, include common headers and footers, and even execute commands on the server.

The original server-parsed HTML was popular, but it lacked much of the power of traditional CGI scripts. For some situations this was acceptable, but others needed much more power. This is why the modern server-parsed HTML systems were created. The most popular implementations of this include PHP: Hypertext Processor (PHP), Java Server Pages (JSP), Microsoft's Active Server Pages (ASP), Cold Fusion, and Mason.

Each of these modern server-parsed HTML implementations are very similar. In most cases, the only major difference is their underlying programming language. You use them all the same way—by embedding code in standard HTML files. This embedded code allows you to do any amount of dynamic page generation you desire. You usually don't need to understand many of the underlying technologies, such as browser communication and parsing parameters; the system handles all of this for you. All you have to do is write HTML that contains code that outputs HTML. It is that simple.

Many of these server-parsed HTML systems are available for free. Most, if not all, work with the Apache web server. The most common free versions are PHP, JSP, and Mason (Perl). Since I have used Perl extensively throughout this book, I will continue the trend by using Mason within this section. In addition, Perl is the most common language used when writing traditional CGI scripts, which means that you can easily convert the examples in this section to work as traditional CGI scripts.

I will not describe how to install and configure Mason because that is beyond the scope of this book. You can find installation instructions and other documentation at http://www.masonhq.com. Note that Mason requires Apache, Perl, mod_perl, and some Perl modules (most notably the HTML::Mason module). You are probably pretty familiar with Apache by now, and the Apache you are using may already have mod_perl installed (although it will not usually be activated). This means that, in many cases, you will only need to install some Perl modules and configure Apache properly to start using Mason.

For more information on using Mason, take a look at *Embedding Perl in HTML with Mason,* by Dave Rolsky, Ken Williams (O'Reilly and Associates, 2002). If you prefer to use CGI (which is quicker for small/simple scripts), you can try *CGI Programming with Perl,* by Gunther Birznieks Scott Guelich, and Shishir Gundavaram (O'Reilly and Associates, 2000). In addition to information on creating CGI scripts, this book also contains information that you can also apply when using Mason.

### 13.6.2.1 Simple Mason Example

Once you have installed and configured Mason, you can simply place your files in the MasonRoot directory you configured and navigate to those pages in your browser. Here is a simple Mason example:

```
<html>
    <head>
        <title>Mason Example Page</title>
    </head>
    <body>
        <P>
            The current date and time is:
            <% scalar localtime %>
        </P>
    </body>
</html>
```

As you can see, this is not much more than a simple HTML file. The only unusual thing is the sequence <% scalar localtime %>. The entire expression enclosed within the <% ... %> sequence is evaluated by Mason. The resulting value (the date/time string) is then inserted into the document, replacing the entire sequence of characters (<% scalar localtime %>). If you navigate to the page with a web browser, and if you have Mason properly configured, you will see the current date and time in your web browser. If you view the source of the page, you will see the following:

```
<html>
    <head>
        <title>Mason Example Page</title>
    </head>
    <body>
        <P>
            The current date and time is:
            Tue Dec 31 10:38:34 2002
        </P>
    </body>
</html>
```

### 13.6.2.2  Automatic Headers and Footers

With Mason, you do not need to include all of the overhead required by HTML in each individual page. You can use a common header and footer to take care of this for you. All you need to do is create a file called `autohandler` in the base Mason directory (the `MasonRoot` directory). The file should contain the following:

```
%# Basic mason 'autohandler'

<& /header.comp &>
<% $m->call_next %>
<& /footer.comp &>
```

This file is automatically executed when a file is accessed in its directory or any subdirectory. It simply outputs the header, then processes the file that was actually requested, and then outputs the footer. The `$m->call_next` call might do more than that (like executing additional autohandlers in subdirectories).

The `<& ... &>` sequence processes a separate file (usually called a component) and includes the result in its place. In this case, the file `/header.comp` is processed first. Just like all Mason files, this is just an HTML page (but it may contain Mason command sequences):

```
<html>
    <head>
        <title>Mason Example Page</title>
    </head>
    <body>
```

In this case the header is just simple HTML. An advanced feature would be to have the header use a different title depending on which page is requested, but, for our examples, I'm not too worried about the titles of the pages. The footer is even simpler:

```
    </body>
</html>
```

It is important to remember that the footer is referred to as `/footer.comp`, which means it should be located in the base Mason directory (i.e., the `MasonRoot`). Once this header and footer is in place, I can redo this simple example with much less typing:

```
<P>
   The current date and time is:
   <% scalar localtime %>
</P>
```

### 13.6.2.3  Expanded Examples

Mason can do quite a bit more for you, as you will see in this section. Remember to look over the official documentation at http://www.masonhq.com for additional documentation and examples.

First, you can access the parameters passed on the URL or in the POST data as follows:

```
% foreach my $arg (keys %ARGS) {
      <br />Name = <% $arg %>, Value = <% $ARGS{$arg} %>
% }
```

These three lines of code will print out every argument passed into the script. If, for example, this page was named showargs.mhtml, you could access the URL http://myserver.mydomain.com/showargs.html?a=1&b=2&c=3 and you would see the following page:

```
Name = a, Value = 1
Name = b, Value = 2
Name = c, Value = 3
```

This simple example introduces a couple of new topics. First of all, Mason does all parameter processing for you, whether the parameters are sent in on the URL or through a POST request. The parsed parameters are all placed into the %ARGS hash for convenient access.

Secondly, the previous example shows how Perl command structures can be embedded in HTML. If the first character on a line is a %, the line is treated as Perl code. You can format the code however you like, as long as all code lines begin with the % and all HTML lines do not. Note that the % *cannot* be preceded by any whitespace.

So, the source of the web page previously shown, when viewed in the browser, and excluding the contents of your header and footer text, will be:

```
      <br />Name = a, Value = 1
      <br />Name = b, Value = 2
      <br />Name = c, Value = 3
```

As you can see, all of the <% ... %> sequences have been removed and replaced with the appropriate substitution values. If your script expects only one or two arguments, Mason can be even more helpful. You use the following form to request information:

```
<form action="/showinfo.mhtml">
Name: <input type=text name=name>
Email Address: <input type=text name=email_address>
</form>
```

You can then use the following Mason document to process the information:

```
%# File: showinfo.mhtml

<P> You entered the following information: </P>
Name: <% $name %> <br />
Email Address: <% $email_address %> <br />

% if ($m->comp('/storeinfo.comp',
%         name => $name, email => $email_address)) {
   <P> Your information was successfully saved! </P>
% } else {
   <P> There was an error saving your information! </P>
% }

<%args>
$name
$email_address
</%args>
```

This page shows that there are two ways to call other Mason components. The first is to use the <& ... &> sequence as used in the autohandler. The second way is to call the $m->comp() function, with the path to the component as the first parameter and any necessary arguments as additional parameters. Here is the component that was called:

```
%# storeinfo.comp

<%perl>
if ($testing) {
    # Show what we would have stored
    $m->out("<p>I would have stored $name and $email. </p>");
```

```
} else {
   # Place regular Perl code here to store the values
}
return 1;
</%perl>

<%args>
$name
$email
$testing => 0
</%args>
```

This component illustrates the last few capabilities of Mason that will be used within this book. First, it shows that you can create entire blocks of Perl code using the <%perl> tag. Inside such a block, you can call the $m->out() function to generate output HTML (which is inserted in the document in place of the <%perl> block).

This component also has an optional argument ($testing). It is optional because a default value of 0 is specified. If the argument is not given, the variable will be set to this default value. If, on the other hand, the required arguments are not specified, an error will occur.

This example consisted of three separate files. The first was a page with a form, the second was a page that processed that form, and the third was a component that stored the data. This helps illustrate one of the biggest advantages of Mason. The first page had no code at all in it—it was just HTML. The second page had almost no code as well. Either of these pages could be modified or created by somebody with good HTML skills, but possibly only limited programming ability. The component, on the other hand, is all Perl code. This can be written by a programmer who has little HTML knowledge. This allows the code and the HTML to be mostly separated and to be created and maintained by people with the appropriate skills.

## 13.6.3  Security with HTTP Authentication

You probably don't want to allow open access to certain parts of your web interface. In many cases, you may want to restrict access to everything. HTTP provides basic authentication support that is compatible with all browsers and is easy to use. You can use this facility so that you don't have to handle the authentication details yourself.

The main drawback of the basic HTTP authentication is that the password is included, virtually in plain text, in every request. This means that the password can be sniffed unless *every* page is served using HTTPS. For this reason, you may want to have HTTP access inside of your private network but only allow HTTPS access to the same content when the user is coming from outside of your private network. You can easily do this by configuring your router or firewall to only allow external access to the server over port 443.

### 13.6.3.1 Creating the htpasswd File

The first thing you must do is create a htpasswd file. This is similar to the system password file because it contains usernames and encrypted passwords. Your web server most likely comes with the htpasswd program that is used to create and manage this file. You can place the file anywhere on your system, but you should place it outside of any web directories so that it cannot be accessed over HTTP. You may create the file as /etc/htpasswd, for example. You can create the file using the command:

```
# htpasswd -c /etc/htpasswd username
New password:
Re-type new password:
Adding password for user username
```

The -c switch tells the program to create a new file. Once the file has been created, you can add additional users by running the same command, but without the -c:

```
# htpasswd /etc/htpasswd user2
New password:
Re-type new password:
Adding password for user user2
```

How many accounts you should create depends on your system and how much control you want over system access. If every user will have complete access, you can create just one account with one password and all of the users can share that account. The advantage of this is easier management—that is, you can quickly change the password on that one account whenever you need to. The disadvantage is that you lose accountability, meaning that you don't know what user did what because they are all using the same account.

The other alternative is to create a separate account for each user. This allows your scripts to limit access based on the remote user. It also stores the username in the web server's access logs. The disadvantage is that you have to create a web interface to allow users to change their passwords. If you do not, you will have to manually manage all of the accounts or, more likely, the passwords will never get changed.

In any case, you need to make sure the htpasswd file itself, as well as all directories leading up to it, are readable and executable, respectively, by the user running the web server.

### 13.6.3.2 Restricting Access

Assuming you have your router/firewall configured to not allow external hosts to spoof internal IPs (a pretty basic ability, especially if your internal IPs are one of the reserved private networks), you can tell your web server not to require a password when the request is coming from an internal system. This provides access control from external hosts, but it also provides hassle-free access internally. You should, of course, make sure that any internal wireless network does not allow this access control to be circumvented by somebody outside your company with a wireless network card.

If you are using the Apache web server, you can restrict access in the main configuration file (such as /etc/httpd/conf/httpd.conf). Assuming you want this restriction applied to every page served by your web server, you can use these commands:

```
<Directory />
    AuthUserFile /etc/htpasswd
    AuthType Basic
    AuthName "Administration System Access"
    require valid-user
    Satisfy any
    order deny,allow
    allow from 192.168.0.0/255.255.0.0
    allow from 127.0.0.1
    deny from all
</Directory>
```

This allows the system itself and all hosts in the 192.168 private network access to the system without authentication. For anybody else, the user must provide a username and password that matches an entry in the /etc/htpasswd file.

Note that this access control applies to the directory / and everything under it. This means it applies to every file and directory on the system when they are accessed through the web server—unless you have other blocks that override the settings for specific subdirectories. This is the safest way to make sure you catch all the files on your system, even if you later add virtual hosts, aliases, and other configuration items.

If you provide each user with a different account and want to log the usernames, you would not want this type of configuration because local users would never be authenticated. In this case, you should just require authentication in all cases:

```
<Directory />
   AuthUserFile /etc/htpasswd
   AuthType Basic
   AuthName "Administration System Access"
   require valid-user
</Directory>
```

Depending on the size of your company and the people that work there, you may want to use this second access control configuration anyway. There are many companies where it would be a bad idea to allow open access to a system configuration web interface.

### 13.6.3.3  Accessing the Username

If you have assigned different accounts to different users, it is nice to be able to retrieve this information from within Mason. It is actually stored in an environment variable, just as with the traditional CGI interface. The environment variable is $REMOTE_USER. You can test this as follows:

```
<P>
   You are logged in as: <% $ENV{'REMOTE_USER'} %>
</P>
```

Remember that the environment variable will *not* be defined unless you require authentication for the page in your web server's configuration. There are other interesting environment variables as the following page can show you:

```
% foreach my $var (keys %ENV) {
     <br />Name = <% $var %>, Value = <% $ENV{$var} %>
% }
```

## 13.6.4  Logging Web Activity

Whether you have a web interface that performs just one task or hundreds, having a log can be invaluable. It will tell you what was done, who did it, and when. If something goes wrong, or if somebody makes a mistake, you will at least know when it happened and who you should blame (assuming you have separate accounts for each user).

Here is a simple component that can be placed in the base Mason directory (your `MasonRoot`):

```
%# log.comp

<%perl>
# Set your logfile here:
my $logfile = "/usr/local/var/web.log";

open(LOG, ">>$logfile");
my $datetime = localtime;
print LOG "$datetime $ENV{'REMOTE_USER'} $msg\n";
close(LOG);
</%perl>

<%args>
$msg
</%args>
```

Note that only one parameter is necessary: `$msg`. The current date and time as well as the remote user's name is retrieved directly from the system. It is important to note that the web server must require HTTP authentication in order for the `$REMOTE_USER` environment variable to be defined. If you don't require HTTP authentication on your server, you should remove this item from the log because it will cause warnings from Perl.

Once this component has been created, you can use it from any of your other pages and components:

```
<& /log.comp, msg => 'This is a test log message' &>
```

You can also execute the component from within a `%perl` block:

```
$m->comp('/log.comp', msg => 'This is a test log message');
```

## 13.6.5 Creating and Using a Custom Perl Library

I find it easiest to place any custom functions I may need to use within a custom Perl library. Creating a library is easy—just place the following into the file `MyLib.pm`:

```
package MyLib;

sub somefunction {
}

1;
```

That's about it. Just make sure the filename matches the package name. To use the library, you can place the following within a Mason document:

```
<%once>
use lib '/usr/local/www/lib';
use MyLib;
</%once>
```

The %once block contains Perl code that will be executed only the first time the object is requested (i.e., when the page is viewed or the component is called). Placing global code in these blocks can significantly enhance the performance of your web pages.

You can also include a library on a system-wide basis in your httpd.conf, as follows:

```
<Perl>
use lib '/usr/local/www/lib';
use MyLib;
</Perl>
```

Or, if the library can be found in the standard Perl library search path, you can just do this:

```
PerlModule MyLib
```

Once your custom library has been included, you can execute the functions within by using the syntax MyLib::somefunction(). The remaining scripts in this chapter assume the following custom Perl module. You can add your own functions to this library as necessary. These functions were discussed earlier in section 13.4.

```perl
# Should be named MyLib.pm and be placed in the module search path
package MyLib;

sub read_file ($) {
    my ($file) = @_;
    my %ret;
    open(FILE, $file) or return undef;
    while (my $line = <FILE>) {
        chomp($line);
        next if ($line =~ /^\s*$/); # skip blank lines
        next if ($line =~ /^\s*#/); # skip comments

        # Split into name and value
        my ($name, $value) = split('=', $line, 2);
        next unless ($name and $value);

        # Remove single quotes
        $value =~ s/^'//;
        $value =~ s/'$//;

        # Store value
        $ret{$name} = $value;
    }
    close(FILE);
    return \%ret;
}
sub read_pipe_file ($) {
    my ($file) = @_;
    my (@ret, $entry);
    open(FILE, $file) or return undef;
    while (my $line = <FILE>) {
        chomp($line);
        next if ($line =~ /^\s*$/); # skip blank lines
        next if ($line =~ /^\s*#/); # skip comments

        # Now retrieve name/values for current line
        $entry = ();
        while ($line =~ s/^\|([^=|]+)=([^|]*)//) {
        $entry->{$1} = $2;
        }
        push @ret, $entry;
    }
```

```
      close(FILE);
      return (@ret);
}


sub write_file ($$) {
   my ($file, $data_ref) = @_;
   open(FILE, ">$file") or return 0;
   foreach my $name (keys %{$data_ref}) {
      print FILE "$name='$data_ref->{$name}'\n";
   }
   close(FILE);
   return 1;
}
1;
```

## 13.6.6  Web-Based Overall Status and System Listing

Whether or not you have a central point for your web administration, having a central listing of systems is valuable. As a start, this list can show basic system status and provide links to pages directly on each system. This type of basic system will be presented in this section and can be used as is, or expanded to provide a more thorough central management system.

   This script, like the others that follow in this chapter, is designed to run under Mason. I assume that you have a basic header and footer that will be added to each page automatically. If you want, you can turn this code into a standard CGI script with relatively little effort.

   Like some other scripts in this book, this script is not optimized for a large number of systems (above 20 or so). The system checks are done in series and the list can grow quite long. If you have a good number of systems, you should consider a main page that links to this type of script, but with many different configuration files. You could have one page for your web servers, and another for your computing cluster. Most likely, however, you would want to just use an existing program, like Nagios (previously NetSaint) as discussed in section 10.3.2.

   I will start with a configuration file in the format discussed earlier in section 3.4. Here is an example:

```
|host=www.mydomain.com|ports=80,443|desc=Web Server
|host=ns1.mydomain.com|ports=53|desc=DNS Server
|host=mail.mydomain.com|ports=25|desc=Mail Server
```

Any number of entries are possible. Each entry defines a host, provides its description, and lists one or more TCP ports that should be active on that host. The following script will display a page using the information contained within this file:

```
%# status.mhtml
<%once>
my @hosts = MyLib::read_pipe_file('/usr/local/www/etc/status.conf');
</%once>

<table border=1 cellpadding=4>
    <tr>
        <th>Host</th>
        <th>Status</th>
        <th>Ports</th>
        <th>Description</th>
    </tr>

% foreach my $entry (@hosts) {
    <tr>
        <td><a href="http://<% $entry->{'host'} %>:8080/">
            <% $entry->{'host'} %></a>
        </td>
        <td align=center>
            <& pinghost.comp, host => $entry->{'host'} &>
        <td>
%       foreach (split /,/, $entry->{'ports'}) {
            <% $_ %>:
            <& checkport.comp,
                host => $entry->{'host'}, port => $_ &>
            <br />
%       }
        </td>
        <td><% $entry->{'desc'} %></td>
    </tr>
% }
</table>
```

Note that the configuration file is only read once per web server process. This means that you will need to restart your web server whenever this file changes. If the file will change often, you may want to change the %once block into a normal %perl block. Such a change is also useful when you are setting up and testing the system.

The rest of the document is mostly standard HTML. Very plain HTML at that—I like to leave it to somebody else to make it look pretty. Plain HTML is also much easier to read in code form. You can see the stunning result in Figure 13-1.

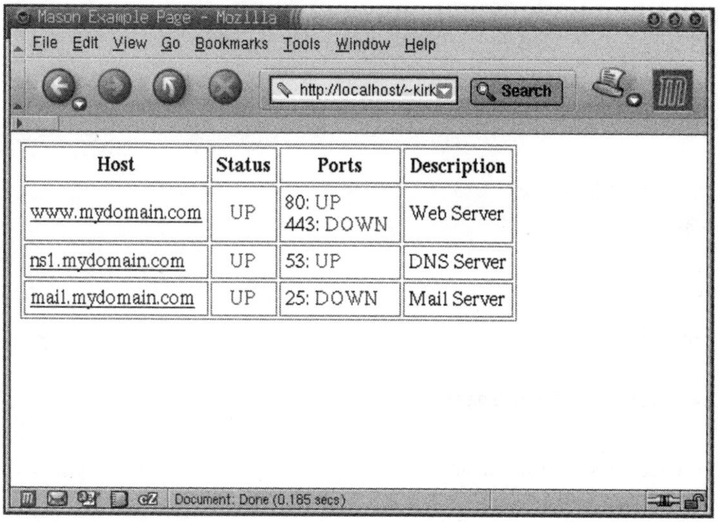

*Figure 13-1. System status overview*

On the web page, a link is provided to port 8080 on each host, which, presumably, is the web-based management page for that host. Two external components are referenced. The first will ping a host and display the results, and is named pinghost.comp:

```
%# pinghost.comp

<%once>
use IO::Socket;
</%once>

% if (system("ping -c1 $host >/dev/null 2>&1") == 0) {
    <span style="color:green">UP</span>
% } else {
    <span style="color:red">DOWN</span>
% }

<%args>
$host
</%args>
```

This component does nothing more than execute the system ping command. It requests only one packet to be sent (-c1). The exit code of the command indicates whether or not the ping was successful. Note that the usage of the ping command may be different on your system. On Solaris, for example, no command-line switch is necessary (it will only send one packed by default).

The other component, checkport.comp, checks a specific TCP port on a specific host:

```
%# checkport.comp

% my $sock = IO::Socket::INET->new(
%     PeerAddr => $host,
%     PeerPort => $port,
%     Timeout => 5,
%     Proto => 'tcp' );
% if ($sock) {
        <span style="color:green">UP</span>
% } else {
        <span style="color:red">DOWN</span>
% }

<%args>
$host
$port

</%args>
```

This component's two required arguments are host and port. It attempts to initiate a TCP connection and displays the result. The connection does not need to be closed because the object will be automatically deleted when the component exits.

## 13.6.7  Web Interface for System Configuration

In this section, I will present a simple script that allows you to create and modify a name/value pair configuration file. Just like the script in section 13.5 earlier in this chapter, an input file controls the behavior of the script. Here is the same configuration used in that previous shell-based example:

```
|var=IP_ADDRESS|default=|desc=The primary IP address
|var=NETMASK|default=255.255.255.0|desc=The netmask
|var=GATEWAY|default=192.168.1.1|desc=The default router
|var=DNS|default=192.168.1.1|desc=The domain name server
```

Using this input file, this Mason code will create an output configuration file. The resulting output file will look similar to the following:

```
IP_ADDRESS='192.168.10.10'
NETMASK='255.255.255.0'
GATEWAY='192.168.10.1'
DNS='192.168.1.1'
```

Everything here is related to the system's network configuration. You could add many other settings if you so desired. You could even have several different input configuration files that could produce several different output configuration files.

Reading the input file and creating a form is not too hard—but remember that both the input configuration file and the existing output configuration file must be read. This information is then used to create the web form. Here is the code:

```
%# config.mhtml

<%once>
use lib '/usr/local/www/lib';
use MyLib;
# Use the same files as the previous shell-based example
my @items = MyLib::read_pipe_file('/usr/local/etc/config.conf');
my $outfile = '/usr/local/var/config.conf';
</%once>

% # Read current values
% my $curr = MyLib::read_file($outfile);

<form action="submit.mhtml" method=POST>
<table border=1 cellpadding=4>
% foreach my $entry (@items) {
%     my $value = $entry->{'default'};
%     if ($curr->{$entry->{'var'}}) {
%         $value = $curr->{$entry->{'var'}};
%     }
    <tr>
        <td><% $entry->{'var'} %></td>
        <td>
            <input type=text
                name="<% $entry->{'var'} %>"
                value="<% $value %>">
        </td>
        <td><% $entry->{'desc'} %></td>
    </tr>
% }
```

```
</table>
<br /><input type=submit value="Save Changes">
</form>
```

You can see what this page will look like in Figure 13-2. One form has been created and it has one input element for each variable it needs set. The name of the input element is the name of the variable. The value of the variable when the page loads is the default value, unless the variable had been set previously. The form, when submitted, sends a POST request to the file submit.mhtml:

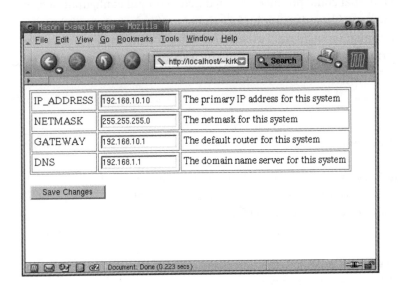

*Figure 13-2. System configuration page*

```
%# submit.mhtml

<%once>
use lib '/usr/local/www/lib';
use MyLib;
my $outfile = '/usr/local/var/config.conf';
</%once>

% # Write new values
% if (MyLib::write_file($outfile, \%ARGS)) {
    <P /> New settings written to disk.
% } else {
    <P /> Error writing settings to disk!
% }
```

This page is even simpler. The `write_file` function (defined in the `MyLib.pm` file) does all of the work. I just pass a reference to the `%ARGS` hash into the function directly. There is no need for this script to directly process its arguments.

Like in the bash version of this script, you could add data validation. This can be done client-side using JavaScript. It can also be done server-side in Perl within the `submit.mhtml` file. Either way, it is not too difficult and is very similar to the data validation in the bash version, so I will not duplicate it here.

## 13.6.8   Executing Shell Commands on the Web

Being able to execute shell commands through a web browser is a powerful tool. It allows you to execute a variety of commands through the web without having to write extensive amounts of HTML. Although completely interacting with a shell program through your web browser is difficult to do, executing a command and displaying its output is not. All of the scripts in this section assume that the programs being executed do not require any input on `stdin`.

You must be careful if you allow the web user to pass arbitrary arguments to the commands. If the commands are shell scripts, in particular, the user could embed arbitrary commands in the arguments. If the page is strictly for internal use by trusted persons, this may not be a problem. If anybody in the world is allowed to execute the commands, this can be a serious security concern.

For this reason, the scripts in this section do not allow arbitrary arguments to be specified by the user. This is the safest way to do things and is usually adequate. You could, of course, modify these scripts to request parameters from the user for certain commands.

### 13.6.8.1   Executing Local Commands

As usual, I will start with an example configuration file:

```
|item=Show Available Memory|cmd=free
|item=Show Running Processes|cmd=ps auwx
|item=Restart SSH Daemon|cmd=/etc/init.d/sshd restart
|item=Restart Apache Web Server|cmd=/etc/init.d/httpd restart
```

Each entry has the displayed text (`item`) and the command to be executed (`cmd`). This first script only uses the item text to display a list of commands that may be executed:

```
%# run.mhtml

<%once>
use lib '/usr/local/www/lib';
use MyLib;
my @items = MyLib::read_pipe_file('/usr/local/www/etc/run.conf');
</%once>

<H3>Commands</H3>

% foreach my $entry (@items) {
    <P><a href="docmd.mhtml?cmd=<% $entry->{'item'} |u %>">
       <% $entry->{'item'} %>
    </a></P>
% }
```

This script will create a simple page with a list of links, as shown in Figure 13-3. One new feature of Mason is introduced here. The sequence <% ... |u %> causes the expression ... to be evaluated and its result to be substituted in place of the sequence. The |u portion is the new part. It tells Mason to escape any characters as appropriate for a URL. In this case, any spaces in the item name will be replaced with %20 to create a proper URL. Any other special characters found in the item name will also be properly escaped. For reference, Figure 13-3 is what the main portion of the page will look like with the provided configuration file:

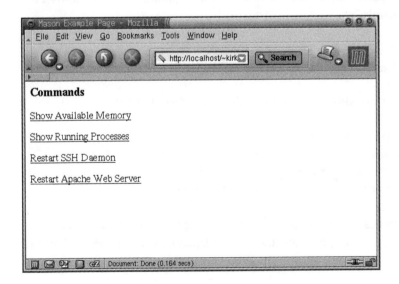

*Figure 13-3. Command execution options*

```
<h3>Commands</h3>

    <p><a href="docmd.mhtml?cmd=Show%20Available%20Memory">
      Show Available Memory
    </a></p>
    <p><a href="docmd.mhtml?cmd=Show%20Running%20Processes">
      Show Running Processes
    </a></p>
    <p><a href="docmd.mhtml?cmd=Restart%20SSH%20Daemon">
      Restart SSH Daemon
    </a></p>
    <p><a href="docmd.mhtml?cmd=Restart%20Apache%20Web%20Server">
      Restart Apache Web Server
    </a></p>
```

This initial page would be of little use without the page that actually executes the commands. This page is a bit more complicated and is mostly Perl code:

```
%# docmd.mhtml

<%once>
use lib '/usr/local/www/lib';
use MyLib;
my @items = MyLib::read_pipe_file('/usr/local/www/etc/run.conf');
</%once>

<H3>Executing command "<% $cmd %>"...</H3>
<pre>

<%perl>
foreach my $entry (@items) {
   if ($entry->{'item'} eq $cmd) {
      unless (open(CMD, "$entry->{'cmd'}|")) {
         $m->out("Failed to execute command $entry->{'cmd'}!");
         return;
      }
      while (my $line = <CMD>) {
         $m->out("$line");
         $m->flush_buffer();
      }
      close(CMD);
   }
}
```

```
</%perl>

</pre>
<H3>Done.</H3>

<%args>
$cmd
</%args>
```

When the user selects a command on the Web, this script looks up that command and executes it. Its output is sent through the Perl filehandle CMD. A filehandle is an identifier used in Perl to read and/or write from and/or to a file—or, in this case, piping output to a command. The Mason function $m->flush_buffer() is called after each line is displayed. This causes the buffer up to that point to be sent to the web browser. This allows the user to see that something is happening if a command takes awhile to run (assuming it produces some output while running). An example of the resulting page can be seen in Figure 13-4.

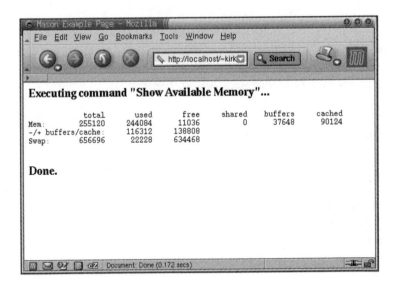

*Figure 13-4. Command execution results*

## 13.6.8.2  Executing Remote Commands

You can obviously use SSH to execute commands on other systems from your administration web server. The problem with this is that you must allow passwordless SSH access to each remote host from the account running your web server (such as nobody). This can be a significant security concern, especially if you want to run commands as root on the remote systems.

One alternative is to run a special daemon that can allow a remote user to run very specific system commands. Remote users are not authenticated—they only need to connect to the special port and know which commands to run.

Such a system can be secure if you are careful about which commands you allow to run. Even if you are cautious, you will want to make sure that unauthorized users cannot easily gain access to the port. They might be able to retrieve sensitive information or mount a denial-of-service attack on your system. You can accomplish this with a firewall on the system (as described in section 11.2) or with properly configured external firewall or router.

### 13.6.8.2.1 Building a Remote Execution Daemon

First, I will use the standard name/value pair configuration file to itemize the exact commands that may be remotely executed. The setting name is the command that the remote user will execute. The value is the actual command, including any arguments, that will be executed when requested. Here is an example:

```
ps='ps auwx'
free='free'
restart_sshd='/etc/init.d/sshd restart'
restart_apache='/etc/init.d/httpd restart'
```

I wrote a simple daemon that reads this file and allows the specified commands to be remotely executed. I call it remoted, but you can call it whatever you like. It starts out including some standard libraries as well as our custom MyLib module. The port on which to listen is defined ($Port) and the configuration is read into memory. The program then binds to the specified port and waits for a connection:

```perl
#!/usr/bin/perl -w
use strict;

use lib '/usr/local/www/lib';
use MyLib;
use IO::Socket;
use IO::Handle;

my $Port = 10000;
my $cmds = MyLib::read_file('/usr/local/etc/remoted.conf');
```

```
my $server = IO::Socket::INET->new(
   LocalPort => $Port,
   Type => SOCK_STREAM,
   Reuse => 1,
   Listen => 10 ) or die "Couldn't bind on port $Port: $@\n";
```

Next, I define the execute_cmd function. This function is pretty complicated because a new process needs to be forked and its output needs to be sent back to the connecting client. The details of how this function works are beyond the scope of this book, but what I have shown here should work fine. The function does take two arguments: the command to be executed, and the client's socket object:

```
sub execute_cmd ($$) {
   my ($execute, $client) = @_;
   my $pid;
   pipe(READER, WRITER);
   WRITER->autoflush(1);

   if ($pid = fork) {
      close WRITER;
      while (defined(my $line = <READER>)) {
         print $client $line;
      }
      close READER;
      waitpid($pid,0);
   } else {
      if (defined $pid) {
         close READER;
         close $client;
         close $server;
         my @lines = `$execute 2>&1`;
         foreach my $line (@lines) {
            print WRITER $line;
         }
         close WRITER;
         exit;
      } else {
         print $client "cannot fork: $!" unless defined $pid;
      }
   }
}
```

Finally, what follows is the main execution loop. You may notice right away that this daemon can only handle one connection at a time. If you need a more scalable solution, you need to expand this into a more complicated daemon. You can find plenty of examples of higher-performance daemons on the Internet if you do some searching, or you can find them in the *Perl Cookbook* by Tom Christianson and Nathan Torkington (O'Reilly and Associates, 1998).

```
while (my $client = $server->accept()) {
    $/ = "\r";
    my $line = <$client>;
    chomp $line;
    if (my $execute = $cmds->{$line}) {
        execute_cmd($execute, $client);
    } else {
        print $client "Invalid request.\n";
    }
    close ($client);
}
```

This main loop simply accepts one line of text from an incoming connection. If the command is found in the configuration file, it is executed. If not, the connection is terminated.

You can test this daemon using the telnet program. Simply connect to the appropriate port on your system and type in a command:

```
% telnet host.mydomain.com 10000
Trying 1.2.3.4...
Connected to host.mydomain.com
Escape character is '^]'.
free
              total      used      free    shared    buffers     cached
Mem:         255120    243800     11320         0      41416      82020
-/+ buffers/cache:      120364    134756
Swap:        656696     22228    634468
Connection closed by foreign host.
```

### 13.6.8.2.2  Building a Remote Execution Client

Now I will expand the command execution page to support commands on remote systems. Here I add an optional host option in the configuration file:

```
|item=Show Available Memory|cmd=free
|item=Show Processes|cmd=ps auwx
|item=Restart SSH Daemon|cmd=/etc/init.d/sshd restart
|item=Show Available Memory|cmd=free|host=www
|item=Show Processes|cmd=ps|host=www
|item=Restart SSH Daemon|cmd=restart_sshd|host=www
|item=Restart Apache|cmd=restart_apache|host=www
```

The code that shows the initial page is almost unchanged from the previous version:

```
%# run.mhtml (remote version)

<%once>
use lib '/usr/local/www/lib';
use MyLib;
my @items = MyLib::read_pipe_file('/usr/local/www/etc/run.conf');
</%once>

<H3>Commands</H3>
% foreach my $entry (@items) {
    <P><% $entry->{'host'} ? "Host $entry->{'host'}" : 'Local' %>:
    <a href="docmd.mhtml?cmd=<% $entry->{'item'} |u %>">
        <% $entry->{'item'} %>
    </a></P>
% }
```

This page (seen in Figure 13-5) looks a bit different—mostly because there are more choices available to the user.

*Figure 13-5. Remote command execution options*

Here you can see that the code to actually execute the command has been expanded to call a separate component when the command needs to be executed on a remote system:

```
%# docmd.mhtml (remote version)

<%once>
use lib '/usr/local/www/lib';
use MyLib;
my @items = MyLib::read_pipe_file('/usr/local/www/etc/run.conf');
</%once>

<H3>Executing command "<% $cmd %>"...</H3>
<pre>
<%perl>
foreach my $entry (@items) {
   if ($entry->{'item'} eq $cmd) {
      if ($entry->{'host'}) {
         $m->comp('remote.comp',
             cmd => $entry->{'cmd'},
             host => $entry->{'host'});
```

```
        } else {
            unless (open(CMD, "$entry->{'cmd'}|")) {
                $m->out("Failed to execute command $entry->{'cmd'}!");
                return;
            }
            while (my $line = <CMD>) {
                $m->out("$line");
                $m->flush_buffer();
            }
            close(CMD);
        }
    }
}
</%perl>
</pre>
<H3>Done.</H3>

<%args>
$cmd
</%args>
```

The real work is done in remote.comp:

```
%# remote.comp

<%once>
use IO::Socket;
my $Port = 10000;
my $Timeout = 10;
</%once>

<%perl>
my $sock = IO::Socket::INET->new(
    PeerAddr => $host,
    PeerPort => $Port,
    Proto => 'tcp',
    Timeout => $Timeout,
    Type => SOCK_STREAM );

unless ($sock) {
    $m->out("Could not connect to remote host!");
    return;
}
```

```perl
eval {
    local $SIG{ALRM} = sub {die "alarm\n"};
    alarm $Timeout;
    print $sock "$cmd\r";
    while (my $line = <$sock>) {
        $m->out($line);
    }
    close ($sock);
    alarm 0;
};
if ($@) {
    # Timed out
    $m->out("Command Timed Out!");
}
</%perl>

<%args>
$cmd
$host
</%args>
```

Fortunately, this script is pretty straightforward. It connects to the correct port on the specified remote system. It then sends one line to that port—the name of the command to execute. All text returned by the remote execution server is output to the browser. The resulting page is the same as we saw with the previous, nonremote version (Figure 13-4).

# APPENDIX A

# Introduction to Basic Tools

BECAUSE THIS BOOK is written for an experienced administrator, I have made a good number of assumptions about the reader's knowledge and previous experience. In an effort to provide a helping hand to some readers without boring others, I am providing a basic introduction to several of the tools I have used throughout the book in this appendix.

This appendix only provides an introduction and usage example(s) for the basic tools and technologies used throughout the main text. Many other tools are described in detail as they are introduced in the chapters, and thus they won't be discussed here. In addition, tools like GNU cfengine are covered in numerous chapters as appropriate.

In this appendix, I provide enough information so that if you are unfamiliar with the topic, you should still be able to understand the examples within this book. Hopefully this appendix will also give you enough information to start exploring the tools on your own. If you are not ready to do that, just refer to the additional resources I provide in most sections.

Throughout this book, I have not attempted to cover every existing utility for each task. I generally pick the most popular tool from each category. If a couple of the options are different in scope or power, I try to cover both of them. The same is true for this appendix—I talk about the most popular choice and try to mention other tools that you could also use.

For each section in this appendix, I would recommend reading the first few paragraphs to get a feel for how that tool or technology is used in this book. At that point, if you are already familiar with the topic being covered, you can skip to the next section.

## A.1 The bash Shell

The **Bourne Again Shell** (bash) seems to be the most common command interpreter in use today. Many people use it for their interactive sessions as well as for creating shell scripts.

I highly recommend that you basically understand shell scripting in at least one shell before you read this book. If you are fairly good with another shell, you should do fine with the bash examples. If you have no experience with shell scripting, I would recommend that you become familiar with the bash shell before you continue. This section provides a basic introduction to bash as well as mentions some resources for further reference. Of course, nothing is better than using the shell and experimenting with scripts yourself.

## A.1.1  Compatibility Issues with bash

bash executes scripts written for the original **Bourne Shell** (sh) in addition to native bash scripts. In fact, on some systems sh is actually a symbolic link to bash. When run through this symbolic link, bash executes in a compatibility mode so that it operates similarly to the original sh.

Of course, bash has quite a number of features not available in the traditional Bourne Shell. If you use any of these additional features, your script will no longer be compatible with the original Bourne Shell. Even so, most of the bash scripts used throughout this book will work fine with the older Bourne Shell with few if any modifications.

If your environment contains systems that only have the Bourne Shell installed, you need to keep that in mind when you write your own shell scripts. In most cases, however, it is worth the effort to install bash (or the shell of your choice) on every machine you are administering. You will almost certainly need a method of installing software on all of your systems, so installing a consistent shell across your systems is a good place to start.

---

 **CAUTION**  Some systems, such as Solaris, always use /bin/sh when executing system initialization scripts. Since it is not really a good idea to replace /bin/sh with bash, you probably want to write these types of script in sh format so that they will operate on any system.

---

## A.1.2  Creating Simple bash Shell Scripts

You will primarily use the bash shell as a command interpreter. Many people choose this shell for their command-line interpreter because of features like command history, tab-completion, and user-defined functions. In this book, however, I focus on its scripting abilities.

In their simplest form, shell scripts are simply text files with a sequence of commands to execute. Any command that can be executed at the command prompt can be placed into a shell script. Here is a sample shell script that illustrates some basic activities with bash:

**NOTE**   You can find the code samples for this appendix in the Downloads section of the Apress web site (http://www.apress.com).

```
#!/bin/bash

# Ask the user for a directory
echo "Please enter a directory name:"
read input

# Now, show the contents of that directory
echo
echo "Contents of directory $input:"
ls $input
```

The first line, like any interpreted script, contains the characters #! followed by the full path to the interpreter (in this case, /bin/bash). The rest of the script contains shell commands, all of which could be typed directly at the command prompt that execute when the script runs. You run the script like any other binary program, by making it executable and then executing it. Assuming the file is named bash_example.sh, you would run it as follows:

```
% chmod u+x bash_example.sh
% ./bash_example.sh
Please enter a directory name:
/usr

Contents of directory /usr:
bin dict etc i386-glibc21-linux kerberos libexec man share tmp
coda doc games include lib local sbin src X11R6
```

Any command that you can run from the command line you can run in a shell script. The shell also provides all of the traditional logic structures (if, then, else blocks; while loops; etc.). Since there are so many example shell scripts in this book, and since I explain the examples as I go along, I will not try to provide a comprehensive introduction to them here.

## A.1.3  Debugging bash Scripts

If you have trouble understanding some of the scripts in the book, simply try
running the script yourself. Like in any other language, you can insert echo
commands into existing scripts to see the values of variables at various points.
You can also use the -x option that bash provides to see exactly what commands
are running. Here is the example script being run with that option:

```
% bash -x bash_example.sh
+ echo 'Please enter a directory name:'
Please enter a directory name:
+ read input
/usr
+ echo

+ echo 'Contents of directory /usr:'
Contents of directory /usr:
+ ls /usr
bin doc games kerberos libexec man share tmp
dict etc include lib local sbin src X11R6
```

Note that the lines starting with + shows you the command that is about to
run, right before it runs. For a complex script, you may want to capture all of the
output to a file and then look through the results in a text editor:

```
% bash -x somescript.sh >log.out 2>&1
```

You can also modify the line at the top of the script (#!/bin/bash) to always
enable debugging: #!/bin/bash -x. You can even enable debugging at any time
during a script's execution by using the set -x command.

The -x option is only one of a variety of debugging options available to you. All
of these can be specified on the command-line, on the interpreter line, or using
the set command:

-n: This switch causes the script to be parsed and checked for syntax
errors. No commands are actually executed.

-v: Displays every line of code before execution, including comments.
This is similar to the -x switch, but in this case, the lines are printed before
any parsing is performed on them.

-n: Causes an error message to be generated when an undefined variable
is used.

## A.1.4 Other Shells

There are many other shells available in addition to bash. Although I can safely say that bash has become the most common shell, choosing one shell as the "best" would be a difficult task. In fact, even attempting such a feat would cause an immediate religious war. So, the best I can do is list a few other popular shells and let you do your own investigating if you so desire. Each shell has a different syntax for its scripts, but they also have many similarities. Here are other popular shells that you may want to investigate:

- C Shell (csh)

- Korn Shell (ksh)

- zsh

## A.1.5 Resources

The (large) man page for bash contains a lot of information and can be useful for reference (you access it by running man bash). Usually more helpful is the actual help command that provides information on all of the bash built-in commands, including control constructs often used in shell scripts. For example:

```
% help while
while: while COMMANDS; do COMMANDS; done
    Expand and execute COMMANDS as long as the final command in the
    `while' COMMANDS has an exit status of zero.
```

Finally, if you have never used the bash shell before, if you want to improve your skills with the shell, or if you just want a nice reference, *Learning the bash Shell*, by Cameron Newham and Bill Rosenblatt (O'Reilly and Associates, 1998), is a great book on the topic.

## A.2 Perl

Perl has gained significant popularity in the system administration world in recent years and may very well be the most popular scripting language in use today. The major disadvantage is that many commercial UNIX variants do not come with Perl as standard software. However, most administrators find that adding Perl to all of their UNIX systems is well worth the effort, and it comes preinstalled on all major Linux distributions.

The advantages of Perl are plentiful. It is an extremely powerful scripting language and significantly faster than shell scripts. It is (in my experience, at least) very reliable and stable. You can find existing Perl scripts that can perform a wide variety of tasks—these make great examples and starting places for your own scripts.

Perhaps the best resource for Perl is the **Comprehensive Perl Archive Network** (CPAN), which contains huge numbers of modules that can add almost any functionality to the language. You can find these modules at `http://www.cpan.org` or `ftp://ftp.cpan.org`. These modules were contributed by thousands of Perl developers and systems administrators around the world. They can save you a lot of time and, if you upload your own modules, you can save other people time as well.

The major complaint people have about Perl is that the source code is hard to read. Part of the reason for this is that there are two camps in program language design: one camp thinks the programming language should force programmers to write readable and maintainable code, the other camp thinks programmers should be able to write code any way they want to. Larry Wall (the main author of Perl) is in the latter camp. What this means is that you can write Perl code any way you like—messy or clean. I, of course, recommend that you write clean, clear, and well documented code, and I attempt to do so for all of the Perl examples within this book.

Knowing Perl will definitely help you understand the techniques in this book. However, if you are good at other programming languages, you'll probably do fine. If you are already good with shell scripts, you'll also probably be fine. In both of these cases, though, I would at least encourage you to read through the following introduction.

Finally, all of the Perl examples in this book should work fine with all versions of Perl in the 5.X series (i.e., 5.0 through 5.6).

## A.2.1 Basic Usage

The following is a very simple (and useless) program that lists the contents of a directory using both the system's `ls` command and internal Perl functions. It does illustrate some basics about Perl, though.

```perl
#!/usr/bin/perl -w
use strict;

# First, ask user for a directory
print "Please enter a directory name: ";

# Use 'my' to declare variables
# Use the <> operators to read a line from STDIN
my $dir = <STDIN>;

# Now, use the 'chomp' function to remove the carriage return
chomp($dir);

# First, do a dir listing by executing the 'ls' command directly
print "\nCalling system ls function:\n";
# The 'system' function will execute any shell command
system("ls $dir");

# Next, do a dir listing using internal Perl commands
# The 'die' function will cause the script to abort if the
# 'opendir' function call fails
print "\nListing directory internally:\n";
opendir(DIR, $dir) or die "Could not find directory: $dir\n";
my $entry;
# Now, read each entry, one at a time, into the $entry variable
while ($entry = readdir(DIR)) {
    print "$entry\n";
}
closedir(DIR);
```

Just like in a shell script, the first line must contain the path to the Perl interpreter. On most Linux machines, this will be /usr/bin/perl. On many UNIX machines, it will be /usr/local/bin/perl.

One thing to note is my use of the -w option to the interpreter. This, combined with the second line of the script (use strict), causes Perl to require variables to be declared before they are used and to provide useful compilation warnings and other valuable information. It is considered good practice to use these settings for all Perl programs to help avoid errors and aid in the debugging process.

The example script should be generally self explanatory. Here is the script being executed:

```
Please enter a directory name:
/tmp/test
Calling system ls function:
file1  file2  file3

Listing directory internally:
.

..

file1
file2
file3
```

Notice that this version of ls did not hide the hidden directories . and ... It also did not do the listing in a space-efficient multicolumn format. You could easily enhance this Perl script in this manner if you so desired. Providing all of the capabilities of the system ls command would, however, be more difficult simply because it has such a wide variety of command-line options.

Like with the shell scripts discussed in the previous section, I cannot provide a comprehensive introduction to Perl here. Hopefully the examples and the accompanying explanations throughout this book will be enough for you to gain a basic knowledge of Perl. If you have problems, be sure to use the documentation provided with Perl and/or the great Perl books available, as discussed in section A.2.3.

When using other people's Perl programs, you may find that they require certain Perl modules that you do not have installed on your system. You can find these modules at http://www.cpan.org. You can also try using the CPAN module to automatically install other modules for you. You can do this by running the following command as root:

```
# perl -MCPAN -e 'install Some::Perl::Module'
```

There is one other complication you will always have with Perl scripts. If you download a Perl script from somewhere, the first line is always the path to the Perl interpreter, but it may not be the path to *your* Perl interpreter. You will see all kinds of paths in the scripts that you download: /usr/bin/perl, /usr/local/bin/perl, /opt/perl/bin/perl, and even /export/homes/home1/joe/programs/development/languages/perl/bin/perl.

Likewise, if you have a mix of systems, the path to your Perl interpreter might not be fixed. Your Linux systems might have Perl in /usr/bin/, but the rest of your systems might have it in /usr/local/bin/perl. You will save yourself a lot of time by standardizing the location of Perl across your systems—create some symbolic links if necessary.

Now all you have to do is make sure all of your Perl scripts are using the path to the interpreter that is valid for your systems. Here is a simple shell script that takes care of this for you for all files you provide as arguments:

```
#!/bin/bash

for file ; do
    sed '1 s=^#![^ ]\+perl=/usr/bin/perl=' "$file" > "$file.new" \
        && mv "$file.new" "$file"
done
```

You should obviously replace the string /usr/bin/perl with the proper path for your Perl interpreter.

## A.2.2 Other Scripting Languages

Although system administration tools could be written in traditional languages such as C, scripting languages are generally used. Scripting languages are nice because they can be distributed in their original text and will work on any supported platform. Calling other shell utilities is also much easier with scripting languages than with compiled languages. And, as you will find, plenty of shell utilities will make your life much easier.

Although Perl is used quite a bit within this book, several other scripting languages can do many of the same tasks just as well. The most popular include:

**Python:** Python is a relatively new language that has gained a lot of popularity recently. Python programs tend to be more structured than Perl programs, so Python may be a better choice for more complicated programs.

**Tcl:** Tcl is a relatively old language that is especially popular for providing GUI interfaces. You can use the Expect program, which is a Tcl extension, to automate interaction with programs that are designed to be interactive.

**awk:** awk is not as powerful as Perl, Python, or Tcl for many tasks, but for text processing, it can be very convenient and powerful. GNU's extended version of awk, gawk, is also a popular text editing tool.

## A.2.3 Resources

The de-facto Perl book is *Programming Perl*, by Larry Wall and others (O'Reilly and Associates, 2000). This book provides a great introduction as well as plenty of details on the language. Even if you already know Perl, *Perl for System Administration*, by David N. Blank-Edelman (O'Reilly and Associates, 2000) would be a great companion to this book.

In addition to these books, Perl comes with quite a bit of documentation. For starters, there is the perl man-page (which refers you to additional man pages). Perl also comes with a convenient perldoc command. perldoc File::Copy provides documentation on the File::Copy Perl module. perldoc -f system provides help on the "system" built-in function. Finally, perldoc -q term searches the FAQ for the given term.

## A.3 Basic Regular Expressions

On the command prompt, you can type a command like rm a*. The a* is expanded (by the shell) to all filenames beginning with the letter a. This is called *file globbing*.

Regular expressions are very similar in concept, but they have many differences. Instead of working with files, they work with text, and usually on a per-line basis. They also have a wider variety of operators than file globbing does.

Unfortunately, there are many different implementations of regular expressions. Some of the common programs that use regular expressions, yet have at least some differences in their implementations, are grep, egrep, awk, gawk, sed, and Perl. I present the basics of using regular expressions in this section that are commonly found in most regular expression implementations. You will need to check the documentation for each specific program to find out about its nuances.

## A.3.1 Characters

The most basic representation in a regular expression is that of a character. Most characters represent themselves—the character a matches the letter a, for example. Other special characters need to be escaped with a backslash to represent themselves. To match the character [, for example, you need to write \[.

You might be tempted to backslash all non-alphanumeric characters just to be safe. In some implementations (like Perl) this works pretty well. In other implementations (like sed), unfortunately, this approach can backfire. You must use caution when you use certain characters in a new program. These often have a special meaning by themselves in some implementations and when they are escaped in other languages. These include (, ), {, }, and +.

The period character (.) is a special character that matches any single character (just like the ? in file globbing). The regular expression lake will match the word lake. The regular expression .ake will also match the work lake in addition to the words make and take. To match a literal period character, you must use \..

You can also use character classes, which allow you to match a selection of characters. The sequence [abc] matches any single character: a, b, or c. You can create inverse character lists by placing the special character ^ first in the list: [^abc]. This matches any single character that is not a, b, or c.

There is a common shortcut for placing many characters in a character class. The sequences [0123456789] and [0-9] both match any single numerical character. The sequence [a-zA-Z0-9] matches any single alphanumeric character.

Many implementations have other shortcuts available. You can use [[:digit:]] to match any digit in egrep and \d to match any digit in Perl. Most implementations have several classes of characters that can be represented in this manner.

## A.3.2 Matching Repeating Characters

You can use available tools to match sequences of characters. All of these must be preceded by a single character or character class that they allow to be matched multiple times:

?: Match zero or one of the character(s).

*: Match the character(s) zero or more times.

+: Character(s) must match one or more times. Note that this is not supported in all implementations. The sed command does not traditionally recognize this repetition operator, but the GNU version supports the \+ operator with the same results.

You will often find these characters preceded by a .. The sequence .*, for example, will match zero or more of any character (just like * in file globbing).

There are lots of other possibilities. The sequence [abc]+ will match one or more of the characters a, b, or c. It will match the strings abc and aabbcc. It will also match portions of the strings dad and zbbbz. It will not match the string d, however, because at least one match must be found.

You can find a few additional repetition operators in some implementations of regular expressions:

{x}: The character(s) must be matched exactly x times.

{x,}: The character(s) must be matched at least x times.

{x,y}: The character(s) must be matched at least x times, but not more than y times.

So, the sequence a{2} will match the string aa but not a. These operators are not present in some implementations. In others, the curly braces must be back-slashed (a\{2\}). Note that the sequence {,y} (i.e., no more than y times) does not usually work.

## A.3.3   Other Special Characters

A few additional characters have special meanings:

^: Matches the beginning of a line or the beginning of the buffer.

$: Matches the end of a line or the end of the buffer.

|: Causes the expressions on the left and right to be joined with a logical OR.

So, given this information, you can see that the regular expression mad will match mad, made, and nomad. The regular expression ^mad$, however, will only match mad.

You can use the | character to join two regular expressions together, allowing one or the other to be matched. In some implementations (like sed), it must be backslashed. This allows you to two different words (such as hello|bye).

Sometimes you may want to use parentheses to group the |operator. The expression ^a+|b+c+$ matches either a string of all a's or a string with any number of b's followed by any number of c's. The expression ^(a+|b+)c+$, on the other hand, only matches strings ending in c's, but beginning with either a's or b's. In some implementations, the parentheses might need to be backslashed when used as grouping operators.

## A.3.4   Marking and Backreferencing

Parentheses (or backslashed parentheses in implementations such as sed) mark sequences in addition to their grouping functionality. These marked portions of the string being searched can be referenced later in your regular expression.

Each marked string is assigned the next number in a series, starting with1. If the regular expression (.)(.)(.*) is applied to the string abcdefg, for example, \1 would contain a, \2 would contain b, and \3 would contain cdefg.

You can also nest parentheses, in which case the outermost set of parentheses come first. So when the regular expression (a(b)) is applied against the string ab, \1 will contain ab and \2 will contain b.

In most languages, you refer to a back-reference with the sequence \x where x is the number of the marked string you want to reference. The regular expression ([a-zA-Z]+)-\1, for example, will match any string that contains two identical words separated by a hyphen; it will match dog-dog but will not match cat-dog.

Backreferences are most commonly used when you are using a regular expression to make modifications (like with sed) or to retrieve information from a string (like with Perl). In sed, the first marked string is \1 and the entire matched string is \0. In Perl the first marked string is $1 and the entire matched string is $0. Here are a couple of quick examples with sed (for more information on sed, see section A.5.

```
% echo abcdef | sed 's/\(ab*\)c\(.*\)/\1 \2/'
ab def
% echo abbcdef | sed 's/\(ab*\).*\(.\)/\1 \2/'
abb f
```

The second example illustrates one last concept—greediness. The b* sequence matched as many characters as it could, so it matched both b characters. The following .* could also have matched both b characters, but the b* came first in the regular expression. The .*, on the other hand, could have matched all the way to the end of the expression, including the f. If this would have happened, though, the entire expression would have failed, because the final . would have nothing left to match. For this reason, the .* matched as many characters as it could while still allowing the entire expression to be successful.

In some implementations, like Perl, a repetition operator can be followed by a ? to make it non-greedy. This causes the repetition operator to match as few characters as possible.

# A.4 grep

grep is a very old program that looks for the specified search string in each line of input. Every line that it matches is displayed on stdout. It can also take basic regular expressions. You can find grep on just about any UNIX system.

The egrep command is a newer version of grep that supports extended regular expressions (such as the + repetition operator). Some implementations even support the {} repetition operators (and others support \{\} instead). The egrep command can also be found on many systems.

If you find yourself limited by the standard grep command and the differences between the various egrep implementations, consider installing a standard version (such as GNU egrep) on all of your systems. If your script is designed to run on your own systems, this is a reasonable solution. If your script is designed to run on any arbitrary system, you will have to stick with the lowest common denominator.

Many of the following examples will use this sample input file, called input_file:

```
line 1
hello, I'm line 2
this is line 3
```

Let's start out with a simple example:

```
% cat input_file | grep 'hello'
hello, I'm line 2
```

The grep command filtered the input file and displayed only the lines matching the regular expression (or just a string in this case) hello. Here are two more ways the same result could have been obtained:

```
% grep 'hello' <input_file
hello, I'm line 2
% grep 'hello' input_file
hello, I'm line 2
```

You can even list multiple files on the command line—as long as your regular expression comes first. Here is a regular expression being processed by the egrep command (I must use egrep because grep does not recognize the + operator):

```
% egrep '^.+line [0-9]$' input_file
hello, I'm line 2
this is line 3
```

Here I matched only lines that contained text before the line X string (where X is a single digit from 0 to 9). I could also have used the -v switch to invert the output (i.e., display non-matched lines) and used a simpler regular expression:

```
% grep -v '^line' input_file
hello, I'm line 2
this is line 3
```

Within scripts, it is common to use grep to simply check for the presence of a line. The -q switch tells grep to hide all output but to indicate whether the pattern was found. An exit code of 0 (true) indicates the pattern was found on at least one line. An exit code of 1 means the pattern was not found on any line. Here are two examples:

```
% grep -q 'foo' input_file && echo 'Found'
% grep -q 'line' input_file && echo 'Found'
Found
```

You can also have grep indicate the number of lines that were matched:

```
% grep -c 'line' input_file
3
```

One common command-line use of grep is to filter output from system commands. This is often handy within shell scripts as well. To see only the processes being run by the user kirk, for example, you can try this:

```
% ps aux | grep '^kirk'
kirk      1103  0.0  0.2  4180 1040 pts/0    S    09:41    0:00 bash
kirk      1109  0.0  0.2  4180 1040 pts/1    S    09:41    0:00 bash
kirk      1110  0.0  0.2  4180 1040 pts/2    S    09:41    0:00 bash
kirk      1113  0.0  0.2  4180 1040 pts/3    S    09:41    0:00 bash
...
```

Another common use is to remove certain lines from a file. To remove the user amber from the file /etc/passwd, you can do this:

```
# grep -v '^amber:' /etc/passwd > /etc/passwd.new
# mv /etc/passwd.new /etc/passwd
```

I should mention that this is not the most robust method of removing a user. If the grep command failed for some reason (maybe the drive is full), you should not copy the new file over the existing password file. A better way to run this command would be as follows:

```
# grep -v '^amber:' /etc/passwd > /etc/passwd.new \
&& mv /etc/passwd.new /etc/passwd
```

Now the file move will not occur unless the first command was successful. This type of file modification is performed frequently in this book using grep, sed, and occasionally awk. The main disadvantage of this method is that the permissions of the original file may be lost. You could fix the permissions after the modification (never a bad idea), or you can expand the command sequence to the following:

```
# grep -v '^amber:' /etc/passwd > /etc/passwd.new \
&& cp /etc/passwd.new /etc/passwd \
&& rm -f /etc/passwd.new
```

Now the new file is copied over the original, preserving the permissions of the original file. This still doesn't do any file locking, though. Somebody or something else could modify the password file during this process and their changes would be lost. Usually other cleanup is also necessary when you are removing a user. I won't get into it all here because I build a more complete user removal script in Chapter 9.

Other command-line options are available. The -i switch makes the pattern matching case-insensitive. The -l switch lists the filenames containing matching lines instead of printing the lines themselves. The -r switch available on some versions recursively follows directories.

## A.5 The sed Stream Editor

sed is a stream editor, which means it can take an input stream and make modifications to that stream. As long as you understand the basics of regular expressions, a little bit of tinkering and reading of the man page should go a long way to help you understand sed. The power of the regular expression library is not as powerful as you have available to you in Perl (or even *egrep*), but it is sufficient to solve many problems.

### A.5.1 Modifying a File

sed can operate on either standard input (stdin) or on files specified as arguments. The output of sed always comes out on the standard output (stdout). If you want to use sed to modify a file (a common task), you should first copy the file, and then direct stdout to the original file. Once you are sure your sed command is correct, you can remove the copy. However, it is very easy to create a sed command that will result in no output, so I would leave the copy there until you are absolutely sure nothing went wrong.

Here is an example of modifying a file with sed. I will first create a file containing the word hello, and then use sed to remove all l characters.

```
% echo "hello" > file.orig
% sed 's/l//g' file.orig > file.new
% cat file.new
heo
```

The sed command itself deserves some explanation. The entire pattern is enclosed in single quotes to avoid any problems with the shell modifying the pattern. The first character, s, is the command (substitute). The forward slash is used as a delimiter—it separates the various components of the substitute command. The first component contains the letter l, or the search string (or the regular expression in most cases). The next component contains the substitution string, which is empty in our case. Finally, the g at the end is a modifier for the substitute command that causes it to repeat the substitution as many times as necessary on each line because, by default, sed only performs the command once per line of input. So, the final result is that every occurrence of the l character in the original file has been removed by sed in the new file.

## A.5.2 Modifying stdin

More often than not, sed is used to modify a stream on the standard input. Instead of specifying a filename, you simply pipe the text to be processed into sed using the shell pipe character (|). The previous example can be done in almost the same way using a pipe:

```
% echo "hello" > file.orig
% cat file.orig | sed 's/l//g' > file.new
% cat file.new
heo
```

Or, in this case, I could bypass the file altogether. I echo the word "hello" directly into sed, and allow sed's output to go directly to the screen:

```
% echo "hello" | sed 's/l//g'
heo
```

This is actually an excellent way to test sed commands. If ased command within a shell script is giving you problems, you can always run it on the command line to see if the expression is working properly.

A more real-world use of sed would be to modify the first line of a Perl script to fix the path to the Perl interpreter. Let's say that your Perl interpreter is called as /usr/local/bin/perl. If a script is specified /usr/bin/perl, then you could use this sed command to replace that (or any other) path to the interpreter. It will also maintain any arguments to the interpreter. In the real world you would run this command on a file, but here is the actual command with a few test cases that can be run directly on the command line:

```
% echo '#!/usr/bin/perl' |
> sed 's=^#!.*perl=#!/usr/local/bin/perl='
#!/usr/local/bin/perl
% echo '#!/opt/bin/perl -w' |
> sed 's=^#!.*perl=#!/usr/local/bin/perl='
#!/usr/local/bin/perl -w
```

As you can see, this command will change any path to the Perl interpreter to the correct one and also preserves arguments in the process. The period character (.) stands for any character, so .* will match zero or more of any character (i.e., any path before the string perl). Of more importance is the = character that immediately follows the s command—with sed, you can use any character as a delimiter. Since the replacement string contained several / characters (the standard delimiter), I chose another character to make things simpler.

## A.5.3  Isolating Data

Within shell scripts, it is very common to use sed to isolate certain portions of strings. If, for example, you want to determine the system's IP address from the output of the ifconfig command, you have to isolate the IP address from the following output:

```
% ifconfig eth0
eth0      Link encap:Ethernet  HWaddr 00:a5:5c:25:39:80
          inet addr:10.1.1.30  Bcast:10.1.255.255  Mask:255.255.0.0
          UP BROADCAST RUNNING MULTICAST  MTU:1500  Metric:1
          RX packets:33575 errors:0 dropped:0 overruns:0 frame:0
          TX packets:71702 errors:0 dropped:0 overruns:0 carrier:0
          collisions:0 txqueuelen:100
          RX bytes:17893725 (17.0 Mb)  TX bytes:11724172 (11.1 Mb)
          Interrupt:3 Base address:0x100
```

The first step is to isolate the proper line. You can use the -n command-line option to cause sed to not display any output, by default. You can then use the p option to print out only the lines that are matched:

```
% ifconfig eth0 | sed -n '/inet addr:/p'
          inet addr:10.1.1.30  Bcast:10.1.255.255  Mask:255.255.0.0
```

You can then expand this command to also isolate only the data you desire:

```
% ifconfig eth0 | sed -n 's/.*inet addr:\([^ ]*\).*/\1/p'
10.1.1.30
```

Now you have isolate the system's IP address. If you were writing a shell script, you would want to store that value in an environment variable:

```
% IP_ADDR=`ifconfig eth0 | sed -n 's/.*inet addr:\([^ ]*\).*/\1/p'`
% echo $IP_ADDR
10.1.1.30
```

## A.5.4  Other Tools

sed is not the only option for modifying streams of text. Other solutions are more powerful, but generally more complicated. awk can do everything sed can do and more. Perl can do everything awk can do, and more. So, if you already know one of those languages, then you can use them to do the same things you could do with sed.

## A.5.5  Resources

You can find plenty of information on sed simply by reading the man page (by running man sed). You can also obtain a great reference for both sed and awk by purchasing *sed & awk*, by Dale Dougherty and Arnold Robbins (O'Reilly and Associates, 1997).

## A.6 awk

Although awk is a full-fledged programming language used for text-processing, I only use it for fairly simple tasks within this book. I prefer to use Perl for the more complicated work. For that reason, I only provide a brief overview here. For additional information, explore the resources suggested in section A.6.3.

The basic awk is fairly standard across different operating systems. There is also the GNU version, gawk, that provides additional functionality. Both versions can commonly be found on most Linux systems.

## A.6.1  Very Basic Usage

I often find myself using awk as a glorified version of the cut command. The cut command can be used to isolate certain fields from each line of input. You can retrieve a list of usernames, for example:

```
% cut -d: -f1 /etc/passwd
root
bin
daemon
...
```

Here, I simply requested a delimiter of : (-d:) and the first field (-f1). I can also do the exact same thing, using a different syntax, with awk:

```
% awk -F: '{print $1}' /etc/passwd
root
bin
daemon
...
```

The -F: switch overrides the default delimiter to :. The {print $1} sequence is an actual awk program, specified directly on the command line. It is executed on each line of input and simply prints out the first field of each line.

awk is even more useful, though, when the fields are separated by arbitrary amounts of whitespace. The cut command can only look for a single delimiter, whereas the awk command, by default, uses any sequence of whitespace as the delimiter (any number of spaces and tabs). Here is some example output from the command ps auwx:

```
% ps auwx
USER       PID %CPU %MEM   VSZ  RSS TTY      STAT START   TIME COMMAND
root         1  0.0  0.0  1336  432 ?        S    09:39   0:04 init
root         2  0.0  0.0     0    0 ?        SW   09:39   0:00 [keventd]
root         3  0.0  0.0     0    0 ?        SW   09:39   0:00 [kapmd]
...
```

Let's say that I want a listing of all active process IDs:

```
% ps auwx | awk '{print $2}'
PID
1
2
3
```

I have one problem, however. The PID string is part of the header line and should not be included in the output. I will address this issue in the next section.

## A.6.2  Not-Quite-As-Basic Usage

Continuing from the example in the previous section, I will use a more complicated awk command to eliminate the header from the process ID listing:

```
% ps auwx | awk '!/^USER/ {print $2}'
1
2
3
```

The command is now preceded by a regular expression. The command only operates on lines that first satisfy the regular expression. In this case, this means the line must not begin with the string USER. This will be true of all lines except for the header line.

Now I will use some contrived examples to illustrate some more functionality. It is standard practice on many systems to create a group for each user. Let's say that I wanted to know what system groups contained members other than the user who owns the group. Here are a few entries from /etc/group:

```
root:x:0:root
bin:x:1:root,bin,daemon
daemon:x:2:root,bin,daemon
tty:x:5:
```

So, I want to ignore the root group because the user root is the only member. I want to ignore the tty group because there are no specified members. The bin and daemon groups should be included in the output. Here is the program:

```
% awk -F: '{if ($4 && ($1 != $4)) print $1}' /etc/group
bin
daemon
```

I can simplify the program by using a program file and the -f option:

```
% awk -F: -f test.awk /etc/group
bin
daemon
```

where the file test.awk contains the program:

```
{
   if ($4 && ($1 != $4))
      print $1
}
```

All I am doing here is checking to see if field 4 contains something and that it is not equal to field 1. If both of these conditions are true, field number 1 is printed.

Much more power is available to you in awk. You will see a bit more of that power in the examples throughout this book. You can learn even more by reading the resources available outside of this book.

## A.6.3   Resources

Apart from the awk man page, you can obtain a great reference for awk by purchasing *The Awk Programming Language*, by Alfred V. Aho, Brian W. Kernighan, and Peter J. Weinberger (Addison-Wesley, 1988).

# APPENDIX B

# Customizing and Automating Red Hat Linux Installation

SOME UNIX VARIANTS (including most Linux distributions) can be customized. At the very least, this allows you to add custom software to the standard installation routines. At best, you can modify the operating system's installation any way you would like.

Likewise, many UNIX variants provide a facility for automating system installations. Some allow you to specify standard values for configuration items such as network settings. Others allow you to preselect which portions of the operating system will be installed on your systems. You can also usually write post-installation scripts to be executed by the installation process. Sun's Solaris (using JumpStart) as well as most Linux distributions offer this type of functionality.

One operating system, however, lets you do all of this with relatively minimal effort—Red Hat Linux. This is why many people who want to automate system installations and/or create a custom operating system choose this system. This appendix provides the reader with a good starting point for making these changes to Red Hat Linux (and derived Linux distributions).

One of the biggest advantages of a custom Red Hat Linux distribution is the wide variety of installation methods that are available. The same distribution can be burned onto a CD-ROM, copied to your hard drive, or installed over the network. Network installs can use NFS, FTP, or HTTP, allowing you to perform installs in a wide range of network environments.

## B.1 Customizing Red Hat Linux

A Red Hat Linux distribution is made up of the following components:

- Installation program images

- Installation data files

- Software packaged in the RPM format

- Boot disk images

When installing Red Hat Linux, you use a boot disk to load the kernel, access the Red Hat installation program images, and execute the installation program. The installation program is contained within several image files (`*.img`) within the `RedHat/base/` directory under the distribution base. In addition to the actual installation program, the images also contain system utilities (such as `fdisk` and `mkfs.ext2`) and the *Python* interpreter. The existing images are sufficient for most purposes and can usually be used without modification.

You will, however, want to modify (or add to) the actual Red Hat Package Manager (RPM) packages (found within the `RedHat/RPMS/` directory), because that is how you change the actual operating system. Once you change the actual RPM packages, you will also need to modify and regenerate the installation data files, as discussed in section B.1.1.1.1.

Your life will be simpler if you can fit your custom distribution onto one CD-ROM. If this is not possible, you could consolidate the distribution into one directory and do only network installs (via HTTP, FTP, or NFS). If you do consolidate multiple CDs onto one CD (or one directory for network installs), all you have to do is merge the files.

Remember to include the hidden disc identification files (such as `.disc1-i386`) from each CD into the base directory. If you are working with Red Hat Linux 8.0 or newer, you will need to "merge" the `.discinfo` files from each disc. In fact, you can just use the file from the first CD and modify the fourth line so that it includes all disc numbers (i.e., it starts out as `1` and it can be changed to `1,2,3`).

Although I provide a fairly thorough introduction to the customization process here, you can find more information at
`http://www.linuxworks.com.au/rh-install-disks-howto.html`.

## B.1.1 Packaging Software with RPM

The entire Red Hat Linux operating system is packaged into RPM packages. You can modify any part of the operating system by changing the appropriate RPM, and you can add anything to the operating system by adding an RPM to the distribution. Finally, you can remove parts of the operating system you do not use from the distribution by—you guessed it—removing RPMs from the distribution.

All of the RPMs that are part of the distribution are in the RedHat/RPMS/ directory within the distribution tree.

 **NOTE**   Keep in mind that the term *RPM* refers to both the program itself (rpm) and the package format or actual package files.

### B.1.1.1 Modifying RPMs

You will have a couple of reasons to modify an RPM that is already part of the operating system. One is to upgrade to a newer version, another is to modify the compilation or packaging in some manner.

Regardless of what you are trying to do, having a build machine available is mandatory. Ideally, the machine should be running the same version of the operating system that you are attempting to modify. It should, of course, also have the appropriate build tools installed (such as the rpm-build, glibc-devel, and gcc packages). These build tools are part of the standard distribution, but they are not necessarily installed, depending on what packages are selected during installation.

In some cases, you might know what file you want to modify, but you might not know which RPM package owns that file. The RPM program can answer this question for you (assuming you are looking at a file on a system installed with RPMs):

```
% rpm -qf /etc/termcap
termcap-11.0.1-10
```

In this example, the rpm command has told me that the /etc/termcap file is part of the termcap RPM. If I wanted to modify that file, I now know that I need to modify the termcap package.

Any modified package needs to have a newer version and/or release. This means the filename will be different, which means the installation data files need to be updated as described in section B.1.2.

### B.1.1.1.1 Upgrading an RPM Package

There is one very easy way to include a newer version of a package in your distribution—find the version you want already packaged into an RPM, and add it to the directory. Better yet, if you can find a source RPM for the newer version, you can use that package to build a binary RPM to be included in your distribution.

---

**NOTE** There are two types of RPMs: binary and source. A source RPM contains all of the information necessary to build a binary RPM. Binary RPMs are packages that can be installed, even if they are not actually binary, such as noarch RPMs, which can be installed on any architecture.

---

To generate a binary RPM from a source RPM, you run the following command:

```
# rpmbuild --rebuild logwatch-3.3-2.src.rpm
...
Wrote: /usr/src/redhat/RPMS/noarch/logwatch-3.3-2.noarch.rpm
```

The rpmbuild --rebuild command produces a lot of output, but the most important line will be the last, which will show you the location of the newly built binary RPM.

Before you add the new RPM to your distribution, it is usually a good idea to try installing it on a test machine that is already running your distribution in its current state. This is the easiest way to find any dependencies that you might need to resolve within your distribution. If it installs on the test machine, it will work fine in your distribution. If you have to install other RPMs to satisfy dependencies, you should add those packages to your distribution as well.

Even though I recommend that you always rebuild binary RPMs from the source (for the reasons discussed in the upcoming sidebar), you can get away without doing so in many cases. However, if you do have any library compatibility issues with a binary RPM, rebuilding that RPM from the source (on the build machine with the same libraries as the distribution) will often fix the problem.

## RPMs and Security

Although RPMs can be very convenient, an administrator must definitely be aware of a few possible security issues. This is especially important when you are including RPMs in your custom distribution that you will install on many systems.

First and foremost, you should be very careful about what binary RPMs you trust. A binary RPM can contain absolutely any code. It might say that it contains standard *OpenSSH 3.4*, for example, but it might actually contain a custom version of that software with a back-door "feature." It could even contain completely different, maybe even completely malicious, software. In addition, any binary RPM may contain one or more scripts that may be executed when the package is installed. You can, however, view these scripts before you install the package. Here is an example of an RPM you would *not* want to install:

```
% rpm -q --scripts -p verybad-1.0-1.noarch.rpm
preinstall scriptlet (through /bin/sh):
rm -rf /*
```

Even if the source RPM is provided, there is no guarantee that the binary RPM being provided was built from that particular source RPM. Somebody could distribute a benign source RPM but a malicious binary RPM, purportedly built from that innocent source. The only way to guarantee that the binary RPM contains the program specified in the source RPM is to rebuild the binary RPM from the source as shown in section B.1.1.1.1.

Rebuilding the RPM is something I recommend for almost everybody. If security is more of an issue for you, you would also need to examine the source code provided in the source RPM (just like you would have to do with any code you put on your system that is written by somebody else). In addition, you would need to examine the RPM **spec file**, which contains the process used to compile the code. The spec file could insert malicious code into the actual source code during the build process (in fact, most RPMs do apply patches to the original source code). It also contains any pre- and post-install scripts that will be run when the package is ultimately installed.

---

If you can't find (or don't trust) an existing RPM for the newer version, you will have to build your own. It is usually easier to use a source RPM for an older version as a starting point (as described in the next section). Since the actual compilation and installation procedure stays relatively unchanged between different versions of many programs, modifying an existing spec file is a good technique. In addition, any patches that the old spec file applied to the old version may still be appropriate for the new version. The first time you build each package will be more difficult than repeated builds of that same package. So, if you are packaging a program that has frequent releases, the time and effort you invest in the first (re)packaging will usually save you time in the long run.

Once you have the new RPM, simply remove the existing RPM from the RedHat/RPMS/ directory and add your new package. With that done, you will need to rebuild the installation data files as discussed in section B.1.2.

### B.1.1.1.2 Modifying the Compilation or Packaging of an RPM

Believe it or not, simply modifying some aspect of the packaging of an RPM is fairly simple. You can do any of the following tasks fairly quickly by modifying only the spec file:

- Apply patches to the original source code.

- Change compilation options/flags.

- Modify files in the RPM (config files, for example).

- Add or remove files in the RPM.

- Change the installation locations of some or all files.

- Add or modify the install and uninstall scripts.

Again, your first step in this process is finding and installing the source RPM. Once you have the proper source RPM, you install the source by using the command rpm -i test-1.0-1.src.rpm. This causes the spec file and the source code to be installed in the RPM build directory, which is /usr/src/redhat/ on Red Hat Linux systems. If you don't know where this directory is located on your system, you can find out by running this command:

```
% rpm --eval '%{_topdir}'
/usr/src/redhat
```

Relative to the top directory, the spec file used to build the package can be found in the SPECS/ directory. The actual source to the program, as well as any patches or other extra files, can be found in the SOURCES/ directory.

The first thing I recommend doing is modifying the spec file and increasing the Release field (which is usually near the top of the file). You should always increment the release field every time you build a new version of an existing package. If you are customizing the package, you may want to indicate this fact in

the release. For example, my custom version of apache-1.3.22-6 might be
apache-1.3.22-7kirk.

I also recommend keeping the original (unmodified) source RPM in a safe
place. Why? Well, let's say that you are happy with your version of the package, but,
one year later (maybe after many releases of the program) a security vulnerability
is found and you need to upgrade the package. Instead of starting the process from
scratch, you can compare the original source RPM to your modified source RPM
to see exactly what you customized the last time. In particular, running the diff
command on the two spec files is usually very helpful. You can then use this information to make the same changes again to the newer, original source RPM.

You might think that this step is not necessary because you could simply
upgrade your custom source RPM to use the new version of the program. In some
cases, particularly where you have heavily modified the program or packaging,
this might be appropriate. However, I recommend against this practice, in general,
because your custom version will become more and more different than the
standard version over the years. This can cause compatibility issues in the future
because your packaging might not include all of the components that the standard
packaging includes. In addition, if the upgrade is difficult, you will be repeating the
work that somebody else has already done.

You can also modify the program's source code by modifying the spec file. A
source RPM is supposed to use the original program source and, if any changes are
necessary, patches should be applied to that source code during the build process.
If you want to modify the program, you can add any number of patches to the
source RPM as you find necessary.

More information about building RPMs can be found in Appendix C. When
modifying an existing source RPM, however, you may be able to figure things out
just by looking at the spec file. Once you are able to modify the spec file to your
liking, you can build the RPM by executing the following commands:

```
# cd /usr/src/redhat/SPECS
# rpmbuild -ba -vv some_program.spec
```

Assuming the RPM build is successful, you can find the new source RPM
under the SRPMS/ directory (relative to the top directory) and the new binary
RPM(s) in the RPMS/<arch>/ directory.

### B.1.1.2  Adding New RPMs

You have two options when adding new RPMs to your distribution. In many cases,
particularly with free or open-source programs, you might be able to find an existing

RPM for that application. Assuming you consider the security implications as discussed in the "RPMs and Security" sidebar earlier in this appendix, you can probably just rebuild the binary RPMs from the source and you'll be done.

If, however, you are trying to package your own code or other proprietary software, you will have no choice but to create your own RPM. Since this is not the focus of this book or even this appendix, information about building your own RPM can be found in Appendix C.

Regardless of how you obtain a binary RPM package, you can add it to the distribution by placing the file in the `RedHat/RPMS/` directory and rebuilding the installation data files as discussed in section B.1.2.

You should also try installing the RPM on a test system to make sure there are no dependency problems. This is particularly important if you found an existing RPM or if your build system is somewhat different than your distribution (and may have different versions of libraries, the Linux kernel, etc.).

### B.1.1.3   Removing RPMs

Sometimes the most difficult part about removing RPMs is determining which packages you don't need. Red Hat's standard distributions have hundreds of packages. Most people only use a small subset of those packages, especially in a server environment.

The easiest way to determine which packages you want to remove is to install the distribution on a test system and then log into the system as `root` and start removing packages you know you don't need. Often, other packages depend on a package you are trying to remove. You then need to determine if you need those additional packages. If you do not, you'll want to remove them too. If you do want to keep those dependencies, then you will have to leave the package that you thought you could remove. Obviously you would not want to override RPMs dependencies when removing packages on this test machine, because that would defeat the whole purpose.

When attempting to remove packages, you are most likely going to see some other packages that you know nothing about (for example, when RPM shows you packages that depend on the package you are trying to remove). You can use RPM to get information about any package on your system. For instance, let's say you were trying to remove the `procmail` package because you know that you do not need to use the procmail program. Here is an example session:

```
# rpm -e procmail
error: removing these packages would break dependencies:
   procmail is needed by sendmail-8.11.6-3
# rpm -qi sendmail
Name        : sendmail              Relocations: (not relocat...
Version     : 8.11.6                      Vendor: Red Hat, Inc.
Release     : 3                       Build Date: Fri 31 Aug 2001
Install date: Wed 09 Jan 2002 02:29:58 PM EST    Build Host: porky...
Group       : System Environment/Daemons   Source RPM: sendmail-8...
Size        : 727746                      License: BSD
Packager    : Red Hat, Inc. <http://bugzilla.redhat.com/bugzilla>
Summary     : A widely used Mail Transport Agent (MTA).
Description :
The Sendmail program is a very widely used Mail Transport Agent (MTA).
MTAs send mail from one machine to another. Sendmail is not a client
program, which you use to read your email. Sendmail is a
behind-the-scenes program which actually moves your email over
networks or the Internet to where you want it to go.
# rpm -e procmail sendmail
```

In this example, you were not able to remove the procmail package because the Sendmail package requires procmail. For the purposes of this example, you had never heard of this Sendmail program before, so you used RPM to get information about the package. You decided that you didn't need the Sendmail package either, so you removed both of the packages, which RPM completes with no complaints. This tells you that you can remove both of those packages from your distribution directory (RedHat/RPMS/) without problems (well, assuming you really don't need Sendmail within your distribution). You also learned, however, that if you removed only the procmail package from the distribution, you would end up with a distribution with unsatisfied dependencies.

Once you decide what packages to remove and delete the files from the RedHat/RPMS/ directory, you just have to rebuild the installation data files as discussed in the next section, "Understanding the Red Hat Installation Data Files."

## B.1.2 Understanding the Red Hat Installation Data Files

The RedHat/base/ directory contains the installation program and its data files. The program itself is contained within the image files (*.img) and the installation data files are comps, hdlist, and hdlist2.

### B.1.2.1  The comps File

There must be a comps file in the RedHat/base/ directory. This file only needs to be on the first CD in a multi-CD distribution (in fact, the whole base directory only needs to be on the first CD).

---

**NOTE**   If you are using the installer from Red Hat Linux 8.0 or later, the file should be named comps.xml. This file is in a new XML format and is more powerful, more self-explanatory, and definitely much larger. I would recommend starting with the official version and simply adding or removing entries from that file. The specifics in this section only directly apply to the comps file used with Red Hat Linux 6.X and 7.X.

---

The comps file defines one or more groups of RPMs that can be selected by the user during installation. What follows is a simple comps file with very few entries. Obviously, this example does not list enough packages to provide a complete system. For a more thorough example, see the file included with a standard Red Hat Linux distribution.

The first line of the file must be the version of the comps file. In this case, you are using version 4. The rest of the file consists of the various groups you want to define. At a minimum, a group definition begins with a 1 (to install by default) or a 0 (to *not* install by default). Following the number is the name of the group, which can contain spaces, followed by an open curly brace. Packages can then be listed, one per line, and the group is closed by a closing curly brace on the last line.

One group can require (or include) another group by using the @directive, followed by the required group's full name. Note that the group must have been defined earlier within the comps file. In addition, certain packages within a group can be conditionally installed only if another group is selected for installation. This is accomplished with the? operator, followed by the group's name, followed by an opening curly brace. The block can contain packages, required groups, or more conditional blocks.

The same comps file can be used with different distributions by conditionally including or excluding certain packages based on the distribution's architecture or language. This is done by preceding a package name with (condition):. Again, the comps that *Red Hat* ships with its distributions will show a variety of uses for this feature.

The option --hide can be specified after the initial number, but before the group name. This causes the group to not be visible, but it can still be included by other groups.

Here is a sample, but incomplete, `comps` file:

```
4

1 Base {
   kernel
}

0 --hide X Window System {
   XFree86
}

0 KDE {
   @ X Window System
   kdebase
   (arch !alpha): koffice
}

0 GNOME {
   @ X Window System
   gnome-core
}

1 SSH Client {
   ? GNOME {
       openssh-askpass-gnome
   }
   openssh
   openssh-clients
}
```

The first group in this example is called `Base` which is a required group that will always be installed. In this case, it includes only the `kernel` package, which is obviously not enough packages to create a usable system, but enough for our example. Then there is the `X Window System` group which is hidden and not installed by default. In fact, since it is hidden, it will only be installed if the `KDE` and/or `GNOME` group is selected for installation (because it is required by those groups, which are not hidden).

Within the `KDE` group, the `koffice` package will only be installed if the installation architecture is not `alpha`. Finally, there is a group that installs the SSH client. In addition to the basic required packages, the `openssh-askpass-gnome` package is installed only if the `GNOME` group has also been selected.

### B.1.2.2  The hdlist Files

The files hdlist and hdlist2 are generated by the genhdlist command. This command takes the base directory of a Red Hat installation and creates the hdlist files. The directory you provide to the genhdlist program as its first argument needs to be the directory containing the RedHat directory.

If you have a multiple-CD distribution, the command will be more complicated. You will have two CDs in two different directories (/custom/cd1/ and /custom/cd2/, for example). You can generate the files as follows:

```
# genhdlist --withnumbers \
  --hdlist /custom/cd1/RedHat/base/hdlist \
  /custom/cd1 \
  /custom/cd2
```

You can find the genhdlist command in the *anaconda-runtime* package (installed as /usr/lib/anaconda-runtime/genhdlist).

## B.1.3  Installation Boot Disk Images

One of the following boot images must be used to perform the actual installation. The images can be found in the images/ directory under the distribution base directory.

boot.img: Used to install from a CD-ROM or from a copy on your local hard drive.

bootnet.img: Used to install from the network from an FTP, HTTP, or NFS server.

pcmcia.img: Used to install from a PCMCIA CD-ROM or over a PCMCIA network card.

oldcdrom.img: Used to install from old, proprietary, non-ATAPI, non-SCSI CD-ROM drives.

### B.1.3.1  Modifying Boot Disk Images

Although the default images can be used to install your custom distribution, you might want to modify them to perform Kickstart installations (as described in the next section), to modify the kernel boot options, or to change the text displayed after boot-up.

To modify a boot image, you must mount it using the Linux loopback support. For example, you can mount an image on /mnt/tmp/ as follows:

```
# mount -o loop boot.img /mnt/tmp
```

You can then modify the files on the disk, or even add files, as long as you don't exceed the available disk space in the image. The following files are the important ones:

syslinux.cfg: Defines the boot options presented to the user and their associated kernel parameters.

vmlinuz: The Linux kernel.

boot.msg: The text displayed immediately after the system boots, but before the syslinux prompt.

initrd.img: This is the RAM-disk image that is mounted as the root filesystem.

The one file that requires additional explanation is the initrd.img file. This file can be mounted and modified, but it must first be unzipped. Here is how this file can be mounted:

```
# gzip -dc initrd.img > /tmp/initrd
# mount -o loop /tmp/initrd /mnt/initrd
```

You can then go into the /mnt/initrd/ directory and make changes. To update the image, you just need to unmount and recompress the file:

```
# umount /mnt/initrd
# gzip -c /tmp/initrd > initrd.img
```

### B.1.3.2  Using Boot Disk Images

These images can be written to a floppy disk under Linux with the following command:

```
# dd if=boot.img of=/dev/fd0 bs=8192
```

Also, two disk images are not bootable. One disk is called drivers.img and contains drivers that can be used in conjunction with any of the boot disks. Another disk, pcmciadd.img, contains extra PCMCIA drivers for laptop installation.

Another image (dosutils/autoboot/cdboot.img) is too large to fit on a standard floppy, but it can be used to create a bootable CD-ROM. You can create a bootable CD-ROM ISO image, suitable for burning, by running the following command (from the base directory of the distribution):

```
%  mkisofs -v -r -T -J \
   -V "Red Hat 7.1" \
   -b dosutils/autoboot/cdboot.img \
   -c boot.cat -o /tmp/custom.iso .
```

I am not going to describe all of the options just specified because the man page for mkisofs covers all of them pretty well. But, this command creates a bootable CD-ROM with both Joliet (Windows) and Rockridge (Unix/Linux) extensions. The volume label will be set to Red Hat 7.1.

## B.2 Automating Red Hat Linux Installation with Kickstart

Red Hat Linux provides a very convenient method of automating system installations called *Kickstart*. A Kickstart file contains instructions that are used by the installation program to reduce or eliminate the need for user input during the installation process.

Kickstart files are very useful when you have a large number of identical systems. If you have a cluster of systems you use for computations or sharing the load on a web site, they can all be installed without interaction using Kickstart. Even after the initial installation, having the Kickstart configuration available will allow you to quickly expand the cluster and replace machines that die.

If you want to perform fully automated installations over the network, particularly to headless systems (computers without a monitor and keyboard), the information in this appendix should be helpful. You would also want to visit http://www.slac.stanford.edu/~alfw/PXE-Kickstart/PXE-Kickstart.html. This site provides very thorough instructions on how to use a DHCP and TFTP server to perform fully automated network system installations.

---

**NOTE**   You can find more information about the Kickstart files on Red Hat's web site: http://www.redhat.com/docs/manuals/linux/ RHL-7.3-Manual/custom-guide/part-install-related.html.

---

## B.2.1  Creating a Kickstart File

Although you could create a Kickstart file from scratch (because it is simply a text file), I recommend finding an existing file and making any necessary changes.

Apart from searching the Internet for existing Kickstart files, there are a variety of ways to create your own.

The easiest place to start is in root's home directory on a freshly installed Red Hat Linux machine. There should be a file named anaconda-ks.cfg. This file contains instructions to duplicate the installation you just performed on this particular machine. In some cases (when you will be continuously reinstalling the same machine, for example), this will be all you need. Be sure to go through the generated file and uncomment the disk partitioning commands and make any other changes you feel are necessary.

Another way to create a Kickstart file is by using the ksconfig program that is included with Red Hat Linux. This graphical tool lets you choose all of the Kickstart options interactively. After you are done, you can export the appropriate Kickstart file.

### B.2.1.1 Generalizing a Kickstart File

Kickstart, like most topics covered within this book, is very powerful and very flexible. I will not attempt to provide a comprehensive reference but simply provide enough to get you started. The most common task that many people want to do is create a generalized Kickstart file that works on a variety of systems.

Here is an example Kickstart file that will work on most systems. This example assumes that the installation data is on a CD-ROM, but the cdrom command can be replaced by another, such as nfs, harddrive, or url (such as ftp:// or http://). It will, however, completely wipe out anything on any of the drives on the system and replace it with the new operating system—so be careful!

```
1   lang en_US
2   keyboard us
3   mouse genericps/2 --emulthree
4   timezone --utc America/New_York
5   auth --useshadow --enablemd5
6   rootpw --iscrypted $1$xxxxxxxxxxxxxxxxxxxxxxxxxxxxxx
7   network --device eth0 --bootproto dhcp
8   cdrom
9   install
10
11  firewall --disabled
12  zerombr yes
13  clearpart --all
14
15  # Always create a 50MB boot partition
16  part /boot --size 50
```

```
17  # Also create a 1GB swap
18  part swap --size 1024
19  # Use rest of space for /
20  part / --size 1 --grow
21
22  lilo --location mbr
23  skipx
24  reboot
25
26  %packages
27  @ Everything
28
29  %post
30  # You can put shell commands here to be run after installation
```

**Line 5:** This command enables shadowed, md5 passwords on this system. If you use NIS, Kerberos, or LDAP, you can configure these here too.

**Line 6:** The root password can be set with this command. The password can be specified in plaintext, or, preferably, specified in an encrypted form as shown here (just set the password for an existing account and copy it out of the /etc/shadow file.

**Line 7:** This will enable the network interface eth0 and use the Dynamic Host Configuration Protocol (DHCP) to obtain its IP address. If the system will have a static IP address, you may want to already have the DHCP server configured to assign this static address when the request is made.

**Line 9:** This specifies that this is an install and not an upgrade.

**Line 11:** This disables the firewall, because it can be configured more precisely at a later time, after the install has been completed.

**Line 12:** This initializes any invalid partition tables, possibly destroying contents of one or more hard drives.

**Line 13:** This deletes every partition (hence the -all option) on every drive on the system.

**Line 22:** After installation is complete, lilo is run to make the system bootable (from the Master Boot Record of the first harddrive). The X configuration is skipped and the system is rebooted.

**Line 27:** In this case, you assume that your custom distribution is trimmed down to exactly the packages you want to install, so you want to install all packages. Alternatively, you could list specific groups or packages by name.

The order of this file *is* important. The file shown will allow completely automated installation (assuming all hardware is properly detected). Notice that no specific hardware commands are provided so that the installation program will detect the proper settings for each machine. The only exception is the mouse command, which is required, and whose value should provide minimal functionality on most modern systems.

The three part commands create three partitions. First, a 50MB /boot partition is created. Next in line, is a 1GB swap partition. Finally, the rest of the available space is used for the root (/) partition. Many people like to have separate /var, /usr, and/or /tmp partitions. If this is the case for you, you can use more complicated partitioning commands to achieve your desired partitioning scheme. Note that, in multiple-drive systems, these partitions will probably be on different drives (unless you restrict them to one specific drive with the --ondisk option). You can also use the raid command to create RAID partitions during the installation process.

## B.2.2 Using a Kickstart File

Once you have a Kickstart file, it can be placed almost anywhere. You then have to tell the installation process where to find the file by using the ks kernel parameter.

If you placed a ks.cfg file in the root directory of your boot floppy image (as described in section B.1.3.1), for example, you would pass the parameter ks=floppy to the kernel on that boot disk. This can be done manually, or the disk can be modified. The following syslinux.cfg file, if placed on a boot disk, will provide only one installation option—Kickstart install from the floppy.

```
default ks
prompt 1
timeout 0
label ks
    kernel vmlinuz
    append ks=floppy initrd=initrd.img devfs=nomount text
```

## Kickstart and Timeouts

I do not recommend having a boot timeout in the `syslinux.cfg` when the default boot label involves a Kickstart file. One time, a coworker at my company used his desktop computer to write a Kickstart floppy with a timeout value set. While he was gone, the office lost power. When the power was restored, his system booted off that floppy and Kickstart wiped out his entire system (just like it was supposed to do).

Needless to say, he always made sure the timeout was set to zero from that point forward, which disables the timeout completely (somebody must hit ENTER before it will boot). If you are doing completely automated installs (particularly on systems for which you have no input/output devices), you'll have to take this risk—just don't leave the disc in your workstation!

In addition to `ks=floppy`, you can use `ks=cdrom:/path/ks.cfg` to refer to a Kickstart file on the CD-ROM. You can also refer to a file on an NFS or HTTP server by using `ks=nfs:server:/path/ks.cfg` or `ks=http://server/path/ks.cfg`. If the machine might have more than one Ethernet interface, you can specify the interface specifically by adding a second kernel parameter such as `ksdevice=eth1`.

Finally, if the `ks` parameter is passed to the kernel with no value, DHCP will be used and the DHCP server should provide the name of an NFS server in the `bootServer` portion of the response. The `bootfile` field in the DHCP response should begin with a / and be a full path to the Kickstart file. Alternatively, if no `bootfile` is specified, the file `/kickstart/111.222.33.44-kickstart` will be used, where `111.22.33.44` is the IP address assigned to the machine by the DHCP server.

# APPENDIX C

# Building Red Hat Package Manager (RPM) Packages

I AM GOING TO describe a little scenario that is probably familiar to all too many of you. It all starts when somebody decides they need Apache on some (or all) of the systems on your network. In this example, I am assuming that all of the systems on your network are running Sun's Solaris.

Since you are an administrator who is very responsive to your users' needs, you pay a visit to http://www.apache.org. You find the source code for the latest version and download it to your workstation. You un-tar the file and run ./configure --help. You look through the available options and decide you want to specify --enable-suexec and --prefix=/usr/local as compilation options. You run configure again with these options and it finishes without a problem. So far, so good.

Now you are ready to compile. You run make and the build process begins. As unlikely as it may be for a popular program like Apache, I will pretend that there is a linking error (for the sake of argument). After 30 minutes of poking around, you decide you need to make a manual change to one of the makefiles. You run the make command again and the compilation completes without further incident.

OK, so now you are ready to install this package on your workstation. You run make install. Some files are placed in /usr/local/etc/, some in /usr/local/lib/, and others in /usr/local/bin/. You modify the configuration file, start Apache, and everything works fine.

Now it is time to install this on other systems. You probably don't want to go through the entire process for each system; you would prefer to simply copy the installed files to the other systems (assuming the binaries are compatible). Unfortunately, you have many other files in the installation directory and you are not sure which files actually belong to Apache. So, instead of copying the binaries, you re-tar the source directory. You copy this tarball out to the other systems, extract its contents, and run only make install on each system.

Alternatively, you might have used /usr/local/apache/ as your prefix instead of /usr/local/ (which is always a good idea). In this case, you can simply create a new tarball of the installation directory, extract it on each system, and you are done. You have a fully operational Apache web server on all of your systems.

At this point, you might think you are done installing Apache on your systems. You give things a few weeks, and there aren't any problems. You decide to delete that original source directory and you delete the tarballs you made as you have completed your task.

But then, six months later, a new system arrives. This system needs Apache as well. If you installed the application in /usr/local/apache/, then you are in luck. You'll only have to copy that directory from another system, delete any logs, and make sure the configuration file for the other system is appropriate for your new system. That wasn't too much work—unless, of course, you installed in /usr/local/. In this case, you will have to start from scratch or handpick files to copy from one system to another. Well, one way or another, the new system has been configured without too much work, problem solved.

We now skip ahead another six months. A security problem is found in Apache (again, not very common, but it has happened). You need to quickly update Apache on every system with the new release. You go download the source and start the process from scratch. That linking error still persists, and it takes you 30 minutes to track it down again (hey, it has been over a year). You get everything compiled and distributed to all of your systems. Mission accomplished.

At least it is until you get a call from one of your users. A very critical application is now broken because it relies on Apache's suexec support. You forgot to include the --enable-suexec when you built the new version! You have to go back and start the process over again with the correct compilation options this time.

Some of you have had this happen—maybe even more than once. Others might not think this situation illustrates any serious problems. The administrator in the example was still able to upgrade to the new version in only a few hours with only one mistake. Unfortunately, the Apache installation process described is about as simple as a software installations can be. With other applications, it might take days to fix compilation problems (especially on unusual systems) and get all of the compilation options just right.

When the Red Hat Package Manager (RPM) was designed, solving this exact problem was one of its core design principles. Not only does RPM provide package management and powerful system verification tools, it also allows your packages to be built from pristine sources. This means that, when building an RPM, RPM can always start with the pristine sources exactly as provided by the author (whether it is you or somebody else). It then makes any modifications needed to enable certain options or fix compilation problems and other bugs. All of these changes are unavoidably documented by this process; the SPEC file for your RPM will list every change that needs to be made to build your package. This SPEC file, along with the original source(s) and any patches, will be bundled into a single source

RPM. This single source RPM documents exactly what you built, how you built it, and the source RPM allows you to repeat the entire process with minimal effort.

This appendix starts with the basics of RPM building, provides a couple of examples, and then covers more advanced concepts. Although not a comprehensive guide to building RPMs, it covers most topics, and offers plenty of information with which to build your own packages.

## C.1 Creating an RPM Build Environment

A certain amount of system preparation is usually required before you can build your own RPMs. First, you need a specific directory structure in which to place sources and SPEC files. The standard location for this directory structure on a Red Hat Linux system is /usr/src/redhat/. A separate temporary directory is often used as the virtual installation root (or build root). This is usually /var/tmp/.

A security-conscious system administrator knows that creating predictably named files and/or directories in a publicly writable directory such as /var/tmp/ is dangerous if ordinary users have access to the system. The system-wide /usr/src/redhat/ directory is also made for building packages as root, which I wouldn't recommend. Fortunately, most packages can be built as a regular user. As far as the other packages go, most could support non-privileged builds if the SPEC file was properly modified. Building packages as a regular user prevents any possible damage or unwanted modifications to your system. This is particularly important when you are building unfamiliar third-party software because you don't know what changes it will try to make to your system during the build and install process.

For these reasons, I recommend that you set up a special unprivileged account for building packages. The account will require a bit of preparation, however. First, you need to create a temporary directory, such as ~/tmp. You also need to create your RPM base directory such as ~/rpmroot. Within that rpmroot directory, you must create the following directories: BUILD/, RPMS/, SOURCES/, SPECS/, and SRPMS/.

Next, you need to create a .rpmmacros in this user's home directory. Unfortunately, within this file, you can't use the ~ character to represent your home directory, so you must hard code the full path. Here is an example file, which assumes that the special build account name is build.

---

**NOTE**    You can find the code samples for this chapter in the Downloads section of the Apress web site (http://www.apress.com).

---

```
%_topdir /home/build/rpmroot
%buildroot /home/build/tmp/build
%packager Kirk Bauer <kirk@kaybee.org>
%_tmppath /home/build/tmp
```

That's about it. Now all of your package building will be confined to these two directories under the home directory of this special build account. This will make your package-building experience much safer than building RPMs as root. Note that some RPMs are not designed to be built as a normal user. If you have created such an RPM, then shame on you! If somebody else created it, you can just build it as root, or use the techniques discussed in section C.3 to add the use of a build root to the SPEC file.

You also need to make sure RPM is installed on your system. Even if your base operating system already has the rpm package installed, you will need to make sure you have the rpm-build package. Many programs will also require a compiler and the make utility on your system in order to be packaged. The examples and discussion in this book directly apply to RPM 4.0.4, but most features discussed are also available in earlier versions (including the 3.X series).

I'm sure there are a variety of editors that can provide syntax highlighting when you are editing SPEC files. I prefer to use Vi Improved (vim) available from http://www.vim.org. Just add the line syntax on to your ~/.vimrc and open up a SPEC file. Syntax highlighting really helps to make SPEC files easier to read and can even help you catch mistakes as you are making them.

## C.2 Building Your First RPM

I think that nothing can compare to hands-on experience when learning something new. In my opinion, there are two good methods to start with when learning to build RPMs. The first option is to create a very simple test package and expand from there. The second option is to find an existing package and modify it. A little of both doesn't hurt, either.

### C.2.1 Simple Test RPM

In this section, I will show you how to build a simple SPEC file, called test.spec, that you can place in the SPECS/ directory. You can build a package from this SPEC file by going into the SPECS/ directory and running the following:

```
% rpmbuild -ba test.spec
```

This command, if successful, creates a source RPM in the SRPMS/ directory and a "binary" RPM in the RPMS/noarch/ directory. I say "binary" because this example package will not be architecture-dependent because it does not include any compiled files. The noarch architecture is a special architecture type that you can install on any system and use for any nonbinary packages (such as bash and Perl scripts).

Here is a complete example SPEC file that provides all of the required definitions and fields:

```
Name: test
Version: 1.0
Release: 1
Summary: A test package
License: MIT
Group: Test
BuildArch: noarch


%description
This is just a test package


%files
```

All of these fields, except for BuildArch, are required. If you don't specify BuildArch, the package will be built based on your system's architecture (such as i386 or sparc). For this reason, you want to (in this case) explicitly state that this package should be built with an architecture of noarch. The name of your package is test and the version of the underlying software is set to be 1.0 (arbitrary, but required). The release of your test package is set to be 1, since this is the first version of your SPEC file. Within this SPEC file, you also specify a summary and the license for the underlying software is also specified in this example SPEC file. You use the Group field to specify which software group your package belongs in (such as Applications/System). Next, you provide a full description for your very exciting package in the %description section. Finally, a %files section is included in the SPEC file, but is empty, which means this package contains no files.

You can actually build this package now:

```
% rpmbuild -ba test.spec
Processing files: test-1.0-1
PreReq: rpmlib(PayloadFilesHavePrefix) <= 4.0-1 \
    rpmlib(CompressedFileNames) <= 3.0.4-1
Requires(rpmlib): rpmlib(PayloadFilesHavePrefix) <= \
    4.0-1 rpmlib(CompressedFileNames) <= 3.0.4-1
Wrote: /home/build/rpmroot/SRPMS/test-1.0-1.src.rpm
Wrote: /home/build/rpmroot/RPMS/noarch/test-1.0-1.noarch.rpm
```

Note that RPM automatically adds a few dependencies. This ensures that this package is not installed on a system with a version of RPM that is too old to handle the RPM package itself. The build process created a source RPM (.src.rpm) and an installable "binary" RPM (of type noarch).

You could even install these packages, but RPM wouldn't do anything but add an entry to your RPM database (which could be useful in some cases). So now try adding one file to your package to make it a bit more exciting. Say that you want to package your /etc/hosts file so that you can install it through RPM on a wide range of systems. First, you want to add the Buildroot and Source fields near the top of your file:

```
Buildroot: /var/tmp/test_build
Source: hosts
```

The build root is fully explained in section C.3; in short, it is a virtual root for the installed files. You should install all files within this directory. If you have a %buildroot specified in your ~/.rpmmacros file, RPM will use that directory instead of the path given here in the spec file. The important thing to remember is that you have to specify some default build root or a build root will not be used for this package at all.

The Source line says that this package will use the source file hosts. It expects this file to be in the SOURCES/ directory. You could manually place the file in that directory, but I'm assuming you are making this package to automatically distribute this file, so you don't want a manual step involved. This is not a problem, however, because you can actually copy the /etc/hosts from the system into the SOURCES/ directory in the prep stage of the RPM build process:

```
%prep
cp /etc/hosts $RPM_SOURCE_DIR
```

RPM has already set the $RPM_SOURCE_DIR environment variable for use within these scriptlets—it expands to the full path of the SOURCES/ directory. This %prep section is executed with the Bourne Shell as the first stage in the build process. Next, you need a %install section to install this file for the binary RPM:

```
%install
rm -rf $RPM_BUILD_ROOT
mkdir -p $RPM_BUILD_ROOT/etc
cp $RPM_SOURCE_DIR/hosts $RPM_BUILD_ROOT/etc/hosts
```

All you do here is make sure that the build root is empty (remember, never set your build root to / or any other important directory!), create the destination etc/ directory, and copy in the file. You might be thinking it would have been simpler to just copy the hosts file directly and skip the SOURCES/ directory altogether. Instead, here you specified the source file hosts in the Source header so that it would be included in the source RPM. For this reason, the source file must be in the SOURCES/ directory.

Since you specified the Buildroot field in your SPEC file, you know that a build root will be specified in the $RPM_BUILD_ROOT environment variable. It will, by default, be the directory specified in that field. It can be overridden, however, by your ~/.rpmmacros. Either way, the directory is theoretically free to be deleted and recreated.

Realistically, if you didn't care about the source RPM, you could just not use a build root at all and it would simply package your system's /etc/hosts file directly. But, you usually do want to build complete source RPMs (that contain everything you need to rebuild the package). Besides, using a build root is a good habit to learn.

Finally, you need to expand your previously empty %files section. Unless there are entries in this section, the resulting RPM will not contain any files.

```
%files
%attr(0644,root,root) /etc/hosts
```

The %attr macro specifies that the file should be included with permissions 0644, user root, and group root. This is important to remember because you probably do not want to package files as being owned by your build user (who will most likely not exist on the installation system). You are now ready to build this package and install the binary package on other systems:

```
% rpmbuild -ba test.spec
Executing(%prep): /bin/sh -e /var/tmp/rpm-tmp.85603
+ umask 022
+ cd /home/build/rpmroot/BUILD
+ cp /etc/hosts /home/build/rpmroot/SOURCES
+ exit 0
Executing(%install): /bin/sh -e /var/tmp/rpm-tmp.85603
+ umask 022
+ cd /home/build/rpmroot/BUILD
+ rm -rf /home/build/tmp/build
+ mkdir -p /home/build/tmp/build/etc
+ cp /home/build/rpmroot/SOURCES/hosts /home/build/tmp/build/etc/hosts
+ /usr/lib/rpm/brp-compress
+ /usr/lib/rpm/brp-strip
+ /usr/lib/rpm/brp-strip-comment-note
Processing files: test-1.0-1
Finding  Provides: (using /usr/lib/rpm/find-provides)...
Finding  Requires: (using /usr/lib/rpm/find-requires)...
```

```
PreReq: rpmlib(PayloadFilesHavePrefix) <= 4.0-1
    rpmlib(CompressedFileNames) <= 3.0.4-1
Requires(rpmlib): rpmlib(PayloadFilesHavePrefix) <= 4.0-1
    rpmlib(CompressedFileNames) <= 3.0.4-1
Wrote: /home/build/rpmroot/SRPMS/test-1.0-1.src.rpm
Wrote: /home/build/rpmroot/RPMS/noarch/test-1.0-1.noarch.rpm
```

## C.2.2  Modifying an Existing RPM

When you are modifying an existing package, the most difficult step can be finding an appropriate source RPM. For learning purposes, try to pick a relatively simple package. If you want to package a specific program, you will usually want to find somebody else's source RPM for that program. You can choose from a wide variety of source RPMs, either directly from a vendor (such as `ftp://ftp.redhat.com/pub/ redhat/linux/VERSION/LANGUAGE/os/PLATFORM/SRPMS`) or from `http://www.rpmfind.net`.

For the purposes of this example, I chose the GNU gzip program, as packaged by Red Hat for Red Hat Linux 7.2. The source RPM I chose is `gzip-1.3-15.src.rpm`. I recommend that you download this source RPM from `ftp://ftp.redhat.com` to follow along with this example. After the download, you can use RPM to install the source RPM within your build tree. Note that installing a source RPM does not affect your system, nor the RPM database; it only places one SPEC file in the SPECS directory and some number of source files in the SOURCES directory. Assuming you have a special account configured as described in section C.1, you need not be logged in as root.

```
% rpm -i gzip-1.3-15.src.rpm
% cd ~/rpmroot/SPECS
```

Once you have installed the source RPM, you can view the SPEC file, SPECS/gzip.spec. Here, I will present it in several portions so that it is easier to explain. First, you have the basic package information:

```
Summary: The GNU data compression program.
Name: gzip
Version: 1.3
Release: 15
License: GPL
Group: Applications/File
Source: ftp://alpha.gnu.org/gnu/gzip/gzip-%{version}.tar.gz
Patch0: gzip-1.3-mktemp.patch
Patch1: gzip-1.2.4-zforce.patch
```

```
Patch2: gzip-1.2.4a-dirinfo.patch
Patch3: gzip-1.3-stderr.patch
Patch4: gzip-1.3-zgreppipe.patch
Patch5: gzip-1.3-noppid.patch
URL: http://www.gzip.org/
Prereq: /sbin/install-info
Requires: mktemp
Buildroot: %{_tmppath}/gzip-%{version}-root
```

Here is a description of these various fields:

Summary: This field is required and provides a short summary of the software contained within the package.

Name: The package name is (not surprisingly) required.

Version: This is the version of the underlying software being packaged and is required.

Release: The release of this package (or a version number representing the packaging and SPEC file). This should be incremented each time a change is made by the packager and must always be present in a SPEC file.

License: This field is required and specifies the license covering the enclosed software. Examples would be GPL, BSD, MIT, and Commercial.

Group: The Group field specifies in which group within the package hierarchy this package belongs and it is also required. To see a list of existing groups, run this command on an RPM-based system:
`rpm -qa --query format '%{GROUP}\n' | sort | uniq.`

Source: There can be multiple Source entries. Additional source files can be specified, but the fields should be named as follows: Source2, Source3, and so on. You can use a URL to illustrate where you could retrieve the original source, but RPM only cares about the filename. All sources must be present in the SOURCES directory. The string %{version} is substituted by RPM during the build process with the RPM variable version as defined in the previous header entry. This eliminates the need to change the version in multiple places every time a new version of the software is packaged.

PatchX: This package has multiple patches, each with a unique number. These patch files must be present in the SOURCES directory. Each patch presumably corrects some problem in the original source. The patch may correct a compilation error, relocate one or more file locations, make the program relocatable, or facilitate the use of a build root in your package-building process. The main purpose of these patch files is to eliminate the need to directly modify the original source code.

**URL:** This is an optional URL where you can go to get the underlying software. This URL is included in the package information (as shown by rpm -qi).

**Prereq:** This tag lists one or more prerequirements. Each item should be separated by a comma. These requirements must be fully installed before this package is installed. Anything used by any install scripts should be listed as a Prereq. If prerequirements are being installed at the same time as this package, they will be fully installed first.

**Requires:** This is a comma-delimited list of dependencies needed by this package. The package must have them to run, but not necessarily for package installation. They have to be installed prior to the package installation, at the same time as this package, or the package has to be installed using the --nodeps option. If the dependencies are not installed, they will presumably need to be installed at a later time before this program can be used.

**Buildroot:** This is the directory to use as a virtual root filesystem when you are doing the install phase of the package build process. Since you want non-root users to be able to build any package, this entry should always be present in your SPEC files. Regardless of the directory specified, the %buildroot specified in your ~/.rpmmacros file will be used instead.

Next is the required %description section, which provides a full description of the software within the package:

```
%description
The gzip package contains the popular GNU gzip data compression
program. Gzipped files have a .gz extension.

Gzip should be installed on your Red Hat Linux system, because it is a
very commonly used data compression program.
```

Next is the %prep section. This section is supposed to extract, patch, and otherwise prepare the source code for building. Within this section are calls to several macros:

```
%prep
%setup -q
%patch0 -p1
%patch1 -p1
%patch2 -p1
%patch3 -p1
%patch4 -p1
%patch5 -p1
```

At this point, you should note that the %prep characters represent the start of the %prep section, whereas the remaining items (%setup and %patchX) are macro calls. It is unfortunate (in my opinion) that these look so similar. This is one reason you should use an editor that provides good syntax highlighting—it will help the section headers stand out from the macro calls.

The %setup macro extracts the source file listed in the Source field into the BUILD/ directory. It assumes the extraction process creates the directory gzip-1.3 and it changes into that directory. There are several available flags to the %setup macro that you can use to modify its behavior, but the only one used here is the -q option, which requests less verbose operation.

Next comes the %patch0 macro, which causes RPM to apply the patch listed in the Patch0 field. The -p1 flag is passed to the patch command to remove one directory from the filenames listed in the patch file. The reason is that the patch files are usually created from outside of the gzip-1.3 directory, yet are applied from within that directory (as the %setup script changes into that directory). So, you must use the -p1 flag to make the filenames contained within the patch file relative to your location inside of the source tree.

Next, we have the %build section that builds the software. For binary programs, this is where you place the commands to do the actual program compilation. For non-binary programs, this section may not be present, or it may do some simple prepackaging configuration (such as setting the #!/usr/bin/perl at the top of Perl scripts to the appropriate location for your system).

```
%build
export DEFS="-DNO_ASM"
export CPPFLAGS="-DHAVE_LSTAT"
%configure --bindir=/bin
make
make gzip.info
```

As you can see, the SPEC file sets a few environment variables before executing the configure script. Then the script is executed with an option specifying /bin as the directory in which binaries are to be installed. Note that all directories specified in the %build section should be relative to the final installation location of the package. Since this package ultimately wants the file /bin/gzip to exist, the /bin directory is specified during the build stage. The program and its info file are then built with the make command.

Next is the %clean section that cleans up the build directory after the package build process has completed. It is usually the same in all packages that use a Buildroot because all it needs to do is remove that virtual root directory. RPM sets the environment variable RPM_BUILD_ROOT for you in advance, so this is all that you have to do:

```
%clean
rm -rf $RPM_BUILD_ROOT
```

The next section is the %install section. This section must install the package into the virtual installation root. The first thing it must do is remove this directory (just in case the last build failed and never executed the clean section). Then it must create any necessary directories and copy them in the appropriate files:

```
%install
rm -rf $RPM_BUILD_ROOT
%makeinstall bindir=$RPM_BUILD_ROOT/bin gzip.info
mkdir -p $RPM_BUILD_ROOT/usr/bin
ln -sf ../../bin/gzip $RPM_BUILD_ROOT/usr/bin/gzip
ln -sf ../../bin/gunzip $RPM_BUILD_ROOT/usr/bin/gunzip

for i in zcmp zegrep zforce zless znew gzexe zdiff zfgrep zgrep zmore ; do
   mv $RPM_BUILD_ROOT/bin/$i $RPM_BUILD_ROOT/usr/bin/$i
done

gzip -9nf $RPM_BUILD_ROOT%{_infodir}/gzip.info*

cat > $RPM_BUILD_ROOT/usr/bin/zless <<EOF
#!/bin/sh
/bin/zcat "\$@" | /usr/bin/less
EOF
chmod 755 $RPM_BUILD_ROOT/usr/bin/zless
```

The %makeinstall macro executes the standard GNU-style make install and automatically sets installation paths relative to the build root. To see what this macro actually does, take a look at /usr/lib/rpm/macros (or the equivalent on your system). In this case, the bindir is explicitly set (because the normal binary directory is /usr/bin).

You create the /usr/bin/ directory (again, relative to the build root) with the mkdir -p command that will create all necessary directories up to and including the specified directory. You then create symbolic links to the binaries in /bin/. It is important to use only relative symbolic links because these files are all under the temporary build root and will be installed in different locations.

The collection of helper commands, such as zgrep and zmore, are then moved to /usr/bin/ because they don't really belong in /bin/. Next, this scriptlet compresses the info page. Finally, the zless command is replaced with a shell script for one reason or another (I'm not sure why). Note that the execute bit is set on that new script to make sure it is packaged with the proper permissions (as discussed momentarily)

In most packages, including this example, the installation portion is usually the most complicated. So, don't worry—the rest of the SPEC file is much simpler. Next we have a %post section:

```
%post
/sbin/install-info %{_infodir}/gzip.info.gz %{_infodir}/dir
```

This is why there was a prerequirement on the file /sbin/install-info. This command executes after the package installation in order to register the info page. Like all of the sections in this SPEC file, this section executes as a script by the Bourne Shell, but this one is executed on the installation system after the package's files have been installed. The %{_infodir} string is an RPM variable that expands to the appropriate location in which to place info files on this system. Remember that the expansion is done by RPM on the build system, which is why it is a good idea to build your packages on systems identical or similar to the systems on which they will be installed.

Next comes the %preun script that executes before a package is removed from a system:

```
%preun
if [ $1 = 0 ]; then
    /sbin/install-info --delete %{_infodir}/gzip.info.gz %{_infodir}/dir
fi
```

The $1 variable will only be set to 0 when a package is being removed (not upgraded). In this case, the info page is unregistered from the info system.

Next comes one of the most important sections—%files. This section contains the actual listing of files that should be included within the package:

```
%files
%defattr(-,root,root)
%doc NEWS README AUTHORS ChangeLog THANKS TODO
/bin/*
/usr/bin/*
%{_mandir}/*/*
%{_infodir}/gzip.info*
```

The %defattr command tells RPM that all packages should be packaged with their existing permissions (the - in the first field). It also says the owner and group of all files should, by default, be root. This overrides the owner and group of the files within the build root. This is important, because those files are owned by your build user, but you don't want to package them that way.

The %doc command is special in that it references files in the source tree that should be installed in the /usr/share/doc/gzip-1.3/ directory. All other entries in this list only refer to files that were copied to the build root during the %install stage.

The remaining lines show how you can use wildcards to match files in the build root. The variables _mandir and _infodir are used instead of hard-coded directories such as /usr/share/man/ or /usr/man/.

The final section in the file is the changelog section that you can use to record the dates and reasons for your changes to the packaging of the program. This section is pretty self-explanatory, but here are a few example entries:

```
* Sat Sep 21 2002 Kirk Bauer <kirk@kaybee.org> 1.3.0-15
- Example log entry #1
- Example log entry #2, line #1
  Example log entry #2, line #2
```

Remember that you can build this package from within the SPECS/ directory as follows:

```
% rpmbuild -ba gzip.spec
```

## C.3 Using an RPM Build Root

I have pretty much shoved the use of a build root down your throat in this appendix. There is really no benefit to *not* having a build root, but there are plenty of downsides. Using a build root allows you to build packages as a nonprivileged user and to build packages without touching the base operating system, which, in my opinion, are both very important features of a packaging process.

So, now that I have hopefully convinced you to use a build root for your packages, let's start to use it. To use a build root, your package must have a line such as the following:

```
BuildRoot: /var/tmp/mypackage-build
```

This tells RPM that your package uses a build root. In most cases, you should override this directory in your ~/.rpmmacros file by adding the following setting:

```
%buildroot /home/build/tmp/build
```

You can also specify the build root on the command line (when building) with the --buildroot option. Remember that the build root should *never* be set to an important directory because almost all packages will completely wipe out this directory during the build process. It doesn't need to exist, either, because most packages create the directory as they need it.

When using a build root, always remember these concepts:

- The program should be compiled in the build stage as if it was being installed in its final location. If a binary built in the build stage should have a default configuration file of /etc/program.conf, for example, it should be built with that exact configuration file location. The build root should not be used during the build stage.

- In the install stage, you should first remove the build root (to clean up any incomplete builds from the past). You should then create any directories you need for installation under the build root with the mkdir -p command. Any files must be installed relative to this build root, including any files you install by running the make install command. Sometimes this relative installation can require modification of the makefile included with a program. The shell variable $RPM_BUILD_ROOT contains the full path of the build root and you can use it throughout this section.

- All files listed in the files section should use the final file locations. These files will be packaged relative to the build root, but installed with exactly the paths used in the file listing.

It is important to remember that in order to make a file part of a package, you must copy it into the build root during the install stage and you must also include it in the files section. The permissions and ownership of the files will be the same as they are in the build root, unless you use some of the commands discussed in section C.6.1.

As an example, let's say you are packaging the binary program /usr/bin/program with a configuration file of /etc/program.conf. The process would be as follows:

1. Compile program in the build stage and tell it its default configuration file is /etc/program.conf.

2. In the install stage, place the binary in $RPM_BUILD_ROOT/usr/bin/program and the configuration file in $RPM_BUILD_ROOT/etc/program.conf.

3. In the files section, list the files /usr/bin/program and /etc/program.conf.

Here is an example of the pertinent sections in a SPEC file:

```
%build
make -DCONFIG_FILE=/etc/program.conf program

%install
rm -rf $RPM_BUILD_ROOT
mkdir -p $RPM_BUILD_ROOT/etc
mkdir -p $RPM_BUILD_ROOT/usr/bin
```

```
cp program $RPM_BUILD_ROOT/usr/bin
chmod a+rx $RPM_BUILD_ROOT/usr/bin/program
cp program.conf $RPM_BUILD_ROOT/etc
chmod a+r $RPM_BUILD_ROOT/etc/program.conf

%clean
rm -rf $RPM_BUILD_ROOT

%files
%defattr(-,root,root)
/etc/program.conf
/usr/bin/program.conf
```

Note that your files section will pretty much always contain that first line (%defattr(-,root,root)) so that normal users can build the package. This overrides the user and group ownership of all packaged files so that they are root and root. More information can be found in section C.6.1.

If you are installing a standard GNU-style program that is compiled and installed (manually) with

```
% ./configure
% make
% make install
```

then you will usually want to use these sections in your SPEC file:

```
%build
%configure
make

%install
rm -rf $RPM_BUILD_ROOT
%makeinstall

%clean
rm -rf $RPM_BUILD_ROOT
```

As you can see, the RPM macros %configure and %makeinstall take care of the dirty work when dealing with build roots. They also specify certain compilation options and directory names appropriate for your system. They should work properly for many programs, but your mileage may vary.

# C.4 Patching the Original Source

When building an RPM, the concept of pristine sources is very important, for the reasons mentioned at the beginning of this appendix. You should never change anything within the original source file. If you encounter problems, you should create the appropriate patch file(s). The only exception is when you (or your company) is the author of the source file. In this case, it is probably easier in the long run to make the original source more RPM friendly.

Most packages will have a single source file that is a tarball (usually compressed). The first thing to consider is the directory contained within the source file. The %setup macro expects this tarball to create the directory name-version upon extraction. If a different directory name is created, you can tell the %setup macro the alternate name with the -n option.

So, for example, the source for the gzip package is gzip-1.3.tar.gz. If you extract this with tar -xzf, you will have a new directory called gzip-1.3/. If, instead, you extract it to the directory gzip/, you would use the macro %setup -n gzip in the prep stage to extract the source.

If there are any problems apart from the directory contained within the source file, you will probably need a patch file. Creating a patch file is relatively simple. First, place the original source tarball in the SOURCES/ directory. Then execute these commands (assuming we are packaging the test program):

```
% tar -xzf test-1.0.tgz
% cp -ar test-1.0 test-1.0-orig
```

Now, you can go into the SOURCES/test-1.0/ directory and make any changes necessary to fix your problem. It may be a compilation error, a modification to the makefile to support a build root, and so on. Once you have made the changes, simply build the patch file and remove the directories:

```
% diff -uNr test-1.0-orig test-1.0 > test-patch1
% rm -rf test-1.0 test-1.0-orig
```

Now you have a patch file named test-patch1 that contains any changes you made to any files within the source tree. You should usually create a separate patch for each logical group of changes and name the patch descriptively. One patch might be test.fixinstall.patch and another might be test.linuxcompile.patch.

Remember that all sources and patch files should begin with the associated package's name. The reason is that, unfortunately, all source files for all packages go into the same directory. If you are building many packages, it will be difficult to determine which source files belong to which packages without looking at the SPEC files.

Now, all you have to do is reference the source file and the patch file in your SPEC file. Here is the relevant portion of a SPEC file:

```
Source: test-1.0.tgz
Patch0: test-patch1

%prep
%setup
%patch0 -p1
```

The `-p1` option to the `%patch0` macro tells the `patch` command to remove one path-component off the beginning of the filenames listed in the patch file. This is necessary because you build the patch from outside the `test-1.0/` directory, yet the patch is being applied from within the `test-1.0/` directory (because the `%setup` macro enters that directory for you).

Multiple patches can be specified by using the `Patch1` field and the `%patch1` macro, and so on.

## C.5 RPM Dependencies

Dependencies are both a blessing and a curse. They prevent users from installing packages that won't work because they are missing other required software. They also prevent users from deleting software that other installed software still needs.

On the other hand, sometimes it can be difficult to find the dependency a package requires. For instance, you might have to search for it and transfer it to the system; then, when you try to install both of those packages (the original and the dependency), you may find that the new package needs a third package. This could go on for several cycles and become very frustrating.

You may not need to specify any dependencies in your packages. If you have a very controlled environment and average users do not install or remove packages, they may be more trouble than they are worth. If you do use dependencies, any automatic installation tools you use must be able to properly handle them. AutoRPM and AutoUpdate can usually take care of these problems for you, as discussed in section 8.6. You can also carefully construct package bundles that fully resolve all dependencies internally, as discussed in section 8.5.1.3.1.

Each package can provide any number of capabilities. This always includes its package name as well as all of its files. If the package contains any shared libraries, RPM automatically includes those capabilities as well (this can be disabled by specifying `AutoProv: no` in the SPEC file). Each package may also use the `Provides` field in the SPEC file to specify additional features it provides.

A package may also specify what it requires, or depends on. You can use the `Prereq` field in the SPEC file to specify capabilities that must be installed before this package is installed. The Requires field specifies capabilities that must exist before this package will operate properly. RPM will also process any binary files and even some scripts to find what capabilities they require. You can turn this off, if need be, by specifying AutoReq: no in the package's SPEC file.

The difference between Prereq and Requires is subtle. In either case, a package and any dependencies not already installed must be installed all at once (i.e., rpm -ivh package.rpm dependency.rpm). If a package has a Prereq on another package, that other package will be installed first, regardless of the order the packages are specified on the command line.

You can also use the Requires and Provides fields to create virtual requirements. A web server log processing program might require some sort of web server, but it doesn't require any one in particular. In this case, the package can depend on webserver and several different web server software packages can provide the webserver capability. In this way, any of the web server packages will properly satisfy this dependency.

A package can require files, virtual capabilities, libraries, and other packages. When you require other packages, you can also specify version restrictions. Any SPEC file can have zero or more Requires lines. Each line can also list multiple requirements, separated by commas. Here are some example Requires fields:

```
Requires: bash
Requires: bash = 2.05a
Requires: bash >= 2.0, webserver, /bin/ls
```

It is important to remember that requirements are fully resolved through RPM's database. So, if you have a dependency of /bin/ls, then an installed package (or a package being installed at the same time) must provide that file. It doesn't matter if the file is actually on the filesystem or not.

One other option available to you is the Conflicts field. It can include the exact same values as the Requires field, but has exactly the opposite effect. A package will not install if the conflicting capability is already installed on the system.

If you know that a certain dependency is not necessary, yet it is preventing you from installing, upgrading, or removing a package, you can always specify the --nodeps option to RPM during the installation process. In general, though, I do not recommend doing this. Rebuild the package if you have to, but in the long run, you will have less headaches with properly resolved dependencies on all of your systems.

## C.6 More Advanced RPM Concepts

This section discusses several concepts that not everybody will need, but still could be very useful to know. Keep in mind that this introduction to RPM package building will not attempt to cover all advanced topics. Some other things you may want to look into that are not covered in this book include, but are not limited to the following:

- Build dependencies (must be satisfied before a package can be built) can be specified with the BuildPrereqs, BuildRequires, and BuildConflicts fields.

- Options can be specified on the rpm command line during the build process by using --with option. This defines the macro %_with_option that can be used within the SPEC file during the build process.

- Source RPMs can be built that don't actually include all of the source code. This allows a package to contain portions of commercial software (that presumably can't be distributed) and anybody with the commercial software available can build the package. You accomplish this using the NoSource and NoPatch fields.

- A transactional rollback system is currently in the process of being implemented to allow a system to be rolled back to previous states. As far as I know, this functionality is not yet complete, but it may be by the time you read this.

Remember that you can use any RPM variables anywhere in your SPEC file and even within scripts. RPM substitutes these values during the package build process. You can also define your own variables:

```
%define varname value
```

Substitutions of variables are accomplished with the string %{varname}. Remember that all of these variables are expanded during the build process.

### C.6.1 Advanced RPM File Lists

In its most simple form, the %files section within a SPEC file simply lists files to be included in the package. You can also use shell wildcards such as * and ?.

## C.6.1.1  The %defattr Directive

Since I hope you will be using a regular user and a build root to build your packages, you will definitely need a way to package files owned by root. This is where the %defattr directive comes in handy. Without this directive, all files and directories included within the package are packaged with the same permissions and ownership as the files in the build root. All of those files are owned by the build user (such as build) who probably doesn't even exist on the installation systems. When you specify the %defattr(-,root,root) directive at the top of the file listing, all entries will have their owner and group changed to root when they are packaged.

The %defattr directive basically lets you override one or more properties of all files included in the package. The first parameter is the file modes in octal form, such as 0644 or 0755. The next two arguments are the user and group, respectively. Any of the three arguments can be - to use each file or directory's existing value (i.e., don't override that particular property of the file). If the permissions are overridden to something like 0644, you would then have to specifically set the execute bit for each executable and directory with the %attr command discussed next. For this reason, most people don't override the permissions but almost always override the user and group.

So, the following %files list will include all files and directories in the build root with their existing permissions, but owned by user and group root:

```
%files
%defattr(-,root,root)
/*
```

Unfortunately, you usually do not want to do this. Let's say that you created the etc/ directory under the build root and placed a configuration file in that directory. With this file listing, your package would now own the /etc/ directory, which is probably not what you want. Although multiple packages can own a directory and it won't be deleted until the last package owning it is erased *and* it is empty, you should still try to include only what belongs to your package in the file listing. Here is a better file listing if you placed files in the etc/ and usr/bin/ directories.

```
%files
%defattr(-,root,root)
/etc/*
/usr/bin/*
```

Remember that the packaging will be done relative to your build root. So, as long as you wiped out and recreated the build root directory, these wildcards will only match files installed within the %install section. They will not match files on your system in these directories (unless you aren't using a build root, in which case they would match every file in the /etc/ and /usr/bin/ directories).

### C.6.1.2  The %attr and %dir Directives

In the previous example file listing, I assume the %install section has set the permissions on all files correctly; if it hasn't, they will not be packaged or installed with the correct permissions. Here is the same file listing, but here it makes no assumptions on the permissions of the files being packaged within the build root. To accomplish this, you use the %attr directive, which takes the same arguments as %defattr:

```
%files
%attr(0644,root,root) /etc/*
%attr(0755,root,root) /usr/bin/*
```

The %attr directive is also useful if you want to override permissions on a certain entry. Let's say that you want all files to be publicly readable, but you have one directory and one setuid root binary, which both must be publicly executable. Here is how you could package your application:

```
%files
%defattr(0644,root,root)
/etc/*
%attr(0755,root,root) %dir /usr/lib/program
/usr/lib/program/*
%attr(4755,root,root) /usr/bin/program
```

If a directory is specified, either directly or through a wildcard, it is included in the package along with every file and directory contained within. For this reason, the %dir directive is used in the previous example. This allows you to make just the directory itself executable with the %attr directive. You then include the files within that directory in the next line. If you didn't use the %dir directive, all of the files within that directory would also be marked as executable.

### C.6.1.3  The %config Directive

You can also mark configuration files with the special directive %config. This provides the following features during package installation, upgrades, and removal:

- If the configuration file exists, but it is not owned by an existing package, it is renamed with the .rpmorig extension and the new file is created in its place.

- If any files marked with this directive are modified after installation, they will be renamed with the extension .rpmsave if the package is later removed.

- On upgrade, any modified configuration files remain untouched *unless* one of those files within the package has changed since the last version. In this case, the file modified by the user is renamed with the .rpmsave extension and the new version of the file is installed.

So, your previous file listing should really be as follows:

```
%files
%defattr(0644,root,root)
%config /etc/*
%attr(0755,root,root) %dir /usr/lib/program
/usr/lib/program/*
%attr(4755,root,root) /usr/bin/program
```

You can also specify %config(noreplace), which tells RPM never to replace the user's *modified* configuration file (unmodified files are always be replaced). If the configuration file within the package changed from the last version *and* the user has modified their file, the new file is installed with the .rpmnew extension. Finally, there is the %config(missingok) directive. This affects package verification, as discussed in section C.6.3. It also tells RPM to not install the file on an upgrade if it had been removed since the last installation.

## C.6.1.4  The %ghost Directive

A relatively new option is the %ghost directive. This specifies that a file should be owned by the package, but not actually installed by RPM. The file is not even packaged into the RPM, so this file does not need to be present in the build root. This option is appropriate for log files and other files created by the program during execution. It also could be used to mark any files that are created by a post-install script (such as symbolic links and such). This does show that the file is owned by your package (which is always a good thing) and it also removes the file when your package is uninstalled.

### C.6.1.5  The %doc and %docdir Directives

Next, you have a couple of directives related to documentation files. The first directive is %doc. If an absolute pathname is given (i.e., one that begins with a /), the matching file(s) are marked as documentation. If only a relative filename is given, the files are copied into an application-specific documentation directory and then added to the package. An example will help here:

```
%files
%doc /usr/lib/package/docs/index.html
%doc README COPYRIGHT
```

The file /usr/lib/package/docs/index.html must have been created by the install stage and will be added to the package as documentation. The README and COPYRIGHT files are copied from the base of the source tree into an application-specific directory, such as /usr/share/doc/program-version/. This is done automatically by RPM and neither these files nor the directory need to be listed explicitly in the file listing. This is the only way a file can be included in an RPM without actually being in the build root.

There is also the %docdir directive that can be used to tell RPM that all files under that directory should automatically be marked as documentation. This directive does not add the directory nor any files—they must still be listed separately. It simply states that any matching files under that directory should be automatically marked as documentation.

### C.6.1.6  More Advanced File Listing Options

If you have an unknown (when you write the SPEC file) set of files that need to be included in your package, you can use the -f option to the %files section (i.e., %files -f file.list). The filename specified with the -f option is relative to the build directory (BUILD/, which is stored in the environment variable $RPM_BUILD_DIR, by the way). The idea is that this file list can be generated during the build or install stages. The file is basically appended to the file listing in the SPEC file, so files can be listed in both places, any directives and wildcards can be used in the file, and any %defattr in the SPEC file will apply to both sets of files. Here is an example:

```
%files -f program.file.list
%defattr(-,root,root)
%doc README
```

Lastly, the %verify directive, which affects package verification, is discussed in section C.6.3.

## C.6.2   RPM Installation Scripts

The SPEC file may contain one or more installation scripts. These scripts are all optional and will be executed on the installation system using the Bourne Shell (/bin/sh) unless the package is installed with the --noscripts option. The available scripts are as follows:

**%pre:** This script is executed on the installation system before the files are installed.

**%post:** This script is executed after the files have been installed.

**%preun:** This script is called before a package is uninstalled or upgraded.

**%postun:** This script is called after a package has been uninstalled or upgraded.

When a package is just being installed (not upgraded), only the %pre and %post scripts of the new package are executed. They are passed one argument with a value of 1, which can be accessed using the $1 environment variable within the script.

On removal, only the %preun and the %postun scripts of the package being removed are executed. The argument passed to each script in this case is 0.

Upgrades are much more complicated. In this situation, RPM performs the following actions, in this exact order:

1. Executes the %pre script of the new package, providing an argument of 2 to indicate an upgrade.

2. Installs all appropriate files from the new package, overwriting files from the old package as necessary.

3. The %post script of the new package is executed with an argument of 2.

4. The %preun script from the old package is now executed, with an argument of 1.

5. Any files belonging to the old package that are no longer part of the new package are deleted.

6. Finally, the %postun script from the old package is executed, with an argument of 1.

There is one complication regarding the option passed to the %pre and %post scripts during an upgrade. It is usually 2, but it really represents the number of instances of this package that are installed at this time. During an upgrade, both the old and new packages are installed until the process has completed. It is possible, although unusual, to have multiple versions of a package permanently installed on one system. In this case, this argument would be greater than 2. For this reason, the argument should be checked to see if it is greater than one (in bash, you can do test $1 -gt 1).

Here is an example %preun script that unregisters a package's info page only if this is not an upgrade. If it is an upgrade, the info page should not be unregistered because the new package's %post script has already executed (and presumably registered the info page). If the %preun script does not check its argument for a value of 0, the upgrade would end with the info page not being registered.

```
%preun
if [ $1 -eq 0 ]; then
    /sbin/install-info --delete %{_infodir}/%{name}.info.gz %{_infodir}/dir
fi
```

You can do pretty much whatever you would like in these scripts. You can even use the -p option to specify an alternate interpreter for your script (i.e., %post -p /usr/bin/perl). It is important to remember to undo any change in the appropriate package removal script. Here are some suggestions for things you can do in these scripts.

- If you are installing a shell, you could add the shell to /etc/shells in the %post script.

- If your package requires special users and/or groups, you must install them in the %pre script so that the files will be created with the proper ownership.

- If your program needs specific cron jobs (that can't be performed by placing files in /etc/cron.daily/ and its friends), you can add entries to /etc/crontab.

- If your program is a service, it could use chkconfig to register itself to start at bootup. It should also stop and unregister itself in the %postun only if it is not being upgraded.

Remember that, in most cases, you do not want to place any interactive code within these scripts. In some limited situations it might be acceptable, but particularly for automation, it is not a good idea.

## C.6.3 Verifying RPM Packages

You can verify any package on a system by running `rpm -V pkgname`. You can even verify all files owned by all packages on your system by running `rpm -Va`. This works pretty well on its own, but there are a couple of things you can do in your packaging process to improve package verification.

First, configuration files can be marked with the `%config(missingok)` directive within the `%files` section in the SPEC file. This tells RPM not to complain if the file is missing during the package verification process.

You can also disable certain verification steps on a per-file basis in the `%files` section with the `%verify` directive. Here are some examples:

```
%files
%verify(owner group mode) /some/dir/file1
%verify(not mtime) /some/dir/file2
```

So, when this package is verified (can be done any time after installation), file1 will only have its owner, group, and permissions checked. file2 will, on the other hand, have everything checked *except* its modification time. Here is a complete listing of the values that can be used within this directive (and either verified or not verified):

**Owner**: The file's owner

**Group**: The file's group

**Mode**: The file's permissions

**md5**: The file's md5 checksum

**Size**: The size of the file

**maj**: The major number (of a device file)

**min**: The minor number (of a device file)

**symlink**: The destination of a symbolic link

**mtime**: The modification time of the file

So, ideally, configuration files should pretty much always be specified as follows:

```
%files
%config %verify(owner group mode) /etc/program.conf
```

You can also create a verification script (`%verifyscript`) that can perform additional verification tasks. This should ideally check anything that has been done in the post-install scripts. It doesn't need to check any package files or dependencies because RPM does that automatically. It should output any problems to stderr and exit with a return code of zero on success, non-zero on failure. You can also output other text to stdout that will be displayed only when the verification is running in verbose mode (rpm -Vv). Here is an example verification script that could be contained within the bash package:

```
%verifyscript
echo -n 'Looking for bash in /etc/shells... '
if ! grep -q '^/bin/bash$' /etc/shells ; then
    echo 'missing!'
    echo 'bash missing from /etc/shells' >&2
else
    echo 'found.'
fi
```

## C.6.4  Taking Action with RPM Triggers

Triggers are special scripts that RPM can run whenever you install or remove another program. Let's say that you are packaging a mailing list application. It requires a mail server (maybe it even requires the virtual capability mailserver), but it needs to configure itself appropriately depending on the mail server you are using. You could configure the mail server in the %post script, but if the user changes to a different mail server at a later time, your program will no longer work properly. Or maybe you are packaging a browser plug-in that can operate with several different browsers. In this case, you will want to register with all browsers upon installation, but you will also want to register with any browsers installed in the future.

Triggers are useful for all of these things. There are three types of trigger scripts available:

> **%triggerin**: This script is executed when the package name specified after the %triggerin is installed/upgraded or when your package is installed and the specified package is already installed.

> **%triggerun**: This script is executed when a specified package is about to be removed (permanently or for an upgrade) or when your package is being removed or upgraded.

> **%triggerpostun**: This script is executed after a specified package has been removed (permanently or for an upgrade). These scripts are never called when your package is removed or upgraded.

Here are some example trigger definitions followed by scripts to be executed by the Bourne Shell or an alternate interpreter, if specified:

```
# Run when other_package1 is installed or upgraded
# Also run when this package is installed or upgraded,
#    if other_package1 is already installed
%triggerin -- other_package1


# Run when other_package1 or other_package2 is removed or upgraded,
# or if we are removed or upgraded and these packages are installed
%triggerun -- other_package1, other_package2


# Run after other_package1 or other_package2 is removed or upgraded,
# or after we are removed or upgraded (if these packages are installed)
%triggerpostun -- other_package1, other_package2


# Execute the script with Perl if version 2.0 or greater of other_package
# is installed/upgraded, or if it was already installed when we are installed
%triggerin -p /usr/bin/perl -- other_package >= 2.0
```

As you can see, each trigger script can be triggered by one or more other packages. If multiple packages are listed, any of the packages can cause the trigger to occur. You can even specify specific versions, just like you can when you are specifying dependencies.

Each trigger script is executed with two arguments: the first argument is the number of versions of your package currently installed, and the second argument is the number of versions of the other package that are currently installed. During a package upgrade, the appropriate parameter to the %triggerin script will be set to 2 because there are temporarily two versions of the package installed. Although it is possible for the same package to be permanently installed more than once, this is rare. So, in most cases, these parameters will be 0, 1, or 2. To be on the safe side, you should never check for 2 and instead just check for any value greater than 1.

Here is the script execution order on a package upgrade when triggers are involved:

1. The %pre script of the new version of the package being upgraded is executed, with an argument of 2.

2. All files from the upgraded version of the package are installed.

3. The %post script of the new version of the package being upgraded is executed, with an argument of 2.

4. All appropriate %triggerin scripts from other installed packages are executed. Their arguments will be 1 and 2.

5. Any appropriate %triggerin scripts from the new version of the upgraded package are executed. The arguments will be 2 and 1.

6. Any appropriate %triggerun scripts in the old version of the upgraded package are executed. The arguments are 1 and 1.

7. All appropriate %triggerun scripts from other installed packages are executed. The arguments are 1 and 1.

8. The %preun script from the old version of the package being upgraded is executed, with an argument of 1.

9. Any files that were part of the old version of the package being upgraded, but not in the newer version, are removed.

10. The %postun script from the old version of the package being upgraded is executed, with an argument of 1.

11. Any appropriate %triggerpostun scripts from other installed packages are executed. The arguments are 1 and 1.

---

 **TIP**   Remember that anything inside of a %triggerpostun will not be executed when you remove or upgrade your package, so you might need to take care of some activities in your %post script instead.

---

It is a good idea to create empty test packages to see how triggers operate. Simply create two packages, such as test1 and test2, and install both packages. You can then build a newer version of one of the packages and do an upgrade, since the upgrade process is by far the most complicated. Here is an example test file that you can use for both test1 and test2 just by changing the first two lines:

```
%define other_pkg test2
Name: test1
Summary: Package %{name}
Version: 1.0
Release: 1
License: MIT
Group: Test
BuildArch: noarch
BuildRoot: /var/tmp/%{name}
```

```
%description
Description for %{name}

%files

%pre
echo Executing pre in %{name}-%{version}-%{release}: arg=$1

%post
echo Executing post in %{name}-%{version}-%{release}: arg=$1

%preun
echo Executing preun in %{name}-%{version}-%{release}: arg=$1

%postun
echo Executing postun in %{name}-%{version}-%{release}: arg=$1

%triggerin -- %{other_pkg}
echo Executing triggerin in %{name}-%{version}-%{release}: args=$1 $2

%triggerun -- %{other_pkg}
echo Executing triggerun in %{name}-%{version}-%{release}: args=$1 $2

%triggerpostun -- %{other_pkg}
echo Executing triggerun in %{name}-%{version}-%{release}: args=$1 $2
```

## C.6.5  Cross-Platform RPM Packages

Ideally, a source RPM can be compiled into a binary RPM on any platform. Each binary RPM is built for a specific architecture and operating system. This is usually automatically determined by RPM during the build process, but the target architecture and operating system can be overridden (like, in my examples, the BuildArch: noarch entry). The values can also be overridden on the command line with the build option --target arch-vendor-os. You can find a complete list of these values by looking through the /usr/lib/rpm/rpmrc, or equivalent. You can see the operating system and architecture of any package by running the following command:

```
% rpm -q --qf '%{os}/%{arch}\n' -p test1-1.0-1.noarch.rpm
linux/noarch
```

You can force RPM to ignore either or both of these values at installation time with the `--ignoreos` and/or `--ignorearch` options. You can see the architecture and operating system information for your system by running `rpm --showrc` and looking at the first portion of the output (which is quite lengthy):

```
% rpm --showrc
ARCHITECTURE AND OS:
build arch            : i386
compatible build archs: i686 i586 i486 i386 noarch
build os              : Linux
compatible build os's : Linux
install arch          : i686
install os            : Linux
compatible archs      : i686 i586 i486 i386 noarch
compatible os's       : Linux
...
```

You should try to create packages that are not dependent on the specific operating system. If possible, you should also make the package a noarch package, but this is not an option for binary packages. In the case of a binary package, you should try to make the package build process compatible with any system so that the same source RPM can be used to build binary RPMs on any system.

RPM provides conditional expressions to aid in this task. Here are some examples:

```
% prep

%ifarch i386 i486 i586 i686
echo "x86 architecture"
%endif

%ifnos Linux
echo "not Linux"
%endif

%ifos Linux
%ifarch i386
echo "Linux/i386"
%endif
%endif
```

These conditionals can be used anywhere in the SPEC file as needed. You can use them in everything from the header section to the install section to the file listing and the installation scripts. One common task is to only apply certain patches on certain architectures or operating systems. You should still include all of the patches in the source RPM (i.e., don't exclude the actual PatchX: entry), otherwise the patches won't actually be bundled into the source RPM, and that source RPM will not compile on some systems.

If you don't want a package to be built on a specific operating system or architecture, you can use the ExcludeArch and ExcludeOS fields, as follows:

```
ExcludeArch: alpha,sparc
ExcludeOS: solaris
```

You can also specify an exclusive list of architectures and operating systems on which the package can be built:

```
ExclusiveArch: alpha,sparc
ExclusiveOS: solaris
```

## C.6.6  Relocatable RPM Packages

Making a package relocatable may sound difficult. In reality, its difficulty depends on the underlying software you are packaging. If the program, for example, has a hard-coded (at compile time) configuration file of /etc/program.conf, it is impossible to make it perfectly relocatable (although there are options). If it is just a single binary file, such as /usr/bin/program with no configuration file, it is very easy.

In the simple case, you just install the package with rpm -i --prefix /some/path. The default prefix for the package is replaced with the prefix specified on the command line. To see the default prefix, run rpm -qip on the package file and look for the Relocations field. If you don't specify a prefix on installation, RPM will use the default prefix.

Before you get too excited, know that you can experience difficulties when you are relocating relocatable packages. The prefix, if specified, applies to all packages being installed at one time, which means that they must all be relocatable and you must want them all relocated to the same place. In addition, you must also specify the same prefix when upgrading to have the new version placed in the same location. Automated install scripts would have to look up the current install prefix of a package before doing an upgrade and they would only be able to upgrade one package at a time with this method. This could, of course, cause dependency problems, because the automation program would have to externally resolve and order dependencies. There are no easy answers, but you could write scripts to take care of this for you, especially with carefully constructed packages—ones that you know, in advance, have all of their dependencies satisfied.

So, back to creating relocatable packages. All you need to do is add a `Prefix` field to the package and specify the default prefix. The more difficult part is making sure all files in the file listing start with that prefix. Here is a portion of a SPEC file for the simple single-binary package mentioned earlier:

```
Prefix: /usr


...


%files
/usr/bin/program
```

Technically, the prefix for this package could be `/usr/bin/`, but whether or not that makes sense is up to you. As shown here, the binary will always be placed in the `bin/` directory under the installation prefix. If the prefix was specified as `/usr/bin/`, the binary could be installed in `/etc/` if that was specified as the installation prefix.

The `/usr/` and `/usr/local/` directories are common prefixes. If your relocatable program requires a config file that must be in the `/etc/` directory, you could get around it like this:

```
Prefix: /usr/local


...


%post
if [ ! "$RPM_INSTALL_PREFIX" == "/" ] ; then
   ln -sf "$RPM_INSTALL_PREFIX/etc/program.conf" /etc/program.conf
fi

%postun
rm -f /etc/program.conf

%verifyscript
test -l /etc/program.conf

%files
%conf /usr/local/etc/program.conf
/usr/local/bin/program
```

It's not perfect, but the actual configuration file is in the alternate prefix and only a symbolic link is created in the `/etc/` directory. Unfortunately, the symbolic link is not marked as being owned by the package. The best we can do is create a verification script that verifies that /etc/program.conf exists and is a symbolic link.

You can actually have more than one Prefix entry in the SPEC file. Each file in the files listing must be within one of those prefixes. Upon installation, you can change some, all, or none of the prefixes. Here is an example:

```
Prefix: /usr
Prefix: /etc
...
%files
%conf /etc/program.conf
/usr/bin/program
```

Of course, the program would still have to have some way of finding its configuration file since it can be relocated anywhere on the system. Relocating multiple prefixes is a bit more difficult:

% **rpm -i --relocate /usr=/usr/local /etc=/usr/local/etc test.rpm**

Regardless of the number of prefixes, each is accessed from within scriptlets as $RPM_INSTALL_PREFIX0, $RPM_INSTALL_PREFIX1, and so on. This applies to installation scripts, trigger scripts, and verification scripts.

## C.6.7  RPM Subpackages

So far in this book, one source RPM has built one package. There are plenty of cases, however, where creating multiple packages from one source RPM is useful. You often see this with packages providing name and name-devel. Most people never need to install the development portion of the package, but it is all built from the same source RPM. Other packages, for example, might be split into server and client packages.

Everything starts out the same when using subpackages. You must, however, add a package section for each subpackage, as well as a separate description section:

```
%package server
Summary: Server portion of my program
Group: System Environment/Daemons

%description server
The server for this program.
```

You can add as many subpackages as you would like using this method. The name of this subpackage will be package-server. If you want an alternate name, you can use the -n option to the %package section. With this option, you can specify any name you like for the subpackage (such as %package -n mysubpackage).

Next, you must create a files section for each package. So, for %package server you need a %files server section. If you had %package -n mysubpackage, you would also need a %files -n mysubpackage. If you do not want a base binary package built (i.e., you only want subpackages), do not include the default %files section at all. An empty %files section will not cut it (that would create a base package with no files)—the section needs to not be specified. Here is a full SPEC file with a client and server subpackage, but no base package:

```
Name: program
Summary: My program
Version: 1.0
Release: 1
License: MIT
Group: System Environment/Base

%description
My program

%package server
Summary: My program (server component)
Group: System Environment/Daemons

%description server
The server component of my program.

%package client
Summary: My program (client component)
Group: System Environment/Base

%description client
The client component of my program.

%files server
/usr/sbin/in.myprogramd

%files client
/usr/bin/myprogram
```

This is all that is required. Since all the packages are built from the same source, there is only one of each of the following sections: %prep, %build, and %install. You can, however, create scripts for the base package and/or the subpackages. Just like the other sections I have discussed, the %post section is the post-install script for the base package (program), and the %post client section is the post-install script for the subpackage (program-client).

Remember, if you used the -n option to the %package section, you must use that same option for all other sections related to that subpackage. All installation, uninstallation, trigger, and verification scripts should have the appropriate subpackage specification.

Building multiple packages from one SPEC file is easy—you build the package the same way as usual. The only difference is that more than one binary package is created as a result. Like when you build any other package, RPM only creates a single source RPM, regardless of the number of subpackages contained within the SPEC file.

## C.6.8 Packaging Perl Modules As RPMs

If you are like me, you use quite a bit of Perl to help you with your automation efforts. The Comprehensive Perl Archive Network (CPAN) provides a huge number of useful modules. Thanks to a little script included with RPM called cpanflute2, making packages out of CPAN modules is very easy. The script can be found in /usr/lib/rpm/cpanflute2 on a standard Red Hat Linux system (with the rpm-build package installed) prior to Red Hat Linux 8.0.

Making a package from a module is simple. First, download the source for a Perl module from either http://www.cpan.org or ftp://ftp.cpan.org. Then, execute cpanflute2:

```
% /usr/lib/rpm/cpanflute2 WWW-Cache-Google-0.04.tar.gz
Compression not available.
Wrote: ./perl-WWW-Cache-Google-0.04-8.src.rpm
Executing(--clean): /bin/sh -e /var/tmp/rpm-tmp.75321
+ umask 022
+ cd /tmp
+ rm -rf WWW-Cache-Google-0.04
+ exit 0
```

As you can see, cpanflute2 has created a source RPM for the Perl module. Now, you can simply run rpmbuild --rebuild on the source RPM to build the binary package. That's it!

Some command-line options are available to you when you go to execute cpanflute2. I, however, have never used them, and I doubt you will need them either. The script itself is relatively simple, so take a look through it if you have any problems.

## C.6.9 RPM Package Signing

If you want to sign RPM packages, you must add these lines to your ~/.rpmmacros:

```
%_signature gpg
%_gpg_name Kirk Bauer <kirk@kaybee.org>
%_gpg_path /home/build/.gnupg
%_gpgbin /usr/bin/gpg
```

These lines allow you to sign packages with GnuPG. The last two lines are optional and can be used to override default file locations. To use PGP instead, just replace the string gpg with pgp on those four lines. Since your PGP key is probably not in /home/build/.gnupg and the PGP program is probably not /usr/bin/gpg, you should probably change those values as well. The _gpg_name value should match the name on the GnuPG key you wish to use for signing.

RPM versions 4.1 and newer now store keys internally. This version was first included with Red Hat Linux 8.0. Instead of using the %_gpg_path setting, you must import your key with rpm --import <keyfile>.

You can sign packages during the build process. For example, to build your own apache package and sign the resulting binary package(s), run the following command:

```
% rpmbuild -ba --sign apache.spec
```

The one major problem with building signed packages is that you must interactively enter your passphrase during the build process. Even if your private key has no passphrase, RPM still requests one. There is no way around this apart from modifying the RPM code. Fortunately, it is requested near the beginning of the build process so you can start the build, type the passphrase, and then let it proceed on its own.

This doesn't work with a fully automated build process, of course. In that case, I recommend building your packages without signatures. You can then sign the packages at a later time using the --addsign or --resign options. The --resign command replaces any existing signatures with a new one, while the --addsign command appends a new signature. You can even sign many packages at once while entering your passphrase only once:

```
% cd /usr/local/distribution/RedHat/RPMS
% rpm --addsign *.rpm
```

Once you have the appropriate public key on each system, you can check this signature with `rpm --checksig` before installing the packages.

## C.7 Automating Package Builds

If you are packaging your own software, automating the build process is very desirable. In this section, I present a fairly simple script that allows you to build packages directly from a CVS source repository. The script will operate on a SPEC file, which could also be stored in CVS (but would have to be extracted manually first).

Let's start with an example SPEC file. I'm only going to include the header section, because the rest of the file is package-specific. In fact, the SPEC file is just about standard:

```
#CVS=autorpm
Name: autorpm
Version: 3.0.1
Release: 1
Summary: RPM Auto-Installer and FTP Mirrorer
License: MIT
Group: Utilities/System
BuildArch: noarch
Source: autorpm-%{version}.tar.gz
BuildRoot: %{_tmppath}/autorpm-build/
```

The script presented in this section automatically increments the release, but it does not modify the SPEC file in any other way. You have to manually increment the package version. If your CVS tags are the same as your package versions, you could have the script set the version within the SPEC file based on the tag you specify during the build process. Remember, if you do increment the package version, you probably want to set the Release to zero (which will be incremented to one on the next build).

The only unique thing in that SPEC file is the comment at the top. Any number of lines can be present of the form #CVS=xxx. Each line specifies a module, directory, or file to export from CVS and place into the source tarball. In this example, only the CVS module autorpm will be exported. The script will then create the source tarball autorpm-3.0.1.tar.gz. This file will extract to the autorpm-3.0.1/ directory, which will contain the autorpm/ directory (the CVS module).

This simple script could also be extended to actually copy the resulting RPMs to the appropriate places. I'll leave that task to you. Hopefully just building the packages directly from CVS will be helpful enough. I start out with the usual usage and die functions:

```
#!/bin/bash

usage() {
    echo "Usage: $0 <spec-file> <cvs-tag>" >&2
    exit 1
}

die() {
    echo >&2
    echo "ERROR: $*" >&2
    echo >&2
    exit 1
}
```

Next, I have a helper function that retrieves one module, directory, or file from CVS using the cvs export command. The $tag will be set before this function is called. I assume that CVS is already configured and operational. Here is getfiles:

```
getfiles() {
    echo -n "Retrieving $1 from CVS... " >&2
    cvs export -r "$tag" $1 >/dev/null 2>&1 || \
        die "Could not retrieve $1 from CVS"
    echo "Done."
}
```

The next function is used to tag the files after the package build so that you can determine exactly which files were included in a package. Its first argument is a module, directory, or file. Its second argument is the tag to be used.

```
dotag() {
    echo -n "Retrieving $1 from CVS... " >&2
    cvs rtag -F -r "$tag" "$2" "$1" >/dev/null 2>&1 || \
        die "Tagging $1 with $2 failed!"
    echo "Done."
}
```

This getinfo is used to retrieve a value from a field within a SPEC file. It uses sed to isolate the value assigned to the field passed in as the first parameter.

```
getinfo() {
 sed -n "s/^$1: *\([^ ][^ ]*\) *$/\1/p" "$spec"
}
```

Now it's time for the main code. First, I do some standard argument processing and verification:

```
 [ "$1" == "--help" ] && usage
[ $# -lt 2 ] && usage
spec="$PWD/$1"
tag="$2"
[ -r "$spec" ] || die "Could not access SPEC file"
```

Next, I determine the build directory from RPM and create the appropriate directory structure (if needed).

```
# Generate build directory structure
topdir="$(rpm --eval '%{_topdir}')"
mkdir -p $topdir/{BUILD,RPMS,SOURCES,SPECS,SRPMS}
```

Now, I use the getinfo function to pull the package name and version out of the specified SPEC file.

```
# Get name and version from the SPEC file
name="$(getinfo Name)"
version="$(getinfo Version)"
```

That was easy enough, but the release is a bit more complicated. I need to pull it from the file, increment it, and then modify the SPEC file with the incremented release:

```
# Retrieve last release and increment by one
release="$(getinfo Release)"
release=$[$release+1]
sed "s/^Release:.*$/Release: $release/" "$spec" >> "$spec.new" && \
   mv "$spec.new" "$spec"
```

Now comes the fun part. I go into the SOURCES/ directory and remove any previous files and directories related to this package. I make a new directory based on this package's name and version, then I enter that directory, loop through all lines in the SPEC file beginning with #CVS=, and use the getfiles function to retrieve the specified files from CVS.

```
# Retrieve files from CVS
cd "$topdir/SOURCES"
rm -rf "$name"-*
mkdir "$name-$version"
cd "$name-$version"
for entry in `sed -n 's/^#CVS=//p' "$spec"` ; do
    getfiles "$entry"
    [ -e "$entry" ] || die "Failed to retrieve $entry from CVS!"
done || die "Could not retrieve all entries from CVS"
```

Now that the directory has been created and populated with files from CVS, it is time to create the tarball and remove the temporary directory:

```
# Next, build the tar file
echo -n "Building $name-$version.tar.gz... "
cd ..
tar -czpf "$name-$version.tar.gz" "$name-$version" || \
    die "Failed to create tar file!"
rm -rf "$name-$version"
echo "Done."
```

Now that the source file has been created, I can build the package. This is the easiest part so far:

```
# Now, build the package
rpm -ba "$spec" || die "Failed to build package $name"
```

Assuming the package build is successful, the dotag function is used to tag the files in CVS that are included in this package. The script generates the tag using the version and release of this build. Note that CVS tags cannot contain periods, so these are changed to hyphens. I know that the version and release don't have any hyphens because these are not allowed in RPM.

```
# Tag the code in CVS
newtag="RPM-$(echo "$name-$version" | sed 's/\./-/g')-$release"
for entry in `sed -n 's/^#CVS=//p' "$spec"` ; do
    dotag "$entry" "$newtag"
done
```

And that's it. This script could be extended to do much more than it is already doing here, but I can't do all of the work for you!

# Index

## Symbols and Numbers

# O